The Languages of Britain

I'm Gwraig

The Languages of Britain

Glanville Price

Professor of Romance Languages,
University College of Wales, Aberystwyth

Edward Arnold

© Glanville Price 1984

First published in Great Britain 1984 by
Edward Arnold (Publishers) Limited
41 Bedford Square
London WC1B 3DQ

Edward Arnold (Australia) Pty Limited
80 Waverley Road
Caulfield East
Victoria 3145

First published in the United States of America 1984 by
Edward Arnold
300 North Charles Street
Baltimore
Maryland 21201

British Cataloguing in Publication Data

Price, Glanville
   The languages of Britain.
   1. Great Britain—Languages
   I. Title
   409'.041   P551.G/

   ISBN 0-7131-6396-8

Text set in 10/11pt Times Compugraphic by Colset Private Limited, Singapore.
Printed and bound by Richard Clay (The Chaucer Press) Ltd. Bungay, Suffolk.

Contents

List of illustrations, maps and figures

Note on references

The list of books and articles at the end of each chapter includes items referred to in the chapter, together in some cases with additional items for further reading that are not specifically referred to in the text. References in the body of the text follow the 'author – date' system – for example, 'Wrenn, 1947: 27' refers to the book listed at 'Wrenn, C.L. (1949). *The English Language.* London: Methuen', and to page 27 thereof.

Acknowledgements

Many more people than I could hope to name individually have helped with the writing of this book, by answering queries, supplying information, or discussing points arising in connection with one chapter or another. To all of them I am grateful. Particular mention must be made of the following, each of whom has read at least one chapter in draft: Mr A.J. Aitken, Ms Delyth Evans, Professor Emrys Evans, Dr Frank Le Maistre, Mr Oliver J. Padel, Professor William Rothwell, Professor Desmond Slay, Professor Colin Smith, Professor Derick Thomson, Mr R.L. Thomson, Dr H. Tomlinson and Professor T. Arwyn Watkins. They have saved me from many errors and omissions, but are in no way responsible for those that remain – particularly since on occasion I have not taken advice offered. I am also most appreciative of the help provided by the staffs of the Library of the University College of Wales, Aberystwyth, the British Library, the National Library of Scotland, the National Library of Wales, and the States of Jersey Central Library.

My thanks are also due to the British Academy for a grant that enabled me to make research visits to Scotland and the Channel Islands in connection with this book, and to the following for permission to reproduce illustrations or maps: the Scottish Development Department (illustration No. 1), the National Museum of Antiquities of Scotland, Edinburgh (illustration No. 2), the National Library of Wales (illustrations Nos. 3 and 4), Edinburgh University Press (map No. 2), Professor Harold Carter (map No. 3).

Mrs Dorothy O. Evans has typed successive drafts with a degree of cheerfulness and skill that can only be fully appreciated by someone who has seen the state of the manuscript she was faced with.

Finally, my heartfelt thanks to my wife for her unfailing help and support. This book is dedicated to her.

Introduction

The subject of this book is the languages that have been spoken for some considerable length of time, or were spoken at some time in the past, in those parts of the British Isles that are subject to the British Crown, i.e. the United Kingdom, the Isle of Man, and the Channel Islands.[1] Irish, therefore, finds a place both by virtue of the fact that it was at one time spoken in some western parts of Wales and elsewhere in the island of Great Britain, and as the traditional language of Ulster. But Irish in what is now the Republic of Ireland is outside the scope of the book.

In general, the languages we are concerned with are each associated with a more or less clearly definable geographical area. The exceptions to this are, on the one hand, Latin and Anglo-Norman, each of which was probably an urban rather than a rural language, perhaps even the language of the ruling, educated and mercantile sections of the community rather than of the mass of the people, and, on the other hand, Romani, the traditional language of the nomadic Gypsies.

What is known of the languages under discussion varies enormously. On the one hand, we have English, Welsh and Scottish Gaelic, which are still spoken and have a lengthy literary tradition to go with them. At the other extreme, we have languages like Pictish and Cumbric, known only from a few fragments and place-names, and Celtic Pictish, whose existence can be established *only* on the basis of place-names and of a few personal names in classical sources. Between, we have a wide range of possibilities. The Norman French of the Channel Islands, though it has little by way of literature and has not been as thoroughly studied as it might and should have been, has not yet disappeared. Manx has little literature but survived until the age of the tape-recorder and so is relatively well known. Anglo-Norman is known from a substantial body of written texts and documents. Though evidence for Irish, Latin, Norse and Romani originating specifically from Britain is somewhat

---

[1] The United Kingdom consists of Great Britain (i.e. England, Scotland, and Wales) and Northern Ireland. The Isle of Man and the Channel Islands are possessions of the British Crown but are not part of the United Kingdom. Man, Jersey, and the Bailiwick of Guernsey (which includes, in addition to Guernsey itself, the islands of Alderney, Sark, Herm and Jethou) are each largely self-governing, though the Westminster Parliament (in which they are not represented) may legislate for them but rarely does. The United Kingdom is also responsible for them in matters of defence and foreign relations. See E.C.S. Wade and G. Godfrey Phillips, *Constitutional and Administrative Law*, ninth edition by A.W. Bradley, London: Longman, 1977, Chapter 3 (pp. 32–41), 'The structure of the United Kingdom', especially 'The Channel Islands' (pp. 38–9) and 'The Isle of Man' (p. 40).

scarce, the languages themselves are known (and, except for Romani, very well known) from other sources. The grammar of Cornish is well enough documented, in spite of a few gaps, but much of the vocabulary is irretrievably lost. Two special cases are British, which represents an earlier stage of Welsh and Cornish for which we have no direct evidence, and Scots, to which, for the sake of convenience, I have devoted a chapter of its own even though I really consider it a dialect of English rather than a distinct language.

One language that is known to have been spoken in part of Britain is omitted altogether, on the grounds that we have no specifically British evidence for it by way either of texts or of place-names indisputably derived from it. This is Flemish. It is known that colonies of Flemings were settled in what is now the south of Pembrokeshire in the twelfth century, but no trace of their language remains, nor do we know how long Flemish continued to be spoken there.

The overall plan of the book, the order in which the chapters are arranged, calls for some explanation. The order can best be described as 'roughly chronological'. By this I mean that I set out with the intention of discussing the various languages in the order in which they arrived in these islands (insofar as that is known), but found it impossible to do so. Three examples will serve to highlight the problem. Where should I bring in Cornish, which, though descended from British which was here long before Latin or English, emerged as Cornish only after the Romans had left and is not attested in writing until long after the English, and their language, had occupied much of the island? And should Scottish Gaelic come before British, on the grounds that the Gaels occupied Northern Ireland (whence they were later to cross to Scotland) before the coming of the Britons, or after, on the grounds that the Britons arrived in Scotland before the Gaels? And is the relevant period for Norman French in the Channel Islands the eleventh century, when the islands first became associated with Britain, or the period, some centuries earlier (but it is impossible to say precisely when), when the speech of Northern Gaul had so far evolved as to be considered French (or at any rate proto-French) rather than Latin?

So, while the plan is, as I have said, 'roughly chronological', I have departed from this to the extent of keeping together chapters on closely related languages. The book therefore falls into the following sections:

I *Early arrivals* – although nothing certain is known about the language of the earliest inhabitants of these islands, there can be no doubt that they had the faculty of speech, and so it seems justifiable to say something about them; then we have a chapter on the language of the Picts who, it is probably safe to assume, were here before the Celts.

II *The Celtic languages* – first the Gaelic languages and then the Brittonic languages, in that order since, in the view of most authorities, the Gaels arrived in Ireland before the Britons reached Britain. Celtic Pictish poses a problem: there can be little doubt that it was brought to Scotland before the coming of the Britons (who were there before the Gaels), but as it can only be discussed in relation to the Brittonic languages, these have to be dealt with first.

III *Latin.*

IV *The Germanic languages* — English and its derivative, Scots, and Norse.

V *French* — the French of the Channel Islands, followed by Anglo-Norman, which was brought relatively late to the main island of Britain and never really established itself.

VI *Romani* — which arrived only in the fifteenth century.

Given the vast difference in what is known about the various languages discussed, I have made no attempt whatsoever to adopt a uniform approach. I have allowed the plan of each chapter to be dictated by what is known about the language in question and by what struck me as particularly important or interesting. The one thing that is common to all chapters is that I am primarily concerned with the languages as social phenomena, i.e. with such topics as the circumstances (where they are known) of their arrival in Britain, with their role as standard or literary languages (but not, except incidentally, with literary history), with their interaction with other languages, with (in most cases) their decline and, except for English, with their disappearance or their present-day struggle for survival. I am not therefore concerned with the grammatical structure of the languages: I cannot do better than refer the reader who is interested in that aspect to the admirable book by Professor W.B. Lockwood, *Languages of the British Isles Past and Present*, London: André Deutsch, 1975.

One important point remains to be made. The most recent arrival discussed in this book is Romani, which has been here for over five hundred years. But a new chapter in the linguistic history of Britain has now begun. In the last century, and particularly in the last half-century, many new linguistic communities have established themselves here. There are, for example, eastern European exiles — Poles, Ukrainians, Latvians, Estonians and others — who settled in Britain during and immediately after the Second World War; in many cases, their traditional languages have been passed on to a second and third generation. There are also the culturally and linguistically varied communities originating from India, Pakistan and Bangladesh, many of them closely-knit communities that may well be expected to resist assimilation and maintain their languages for some considerable time to come. In London and some of the industrial cities of the Midlands, there are now substantial communities of Turkish-speaking, Greek-speaking, Italian-speaking, Spanish-speaking, and other European workers, who may or may not remain indefinitely. A census taken by the Inner London Education Authority in 1978 of pupils in its schools whose first language was not English identified 131 such languages, twelve of which (in order of number of speakers: Bengali, Turkish, Greek, Spanish, Gujerati, Punjabi, Italian, Urdu, Chinese, French, Arabic and Portuguese) were each the first language of over a thousand pupils, while the range of languages encountered in, for example, Leicester includes Latvian, Ukrainian, Polish, Chinese, Punjabi, Gujerati, Bengali and Italian.[2]

---

[2] See the Commission for Racial Equality, *Ethnic Minority Community Languages: A Statement,* London, 1982, p. 2.

It is too early to tell how many of these relatively recently arrived languages will survive for more than two or three generations. If many of them do, then someone will have ample material for another book.[3]

---

[3] The Runnymede Trust has already produced the following papers: Verity Saifullah Khan, *Bilingualism and Linguistic Minorities in Britain*, 1977; K. Campbell-Platt (revised by S. Nicholas), *Linguistic Minorities in Britain*, 1978. See also Verity S. Khan 'The "mother-tongue" of linguistic minorities in multicultural England', in *Journal of Multilingual and Multicultural Development*, 1 (1980)): 71–88.

Part I Early Arrivals

1   Prehistoric Britain

Britain and Ireland have existed as such, i.e. as islands, for perhaps no more than 8,000 years. Before that, they formed part of the north-west European land-mass. But traces of habitation by men − or men-like beings − go back much further, and the first Stone Age men may well have visited these parts a quarter of a million years ago.[1]

Writing of the people of the Earlier Upper Palaeolithic period ('Upper Palaeolithic' = 'Late Old Stone Age'), J.B. Campbell comments (1977:v):

> I see what I call the Earlier Upper Palaeolithic . . . peoples as having ultimately disappeared from Britain owing to the maximum ice advances of about 18,000 to 16,000 years ago, whilst the Later Upper Palaeolithic . . . peoples went on to become the ancestors of the native Mesolithic [= Middle Stone Age] population and in a sense the first 'British' population who managed to stay.

Traces of Earlier Upper Palaeolithic man are found in the Paviland Cave in the Gower Peninsula, in Devon, Somerset, Derbyshire, Suffolk and elsewhere, while evidence for the Later Palaeolithic period (13,000 BC to approximately 9000 BC) comes from caves in many parts of England and Wales, among them Devonshire, the Mendips (including the famous Gough's Cave at Cheddar), Hampshire, Herefordshire, Derbyshire, Lancashire, Yorkshire, and North and South Wales. During the Mesolithic period, the remaining native population was supplemented by at least three different streams of immigrants that came in from the east, the south and the south-west respectively (see Hawkes, 1948:20).

Although it is most unlikely that pure-blooded descendants could now be found of any of these early racial groups, the ethnic 'mix' is certainly different in different parts of the country and it is not beyond the bounds of possibility that communities owing a significantly higher proportion of their genes to their prehistoric forebears than do the generality of Britons may still be found in some of the remoter parts of the Welsh mountains (and perhaps elsewhere). Professor E.G. Bowen notes (1957:132) that many inhabitants of the Plynlimon moorland and the Black Mountain country of Carmar-

---

[1] The earliest known 'Briton' is the so-called 'Swanscombe Man' (who may have been a woman), parts of whose skull were found in a gravel quarry at Swanscombe in the lower Thames valley in 1935. He or she was of a different species from *homo sapiens*, perhaps of a species akin to Neanderthal man. For a recent study of the earliest inhabitants of these islands see Alex Morrison, *Early Man in Britain and Ireland*, London: Croom Helm, 1980.

thenshire have dark hair and eyes, swarthy skins, long, narrow heads, brow ridges that often stand out strongly, broad cheek-bones and noses, and prominent mouths, and wonders whether they could be descendants of the original Upper Palaeolithic and Mesolithic inhabitants driven by later immigrants into the hills. Basing his conclusions on research into blood-group distributions in Wales (see Mourant and Watkin, 1952, and Watkin, 1956), which seemed to show that populations with high B frequencies were among the earliest arrivals in Wales, he continues (*ibid.*, 133):

> The genes inference . . . is that the marked B gene frequencies found in the Plynlimon and Black Mountain regions of Wales represent the survival there of very early human stocks.

However this may be, it seems probable that, during the Palaeolithic and Mesolithic periods, the population of the area that was to become the British Isles was very small, to be numbered perhaps in hundreds rather than thousands, and that they migrated from one area to another as the seasons and the need to find fresh food supplies dictated. And, of course, we know absolutely nothing of the language or languages they spoke. The most we can say is that it is reasonable to assume that they did in fact use language and that, given the diversity of their origins, a variety of languages were in use.

Human society in the Palaeolithic and Mesolithic periods was characterized by a subsistence economy based on hunting (including fishing) and gathering. Some five or six thousand years ago, the first communities characterized by a more advanced economy based on farming arrived in these islands. We have now reached the Neolithic period or New Stone Age (which in Britain probably lasted from about 3500 BC or a little earlier to a little after 2000 BC) and are approaching the dawn of civilization.

We know no more about the languages of Neolithic man, in Britain or elsewhere, than about those of his predecessors. Two eminent Celtic scholars, John Morris Jones and Julius Pokorny, argued vigorously (Jones, 1889; Pokorny, 1926–30) that Welsh and Irish respectively have many syntactical features that seem not to be generally characteristic of the Indo-European languages but which do have striking parallels in the Hamitic languages of North Africa, and in particular in Ancient Egyptian and its descendant, Coptic, and in Berber.[2] They point out furthermore that anthropological evidence is consistent with the view that some pre-Celtic stratum in the population could have migrated to Britain from North Africa via Spain and France. They are therefore led to the view that the features in question are derived from a pre-Celtic and probably Hamitic substratum. What this implies is that, when the pre-Celtic population mixed with the incoming

---

[2] Some of the features quoted by Jones are quite striking − e.g. the fact that the verb takes a 3rd person singular form when the subject is a plural noun (Welsh *daethant* 'they came' but *daeth y dynion* 'the men came'), or the use of the same preposition (in Welsh, *yn*) in a wide range of syntactic functions, e.g. to introduce a present participle (*yn caru* 'loving'), to introduce the complement of verbs of being and becoming (*mae ef yn was* 'he is a servant'), to form adverbs (*ebrwydd* 'sudden', *yn ebrwydd* 'suddenly'), etc., etc.; but many are trivial (such as the fact that adjectives follow the noun), or easily paralleled elsewhere (such as various features of word order), or far-fetched.

Celts, a mixed language resulted which was basically Celtic but which contained various syntactical features carried over into it from the other languages (just as, for example, the Anglo-Irish construction 'I am after seeing him', meaning 'I have seen him', is composed of English words but reproduces a typically Irish − and, indeed, Welsh − grammatical construction). This is an intriguing hypothesis, supported by a certain amount of circumstantial evidence (linguistic and anthropological parallels), but it is at best a hypothesis and, by the nature of the evidence, must remain an unproven one.

An immense and far-reaching technological advance in the history of mankind occurred when men learned to extract, smelt and cast metal, in particular copper, and then to make bronze which is both harder than pure copper and more easily cast. There seems little doubt that the introduction of copper- and then bronze-working into Britain is to be associated with the people usually known as 'Beaker Folk', so termed because of their custom of placing pottery beakers or drinking vessels of a distinctive shape in their graves, who probably arrived from the continent around the middle of the third millennium BC.

Once again, anthropological evidence suggests that some communities in Wales still retain physical features inherited from this prehistoric population. Referring to the tall, broad-headed people with lightish colouring still to be found in parts of the Dee, Wye, Usk and Tywi valleys and sporadically in the Vale of Glamorgan, Bowen comments (1957:135):

> On skeletal evidence such types appear closely related to the people who made Beaker pottery . . . and whose burials are found in much the same localities. The blood group evidence of modern times indicates that people apparently associated with these various racial types in Wales are sharply off-set from the apparent descendants of Palaeolithic man on the moorlands in that they possess a low B gene frequency.

In some parts of the world, the languages of Bronze Age populations have come down to us. For example, the language of the inscribed tablets (dating from *c.* 1500−1100 BC) in the so-called 'Linear B' script of the Bronze Age civilization of Minos and Mycenae has been shown to be an early form of Greek. But the Bronze Age languages of Britain (and of Western Europe generally) are completely unknown − unless, that is, those who maintain that the Beaker Folk were in fact Celts are right. Or there is one other possibility. We may perhaps still possess a few (unfortunately unintelligible) words and phrases in a pre-Celtic language, if that is what the fragmentary and problematic inscriptions known as Pictish really are (see Chapter 2).

It often seems to be the case that waterways are more likely than names of hills or human settlements to retain their original names when an area is occupied by a community speaking a different language. So, if any pre-Celtic elements remain anywhere in the place-names of Britain, the most likely place to find them would be in the names of rivers and streams. But if there are any such elements, they are not easily identified. One of the foremost authorities on the place-names of England, Eilert Ekwall, in his book on the names of English rivers, while not excluding the possibility that some unexplained river-names *may* be pre-Celtic, argues that 'pre-Celtic origin should be kept as a rather remote contingency' and tersely comments (1928:lv):

I cannot point to any definite name that strikes me as probably pre-Celtic.

One the other hand, Professor W.F.H. Nicolaisen has recently argued persuasively (1976:173–91) that various Scottish river-names (including (*Black*)*adder, Ale, Ayr, Farrar, Naver, Shiel*) are Indo-European[3] but *not* Celtic, and so presumably pre-Celtic. If so, then 'when the Celts first arrived in Scotland, there were already people present who, as immigrants from Europe centuries before them, had introduced an Indo-European language to the British Isles' (*ibid.*, 191).

Who the earliest inhabitants of Britain were and what their languages were is, then, very much of a mystery. The earliest arrivals to have any kind of recognizable identity were the Celts, in the sense that 'the peoples speaking a Celtic language[4] are the earliest Britons of whom we have written records' (Chadwick, 1964:19).

The Celtic languages can be divided into two main groups, known conventionally as Q-Celtic and P-Celtic. This curious terminology is based on a significant difference in the phonetic development of the two groups. Indo-European seems to have a consonant that can be represented as $[k^w]$ – it was a *k* sound pronounced with the lips rounded, like the *qu* of English quart, etc. To use a technical term, this sound has two 'points of articulation': the tongue is raised until it touches the velum or soft palate (as for the *k* sound in *calm*) but at the same time the lips are drawn together until they almost, but not quite, touch. In languages where this sound occurs, it frequently changes to a *p* – i.e., instead of the flow of air being stopped at the velum, it is stopped at the other point of articulation, i.e. the lips (one can compare, for example, Greek *hippos* 'horse', where this has occurred, with the related Latin form *equus*, where it has not, or Romanian *patru* 'four' with Latin *quattuor* from which it derives). This development took place both in the Celtic speech of Gaul, Gaulish, and in what is known as Brittonic or Brythonic, the branch of Celtic from which Welsh, Cornish and Breton are derived; these two sub-branches of Celtic are therefore grouped together as P-Celtic. On the other hand, the Goidelic or Gaelic languages (which, in their modern forms, are

---

[3] The Indo-European family of languages includes nearly all the languages now spoken in Europe (the major exceptions being Basque, Finnish, Hungarian and Turkish) and a number of extinct and extant Asian languages (including Persian, Sanskrit, Hindi, and a number of other languages of the Indian sub-continent). See W.B. Lockwood, *A Panorama of Indo-European Languages*, London: Hutchinson, 1972.

[4] There is no necessary connection between race and language. To take an obvious example, the fact that a child of, say, Polish or Asian parents may grow up in Britain speaking as his first language a Germanic tongue, namely English, does not of course imply that he has inherited any of his genes from the Angles, Saxons and Jutes who first brought the English language to these shores. Indeed, few if any Englishmen are likely to be of pure Anglo-Saxon descent. Likewise, although the French language is derived from Latin, the French people probably have very much more Celtic and Germanic blood than Roman in their veins. So, when speaking of 'Celts', we are really using this as a convenient abbreviation for 'the Celtic-speaking peoples' (who may well have been, at the time in question, pure-blooded Celts, but this is of little consequence for our purposes).

Irish, Scottish Gaelic and Manx) did not share this development but, for a while, retained the [kʷ], written as Q, though it has since been simplified to [k], written C; these are therefore the Q-Celtic languages. The point is well illustrated by the following pairs of words:

Irish	*Welsh*	
(Q-Celtic)	(P-Celtic)	
cé	pwy	'who'[5]
ceathair	pedwar	'four'[5]
ceann	pen	'head'
ċoire	pair	'cauldron'
cruth	pryd	'appearance'

The Celts appear on the world scene in the sixth century BC, in parts of the territory now consisting of Bavaria, Switzerland, Austria, Bohemia and Hungary, which makes them 'the first great nation north of the Alps whose name we know' (Powell, 1948:13). It is far from clear when the first Celtic-speaking tribes arrived in the British Isles, or how many other waves of Celts were to follow them in later centuries, or what precisely were the ethnic and linguistic relationships between the different waves. Various interpretations of the evidence – or, rather, the relative lack of evidence – seem to be possible. One, which is preferred by the eminent Celticists Myles Dillon and Nora Chadwick, is that the Bronze Age Beaker Folk who arrived around 2000 BC were Celts (see Dillon and Chadwick, 1967:4–5). At the other extreme is the view (which Dillon and Chadwick acknowledge is also tenable) that the first Celts to arrive were the Iron Age people who came in successive waves from the mid-sixth century to the early first century BC (when, as Caesar tells us, in the first documented reference to the coming of the Celts to Britain, some of the Belgae crossed to Britain from northern Gaul). An intermediate position is adopted by Leslie Alcock who argues (1970:56) that the archaeological evidence leads to the conclusion that there was 'by 700 BC, the presence of a military aristocracy in Britain and Ireland; and it would be difficult to deny this aristocracy the title Celtic. We can therefore postulate a common Celtic culture on both sides of the Irish Sea in the seventh century BC.'

Nor do we know for certain whether the earliest Celts to reach Ireland first passed through Britain or whether they made their way there directly from the Continent. And did the distinction between P-Celtic and Q-Celtic arise before some of the Celts left the mainland of Europe, or after they had settled in these islands? And, on the former assumption, which waves spoke P-Celtic (or an earlier form of it) and which spoke Q-Celtic? Thomas O'Rahilly, for example (1946:20), argued an unorthodox case with reference to Ireland, namely that, in the last five centuries BC, there were four waves of Celtic invaders, of whom the first three (who also, at the same time or earlier, invaded Britain) were P-Celts, and only the last arrivals, who reached Ireland directly from Gaul, were Goidels, i.e. Q-Celts.

Dillon and Chadwick, however, find O'Rahilly's demonstration unconvincing, and argue (1967:5) that 'the notion that this more archaic language

---

[5] Compare the corresponding Latin forms *quis* 'who?' and *quattuor* 'four', which retain the Indo-European [kᵂ] as *qu-*.

[i.e. Goidelic] was brought latest . . . is inherently improbable. We think it more likely that Goidelic was first established in Ireland, and that Brythonic [i.e. P-Celtic] tribes made settlements there, just as Irish settlements were made in Wales both north and south'. Likewise, Alcock maintains (1970:55) that

> there is no evidence for a primary or general Goidelic settlement in Britain. The evidence for Goidels is confined entirely to the western fringe of this island, and their presence can best be accounted for by historically-documented migrations *eastward* over the Irish Sea in the late fourth and fifth centuries AD.

He further presumes that the original Celtic-speaking colonists 'spoke a more or less common language at the time of their arrival here. The development of the P and Q variants of Celtic speech then took place largely in these islands, though it is known that further Brythonic invasions reinforced Southern England in later centuries' (*ibid.*).

I shall not attempt to enter further into these questions where even specialists find it impossible to arrive at a consensus. What is certain is that, whatever may have been the factors that brought this about, before the beginning of the Christian era Ireland was mainly Goidelic-speaking and Britain predominantly Brittonic-speaking, but that there was much traffic in both directions.

References

Alcock, Leslie (1970). 'Was there an Irish Sea culture-province in the Dark Ages?' in Donald Moore (ed.), *The Irish Sea Province in Archaeology and History*, Cardiff: Cambrian Archaeological Association, pp. 55–65.

Bowen, E.G. (1957). 'Race and culture', in E.G. Bowen (ed.), *Wales. A Physical, Historical and Regional Geography*, London: Methuen, pp. 131–40.

Campbell, John B. (1977). *The Upper Palaeolithic of Britain. A Study of Man and Nature in the Late Ice Age*. 2 vols. Oxford: Clarendon Press.

Chadwick, Nora (1964). *Celtic Britain*. 2nd impression, revised. London: Thames & Hudson. (1st ed., 1963)

Dillon, Myles, and Nora K. Chadwick (1972). *The Celtic Realms*. 2nd ed. London: Weidenfeld & Nicolson. (1st ed., 1967)

Ekwall, E. (1928). *English River-Names*. Oxford: Clarendon Press.

Hawkes, Jacquetta and Christopher (1948). *Prehistoric Britain*. London: Chatto & Windus.

Jones, J. Morris (1899). 'Pre-Aryan syntax in insular Celtic' (dated 1899), in John Rhŷs and David Brynmore-Jones. *The Welsh People*, London: Fisher Unwin, 1900 (4th ed., 1906), pp. 617–41.

Mourant, A.E., and I.M. Watkin (1952). 'Blood groups, anthropology and language in Wales and the western countries.' *Heredity*, 6:13–36.

Nicolaisen, W.F.H. (1976). *Scottish Place-names. Their Study and Significance*. London: Batsford.

O'Rahilly, Thomas F. (1946). *Early Irish History and Mythology*. Dublin: The Dublin Institute for Advance Studies.

Pokorny, J. (1926–30). 'Das nicht-indogermanische Substrat im Irischen.' *Zeitschrift für celtische Philologie*, 16 (1926–27), 95–144, 231–66, 363–94; 17 (1927–28), 373–88; 18 (1929–30), 233–48.

Powell, T.G.E. (1958). *The Celts.* London: Thames & Hudson.

Watkin, Morgan (1956). '*ABO* blood groups and racial characteristics in rural Wales.' *Heredity*, 10:161–93.

2 Pictish

In 1955, F.T. Wainwright edited a volume of studies by various scholars under the title *The Problem of the Picts* (see References). The only criticism one might make of this title is that it suggests that there is only one problem associated with the Picts, whereas in reality there are several. In the words of Isabel Henderson (1967:12):

> The Picts have acquired the reputation of being quite the darkest of the peoples of Dark Age Britain. As the formidable enemies of the Romans swarming over Hadrian's Wall the Picts are familiar enough, but before and after this break in the clouds all is obscure and what people remember best about the Picts is that very little is known about them.

The most intriguing problem, perhaps, but one that is beyond the scope of this book, is that of the truly enigmatic symbols that are found carved on standing-stones of the fifth to the ninth centuries (and very occasionally on pieces of silverware and other artefacts) over a vast area of the north of Scotland.[1] The very name of the Picts, too, is problematic. Is the word *Picti*, which occurs in Latin, merely the Latin *picti*, i.e. 'the painted ones', and if so, precisely what does it mean? Does it refer to their practice, mentioned by various Latin writers, of painting and tattooing themselves? Or, says Dr Henderson (1967:51), 'it could also be a translation of a very early British collective name, *Pritani*, which may mean "the people of the designs", and which came to be used in the form *Priteni* to refer exclusively to the peoples north of the Forth'. Or is it a different word altogether, perhaps an adaptation of some name that the Picts applied to themselves?

Where did the Picts come from, and what in the end became of them? Here we have more mystery. There is, as Isabel Henderson says (1971:52), 'no trace of the *Picti* having arrived at some point in time to settle in North Britain in the way that the Scots arrived in Argyll and the Anglo-Saxon peoples arrived in the south'. They are first referred to as *Picti* in a Latin poem of AD 297 but there can be no reasonable doubt that they had been dwelling in much of Scotland north of the Forth for some considerable time before that. Indeed,

---

[1] On the Pictish symbols, see in particular J. Romilly Allen and J. Anderson, *The Early Christian Monuments of Scotland* (Edinburgh, 1903), R.B.K. Stevenson, 'Pictish art', in Wainwright (ed.), 1955:97–128, and Charles Thomas, 'The interpretation of the Pictish symbols', *The Archaeological Journal*, 120(1963) : 31–97.

it is highly probable that the Caledonii, the Venicones, the Vacomagi, and the Taezali, mentioned by Ptolemy in the second century, and other peoples named by later writers, were in fact Pictish tribes. There are various references to the Picts over the next few centuries — we have lists of the names of Pictish kings, beginning with that of Bridei in the sixth century, we know they were evangelized by Columba, mention of their wars with other peoples occupying parts of Scotland (the Britons, the Northumbrian Angles, and the Scots) has come down to us, a Pictish bishop attended a council in Rome in 721, and in or about 843 Kenneth mac Alpin, king of Scots, also succeeded (in circumstances that are not clear) to the throne of Pictland. Thereafter, the Picts disappear from history. It is highly unlikely that they were exterminated, or expelled from the areas they still occupied. What is much more probable is that they were gradually assimilated by the Scots.

The problem that is of direct concern to us is that of the language or languages spoken by the Picts — and what is now established beyond doubt is that, though we know very little about either, at least two languages were spoken in the area and at the period in question. One of these, as we shall see in chapter 11, was a form of Celtic, and we shall refer to it as 'Celtic Pictish'. The other, which we shall refer to for convenience merely as 'Pictish', is the subject of the present chapter.

The fact that there were these two languages has been clearly demonstrated by Professor Kenneth Jackson, who surveys (1955:133–49) all the available evidence. Taking the evidence as presented by Jackson, but setting it out differently (and only in summary form), we can show that it falls into three categories. First, there are statements made by early medieval writers who clearly recognized the existence of a Pictish language, even though their comments are not such as to enable us to come to any conclusions about the nature of that language. We are told by Adamnan in his *Life of St Columba*, completed between 692 and 697, that Columba needed an interpreter in dealing with the Picts, which suggests that, whatever their language may have been, it was either not Gaelic or, if it was, then it was a very different kind of Gaelic from that spoken by Columba. Some forty years later, the Venerable Bede, in his *Ecclesiastical History of the English People*, which he completed in 731, refers to the existence in his day of four peoples, each speaking a different language, namely the English *(Angli)*, the Scots (i.e. Gaels) *(Scotti)*, the Britons *(Brettoni)* and the Picts *(Picti)* — though, again, this is not enough to warrant the conclusion that Pictish was necessarily unrelated to either Gaelic or Brittonic. Secondly, there is the evidence for Celtic Pictish, which we shall discuss in the appropriate place (see pp. 155–6). Finally, we have the evidence for the other (and presumably earlier) Pictish language, to which we now turn our attention.

Classical and early medieval sources provide for Pictland, among a large number of certain or probable Celtic names, a few that cannot be shown to be Celtic and so may well be pre-Celtic. These range from the names of the four tribes mention by Ptolemy, the Caledonii, the Venicones, the Vacomagi, and the Taezali, to some of the names figuring in the list (perhaps dating from the ninth century but based on earlier sources) of Pictish kings, including Bridei, Derelei and Bargoit.

Our main source for Pictish, however, is a couple of dozen brief inscriptions,[2] mainly in Ogams (see pp. 28–9 below), dating probably from the eighth and ninth centuries, carved on standing stones from various localities in those parts of Scotland known to have been occupied by the Picts. These inscriptions, as we shall see, seem to be almost completely unintelligible, and though some scholars in the past argued that the language in question was Celtic, either P-Celtic or Q-Celtic,[3] this view is now completely abandoned.[4]

One of the first to suggest that Pictish was not merely not Celtic but not even Indo-European[5] was Sir John Rhŷs, who at one time (1892–3) propounded but later (1897–8) abandoned the view that it was an Iberian language related to Basque (a view that, as we shall see, has recently been revived by Henri Guiter).

In 1940, R.A.S. Macalister devoted a major article to the problem, discussing every inscription at great length. We shall return to Macalister's interpretation later. Meanwhile, we can quote his conclusion (1940:223) which is:

> For me one thing is absolutely certain. The language of which a few disconnected scraps are recorded in the inscriptions studied in these pages, whatever it may be, is altogether independent of Celtic.

This rather negative statement is almost certainly true, but the positive side of Macalister's commentary does not carry conviction. The corpus of evidence available for analysis is, after all, very restricted, namely twenty-two inscriptions (Macalister rejects the others that are usually assumed to be Pictish), all of them brief and some of them damaged or difficult to decipher. On this slender and uncertain basis, Macalister considers that he can come to valid conclusions both about pronunciation and about some aspects of Pictish grammar (such as that Pictish is an inflected language in which 'the relation [e.g. the genitive relation] between substantive and substantive is expressed by suffixes', *ibid.*, 220, and that it has grammatical gender). He also proposes translations of some of the inscriptions. We can take by way of example one of the longest of the inscriptions, from Lunnasting in Shetland, which Macalister reads as follows (there is some doubt about two or three characters):

ETTYCUHETTS AHEHHTTANNN HCCVVEVV NEHHTONN

Macalister makes (*ibid.*, 210–12) a number of bold assumptions on the basis of which he arrives at his grammatical analysis and his tentative translation. The -S of the first group (or word, if it is a word) is equated with the final -ES found in another inscription and, for no very good reason, is taken to be 'a Pictish feminine suffix' added to a personal (female) name ETTYCUHETT.

[2] The most recent and most thorough survey of these inscriptions is provided by Oliver J. Padel's unfortunately unpublished M. Litt. thesis (1972).

[3] On the terms 'Q-Celtic' and 'P-Celtic' see p. 16 above.

[4] For a summary of the various hypotheses advanced regarding the linguistic position of Pictish, see Jackson, 1955:130–2.

[5] On the Indo-European languages, see Chapter 1, note 3, p. 16.

The second 'word' is analysed as AHEHHT, translated by what Macalister himself recognizes is no more than a 'provisional guess' as 'husband', and -ANNN, which he had already argued in respect of another inscription could be a feminine possessive suffix. HCCVVEVV is perhaps 'a clumsy way of spelling the word which [on another Pictish stone] appears as KEVV' – 'let us provisionally translate this word . . . as "stone" ', he says. NEHHTON is plausibly identified with the known Pictish name 'Nechton'. We therefore get a word-for-word translation 'of-Ettycuhett / (of) her husband (?) / (the) stone / (of) Nechton', i.e. 'The grave of Ettycuhett's husband Nechton'.

All this is too speculative and indeed fanciful to carry conviction, and it brought down on Macalister's head the charge that he was so sure of his interpretations that he went in for 'correcting the engravers when their Pictish was ungrammatical' (Jackson, 1955:131).

The most recent attempt at solving the Pictish problem has been made by a French scholar, Professor Henri Guiter (1968), who concludes that Pictish was a form of Basque. This is not as implausible as might at first seem, as it is well within the bounds of possibility that, among the many peoples that migrated around the coasts of Western Europe in the prehistoric period and later, a Basque-speaking people may have made their way as far north as Scotland. Before we can discuss this theory further, however, we must turn to consider the Pictish inscriptions themselves and, in particular, the problem of arriving at acceptable readings of them.

Illustration 1. Pictish inscription in Latin characters on the 'Drosten Stone'. (Crown copyright)

Two of the inscriptions are in Latin characters. The first of these, on a slab now in the church at Fordoun, probably dates from the eighth century. It is in poor condition and indistinct, but most authorities agree that the reading is:

PIDARNOIN

in which IDARNOIN may well be a personal name. The other, carved on one of the edges of a stone cross now in the museum at St Vigeans (near Dundee) (illustration **1**), is in what is considered to be a late ninth-century script and presents no problems at all so far as the actual characters used are concerned. It reads:

DROSTEN
IPEUORET
ETTFOR
CUS

It is generally accepted, on the basis of a comparison with names occurring in the lists of Pictish kings or in the Brittonic languages, that *Drosten, Uoret* and *Forcus* are personal names. *Ett* has sometimes been taken to be a mis-spelling of Latin *et* 'and' (but no arguments are advanced in favour of the assumption), and *ipe* is problematic.

The other Pictish inscriptions are all in the Ogam alphabet, which, as we shall see when we come to discuss early Irish (see below pp. 28–9), consists of groups of strokes cut along a base line, each group corresponding to a letter of the Latin alphabet. Apart from the Pictish inscriptions in Scotland, all of the Ogam inscriptions, not only in Ireland but also in the Isle of Man, Wales and Cornwall, are in Irish, and there can be no reasonable doubt that the Picts borrowed this alphabet from the Gaels.

There is no reason not to assume that a given combination of strokes has the same alphabetical value in the Pictish Ogams as in the Irish Ogams. But this does not mean that there is no problem in deciphering the inscriptions. First, some of the inscriptions are broken, so, to take a simple example, it may not be certain whether two strokes at the beginning or end of an inscription represent a complete character or all that is left of an original group of three, four or five strokes. Then it may be uncertain whether a group of four strokes is to be taken as a single group (i.e. K) or as two groups of two strokes (i.e. D + D). To complicate the problem further, it is not always certain whether an apparent scratch on a stone is deliberate, i.e. part of the Ogam inscription, or a mere crack or flaw of no significance.

The crucial importance of the transcription of the Ogams emerges very clearly when we come to consider Guiter's theory that Pictish is closely related to Basque. This can be easily illustrated by taking the brief inscription on a stone from Keiss Bay, on the east coast of Caithness (illustration **2**). Rhŷs and Macalister agree on a reading that differs considerably from Guiter's:

Guiter	N	AU	K	E	T	AGO	N	A
Rhŷs, Macalister	N	E	HT	E	T	R		I

Guiter interprets the inscription, on the basis of Basque, as follows:

(i) NAUKE = Basque *nauke*, from *nau* 'he possesses me' + a suffix *-ke*, which gives the verb the value of a 'conjectural present' tense, to be translated here as a future tense.

(ii) TAGONA = Basque *dagona*, from *dago* 'he is', + *-n-* (corresponding to a relative pronoun), + *-a* which specifies 'definiteness'.

The proposed translation is therefore: 'He will (doubtless) possess me, he who is here.'[6] The similarity between what is claimed to be the Pictish inscription and the Basque equivalent is certainly very striking − but, as we have seen, all depends on whether or not one accepts Guiter's reading, which is not that of the Celticists.[7]

The most one can say at this stage in favour of Guiter's interpretation is that he puts forward a tantalizing hypothesis, and one that is not *a priori* implausible. Against it must be set the fact that it depends on an interpretation of the Ogams that has not yet been accepted by Celticists as valid. There is the further consideration, though admittedly a highly subjective one, that some of the translations proposed by Guiter strike one as exceptionally fanciful and not at all the kind of thing one expects to find in Dark Age inscriptions, whatever their provenance. Three examples by way of illustration:

(i)   (Lunnasting, Shetland) 'Because of Etxeko, I was in grief, without will-power.'[8]

(ii)   (Golspie, Sutherland) 'Aldalurrekoa attacked the bear.'

(iii) (A tripartite inscription from Brodie, Moray). 'I, Idarrako, depart. He departs, melancholy, so let him have need of tears. On the place where he lies, the supply of earth that he bears has burned him. He is asleep beneath the snow. Arise! He has a stream of moans.'[9]

We have no idea how long Pictish survived as a spoken language. Though the inscriptions probably date from the eighth and ninth centuries, it does not necessarily follow that the language was still then in everyday use. It is at least possible, as has been suggested by Jackson (1955:154) and Oliver Padel (1972:38), that a Celtic-speaking population adopted an earlier, non-Indo-European, language for ritual or commemorative purposes and that, consequently, it remained in use for epigraphic purposes even after it had been replaced by Celtic as an everyday spoken language.

---

[6] Guiter's French rendering (1968:299) is: 'Il me possédera (sans doute), celui qui est ici.'

[7] In fact, though there is considerable doubt about the interpretation of some of the inscriptions (or parts of them), the Keiss Bay inscription is a particularly clear one (Padel, 1972:107, refers to 'the great clarity with which the inscription has survived') and, in this case at least, Guiter's transcription is certainly to be rejected.

[8] 'A cause d'Etxeko, j'étais dans la douleur, sans volonté' (Guiter, 1968:293).

[9] 'Moi, Idarrako, je m'en vais. Il s'en va mélancolique: ainsi, qu'il ait besoin de pleurs.' 'Sur sa couche l'apport de terre qu'il supporte l'a brûle'. 'Il est endormi sous la neige. Lève-toi. Il a un torrent de plaintes' (Guiter, 1968:303). In fact, Oliver Padel (1972:69) says of this set of three inscriptions that they are 'worn to the point of being nearly indecipherable' and (*ibid.*, 73) that they are 'too fragmentary to be of very much use linguistically'.

Illustration 2. Pictish Ogam inscription on the Keiss Bay stone.

References

Guiter, Henri (1968). 'La langue des Pictes.' *Boletín de la Real Sociedad Vascongada de los Amigos del País* (San Sebastián), 24:281–321.

Henderson, Isabel (1967). *The Picts*. London: Thames & Hudson

—(1971). 'The problem of the Picts', in Gordon Menzies (ed.), *Who are the Scots?* London: BBC, pp. 51–65.

Jackson, K.H. (1955). 'The Pictish language', in Wainwright 1955, pp. 129–66.

Macalister, R.A.S. (1940). 'The inscriptions and language of the Picts', in John Ryan (ed.), *Essays and Studies presented to Professor Eoin MacNeill*, Dublin: At the Sign of the Three Candles, pp. 184–226.

Padel, Oliver J. (1972). 'Inscriptions of Pictland.' Unpublished M. Litt. thesis, University of Edinburgh.

Rhŷs, John (1982–93). 'The inscriptions and language of the northern Picts.' *Proceedings of the Society of Antiquaries of Scotland*, 26:263–351; 'Addenda and corrigenda', *ibid.*, 411–12.

—(1897–98). 'A revised account of the inscriptions of the northern Picts.' *Proceedings of the Society of Antiquaries of Scotland*, 32:324–98.

Wainwright, F.T. (ed.) (1955). *The Problem of the Picts*. Edinburgh: Nelson.

3   Irish in Early Britain

There is, as we shall see, firm evidence that some western parts of Wales and England were at some stage occupied by Irish-speaking communities of Goidels. Some scholars[1] once held that these were the remnants of the earliest waves of Celtic-speaking immigrants who, in their view, first occupied Britain and only later crossed to Ireland. Among those to look at things in this way was the first Professor of Celtic at Oxford, Sir John Rhŷs, who wrote that, at one stage:

> All the British Islands may be treated as Goidelic, excepting certain parts where the neolithic natives may have been able to make a stand against the Goidels; but at a later period there arrived another Celtic people with another Celtic language, which was probably to all intents and purposes the same as that of the Gauls. These later invaders called themselves Brittones and Belgae, and seized on the best portions of Britain, driving the Goidelic Celts before them to the west and north of the island (Rhŷs, 1908:217–18).

This view is, as we have seen (pp. 17–18), now generally regarded as untenable.

There are a number of Irish words in Welsh that must have entered the language during the Dark Age period (see p. 33 below), but these do not in themselves prove that there were Irish-speaking communities on Welsh soil. The strongest evidence for the existence of such communities is provided by the Irish inscriptions in the so-called 'Ogam' script found in Wales and other western parts of this island. Ogam is a method of representing characters of the Latin alphabet by means of notches and grooves cut on stone slabs. The vowels are represented by notches in one edge[2] of the slab, and the consonants by grooves cut on one side or the other of the edge or obliquely across it (fig. 1). Although these combinations of notches and grooves look nothing like the usual characters of the Latin alphabet, they do stand for Latin letters[3] and do not constitute a different alphabet. The point will perhaps be clear if one thinks of the morse code in which different sequences of dots and dashes, whether expressed visually by means of

---

[1] For a brief account of their views, see Charles Thomas, 1972:253–4.

[2] Usually a vertical edge, but occasionally a horizontal one. (In the case of the Pictish Ogams – see pp. 24–5 – the baseline may be drawn on the face of the slab, as shown in illustration 2, p. 26.)

[3] For an ingenious theory that provides at least a possible explanation of what is, on the face of things, the curious grouping of the letters, and in particular of the consonants, see James Carney, 'The invention of the Ogom [sic] cipher', *Eriu*, 26 (1975); 53–65.

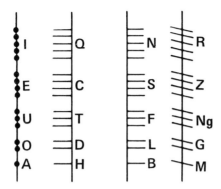

Fig. **1.** The Ogam alphabet

flashing lights or audibly as 'buzzes', correspond *specifically* to letters of the Latin (and not, say, the Greek or Russian or Arabic) alphabet – e.g.:

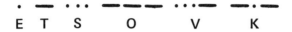

The origins of Ogam are unknown. Two recent, and not necessarily contradictory, suggestions are that it is based on 'the very similar system of notches and wooden rods used in counting sheep, the well-known tally-sicks' (Jackson, 1953:152), and that 'it was evidently a ceremonial script, for we find it only on memorial stones, and in the sagas it is associated either with funeral rites or with cryptic messages' (Dillon and Chadwick, 1972:198).

The great majority of the Ogam inscriptions are to be found in Ireland itself, where about 300 of them survive, mostly in the south-west. It is difficult, and in some cases virtually impossible, to date them with any great precision. Most of them probably date from the fifth and sixth centuries, though some could be earlier and some are certainly later (seventh or perhaps even eighth century).

Our immediate concern, however, is with the fifty-seven Ogams outside Ireland. Of these, forty are in Wales (mainly in the south-west) (map **1**, p. 32), eight in Cornwall and Devon, one in Hampshire, six in the Isle of Man and two in Argyll. One important distinction is that, whereas in Ireland the inscription is only in Irish, forty-four of the fifty-seven Irish Ogam stones found outside Ireland also bear an inscription in Latin (which in all but two cases, both in Wales, is the almost exact equivalent of the Ogam inscription) or, at the very least, a Celtic name in normal Latin letters. Although it is far from easy to date the Latin inscriptions, they do provide some help, and Kenneth Jackson suggests (1950:205) that some twenty-seven or twenty-eight of the thirty bilingual inscriptions belong to the period between about 450 and 600, the remaining two or three being from the early seventh century.

The inscriptions are in general very brief, and what Nash-Williams (1950:6) says of the Ogam stones in Wales is also true of the others:

The language of the Ogam inscriptions is purely funerary, and is limited in the main to the use of the personal name, either simply or in various combinations.

Where the inscription consists of only one word, a personal name, this is in the genitive case and so must be interpreted as meaning something like 'the stone (or memorial) of . . .'. A stone from Jordanston (Pembrokeshire) for example has, in Ogam, only DOVAGNI, i.e. '(The stone of) Dovagnus' (though in this case, as in some others, the Latin version is a little fuller, viz. TIGERNACI DOBAGNI, i.e. '(the stone of) Tigernacus Dobagnus'). Among the longer inscriptions are:

(i)   (from Eglwys Cymyn, Carmarthenshire) (Nash-Williams, 1950:109):
      Irish: INIGENA CUNIGNI AUITTORIGES
      Latin: AVITORIA FILIA CUNIGNI
      i.e. 'Avitoria the daughter of Cunignus'.
(ii) (from Cilgerran, Pembrokeshire) (Nash-Williams, 1950:184):
      Irish: TRENAGUSU MAQI MAQITRENI
      Latin: TRENEGUSSI FILI MACUTRENI HIC IACIT
      i.e. '(the stone of) Trenagussus son of Maquitrenus' (with in addi-
      tion, in Latin, '(he) lies here' − a formula that frequently occurs in
      the Latin inscriptions but never in the Irish).
(iii) (from St Dogmaels, Pembrokeshire) (Nash-Williams, 1950:213):
      Irish: SAGRAGNI MAQI CUNATAMI
      Latin: SAGRANI FILI CVNOTAMI
      i.e. '(the stone of) Sagra(g)nus son of Cunotamus'.

The amount of linguistic information to be culled from the Ogam inscriptions is therfore limited, but not negligible, as Jackson in particular has shown. An interesting feature of a stone from Castell Dwyran (Carmarthenshire), probably dating from about AD 550, is that it illustrates strikingly the different forms of the same name in Q-Celtic and P-Celtic: whereas the Ogam inscription reads VOTECORIGAS '(the stone of) Votecorix', the Latin version has MEMORIA VOTEPORIGIS PROTICTORIS 'The memorial of Voteporix the Protector' − we therefore have the Q-Celtic/P-Celtic alternation *VoteCorix/VotePorix*. As far as grammar goes, the inscriptions give us numerous examples of the genitive case and little else. The vocabulary, apart from the proper names, is limited to such words (in the genitive) as MAQI 'son' (a number of instances), one example (quoted above) of INIGENA 'daughter', AV (V) I 'grandson' or 'descendant', together with 'MOSAC, a common-noun of unknown meaning rendered in the Latin . . . as PVVERI [i.e. "of the boy"]' (Jackson, 1953:171). Jackson makes shrewd use of these and other linguistic features of the inscriptions to argue convincingly that Irish remained as a spoken language in western Britain at least until the sixth or even the seventh century.

We now turn to the problem of identifying, at least approximately, the areas where the Irish in fact settled.

The earliest serious Irish raids seem to have been on south-west Wales, probably around AD 270–275, from which time 'the pressure of pirates and invaders upon the western coasts of Britain was second only to that of the Teutonic peoples upon the eastern and southern shores' (Wheeler, 1925:234). Indeed, these incursions soon developed into something much more than raids, since there is evidence that, perhaps as early as the late third century, settlers from the Déisi tribe of Co. Waterford established a dynasty of Irish kings in south-west Wales (Dyfed),[4] where they continued to rule until the tenth century. This does not of course necessarily imply either that the British population was driven out of the area or that British ceased to be spoken there. On the contrary:

> It is clear that the Irish who had settled in this part of Dyfed lived side by side with the British-speaking population on terms of close relationship. . . . 'Raiding' is here an irrelevant word, and the idea of conquest is contrary to the evidence. Everything points to a peaceful penetration (Chadwick, 1976:32).

From Dyfed, the Irish seem to have thrust further east, where they founded the tiny kingdom of Brycheiniog, whose name remains in that of the former county of Brecknock (in Welsh, *Brycheiniog*) (now forming the southern part of the county of Powys), and, in English only, in the name of its county town, Brecon (in Welsh, *Aberhonddu*). The ruling dynasty of Brycheiniog, claiming descent from an Irish prince, Broccán (or in Welsh, Brychan), and a Welsh princess, Marchell, lasted from the fifth to the tenth century. It is noteworthy that this area has a greater number of Irish inscriptions than any other part of Wales except Dyfed (map 1).

Further south, although little is known from historical sources, it is generally agreed that Irish colonies were established in Cornwall and Devon. The existence of six Ogam inscriptions in Cornwall and two in Devon, and the evidence provided by recent archaeological field-work, lead Professor Charles Thomas to suggest (1973–74:6) that Irish-speaking settlers reached the area in two waves, one affecting north-east Cornwall and part of west Devon from the late fifth century AD, and the other reaching west Cornwall and the Isles of Scilly in the following century.

That the Irish settled in North as well as in South Wales, though apparently much less densely, is indicated not only by the presence in that area of three Irish inscriptions but also by place-names that either make reference to the Irish or are of Irish origin:

> The peninsula of Caernarvonshire, and also Anglesey and West Merioneth, were settled by Irish about the same time as Dyfed, and the Irish language was spoken all over the area . . . and is deeply embedded in place-names. At the head of Afon Lledr in Caernarvonshire is *Llyn Iwerddon*, 'Lake of Ireland'. Lower down, near the falls of the Conway River is a hill or place called *Iwerddon*, 'Ireland', and half-way between

---

[4] The kingdom of Dyfed covered a smaller area than the present county of that name, corresponding more closely to the former county of Pembroke and western Carmarthenshire.

is *Dolwyddelan*, 'Gwyddelan's meadow', Gwyddelan being derived from *Gwyddel*, 'a Gael', an Irishman. . . . The Irish of Caernarvonshire, however, came apparently from further north than those of Dyfed, for the northern peninsula was known, and is still known today, by the name of *Lleyn*, from Irish *Laigin*, 'the Leinstermen', while the little village on Nevin Bay still bears the name *Porth Dinllaen*, 'the harbour of the fort of the Leinstermen' (Dillon and Chadwick, 1972:40).

Map 1. The distribution of stones with Irish Ogam inscriptions in Wales.

Specific reference to the presence of Irish settlers in north-west Wales is found in the ninth-century *Historia Brittonum* ('History of the Britons') by Nennius (who perhaps drew on seventh-century sources). According to Nennius, a force of Britons led by Cunedag (or, to give him the modern Welsh form of his name, Cunedda) moved from an area in south-east Scotland to north-west Wales to combat the Irish settlers in that area, and, according to Nennius (whose account may or may not be accurate), he succeeded in expelling them. It is not certain precisely when this migration took place, though a date around AD 400 seems probable. Nor is it known why Cunedda and his men travelled what was at that time a considerable distance to drive out the Irish from an area with which they had no direct connection. It has been plausibly suggested (see Collingwood and Myres, 1937:289−90) that they went at the instigation of the Romans, following their widespread practice of transplanting a tribe from one frontier district of the Empire to another to act as a local militia.

That there was much contact of many kinds, peaceful (religious and commercial, for example) as well as hostile, between the various populations making up what has been called 'the Irish Sea province' is beyond all doubt,[5] and its linguistic effects are to be found both in the numerous words of Welsh origin in Irish (which are beyond the scope of this book) and in the Irish loan-words in Welsh. The latter include *brat* 'rag, apron' (Irish *brat* 'cloak'), *brechdan* 'bread-and-butter, sandwich' (Old Irish *brechtán* 'bread-and-butter', now *breachtán*), *cerbyd* 'vehicle' (O. Ir. *carpat* 'war chariot', now *carbad*), *codwm* 'a fall' (Ir. *cutaim* 'a fall'), *cogor* 'chattering' (O. Ir. *cocur* 'whisper', now *cogar*), *croesan* 'buffoon, jester' (O. Ir. *crossán* 'buffon, jester'), *dengyn* 'grim, stubborn, inflexible' (O. Ir. *dangen* 'strong, firm', now *dáingean*), *dichell* 'trick, stratagem' (Mid. Ir. *díchell* 'concealment'), *tolc* 'dent' (Ir. *tolc* 'tear') (Lewis, 1946:82−4). A few Welsh place-names are also probably of Irish origin, including in particular a number of names of rivers and streams ending in *-ach* or *-an* (see Thomas, 1938), such as *Clarach* (Ir. *claragh* 'level place') or *Desach* (which may perhaps include the name of the invading tribe of the Déisi, though the fact that the stream in question is in North Wales whereas the Déisi settled mainly in south-west Wales is perhaps a counterindication). Were the study of Welsh place-names further advanced than it is, more might well have been said about this. Meanwhile, the following comment by Professor D. Simon Evans (1979:25) will serve to draw attention to the potential interest of place-names in this connection:

> As we are reminded by the late Professor Melville Richards [Richards (1960)], the Ogam stones were erected to commemorate members of the ruling class: their absence in certain areas, such as those north of Teifi, may only indicate that the Irish were not in power there when such stones were being erected. They may well have been present in some of

---

[5] Various archaeological, historical, literary, ecclesiastical and architectural aspects of this multi-faceted relationship were discussed in the papers given to a conference held by the Cambrian Archaeological Association at Aberystwyth in 1968 and since published under the title *The Irish Sea Province in Archaeology and History*, ed. Donald Moore, Cardiff: Cambrian Archaeological Association, 1970.

these parts, and their language spoken. Evidence for this could be forthcoming from a detailed and exhaustive study of place names. Professor Richards has already shown how names in *Cnwc* 'hillock' (Irish *cnoc*) suggest considerable Irish influence in Ceredigion south of the Ystwyth. . . . We do then have evidence suggesting that at an earlier time Irish may well have been more prevalent, in Ceredigion, and also in other areas, such as the north-west, in Anglesey and Caernarvon.

How long did Irish remain as a spoken language in those western parts of this island where it is known to have been introduced? As far as North Wales is concerned, one cannot accept at its face value Nennius's statement that the Irish were totally expelled by Cunedda and his followers, which would have been about the year AD 400, since their inscriptions show that the Irish were still there, and still using Irish, as late as the sixth century. There are however only three such inscriptions in North Wales, and Charles Thomas may well be right in arguing (1972:260) that this indicates not only that Irish settlements must have been 'far less intensive' and 'more localised' in that area than elsewhere but that they were 'more swiftly assimilated'.[6] Jackson (1953:171) regards it as certain, on the basis of the Ogam inscriptions in Dyfed and of features of the spelling of various Irish names in the corresponding Latin inscriptions, that Irish was still spoken in south-west Wales in the second half of the sixth century and probably even in the seventh century.[7] Similarly the forms of Irish names occurring in Latin inscriptions in Devon and Cornwall suggest that, there too, Irish survived into the sixth and perhaps as late as the seventh century (*ibid.*, 172).[8] There was presumably a period – perhaps a lengthy one – of bilingualism before Irish died out in the areas in question and the population of Irish or mixed Irish and British descent became absorbed into the British-speaking population.

Before we leave the question of Irish speech in Wales, we must consider the curious problem of numerals (up to '20') of undoubted Irish origin identified

---

[6] It is difficult to credit the very different conclusion to which W.J. Gruffydd claimed (1928:342) that all observation led him, namely that part of north-west Wales 'was Irish in speech, probably in the remote parts, up to the Norman Conquest'.

[7] D. Simon Evans has recently suggested, though only tentatively, that the existence in Wales of nine stones bearing inscriptions in Ogam only (four in Pembroke, two in Brecknock, one each in Ceredigion, Carmarthen and Glamorgan) may indicate areas of more intensive Goidelic or Irish culture, where Irish alone may have been spoken (Evans, 1979:33). Had the stones in question been more or less concentrated in one or two areas, one might perhaps have had some sympathy for this view, but the fact that they are so scattered argues against it. In general, Evans agrees with Jackson, and considers that 'one is justified in regarding the circumstance that no Ogam stones are found later than around 600 as very suggestive. There is no evidence from any other source that Irish as a living language survived in Wales beyond this time, and it is hardly likely that it was much in use after about the middle of the seventh' (*ibid.*, 27).

[8] Charles Thomas's conclusion (1973–74:6) is not much different: 'On the reasonable assumption that an inscription with an Irish name (in Ogam, or Roman letters) marks the grave of an Irish-speaker, and that where all inscriptions in a district are in Ogam this implies at least the adoption there of an Irish mode of commemoration, then we can state that there were Irish-speakers in north-east Cornwall and west Devon *c*. AD 500, and for some time afterwards.'

and collected in Cardiganshire between the wars by a local antiquarian, David Thomas, who (1939:105) considered them 'a linguistic discovery of the greatest importance'. He had originally published seven versions of these numerals (Thomas, 1924), and by 1939 had recorded 39 versions (33 from Cardiganshire, the others from neighbouring counties) (Thomas, 1939). The closeness of these forms to Irish is clearly illustrated by the following set from Llanwnen which can be taken as fairly typical:[9]

	1	2	3	4	5
Llanwnen	ên	dôr	dâr	câr	cŵi
Irish	(h)aon	dó	tri	ceathair	cúig
	6	7	8	9	10
	sich	soch	nich	noch	de
	sé	seach	hocht	naoi	deich

(Note (i) that the circumflex accent of *ê, ô*, etc, indicates a long vowel, (ii) that *ŵ* in *cŵi* represents a vowel similar to *oo* in *boot*, and (iii) that *(h)oan, ceathair* and *naoi* are pronounced rather like *ên, kyáhir* and *nê* respectively.)

Thomas's 1924 article attracted the attention of the eminent Norwegian Celticist, Alf Sommerfelt who, the following year, published an article (Sommerfelt, 1925) in which he argued not only that the numerals in question were indeed Irish but that certain phonetic features indicated that they derived from a form of Irish that was earlier than that of the most ancient Irish manuscripts. One might reasonably assume that, if Sommerfelt is right, then these numerals must have been handed down since the time of the Irish settlements in the area, i.e. from the seventh century or earlier. Sommerfelt however does not say this and, indeed, in answer to objections from another distinguished Celticist, Julius Pokorny, who had argued (Pokorny, 1928) for a recent origin for the numerals in question, Sommerfelt, while maintaining his view as to the ancient origin of the numerals, defended himself (Sommerfelt, 1929) against the charge that, if we were right, they would have to have been preserved for some 1300 years in a Welsh-speaking milieu. But in that case, where did they come from, and when? These are questions Sommerfelt does not ask, let alone answer, though he seems not to have abandoned his theory, as the two articles in question were reprinted nearly forty years later (Sommerfelt, 1962). His theory was indeed accepted by some Celticists but has recently been effectively demolished by David Greene who argues (1975 – 76:311) that 'Sommerfelt's interpretation is, in spite of its august backing, so improbable as not to deserve further consideration'. It seems much more likely that Greene is on the right track in stressing the presence in the area of itinerant Irish workers (who had gone there to work in the lead-mines), and in concluding (*ibid.*, 309) that the Irish-speakers from whom the numerals in question were derived 'were not ancient Goidels, but simple Irish wanderers of the eighteenth century'.

[9] Most of the other sets, however, have *ên* for 'one', *câr* for 'three' and *côr* for 'four' (presumably because of a tendency to introduce both rhyme – *ên, dôr / câr, côr* – and alliteration – *câr/côr* – when the numerals became a jingle rather than a normal, everyday method of counting); cf. the 'Anglo-Cymric score' (pp. 150–2 below).

What of Irish further north and, to begin with, in the north-west of England? The presence of Irish raiders was certainly felt there, perhaps as early as Roman times (see Chadwick, 1976:34). But were there any Irish settlements? No Irish inscriptions are known in that area, but this in itself does not constitute proof that there were no such settlements. The existence of Irish place-names (though admittedly only a handful) in Cumberland – e.g. *Greysouthern* ('Suthan's cliff', from an Irish personal name and *craicc* 'crag, rock, cliff') and *Ravenglass* ('Glas's share' from the personal name *Glas* and Irish *rann* 'part, share') (Ekwall, 1960: xxiii, 205, 381) – may perhaps suggest that Irish influence in that area could have amounted to something more lasting than coastal raids. But it would be dangerous to build too much on these, as it is not certain that these names can be attributed to Goidels of the period we are at the moment interested in. An alternative explanation is that they are due to the influence of Scandinavians who crossed from Ireland to Cumberland in the tenth century. These Viking communities had become so far Celticized during their stay in Ireland that 'they had adopted the Irish method of forming compounds by placing the defining element last' (Reaney, 1960:69) as in such Cumberland names as *Dalemain* 'Máni's valley', *Gillcamban* 'Camban's ravine'. They also introduced at least one place-name element that they had themselves borrowed from Irish, viz. Old Norse *erg* 'shieling, hill pasture', from Irish *airghe*, which occurs in numerous place-names in north-west England, including the first syllables of *Arrowe, Argam, Arkholme*, and the final syllable of *Torva, Berrier*, and *Mozergh* (*ibid.*, 98). So it is a not unreasonable assumption that 'what Gaelic influence there is on [English] place-names is due almost entirely to the immigration of Irish-Norwegian vikings into the north-west in the tenth century' (*ibid.*).

There remain to be mentioned the Isle of Man and Scotland.

The presence of six Ogam inscriptions in Man is sufficient to indicate that Goidels arrived in the island not later than the fifth century and perhaps earlier. They found there a British-speaking population. However, whereas in Wales and south-western England the Irish-speaking community was eventually absorbed into the British-speaking population, here the reverse was the case. In Man, it was British that died out, and Goidelic that survived – for several centuries at least, after which it was to die out, as we shall see in Chapter 6, 'Manx'.

It was probably in the second half of the fifth century that the Goidels of Dálriada (in Antrim) crossed to Argyll where a new Dálriada in due course came into being. The Gaels of Scotland maintained close links and a community of language with their ancestral homeland in the north of Ireland and one can properly use the term 'Common Gaelic', or indeed 'Irish', with reference to the Goidelic speech of Ireland, Scotland and Man for a period of several centuries after the initial invasion. Jackson's conclusion (1951:91–2) is that 'there is absolutely nothing to suggest that the Gaelic of Ireland, Scotland and Man differed in any respect before the tenth century; and on the contrary, there is body of decisive positive evidence tending to show that so far as we can tell they were identical', and that, though some difference between Western Gaelic (i.e. Irish) and Eastern Gaelic (i.e. Scottish and Manx Gaelic) began to appear in the tenth century, they 'continued to be one language, sharing many new developments in common, from the tenth until the thirteenth century'. And even after the separation from Irish in the thirteenth century, Scottish Gaelic and Manx continued for the most part to develop as one language until, probably, the fifteenth century.

We shall trace the fortunes of the two branches of Eastern Gaelic in the chapters devoted to Scottish Gaelic and Manx respectively.

References

Alcock, Leslie (1970). 'Was there an Irish Sea culture-province in the Dark Ages?', in Donald Moore (ed.), *The Irish Sea Province in Archaeology and History*, Cardiff: Cambrian Archaeological Association, pp. 55–65.

Bowen, E.G. (1956). *The Settlements of the Celtic Saints in Wales*. 2nd ed. Cardiff: University of Wales Press. (1st ed., 1954).

Chadwick, Nora K. (1964). *Celtic Britain*, 2nd impression, revised. London: Thames & Hudson. (1st ed., 1963).

Collingwood, R.G., and J.N.L. Myres (1937). *Roman Britain and the English Settlements*. 2nd ed. Oxford: Clarendon Press. (1st ed., 1936).

Dillon, Myles, and Nora K. Chadwick (1972). *The Celtic Realms*. 2nd ed. London: Weidenfeld & Nicolson. (1st ed., 1967).

Ekwall, E. (1960). *The Concise Oxford Dictionary of English Place-Names*. 4th ed. Oxford: Clarendon Press. (1st ed., 1936).

Evans, D. Simon (1979). 'Irish and the languages of post-Roman Wales.' *Studies*, 68:19–32.

Greene, David (1975–76). 'The Irish numerals of Cardiganshire.' *Studia Celtica*, 10–11:305–11.

Gruffydd, W.J. (1928). *Math vab Mathonwy*. Cardiff: University of Wales Press.

Jackson, Kenneth (1950). 'Notes on the Ogam inscriptions of southern Britain', in Sir Cyril Fox and Bruce Dickins (eds.), *The Early Cultures of North-West Europe*, Cambridge: University Press, pp. 199–213.

—(1951). 'Common Gaelic.' *Proceedings of the British Academy*, 37:71–97.

—(1953), *Language and History in Early Britain. A Chronological Survey of the Brittonic Languages, 1st to 12th c. AD*. Edinburgh: University Press.

Lewis, Henry (1946). *Datblygiad yr Iaith Gymraeg*. 2nd ed. Cardiff: University of Wales Press. (1st ed., 1931).

Meyer, Kuno (1895–96). 'Early relations between Gael and Brython.' *The Transactions of the Honourable Society of Cymmrodorion*, pp. 55–86.

Nash-Williams, V.E. (1950). *The Early Christian Monuments of Wales*. Cardiff: University of Wales Press.

Pokorny, Julius (1928). 'Zu den irischen Zahlwörten in Südwales.' *Zeitschrift für celtische Philologie*, 17:261–62.

Reaney, P.H. (1960). *The Origin of English Place Names*. London: Routledge & Kegan Paul.

Rhŷs, John (1895). 'The Goidels in Wales.' *Archaeologia Cambrensis*, 5th series, 12:18–39.

—(1908). *Celtic Britain*. 4th ed. London: SPCK. (1st ed., 1884).

Richards, Melville (1960). 'The Irish settlements in south-west Wales. A topographical approach.' *Journal of the Royal Society of Antiquaries of Ireland*, 90:133–62.

Sommerfelt, Alf (1925). 'Des noms de nombre irlandais au Pays de Galles.'

Avhandlinger utgitt av Det Norske Videnskaps-Akademi, Hist.-Filosof. Klasse, n.2.

—(1929). 'Sur les noms de nombre irlandais trouvés au Pays de Galles.' *Norsk Tidsskrift for Sprogvidenskap*, 3:259–63.

—(1962). *Diachronic and Synchronic Aspects of Language. Selected Articles*. The Hague: Mouton. (Sommerfelt, 1925 and 1929, are reprinted as pp. 259–65 and 266–9 respectively.)

Thomas, Charles (1972). 'The Irish settlements in post-Roman western Britain: a survey of the evidence,' *Journal of the Royal Institution of Cornwall*, 6:251–75.

—(1973–74). 'Irish colonists in south-west Britain.' *World Archaeology*, 5:5–13.

Thomas, David (1924). 'An old system of numeration found in south Cardiganshire.' *Transactions of the Cardiganshire Antiquarian Society*, 3:9–19.

—(1939). 'Old Goidelic numerals.' *Transactions of the Cardiganshire Antiquarian Society*, 14:105–17.

Thomas, R.J. (1938). *Enwau Afonydd a Nentydd Cymru*. Cardiff: University of Wales Press.

Wheeler, R.E.M. (1925). *Prehistoric and Roman Wales*. Oxford: Clarendon Press.

4 Irish in Northern Ireland

Ulster, one of the five ancient provinces of Ireland, consists of nine counties. When Ireland was partitioned under the Anglo-Irish treaty of December 1921, which came into effect in 1922, three of the Ulster counties, Donegal, Cavan and Monaghan, were incorporated in the Irish Free State (later to become the Republic of Ireland). The other six, Antrim, Armagh, Down, Fermanagh, Londonderry and Tyrone, remained within the United Kingdom as the province of Northern Ireland. (Although the term 'Northern Ireland', with reference to 'the six counties' — as the area is sometimes known, particularly in the Republic — is strictly applicable only to the post-partition period, we shall, for convenience, sometimes use it when referring to earlier periods also.)

Our concern in this book is with those languages that are, or have been, spoken within the bounds of the United Kingdom of Great Britain and Northern Ireland as at present constituted, together with the Isle of Man and the Channel Islands. We shall therefore not, except very occasionally for purposes of comparison, refer in detail to the history of the Irish language in what is now the Republic, or to its present sociolinguistic situation in that country. However, a few brief general paragraphs on the history of the language in Ireland as a whole are necessary by way of introduction.

As we saw in the chapter on 'Prehistoric Britain' (see in particular pp. 17–18), the Goidels, or Gaels, first reached Ireland in prehistoric times. Thereafter, with the exception of settlements of Vikings (and perhaps, earlier, of Britons) around the coast, their descendants were to remain for centuries the unchallenged occupants of the whole island.

A century after the Norman Conquest of England, Henry II authorized an invasion of Ireland in 1169. Three years later, he himself visited the country, the native Irish kings were forced to recognize him as overlord, and the whole country was placed, at least nominally, under Norman administration. So began the English involvement with Ireland.

A period of linguistic as well as political and social tension between the native Irish and the occupying Anglo-Norman communities followed, a period during which the Irish language was not by any means always the loser. On the one hand, Edward III's Statute of Kilkenny of 1366 decreed that Irishmen living among the English-speaking settlers were to adopt English on pain of forfeiting their lands. But on the other hand, 'the gradual pushing back of English influence [in the fourteenth and fifteenth centuries] until it was confined to a strip of territory along the East coast and a sprinkling of walled towns and castles elsewhere was as marked in the linguistic sphere as in

39

the field of politics and military conflict' (Ó Fiaich, 1969:102). Indeed, in the fifteenth century even some of the Anglo-Irish noblemen spoke Irish as well as English and by the end of the century the tide was running strongly in favour of Irish, which was to hold its own until well into the sixteenth century.

But the tide turned. We cannot here sketch, even in broad outline, the complex and shifting patterns of factors as a result of which the Irish language has been 'steadily pushed back towards the peninsulas and islands of the western and south-western seaboards, into narrow glens, and up the sides of mountains' (Wall, 1969:81). For this, I refer the reader to Maureen Wall's essay from which I have just quoted. Mention must however be made of the influence of English landowners who were brought in in the seventeenth century when many of the old aristocracy were dispossessed. Their ascendency perhaps marks the real beginning of the decline of Irish, which came to be excluded in due course from all legal and administrative functions and from the higher levels of commercial activity. Consequently, by the beginning of the nineteenth century,

> Irish had ceased to be the language habitually spoken in the homes of all those who had already achieved success in the world, or who aspired to improve or even maintain their position politically, socially or economically. The pressures of six hundred years of foreign occupation, and more particularly the complicated political, religious and economic pressures of the seventeenth and eighteenth centuries, had killed Irish at the top of the social scale and had already weakened its position among the entire population of the country (Wall, 1968:82).

Among the poverty-stricken and illiterate peasants, however, it was to remain in general use until well into the nineteenth century, except in those parts of the north that had been colonized from outside Ireland (see below).

Among the factors leading to the decline and eventual collapse of Irish even among the common people of Ireland, Maureen Wall draws particular attention to the anglicizing influence of the so-called 'National' schools that were established throughout Ireland from 1831 onwards, and more especially to the Famine of 1845, which led to the death of an estimated one and a half million people, while a further million emigrated in the course of the next five or six years. A great proportion of these can safely be assumed to have been Irish-speakers (see Wall, 1969:87).

A question relating to ability to speak Irish was first included on the decennial census form in 1851. According to that Census there were 1,524,286 Irish-speakers (of whom 319,602 were returned as speaking Irish only). This represented 23.3 per cent of the total population. Thirty years later, the number of Irish speakers (i.e. the total of those speaking both languages and of those speaking Irish only) had dropped by more than a third to 949,932 (18.2 per cent), while the number of those who spoke Irish only had fallen by four-fifths to 64,167. Thirty years later again, in 1911, the date of the last Census held in a united Ireland, the number of Irish-speakers was down to under two-thirds of what it had been in 1881, viz. 565,573 (13.3 per cent of the total population), while the number of those who spoke Irish only had been reduced by almost three-quarters to 16,873.

We now turn to consider the decline of Irish specifically in Northern Ireland.

The one factor that distinguishes the north fundamentally from the rest of the island, and it is this factor that is at the root of Ireland's present tribulations, is that, of all the Irish provinces, Ulster was by far the most deeply affected by the 'plantations'. The policy of bringing into Ireland settlers from outside began in the sixteenth century, but was most vigorously prosecuted and successfully implemented in the seventeenth. A major Irish insurrection, led by Hugh O'Neill, Earl of Tyrone, was finally crushed in 1603. Four years later, O'Neill, and his ally, Rory O'Donnell, Earl of Tyrconnell, both of whom had been pardoned by James VI and I, deemed it prudent to escape to the continent with a large band of their followers (the incident has come to be known as 'the Flight of the Earls'). This was construed by the government in London as a treasonable act and the extensive estates in Ulster of the earls and their associates were declared forfeit to the crown. The opportunity was seized to settle on the confiscated lands Protestant and English-speaking colonists or 'planters', mainly from Lowland Scotland. Further plantations took place after Cromwell's conquest of Ireland in 1649–50 and after William III's defeat of the Catholics under James II at the Battle of the Boyne in 1690.

The intrusion into Northern Ireland of a politically and economically dominant English-speaking minority inevitably had far-reaching linguistic consequences. These were, however, long-term rather than immediate, and it is certain that in much, though perhaps not all, of the area the great mass of the native population and their descendants remained Irish-speaking for a considerable period. Even in the most heavily anglicized county, Down, a number of Irish-language poets flourished in the seventeenth and eighteenth centuries (Ó Casaide, 1930:4–8). Nor was the use of the native tongue restricted to Catholics – in 1716 for example, it was reported at a Presbyterian synod that various ministers and licenciates were in the habit of preaching in Irish at a number of places in counties Londonderry, Antrim, Down, Armagh and Tyrone (*ibid.*, 10).

Contemporary evidence indicates, however, that, in Co. Down at least, the position of Irish had been seriously undermined by the middle of the eighteenth century. Walter Harris states in his book, *The Antient and Present State of the County of Down* (1744), that 'the Irish Tongue is in a manner banished from among the common People, and what little of it is spoken can be heard only among the inferior Rank of Irish Papists' (Ó Casaide, 1930:12).

For the position of Irish in the early part of the nineteenth century, we have various sources, none of them, unfortunately, as informative as they could easily have been. The first of these is the county-by-county *Statistical Survey* published by the Royal Dublin Society, mainly, as far as the Ulster counties go, in the period 1802–1804, though the volume for Antrim was not published until 1812 and the one for Fermanagh never appeared. The scant attention paid to the language is highlighted by the fact that the author of the *Statistical Survey of the County of Antrim*, the Rev. John Dubourdieu, out of 742 pages devotes only six lines (in a two-page section entitled 'Language of the Inhabitants, Cloathing, Use of Spirits or Beer'!) to the Gaelic language:

> All speak English; and the descendants of the first Scotch settlers speak also a dialect of the Celtic, said to be a mixture of the Highland language and that, which the ancient inhabitants spoke: but it is not easily understood by those, who speak either Erse [= Scottish Gaelic] or Irish well (Dubourdieu, 1812:497).

The volume on Armagh says that English is general, those on Londonderry and Down comment that Irish is spoken in mountainous districts, and that on Tyrone states that English is the more prevalent language except in the wilds of Munterloney (chiefly in the barony of Strabane) (see Ó Cuiv, 1951:81–4). A pamphlet by Whitley Stokes, *The Necessity of Publishing the Scriptures in Irish* (1806), observes that Irish was spoken by 'a few' in Antrim, Armagh and Down, that there was scarcely any Irish in Fermanagh, and that Irish and English were spoken 'half and half' in Tyrone (no comment is made on Co. Londonderry) (*ibid.*). Edward Wakefield's *An Account of Ireland, Statistical and Political* (1812) informs us that in the mountainous districts of the four northern counties, Antrim, Londonderry, Armagh, and Down, the descendants of the original habitants 'who retired for shelter to remote places, when the fertile parts felt into the hands of their powerful invaders . . . retain the ancient Irish language, and to them it is chiefly confined' (Wakefield, 1812, Vol. II:730).

The most specific, though still far from detailed, comments to be found in our early nineteenth-century sources are made in the volume of parish surveys published by William Shaw Mason, under the title *A Statistical Account, or Parochial Survey of Ireland* (3 vols, Dublin, 1814–19). From this we learn that Irish was spoken universally in Creggan (Armagh), generally in Ardclinis and Laid (Antrim) and in Dungiven (Londonderry), that it was also spoken in the upper part of Dunaghy and in Ramoan (Antrim), that it was declining in Killelagh, Maghera and Tamlacht (Londonderry) and in Errall-Keroge (Tyrone), that a few could speak it at Ballymoyer (Armagh), and that the remaining Irish-speakers in Templecarne (Fermanagh – this is one of the few references we have to Irish in that county) preferred English (Ó Cuiv, 1951:81–5). In 1874, the Revd Abraham Hume[1] claimed that, though it had since disappeared, Irish was spoken as recently as 1820 from Ballynahinch to near Newry and Newcastle, i.e. in central Down, north of the Mourne Mountains. Evidence for north-western Down is provided by the comments of John O'Donovan who toured the county in 1834 in connection with the Ordnance Survey. It had already disappeared from Magheralin and Dromore (where the last speaker had died a few years before). Further south, he met the last speakers of Irish, aged 84 and 100 respectively, in Newry and Donaghmore.

Not surprisingly, Irish seems to have persisted longer in and around the mountains themselves. An account of 1843 tells us that, though an Irish-speaking population that had existed near Downpatrick (some 30 miles south-east of Belfast) about a century earlier had by then completely disappeared, the language remained in 'the mountainous districts' (which, in the

---

[1] My source for the comments made by Hume and other nineteenth-century writers is Ó Casaide, 1930:54–7.

context, almost certainly means the Mourne Mountains) and in the neighbourhood of Carlingford Lough (south of Mourne). Even as late as 1880, W.H. Patterson, in his *Glossary of Words in Use in the Counties of Antrim and Down*, quotes a correspondent who informed him that there were 'a good many Irish-speaking people' in the neighbourhood of Hilltown (on the northern edge of Mourne).

West of Co. Down is Co. Armagh. Patterson tells us that when the Irish-speakers from Down frequented fairs at Newtown Hamilton and Crossmaglen, in eastern Armagh, 'they meet numbers of people who speak English very imperfectly, and with these people the Down men converse altogether in Irish'.

As we shall see, Irish remained until relatively recently in the Glens of Antrim (in the extreme north-east of Ireland). Along the north-east coast, however, Abraham Hume, in his book of 1874 referred to above, comments that, though Irish had been spoken 'so late as 1820 . . . from Ballycastle, by Cushendall, to near Glenarm', there, as in central Down, in his own day there was 'little to be found of it beyond single words'.

Writing in 1857, i.e. shortly after the publication of the first census report to include a question on the Irish language, John O'Donovan reported that Irish was 'a good deal spoken' in the Glens of Antrim, and also 'very much spoken . . . in the mountainous parts of Londonderry, Tyrone and Down, particularly along the Mourne Mountains'. These comments are borne out, at least in part, by the figures for the 1851 Census. The figures for that Census (which accords separate status to Belfast and Carrickfergus, instead of including them under Co. Antrim) are:

	Speaking Irish only	Speaking English and Irish	Total	Irish-speakers as a Percentage of total population
Antrim	11	3,022	3,033	1.2%
Armagh	148	13,588	13,736	7%
Belfast	–	295	295	0.3%
Carrickfergus	–	15	15	0.2%
Down	2	1,151	1,153	0.4%
Fermanagh	10	2,694	2,704	2.3%
Londonderry	28	5,378	5,406	2.8%
Tyrone	405	12,487	12,892	5%
Total	604	38,630	38,234	2.6%

Figures by county, however, conceal sometimes wide differences between different parts of the same county. Although the same objection applies to some extent even to figures by barony (the smallest territorial unit for which figures were given), these latter do enable us to draw attention to a few baronies in which the proportion of Irish-speakers was still relatively high (see Ó Cuív, 1951:81–5, and end-map). In particular, Irish-speakers counted for

15 per cent in the barony of Lower Glenarm (Antrim), 19 per cent in Upper Fews (Armagh), 24 per cent in Upper Strabane (Tyrone), and 29 per cent in Upper Orior (Armagh). In no other barony did the proportion reach 10 per cent (the next highest was West Omagh, in Tyrone, with a mere 7 per cent).

Ten years later the figures for the six counties as a whole were:

Irish only	Irish and English	Total	%
511	27,938	28,449	2%

70 per cent of the Irish-speakers were in Tyrone (10,860) and Armagh (8965). It is clear that, by 1861, monoglot speakers of Irish were an almost negligible element in the population and that the language had almost or entirely disappeared from large tracts of the province.

The figures for monoglot speakers of Irish fell to 242 in 1871, to 92 in 1881, and to a mere 14 in 1891. In the same period, the total figures for Irish speakers had also declined dramatically, from 38,234 in 1851 to 15,849 in 1891, a drop of 59 per cent. It is widely accepted that the Census figures for 1851, 1861 and 1871 may underestimate the numbers of Irish-speakers in consequence of the way in which the question was included on the form (in a footnote, rather than in a separate column). If so, then the figures also fail to reveal the full extent of the decline in Irish during the second half of the nineteenth century.

The county-by-county figures for 1891 are:

	Speaking Irish	Percentage of total population
Antrim	885	0.4%
Belfast City	917	0.4%
Armagh	3,486	2.4%
Down	590	0.3%
Fermanagh	561	0.8%
Londonderry	2,723	1.8%
Tyrone	6,687	3.9%
Total	15,849	1.3%

Apart from Upper Strabane (Tyrone), where 3181 Irish-speakers represented 19.2 per cent of the population, the proportion nowhere reached 10 per cent. The figures and proportions for those baronies that still had more than 10 per cent of Irish speakers in 1851 were: Lower Glenarm (Antrim), 370 (4.4 per cent); Upper Fews (Armagh), 940 (6.6 per cent); Upper Orior (Armagh), 2355 (9.2 per cent). The baronies of East Omagh, West Omagh and Upper Dungannon, all in Tyrone, had proportions of 4.2 per cent, 4.2 per cent and 3.4 per cent respectively. In no other barony in the province did the proportion reach 3 per cent. (See Ó Cuív, 1951:81–5, and end-map).

The 1891 figures are perhaps the last really reliable ones for the numbers of native-speakers:

> By 1901 the effects of the Gaelic Revival were reflected in the Census Returns, for although the number of Irish speakers continued to fall in the Gaeltacht areas, elsewhere in the country increases were recorded. Whereas in 1851 there was underestimation, from 1901 on we are faced with overestimation (Ó Cuív, 1951:27).

The figures for Irish-speakers in the six counties in 1901 and 1911 respectively are 21,452 (with only 8 monoglots, mainly elderly) and 28,279 (including 4 monoglots, all aged under 10, who could presumably be expected to learn English in due course).

Since partition, a question relating to ability to speak Irish has no longer been included on census forms in Northern Ireland. Two things are however clear.

On the one hand, both in consequence of the Gaelic Revival, fostered by the Republic's energetic policy of promoting Irish, and in reaction to the official British attitude which is at worst hostile and at best indifferent (Irish has no official status in Northern Ireland), Irish plays an important role in Republican circles. But the role of Irish (and of other languages, such as Welsh) as a second language is a topic beyond the scope of this book (on this, see Stephens, 1976:138–41).

On the other hand, as a traditional spoken language, Irish in Northern Ireland is virtually extinct, even in Tyrone in parts of which, as we have seen, it was spoken by 19 per cent of the population less than a century ago.

As it happens, the last stages of Irish in different parts of the north were chronicled by scholars (mainly foreigners) who undertook the task of preserving for posterity what could be recorded of the Irish of Armagh, Antrim and Tyrone before it was lost for good. In 1923, the Norwegian scholar Alf Sommerfelt had the opportunity of studying the language of one of the last surviving speakers of Armagh Irish. His informant was a native of Ballsmill, a village just to the north of the (now international) border between Co. Armagh and Co. Louth. At the time of his birth, in 1845, the area was entirely Irish-speaking and the boy 'probably spoke little or no English till he came to Dundalk at the age of fourteen' (S. Ó Ceallaigh, in Sommerfelt, 1929:107). Yet less than eighty years later, the same area was entirely anglicized.

Professor Heinrich Wagner's *Linguistic Atlas and Survey of Irish Dialects* (Wagner, 1958–69) includes only two points in Northern Ireland, Creggan in Co. Tyrone and Rathlin Island (Antrim). It was already too late, if only just too late, to retrieve anything of the dialects of Co. Derry, Co. Fermanagh and the mainland of Co. Antrim. By the time Wagner began his survey in the early 1950s, Irish had 'almost disappeared from *East Ulster*' – but, he says, twenty years previously he would have been able to find 'excellent subjects' in most northern counties, including not only Louth and Monaghan in the Republic, but also Armagh, Fermanagh, Derry and Antrim (Wagner, 1958–69:I, xiv). However, when in 1950 and 1952 he sought out the last remaining Irish-speakers in a few mountain valleys in north Tyrone (in particular, the Creggan, Glenlark, Glenelly and Altacamcossy areas), he was able to find about a dozen of them. Only one of these could speak Irish as fluently as English and of his six principal informants, aged from about 60 to 84, he says: 'Their language . . . has not the virility or versatility of a living dialect but rather the corruption and inarticulation of a dying tongue' (Stockman and Wagner, 1965:44).

'Native Irish', Wagner tells us (1958–69:I, xiv) 'is dead in County Antrim, apart from Rathlin Island . . ., where a few good speakers can still be found'. As far as the Glens of Antrim go, Nils Holmer reports (1940:5) that, when he visited the area in 1937, 'only three or four people could be found who might be called "native speakers" of the Antrim dialect, and even these people were by no means fluent speakers of Irish' – though the parents of many people still living had in fact had Irish as their first language (*ibid.*, p. 10). But, though, as Wagner says, Gaelic persists in Rathlin Island, it has to be pointed out that Rathlin Gaelic is not, strictly speaking, Irish. The island is some three miles off the Irish coast and only 14 miles from Scotland and, according to popular tradition, was occupied by Scottish settlers in the seventeenth century, the previous population having been reportedly massacred by English troops in 1575 (O'Rahilly, 1932:164, note 2). The most recent scholar to devote his attention to the subject takes the view that 'the Gaelic of Rathlin . . . lies between Irish and Scottish Gaelic, and is clearly distinct from both' (Ó Baoill, 1978:viii–ix). On the other hand, Nils Holmer, in his book on Rathlin Gaelic, to which Ó Baoill refers on the page in question, considers that in many, though not all, respects Rathlin Gaelic is closer, in terms of phonology, morphology and vocabulary, to Scottish Gaelic than to Irish and accepts O'Rahilly's view (1932:191, note 1) that it is 'essentially a Scottish dialect' (Holmer, 1942:132), a view that that is shared by Wagner (1958–69;I, xiv). Any differences between the dialect of Rathlin and present-day Scottish Gaelic dialects might well be explained, Holmer suggests (1942:133), if it could be assumed that (as is by no means improbable) the seventeenth-century colonists hailed from Ayrshire and spoke the now extinct Ayrshire dialect of Gaelic. But even on this relatively isolated island, the situation of Gaelic is precarious. When Holmer went there in 1937, he was able to find, out of a total population in residence of something under 200 (a further sixty or so being temporarily absent, working in Ireland or Scotland), only nineteen, aged for the most part over sixty 'who still speak (or rather remember how to speak) Irish' (Holmer, 1942:1). He later comments specifically that, of those few who actually use the language, 'English is used to at least an equal extent. By the majority of the Irish speakers Irish is remembered merely as something of the past' (*ibid.*, 7).

References

Dobourdieu, John (1812). *Statistical Survey of the County of Antrim*. Dublin.
Holmer, Nils M. (1940). *On some Relics of the Irish Dialect Spoken in the Glens of Antrim*. Uppsala: A.-B. Lundequistska Bokhandeln, Leipzig: Harrassowitz.

—(1942). *The Irish Language in Rathlin Island, Co. Antrim*. Dublin: Royal Irish Academy.

Ó Baoíll, Colm (1978). *Contributions to a Comparative Study of Ulster Irish and Scottish Gaelic*. Dublin: Institute of Irish Studies, University of Belfast.

Ó Casaide, Séamus (1930). *The Irish Language in Belfast and Co. Down, AD 1601–1850*. Dublin: M.H. Gill & Son.

Ó Cuív, Brian (1951). *Irish Dialects and Irish-speaking Districts*. Dublin: Institute for Advanced Studies.

—(ed.) (1969). *A View of the Irish Language*. Dublin: Stationery Office.

Ó Fiaich, Thomás (1969). 'The language and political history', in Ó Cuív (ed.) (1969), pp. 101–11.

O'Rahilly, Thomas F. (1932). *Irish Dialects Past and Present*. Dublin: Browne & Nolan.

Sommerfelt, Alf (1929). 'South Armagh Irish.' *Norsk Tidsskrift for Sprogvidenskap*. 2:107–91.

Stephens, Meic (1976). *Linguistic Minorities in Western Europe*. Llandysul: Gomer Press. ('The Gaels of Northern Ireland', pp. 123–44.)

Stockman, Gerard and Heinrich Wagner (1965). 'Contributions to a study of Tyrone Irish.' *Lochlann*. 3:44–236.

Wagner, Heinrich (1958–69). *Linguistic Atlas and Survey of Irish Dialects*, 4 vols. Dublin: Institute for Advanced Studies.

Wakefield, Edwards (1812). *An Account of Ireland, Statistical and Political*. 2 vols, London.

Wall, Maureen (1969). 'The decline of the Irish language', in Ó Cuív (ed.) (1969), pp. 81–90.

5 Scottish Gaelic

Scottish Gaelic is one of the three literary languages of twentieth-century Britain. And if Gaelic literature lacks the variety and the volume, and indeed the prestige, of Welsh literature, let alone English literature, and is nowadays accessible only to a diminishing readership, it is nevertheless universally recognized as an authentic component of the western European literary heritage.

The earliest Gaelic text we have from Scotland, dating from the twelfth century, hails from a (long since vanished) Celtic monastery at Deer in Buchan, some twenty-five miles north of Aberdeen. It consists of six brief passages, in five different hands, one relating to the foundation of the monastery and the others to various grants of land and privileges made to it. But if those notes are undeniably both Scottish and Gaelic, they are not 'Scottish Gaelic' insofar as that term relates to a specifically Scottish and non-Irish form of the language. There are indeed a few minor phonetic and morphological features that may or may not represent 'the faint beginnings of one or two popular Scottish Gaelic characteristics' (Jackson, 1951:88), but, in its essentials, the language is identical with the Irish of the same period (see Jackson, 1972:149).

There can be no reasonable doubt that, as in Ireland and Wales, bards and bardic verse flourished in early Gaelic Scotland, but none of this early literature remains. The oldest surviving examples are in manuscripts dating from the beginning of the sixteenth century, foremost among them the anthology of poems known as the Book of the Dean of Lismore. We have in this and other manuscripts about eighty-six poems from the period 1450–1550, and another forty from the seventeenth century, many of the latter being the work of members of the distinguished MacMhuirich family of Bards.

In spite of the many powerful forces working against Gaelic, which we shall discuss later, poetry flourished in the eighteenth century, with a renewing of themes and forms, under the influence particularly of one of the greatest figures in the history of Gaelic literature, Alasdair MacMhaighstir Alasdair or Alexander McDonald (see in particular Thomson, 1974:157–80), and his younger contemporary Donnchadh Bàn Mac an t-Saoir or Duncan Ban Macintyre (*ibid.*, 180–90).

Strangely, perhaps, when one considers the importance of the Romantic and post-Romantic periods in other western literatures, the nineteenth century is a period of qualitative decline. This can plausibly be attributed to the economic and social pressures (foremost among them the infamous 'Clearances' to which we shall return later) that, in the late eighteenth and early nineteenth centuries, led to a far-reaching depopulation of the Highlands. Perhaps even more strangely, given the catastrophic decline in the Gaelic-speaking population, our own time has witnessed a remarkable renaissance (see in particular Thomson, 1974:249–95), with poets such as Somhairle MacGhilleEathain (Sorley Maclean, born 1911), Deòrsa Caimbeul Hay (George Campbell Hay, born 1915) and Iain Mac a' Ghobhainn (Ian Crichton Smith, born 1928), to name but three who, by publishing in both Gaelic and English, have made for themselves a reputation that extends far beyond the bounds of Scotland.

The tradition of prose writing is much weaker, and, at least until very recent times when a determined effort has been made to cultivate prose literature, has been largely restricted to folk-tales (often based on oral tradition),[1] essays and religious writings. Writing in 1960, the Rev. T.M. Murchison, having first drawn attention to the wealth of Gaelic 'oral prose', of which little has been recorded and even less printed, and then to the existence of translations of the Scriptures (see below) and of various English religious works, continues:

> Original Gaelic prose is the latest development of all, and, by comparison with the other branches of Gaelic literature, such as poetry, oral prose and translated prose, it is – or was until with the past fifty or so years – comparatively meagre. It may be said to have begun with the Gaelic periodicals edited by Norman Macleod[2] . . . and others last century (Murchison, 1960:xvi).

In this connection, it is worth noting that both printing and translations of the Scriptures came late to Gaelic. The first book to be printed in Gaelic was a translation (1567) by Bishop Carswell of John Knox's Liturgy or *Book of Common Order*. The Gaelic New Testament however was not printed until 1767 (i.e. exactly two hundred years after the first publication of the Welsh New Testament), and it was not until 1801 that a complete Old Testament (published in four parts, the first of which came out in 1783) was available.[3]

But who are the Gaels of Scotland?

The Gaels were the original Scots – not in a chronological sense, for the Picts, the Britons, and doubtless others, were there before them, but in the sense that it was the Gaels who brought to 'North Britain' the name by which it is now known. The 'Scotti' of 'Scotia' (i.e. Ireland) may have set foot in the northern part of Britain as well as many more southerly parts as early as the fourth century (see Chapter 3, 'Irish in Early Britain', and particularly p. 36), but it was probably not until the latter part of the fifth century that

---

[1] By way of example, see *Stories from South Uist*, told by Angus Maclellan, translated by John Lorne Campbell, London: Routledge & Kegan Paul, 1961.

[2] A collected edition of Norman Macleod's writings, from 1832 onwards, was published in 1867 under the title *Caraid nan Gàidheal*, 'Friend of the Gaels'.

[3] Before this, some use had been made of the Bible in Irish – in 1690, for example, the General Assembly of the Church of Scotland distributed 'over 3000 Irish Gaelic Bibles, New Testaments and Catechisms to Highland parishes but unfortunately few could read them' (Donn, 1963:349).

they began to settle there. The decisive event, which took place around AD 500, was the establishment of a permanent colony in present-day Argyll, under the leadership of Fergus Mór, an event that has been described as arguably 'the single most important event in Scotland's history' (Bannerman, 1971:66).

The Scottish – i.e. Gaelic – kingdom of Dálriada (the name had originally been applied by the Scots to their earlier territories in County Antrim, but was retained for their new colony across the North Channel) corresponded closely to what was later to become the counties of Argyll and Bute. More precisely, it included by the seventh century the southernmost islands of the Inner Hebrides (principally among them Mull, Iona, Coll, Tiree, Colonsay, Jura and Islay), the almost land-locked islands of Arran and Bute, and the Ardnamurchan, Cowal and Kintyre peninsulas and a stretch of territory in between.

The evolution of relations between the Scots and, on the one hand, the Picts to the east and north of them, and, on the other, the Britons to the south-east of them, and, later, the Angles who in the seventh century moved into south-east Scotland, is far from clear. What is certain, however, is that in or about 843 the Picts were united with the Scots under the rule of Kenneth mac Alpin and that, in the early eleventh century, the former British territories in the south-west were absorbed into the Scottish Kingdom (see p. 147). It is likely that, for a time, there was a substantial amount of Gaelic/British bilingualism, resulting in 'a strongly pervasive [British] influence on [Gaelic] syntax, so that Gaelic syntax has many points of close similarity with modern Welsh' (Thomson, 1976:4).

As we have seen (p. 36), the terms 'Common Gaelic' or even 'Irish' can legitimately be applied to all varieties of Gaelic, i.e. Scottish Gaelic and Manx as well as the Gaelic of Ireland, for a period of several centuries after the original occupation of Argyll. The authoritative view of Professor Kenneth Jackson (1951:91–2) is that differences between Scottish Gaelic and Manx on the one hand and Irish Gaelic on the other first appear in the tenth century (i.e., several hundred years after the invasion), and that they can continue to be considered as locally differentiated dialects of the same language as late as the thirteenth century.

Although the south-east of Scotland, i.e. the area occupied by the Northumbrian Angles, and the extreme north-east, i.e. Caithness, which was under Norse occupation, were probably never predominantly Gaelic-speaking, it can reasonably be assumed (and the assumption is supported by the widespread distribution of place-names of undoubted Gaelic origin) that, by the eleventh century, Gaelic, and in general Gaelic only, was spoken over much or all of the rest of mainland Scotland and the islands off the west coast. (The Outer Isles were for a time Norse-speaking but later, perhaps during the twelfth century, they were re-Gaelicized.)

But already, at this early period, the seeds of the anglicization of Gaelic Scotland were being sown (see Murison, 1974). A recent comment that 'from the eleventh/twelfth centuries . . . we begin to think of the "survival" more than of the natural development of Gaelic' (Thomson, 1976:4) has an ominous ring.

Malcolm Canmore (1058–93), the last King of Scots whose native tongue was Gaelic, had spent fifteen years in exile in England, had gained the throne thanks to English help, and married a princess of Wessex, Margaret. In this way the English language and English customs became established at the Scottish Court. The process of anglicization was accentuated in the first half of the twelfth century by the introduction of the feudal system during the reigns of Alexander I and David I, the sons of Malcolm and Margaret. Ever increasing contacts, both peaceful and hostile, with England (now under Anglo-Norman rule) were to lead to a strengthening of the position of both English and French at the Scottish court and among the Scottish nobility, and by the time of the last king of the House of Canmore, Alexander III (1249–86), there can have been but little by way of a 'Gaelic presence' in ruling circles.

The author of a recent book on Gaelic suggests that 'in view of the impact of an English-speaking elite, it may be that the adoption of English by the Scottish court in the fourteenth century is more crucial to the ultimate retreat of Gaelic than any other single factor' (Dorian, 1981:40). Perhaps more important, however, even than the influence of the court in fostering the anglicization of the middle and lower classes was that of the burghs. These were, fundamentally, communities of outsiders, founded in most cases in the eleventh and twelfth centuries as military establishments but which quickly developed into trading centres, many of whose inhabitants were English, Flemish or Scandinavian merchants and craftsmen, 'little groups of Teutonic aliens . . . who must have involved the common people in their unfamiliar language for so many of the ordinary economic transactions of life' (Smout, 1969:32).

It is uncertain not only how but when the central Scottish Lowlands became anglicized, but the evidence suggests that by the end of the fourteenth century, if not earlier, the area was largely English-speaking, though north of the Forth and Clyde, Gaelic was probably, apart from the burghs, still the usual language of the mass of the population:

> The classic statement is that of Fordun in the later fourteenth century, 'The manners and customs of the Scots vary with the diversity of their speech, for two languages are spoken among them, the Scottish [i.e. Gaelic] and the Teutonic, the latter of which is the language of those who occupy the seaboard and plains, while the race of Scottish speech inhabits the highlands and outlying islands' to which may be added Major's remark after making a similar statement in his *History* in 1521, 'but most of us spoke Irish a short time ago' (Murison, 1974:76).

Gaelic was still spoken, though to what extent is far from clear, in south-west Scotland in the mid-sixteenth century (Lorimer, 1949). However, by that time knowledge of Scots was already widespread, and by the end of the seventeenth century and perhaps earlier Gaelic was probably extinct, though it may have lingered on for a time in some parts, especially in Glenapp (see Lorimer, 1953:42).

Although, throughout the Middle Ages, Gaelic played little part in the administrative life of Scotland, being passed over in favour of Latin, English or French, there was one significant exception. This was the Lordship of the Isles, a large and powerful province that included not only the Western Isles but many parts of the north-western mainland and which was virtually independent from the twelfth century until it was brought under the authority of the crown in 1493, in the reign of James IV.[4] Throughout its existence, the Lordship was 'a centre of Gaelic power and an integrated society' (MacKinnon, 1974:24), and it has been argued that it should be seen as 'a contributory factor in the continuing existence of the Gaelic language and culture in Scotland today' (Bannerman, 1977:208).

The fact that, in the sixteenth and early seventeenth centuries, the almost totally anglicized Lowlands dominated the political life of Scotland was to lead to considerable hostility to the Highlanders, their religion (for the Reformation had so far left them largely untouched), their way of life, and their language. This is vividly illustrated by the views expressed by James VI in his book of advice to his son and heir, *Basilikon Doron*, published in 1599, four years before he ascended the throne of England as James I:

> As for the Hie-lands, I shortly comprehend them all in two sorts of people: the one, that dwelleth in our maine land, that are barbarous for the most part, and yet mixed with some shewe of civilitie: the other, that dwelleth in the Isles, and are alluterly barbares, without any sort or shew of civilitie (James VI, 1599:159).

And, to deal with the islanders in particular, he advises:

> Follow forth the course I have intended, in planting Colonies among them of answerable In-Lands [i.e. Lowlander] subjects, that within short time may reforme and civilize the best inclined among them; rooting out or transporting the barbarous and stubborne sort, and planting civilitie in their roomes (*ibid.*).

Gaeldom, then, is in effect declared to be a bad thing, fit only for destruction. And a like attitude was to determine official policy towards the Gaels and their language for a century to come, beginning with the notorious 'Statutes of Iona' of 1609, when a group of clan chiefs were forced to give their assent to a number of terms for the future governance of the Highlands and Islands. These statutes provided *inter alia* that at least the eldest child of 'every gentilman or yeaman within the saidis Islandis' or of anyone 'being in goodis worth thriescoir kye ["cows"]' was to be educated at 'the scuillis in the Lowlands' and brought up in such a way that 'they may be found sufficientlie to speik, reid and write Inglische' (quoted after Macleod, 1963:307).

Full official sanction to the Statutes was given by an Act of the Scottish Privy Council of 1616. The preamble recommends the setting up of schools in order that the 'Inglishe toung be universallie plantit' and that 'the Irishe

---

[4] It is worth mentioning, however, that in the interests of communication with his Highland subjects James acquired some substantial knowledge of Gaelic – the last King of Scots to do so.

language, which is one of the cheif and principall causis of the continewance of barbaritie and incivilitie amongis the inhabitantis of the Iles and Heylandis, may be abolisheit and removit' (quoted after MacKinnon, 1974:35–6).

This Act was the forerunner of various other measures designed to put an end to the 'barbarous' language and culture of Gaeldom. In particular, the Scottish parliament in 1631 confirmed the Statutes of Iona and the 1616 Act of the Privy Council, and in 1646 enacted that the Statutes should be implemented and that an English school should be established in every Highland parish. (Though the act was repealed in 1662, it was in effect, re-enacted in the 'Act for the Settling of Schools' of 1696.)

The attitude of official and religious bodies towards Gaelic was to continue to be largely unsympathetic, and at worst actively antagonistic, until well into the second half of the eighteenth century. The attitude of the Church of Scotland was ambivalent. In its eyes, Gaelic was associated with popery and so the goals that the Church set itself included the conversion of the Highlands not only to the presbyterian religion but to the English language. On the other hand, the task of evangelizing the still extensively monoglot Gaelic population dictated that, though education was to be in English, preaching would of necessity have to be carried on also in Gaelic.[5] Consequently, from 1690 onwards the General Assembly of the Church of Scotland adopted various measures recognizing the need for exercising the Church's ministry through the medium of Gaelic (or, as the text of the relevant acts usually has it, 'in the Irish language') and designed to ensure an adequate supply of Gaelic-speaking ministers (see Durkacz, 1981).

But if the attitude of the established Presbyterian church was no better than grudgingly tolerant, that of the SSPCK (i.e. the Society in Scotland for Propagating Christian Knowledge – and, though the initials 'SPCK' are often used to refer to it, a different body from the English SPCK) was determinedly hostile. The Society was founded in 1709 for the express purpose of establishing charity schools in the Highlands. Its attitude to Gaelic was made clear as early as 1716 when it was stated that nothing could be as effective for bringing the Highlanders under control and 'making them usefull to the Commonwealth' as teaching them their duty to God, King and country and 'rooting out their Irish language' (see Campbell, 1950:55). This hostility was to be expressed again on numerous occasions in ensuing years when one or other of the Society's schoolmasters was reprimanded for teaching his pupils to read the Gaelic catechism and psalms and the (Irish) Bible (see Macleod, 1963:308–11).

The tribulations of the Gaelic community were magnified and multiplied after the defeat of the 1745 Rebellion under the Young Pretender, after which the spirit of the Gaels was broken and, as John Lorne Campbell somewhat bitterly expresses it (1950:58), 'the Highlands and Islands lay defenceless before the parochial and SPCK schoolmasters'.

---

[5] For example, an Act of the General Assembly of 1699, prescribing the appointment of Ministers 'who have the Irish language' to Highland parishes and the use of Gaelic for preaching and for teaching the Catechism, also calls for the provision of English schoolmasters in all Highland parishes.

But worse was to come. The shameful 'Clearances' (see Prebble, 1963), which began in 1782 and continued for over seventy years, resulted in large-scale depopulation of the Gaelic-speaking parts of the mainland of Scotland. 'In terms of a Gaelic speech community this could be regarded as the removal of its heartland. *Effectively this was to reorientate the linguistic geography of Scotland in reducing the Gaelic areas to the very fringes of northern and western coastal areas and to the Hebrides*' (MacKinnon, 1974:47).

On the other hand, the late eighteenth century also saw the awakening of a more enlightened attitude towards Gaelic, particularly in the field of education. Even the SSPCK adopted a more tolerant standpoint, the first manifestations of which were its publication of the Gaelic New Testament in 1767 and, in the same year, a decision 'that the Society's regulations enjoining the schoolmasters not to teach the scholars Earse be altered and that in time coming schoolmasters in those places in the Highlands where the Earse language is generally spoken be enjoined to teach their scholars to read both Earse and English' (quoted after MacLeod, 1963:310). (It is worth noting that the word used is not merely 'allowed' but 'enjoined'.) The situation of Gaelic was now better in the SSPCK schools than in the parish (i.e. state-controlled) schools, where English continued as the only authorized medium of instruction. Furthermore, the Society (which by 1811 was educating 16,000 pupils in 290 schools in the Highlands and Islands) resolved in 1824 that Gaelic-speaking children should first be brought to read Gaelic and only later English, and in 1828 Gaelic text-books were introduced.

The foundation in 1811 of the Edinburgh Society for the Support of Gaelic Schools and of similar societies in Glasgow and Inverness in 1812 and 1818 respectively marked a significant advance in the field of education.[6] All three societies adopted the principle of 'circulating schools', whereby an itinerant teacher would stay in an area for a limited period and then, having taught a number of people (of all ages) to read, would move on to another locality. The effect of the combined efforts of the three societies (the Edinburgh society alone is estimated to have taught 100,000 people to read Gaelic by 1861), and of those of the SSPCK, was to ensure that, by the second half of the nineteenth century, at least a moderately high level of literacy was widespread throughout the *Gàidhealtachd* or Gaelic-speaking area. (Between 1830 and 1900, over 900 books were published in Gaelic – MacKinnon, 1974:51.)

From the passing in 1872 of the Education Act (Scotland) instituting compulsory and universal education from the age of five to the age of thirteen, until after the Second World War the situation of Gaelic in primary schools was lamentably unsatisfactory (see Campbell, 1950:69–86; MacLeod, 1963:319–24; MacKinnon, 1974:54–60). (In secondary schools, things were better in the inter-war period.) The 1872 Act itself took no cognizance of the existence of Gaelic – it is not even mentioned – and so made no provision whatsoever for it either to be taught as a subject or to be used as a medium of

---

[6] The Edinburgh Society had an explicitly evangelical approach, its sole aim being 'to teach the inhabitants to read the Holy Scriptures in their native language' (quoted after MacLeod, 1963:313), whereas the other two societies were more concerned with teaching Gaelic as such (and also taught English and arithmetic).

instruction. Consequently, not only was the opportunity lost of consolidating the work done by the pre-existing Gaelic schools but 'one of the most promising developments in the history of Highland education was ignored, and the possibility of establishing a tradition of Gaelic literacy throughout the Highlands was destroyed' (MacLeod, 1963:320).

In spite of protests over the years from numerous quarters, little improvement was to be effected for a long time to come. In 1875 Inspectors of Schools were authorized (but not required) to test the comprehension of Gaelic-speaking children in Gaelic rather than English — a measure of little value when three out of four inspectors in the area were opposed to the teaching of Gaelic and one went so far as to say in 1878 that he would 'regard the teaching of Gaelic in schools in any shape or form as a most serious misfortune' (quoted after Campbell, 1950:70). Also in 1878, however, School Boards were further authorized to allow the teaching of Gaelic during ordinary school hours and to pay part of the salary of teachers of . . . 'Gaelic, drill, cooking or any other special subject' — though, in practice, this permissive regulation seems to have had little effect. (It should be noted that when in 1876 the Scottish Education Department asked all School Boards in the Highlands whether they would be disposed to support an application by the Gaelic School Society for special grants from the SED to encourage the teaching of Gaelic, of 90 boards that replied, 25 were opposed to the suggestion, including those from such strongly Gaelic-speaking areas as Coll, Glengarry, Glenshiel, Lochcarron, Sleat and Strath ('The reply of School Boards . . .', 1877).)

Although the Scottish Education Department sanctioned the use of Gaelic in infant and junior classes (but no higher up the school) in 1885, there was little significant change in the situation of Gaelic in primary schools until well into the second half of the twentieth century. The Education Act of 1908 made no significant recommendation on the subject and, though the so-called 'Gaelic clause' of the 1918 Act did make specific mention of the problem, the 'clause' amounted to little more than a parenthetical passing reference: 'It shall be the duty of every education authority . . . to prepare . . . a scheme for the adequate provision . . . of all forms of primary, intermediate and secondary education in day-schools (including adequate provision for teaching Gaelic in Gaelic-speaking areas.)' In practice, the effect was again minimal. There was indeed greater emphasis on teaching Gaelic as a subject, particularly at the secondary level, but the general pattern was still:

> one of using Gaelic only when necessity dictated its use. As soon as the Gaelic-speaking pupil had acquired a modest acquaintance with English, Gaelic was almost completely discarded until its study was taken up in a desultory manner in the upper primary classes (MacLeod, 1963:324).

The view that, all in all, the Education Act of 1872 and later developments in the field of public education were detrimental to the cause of Gaelic has often been expressed, most recently by Kenneth MacKinnon (1977:35):

> Unfortunately for Gaelic as an institution in social life, the system of Gaelic-language schools established in the Highlands chiefly through

the charitable efforts of exiled Gaels were (*sic*) replaced after 1872 by English-language public authority schools, mediating new values almost exclusively through English.

There were to be no further developments of much substance until after the Second World War – by which time it was already too late. But before discussing the present position of Gaelic, we shall trace briefly its decline over the last two hundred years.

Usable figures for numbers of Gaelic-speakers were first provided at the 1891 Census. (Statistics were in fact obtained in 1881, but in that year only those who claimed to speak the language 'habitually' were enumerated.) Some evidence, fragmentary, unsystematic and to some extent impressionistic though it is, is however provided for the time a century before that by comments made by the contributors (in most cases, ministers of the Church of Scotland) to Sir John Sinclair's parish-by-parish *Statistical Account of Scotland* (Sinclair, 1791–99).

The *Statistical Account* (supplemented by the *New Statistical Account* of 1834–45 – see below – for some areas on which the 1791–99 *Account* is silent) reveals (see Price, 1978–79:240–4) that, in the 1790s, Gaelic was well maintained everywhere in Sutherland (and, on the north coast, even further to the east in the parish of Reay, in Caithness), in virtually the whole of Ross and Cromarty (except for the eastern part of the Black Isle which was already almost wholly anglicized) and Inverness-shire (with the possible exception of the town of Inverness itself). Further to the south-east, Gaelic seems to have been well maintained (though sometimes in a bilingual situation) in the northern and central Grampians (i.e. the mountainous southern part of the counties of Nairn, Moray, and Banff, and the extreme west of Aberdeenshire). Further south again, an area covering almost the whole of the mountainous part of Perthshire west of Glen Shee and extending southwards on either side of Loch Lomond into the mountainous parts of Stirlingshire and Dumbartonshire was still Gaelic-speaking, as were, in the west, the whole of Argyll (though anglicization was well advanced in the town of Inveraray and perhaps also Campbelltown), and at least the two main islands of the county of Bute, viz. Bute and Arran.

The *Account* also paints a picture – albeit a sometimes obscure one – of the different stages reached by the process of anglicization in various parts of the country (see Price, 1978–79:242–4). The early stages are to be seen in those parishes whose inhabitants (or some of them) can understand and in some cases read English. Then there are the parishes where some English is not merely understood but spoken, even if only to a limited extent, particularly for transacting business. A fairly general use of English, at least as a second language, is noted in respect of a number of parishes, particularly those on the edge of the Gàidhealtachd, such as the east coast parishes of Ross, some of the Argyll parishes, and Kingarth on the Isle of Bute. English seems to have been as prevalent as Gaelic in some of the parishes south of the Moray Firth (Ardesier, Cawdor, Kirkmichael), while an advanced stage of anglicization is observable in such parishes as Strathdon (Aberdeenshire), where Gaelic is said to be 'much on the decline', and Rhu (Dunbarton) where

'English is generally spoken, but many understand and frequently converse in Gaelic'.

Anglicization seems to be mainly attributed in the *Account* to two causes. The anglicizing effect of contact with the Lowlands, especially by way of transacting business and through the widespread practice among young Highlanders of going into service in 'the low country', is often mentioned while the anglicizing influence of the schools is referred to (sometimes with approbation) in the reports on a number of parishes. A linguistic class distinction is occasionally noted as, for example, in the report on Callander (Perthshire) where 'the language spoken by persons of rank and liberal education is English; but the language of the lower classes is Gaelic'.

Some forty years later, from 1834 to 1845, there appeared (in fifteen volumes) a *New Statistical Account of Scotland*, which, though again only sporadically and impressionistically, makes often interesting and sometimes illuminating comments on the extent to which Gaelic was then spoken and, not infrequently, on the reasons for its decline. Some of the contributors make specific comparisons with the situation as it had been forty years before.

The comments on parishes in Sutherland, the mainland parishes of Ross & Cromarty, and Inverness-shire reveal that, in general, Gaelic is still standing up moderately well in the 1830s. However, the use of English is widespread and very much on the increase, and in some areas is said to be 'daily gaining ground' or 'advancing rapidly', whereas, in a number of parishes, Gaelic is said to be 'losing ground', sometimes rapidly, and a couple of commentators, those on Kingussie & Insh and on Moy & Dalarossie (both in Inverness-shire), forecast its eventual total extinction in their areas. As for the town of Inverness itself, many of the rising generation are said to be 'totally ignorant' of the language.[7]

Further south, the situation, as might be expected, is worse. South of the Moray Firth, Gaelic is still in general use in the parishes of Cawdor (Nairn), Cromdale (Moray), and Kirkmichael (Banff), but in all three English is also by now well entrenched. Forty years later James A.H. Murray, basing his assessment on reports from correspondents, was to state that, though a few natives still spoke Gaelic in the parish of Ardclach, elsewhere in Nairn it was 'gradually disappearing, most of the young people being quite ignorant of it'; it was still used in public worship in Abernethy and Duthil (Moray) and Kirkmichael and Tomintoul (Banff), but no longer at any church in Aberdeenshire, although 'it is still used in ordinary conversation by a considerable proportion of the population of Glengairn, Crathie and Braemar' (Murray, 1870−72:234−5).

In Perthshire, Gaelic, according to the *New Statistical Account*, was still in general use in Balquidder, Blairatholl & Strowan, Blairgowrie, Dowally, Dull, Killin, Little Dunkeld, Logierait, Moulin and Weem, though in nearly

---

[7] This is in marked contrast with the situation as it had been in 1704, when a Church of Scotland commission reported that some 3000 parishioners in Inverness (over three-quarters of the total population) could not understand English, while about 900 spoke both languages and only 40 could speak English only (Durkacz, 1981:152).

all of these parishes the generality of the population seems to have been bilingual, and in Comrie English was gaining rapidly while Gaelic was losing ground at Fortingall.

In the mainland parts of Argyll, Gaelic was still generally spoken, though the reports on parish after parish comment that it was or had been for some time losing ground, or that English was generally understood and gaining ground. It would appear that only in the mountainous and partly island parish of Appin & Lismore were there still many who did not understand English.

On the southern fringes of the Gàidhealtachd, some Gaelic was still spoken at Buchanan in Stirlingshire and, though it had rapidly lost ground in the preceding forty years, it was still generally understood at Arroquhar in Dunbartonshire. (Murray was to report, 1870–72:235–6, that Gaelic was still spoken in Buchanan and that, in Arroquhar, it was 'still in general use, but receding'.)

Of the two main islands of the County of Bute, in the Firth of Clyde, Gaelic still prevailed in Arran in the 1830s but on the Isle of Bute was in the main spoken only by the older generation.

In the Hebrides, the picture was in general much brighter. In Lewis, Gaelic was still the first or only language of the natives, even in Stornoway where 'the principal inhabitants', though preferring English, also knew Gaelic. In Harris, the Uists and Barra, Gaelic was universally spoken and was the only language in common use. It was also well maintained in Skye, though there the influence of English was appreciably greater than in the Outer Isles. Further south, in the Argyllshire islands of Tiree (the parish also includes the island of Coll), Mull, Islay and Gigha (there is no relevant comment on Jura), the language mainly spoken was Gaelic though knowledge of English was widespread.

The authors of the reports on those parishes where there had been a marked decline in Gaelic in their own lifetime are often in no doubt as to the reasons. Time and time again they point to the influence of the schools, to 'the desire which is now very prevalent among parents of the lower classes to have their children taught to read and understand English' (report on Kilmuir Easter, *New Statistical Account*, XIV, 306–7), and to increased relations with outsiders (by way of trade, or because of an influx of southerners, or time spent by young people in service outside the Gaelic area). Most of the comments are neutral in tone, though some express regret at the decline Gaelic, while one or two are hostile, such as the following, from the report on the parish of Kilcalmonnell & Kilberry in Argyll: 'The Gaelic is the vernacular language of the parishioners, but the English is displacing it, and the sooner it overmasters it better' (VII, 410).

From 1891 onwards, we have for each decennial census figures for those who were returned as being speakers of Gaelic (see Price, 1966). The steady decline in the language over a period of ninety years is well illustrated by the following table:

	Gaelic only	Gaelic and English	Total
1891	43,738	210,677	254,415
1901	28,106	202,700	230,806
1911	18,400	183,998	202,398
1921	9,829	148,950	158,779
1931	6,716	129,419	136,135
1951	2,178	93,269	95,447
1961	974	80,004	80,978
1971	477	88,415	88,892
1981			79,307

One can only guess at the reasons for the totally unexpected increase of over 10 per cent in the number of bilinguals between 1961 and 1971. It can be assumed that a number of people had meantime acquired a good knowledge of Gaelic as a second language, though it is difficult to accept that over 8000 had done so. It is quite possible that some who could express themselves in Gaelic to some extent but did not normally use it and were more at home in English did not put themselves down as Gaelic-speakers in 1961, but changed their mind ten years later. However that may be, the figures are so astonishing as to leave one with serious doubts about taking them at their face value. As for the 477 monoglots, the Census Office itself felt it necessary to take the highly unusual step of tracing as many as possible of the individuals concerned in the records for the previous Census. This was not possible where people had meanwhile changed their address, but enough were found to lead the Census officers to reject the 1971 figures: of 109 monoglots traced, 46 had stated in 1961 that they were bilingual and 33 had then declared that they did *not* speak Gaelic (*Census 1971*, p. viii). It has however been argued (MacKinnon, 1978:4) that 'the 46 bilinguals who had seemingly become monoglots 10 years later might not be too unreasonable a phenomenon', since there are known to be 'older Gaelic speakers in remote situations who were bilingual in their schooldays and youth but have reverted to a Gaelic-only state in their declining years'.

That said, and with obvious reservations in respect of the 1971 figures, we can now look more closely at the evidence for the decline of Gaelic provided by the census reports. (At the time of writing, details of the information provided by the 1981 census for territorial units smaller than the 56 districts into which Scotland is divided are not yet available.)

The *Gàidhealtachd* can be conveniently divided into three areas: a mainland zone, the Inner Hebrides, and the Outer Hebrides.

The mainland zone consists of the former county of Sutherland, the mainland parts of Argyll, Inverness and Ross & Cromarty, and the so-called 'Highland District' of the county of Perth. Parts of this area that were predominantly Gaelic-speaking within living memory are now completely anglicized. As recently as 1914, the Professor of Celtic at the University of Edinburgh could state in his inaugural lecture that 'West and North Perthshire is largely Gaelic speaking' (Watson, 1914:73). But in 1971, in the

Highland District, there were only 485 Gaelic-speakers out of a total population of 11,355, i.e. 4.3 per cent. Gaelic has also virtually disappeared from the east coast of northern Scotland, as is shown by the percentages in the tables below (rounded up or down to the nearest whole number, except in the case of percentages ending in .5) for some representative parishes in that area:

	1891	1921	1961	1971
Loth (Sutherland)	51%	22%	7%	5%
Fearn (Ross & Cromarty)	63%	32%	6%	5%
Ardeseir (Inverness)	45%	7%	2%	3%

(In 1971, these three parishes numbered 95 Gaelic-speakers out of a total population of 2515.)

A similar decline is revealed for inland areas of the three counties in question, though generally speaking it has not gone quite as far as on the coast, but the only part of the mainland where Gaelic is now at all widely spoken is in the extreme north-west and along the (sparsely populated) west coast north of Loch Linnhe and the South of Mull. Writing in 1914, W.J. Watson, while observing that throughout the Gaelic-speaking area 'bilingualism of a sort is the rule', added the qualification that 'on the whole the West Coast man uses Gaelic for his ordinary purposes, though he can speak and read English; the East Coast man is apt to use English, even though he can speak Gaelic' (Watson, 1914:74). But even on the west coast there has been a marked decline this century, as is shown by the following percentages for the four north-western parishes in Sutherland (numbering a total of 885 Gaelic-speakers in 1971):

	1891	1921	1961	1971
Tongue	85%	78%	44%	38%
Durness	84%	75%	40%	37%
Eddrachillis	85%	73%	47%	36%
Assynt	87%	76%	45.5%	31%

Of the mainland parishes further south, only one, namely Applecross (Ross & Cromarty) − an area which 'although on the mainland, resembles an island, in that its main communications are by sea' (Gordon, 1951:254) − had a majority of Gaelic-speakers in 1971 (295 out of a total population of 550, i.e. 54 per cent − a substantial drop since 1961 when 71.5 per cent spoke Gaelic), and only four other parishes (Gairloch, Lochcarron and Glenshiel, in Ross & Cromarty, and Ardnamurchan − which had 61.3 per cent in 1961 − in Argyll) had over 40 per cent and another three (Lochalsh and Kintail in Ross & Cromarty and Arisaig & Moidart in Inverness) had over 30 per cent.

An analysis by age-groups gives little cause for optimism. It we take, by way of example, the data provided by the 1971 report for the county of Ross & Cromarty, we find that, whereas 54 per cent of those aged over 70 spoke Gaelic, only 37 per cent of those in the age-group 40−49 and only 23 per cent of those in the age-group 5−14 did so. Indeed, in the whole of Scotland only 8015 children in the age-group 5−14 spoke Gaelic. Worse, the number of speakers on the mainland was minimal. It is not possible to distinguish in all cases between the islands and the mainland, but if we take the figures for

Sutherland, Ross & Cromarty, and the Lochaber and Inverness Districts of the Highland Region and exclude those for the Skye and Lochalsh District of that region and for the Western Isles, we arrive at a total of only 695 Gaelic-speakers in the age-group 5–14.

The Census reports, however, valuable though they are, are a somewhat unsubtle measure for gauging either the vitality or the viability of a language. Fortunately, our view of Gaelic can be refined on the basis of a number of other reports and studies that have appeared in the last quarter of a century. And it must be said at the outset that the picture they present is, in general, even gloomier than one based solely on the census figures.

We have already seen that Gaelic is best maintained in the islands, and particularly in the Western Isles. This emerges with striking, and even shocking, clarity from a report, *Gaelic-speaking Children in Highland Schools*, published in 1961 (see *Scottish Council for Research in Education*, 1961), a report that concludes that 'the position of Gaelic in the Highland community is far worse than it was as revealed by the 1951 census' (p. 63). A table (pp. 70–1) gives, for each class from Primary I to Primary VII in each school district in the counties of Sutherland, Ross & Cromarty, Inverness and Argyll, and on the basis of a survey made in 1957, the distribution of pupils according to their first language, 'first language' being defined as 'the language in which the child is more at ease and the one which he tends to use first in conversation' (p. 23). From this table we can abstract the following information, which shows that Gaelic was maintained in the Outer Isles, less well in Skye, Coll and Tiree, that its position was already seriously undermined in the islands of Mull (with Iona) and Islay, and that, with the exception of the remote western peninsula of Ardnamurchan and around Loch Carron, it had collapsed on the mainland (see table below).

	Gaelic as first language	Total number of pupils	% Gaelic
I Islands			
(i) Outer Isles (Lewis, Harris, N. & S. Uist, Barra)	3,065	4,201	73%
(ii) Skye	465	915	51%
(iii) Coll and Tiree	60	149	40%
(iv) Islay	81	472	17%
(v) Mull and Iona	22	264	8%
Total for islands	3,693	6,001	62%

(The percentages for the various Outer Isles were: Lewis, 66%; Harris, 94%; N. Uist, 88%; S. Uist, 82%; Barra, 84%.)

	Gaelic as first language	Total number of pupils	% Gaelic
II Mainland			
(i) Ardnamurchan (Argyll)	36	179	20%
(ii) Loch Carron (Ross)	19	145	13%
(iii) Rest of Argyll	19	5,177	0.4%
(iv) Sutherland	2	1,571	0.1%
(v) Rest of Ross & Cromarty	20	4,202	0.5%
(vi) Inverness	40	7,627	0.5%
Total for mainland	136	18,901	0.7%

In 1957, then, i.e. over a quarter of a century ago, in mainland Scotland there were only 136 pupils of primary school age whose first language was Gaelic. The report's terse comment (p. 25) that 'in the county of Sutherland . . . the bilingual problem can be said to have disappeared from the primary school' (a comment that could unfortunately be applied with almost equal validity to almost the whole of what used to be the mainland Gàidhealtachd) is confirmed by a recent study of the decline, leading to imminent extinction, of Gaelic on the east coast of Sutherland. Such bilingualism as still exists there is unstable:

> It is only the last stage of a general transition from nearly universal monolingualism in Gaelic to nearly universal monolingualism in English. . . . On the basis of evidence from the two *Statistical Accounts*, it can be assumed that the transition period began during the first half of the nineteenth century. It will close with the death of ESG [East Sutherland Gaelic] in the early decades of the twenty-first century, when (assuming healthy life expectancies) even the youngest of today's semi-speakers will be disappearing from the scene (Dorian, 1981:94).

At the other extreme of the remaining Gàidhealtachd, this situation was perhaps reached even earlier. When Nils Holmer visited Arran (where 605 Gaelic-speakers were enumerated in 1931) in 1938, he found that, although a fair number of people, particularly in the south of the island, were still able to speak, and in some cases, read and write Gaelic, 'there was no single person of those I met who used Gaelic in every-day conversation' (Holmer, 1957:viii). In Kintyre too (1179 Gaelic-speakers in 1931), he found that few people actually used the language and expressed the view that 'of most of the people here registered as Gaelic speakers it may rather be said that they still remember Gaelic than speak it' (Holmer, 1962:1).

Apart from a few vestigial remnants on the mainland, the Scottish Gàidhealtachd is, then, now restricted to the islands − and in particular to the Outer Isles for, as we have seen, its position is already gravely weakened on the southern (Argyllshire) isles and anglicization is well advanced even on Skye. But even in the Outer Isles, the language is under threat. The capital of Lewis, Stornoway, in particular, is almost lost. The 1957 survey of Gaelic-speaking schoolchildren (Scottish Council for Research in Education, 1961) revealed that only 28 primary school pupils out of 667 in Stornoway, i.e. a mere 4 per cent, gave Gaelic as their first language. This bears out the comments made in 1955 by Arthur Geddes (1955:93) that 'most of the children of the town speak no Gaelic and many hardly understand it'. He even goes so far as to claim that 'the Lewis crofters' children still speak Gaelic, but children in Stornoway ceased to do so forty or fifty years ago' (*ibid.*, p. 9) (i.e., before the First World War). If the influence of Stornoway has not yet seriously affected the adjacent rural areas, one wonders how long it will be before this happens.

In neighbouring Harris − it forms the southern part of the same island − one sees the beginnings of a similar evolution. A recent survey shows that the proportion of primary school children having Gaelic as their first language dropped from 94 per cent in 1957 to 67 per cent in 1972−73. Here too, there was a marked difference between the capital, Tarbert (52 per cent), and the rural areas (87 per cent) (MacKinnon, 1977:77–8). This survey also highlights significantly different degrees of language maintenance between different social groups. The figures in the table below, for children in the 5–7 age group in 1972–73 and those in the 11–13 age group in 1974–75, are for native Harris children only, i.e. they exclude the children of incoming families (who might be presumed to be in general English-speaking) (see MacKinnon, 1977:85):

Occupational class of parent:	Gaelic-speaking Number	%
Professional	6	17%
Public servants	12	50%
Commercial	7	57%
Technical	26	65%
Agricultural	42	88%
Manual	57	91%
Unemployed	7	86%

Perhaps the factor that weighs – or, at least, has weighed in the past – most heavily against Gaelic has been indifference or even hostility towards it on the part of Gaelic-speakers themselves who, seeing the restricted role it occupies in their society as compared with English (see Thomson, 1979), have all too often come to the inconsequential but, in the circumstances, understandable conclusion than it is itself in some way inferior and unworthy of respect. This attitude has its roots a long way back in the past. Quoting MacKinnon's observation that 'by the thirteenth century Gaelic had ceased to be a socially dominant language' and that in central and southern Scotland it was 'restricted to the common people' (MacKinnon, 1974:25), Nancy Dorian adds:

If not in the thirteenth century, then at least in the fourteenth, more could be said: Gaelic had not only ceased to be socially dominant; it had ceased to be socially acceptable. It had come to be looked on as the language of a wild, even savage, people: the Highlanders (Dorian, 1981:16).

Typical of more recent comments are the following (which could easily be multiplied);

'There exists an animus against the language.' 'Parents object to Gaelic as a waste of time' (Teachers' comments quoted in An Comunn Gàidhealach, 1936:8).

   The linguistic attitude [in Lewis] is largely one of indifference. Although many speakers take a certain pride in their Gaelic mother tongue, they are fully aware of the practical advantages of English (Oftedal, 1956:14).

   Arran is an island of scholars and a great many of the Gaelic speakers can read and write the language, but unfortunately there is a general disregard for the native dialect (Holmer, 1957:viii).

> Only a minority of Gaelic-speaking parents are actively interested in
> an improvement of the position of Gaelic in schools. The majority of
> parents, while kindly disposed, are apathetic and some are either
> secretly or actively hostile (Smith, 1968:65).

These comments are all, of course, to some extent impressionistic.
However, the results of a carefully devised investigation in Harris in 1973,
'Attitudes to Gaelic amongst the adult population' (in MacKinnon,
1977:157–67), while demonstrating the existence of a relatively high degree
of language-loyalty among the crofting community, noted that sections of
the manual occupational category regarded Gaelic as 'an impediment
towards educational advancement and mobility of their children' (162). Most
worrying of all was the fact that younger women, i.e. those in the 18–39 age-
group, showed significantly less language-loyalty than either men in the same
age-group or older women. This, says MacKinnon, 'does not augur well for
the future prospects of Gaelic language-maintenance. These are the mothers
or mothers-to-be of the ensuing generation' (161).

It is difficult not to be profoundly pessimistic about the future of Gaelic.
One is tempted to ask, not 'Can Gaelic survive?' but 'How long can Gaelic
survive?' A quarter of a century ago, the Professor of Celtic at the University
of Edinburgh expressed the following sombre view:

> Taking all the facts together, the writer believes that Scottish Gaelic will
> be quite extinct by the middle of next century, if not before, unless some
> new factor is introduced which radically alters the present situation
> (Jackson, 1958:230).

Has any such factor since entered the situation? Perhaps. In reality, a number
of new factors have been brought in – it remains to be seen whether they can
bring about a change so far-reaching that the ebbing tide of Gaelic can be
stemmed before it is too late.

There have certainly been improvements in the field of education – or,
more precisely, an opportunity for improvement has been offered, but there
has been a regrettable failure to take full advantage of it. *The Schools
(Scotland) Code 1956* (reinforced by the *Education (Scotland) Act,* 1962)
states quite clearly that:

> In Gaelic-speaking areas reasonable provision shall be made in schemes
> of work for the instruction of Gaelic-speaking pupils in the Gaelic
> language and literature, and the Gaelic language shall be used where
> appropriate for instructing Gaelic-speaking pupils in other subjects.

One notes the expressions 'shall [i.e. not 'may'] be made' and 'shall be used'.
There is however a major weakness in the statement and it lies in the
vagueness of the terms 'reasonable provision' and 'where appropriate', and
this has had unfortunate consequences:

> The terms of the code have often been narrowly interpreted at Authority
> and school level, and provision has in general been related much more
> to the teaching of Gaelic as a subject than to its use as a medium in
> bilingual education programmes (MacLeod, 1978:45).

There are of course severe practical problems, not least among them the acute shortage or, in some respects, total unavailability of teaching materials in Gaelic. But, as MacLeod put it in an earlier article (1963:328), 'one of the chief difficulties in establishing Gaelic as an integral part of the curriculum was the prevailing attitude towards the use of the language in the classroom situation' – there is no quick way of overcoming the deeply entrenched tradition that 'the classroom is the exclusive province of English' (*ibid*). Indeed, it seems that the term 'bilingual education' is taken in a much more restricted sense in Scotland than in Wales. Furthermore, 'nowhere . . . is Gaelic used as an "official" or "administrative" language in the school' (MacKinnon, 1977:61) – which, of course, only serves to accentuate the inferior status of Gaelic.

Nevertheless, there *has* been progress in the field of education, since a determined attempt was made from the late 1950s onwards to enhance the status of Gaelic in the schools of Inverness-shire. 'The experiment was in some respects less vigorously conducted than was hoped, but it was an important turning point' (Thompson, 1976:7) – and it was to serve as a useful foundation on which Comhairle nan Eilean, the local government authority responsible for the newly-established Western Isles District, could build after 1975. Here we have an Education Authority that seems to be genuinely seeking the substance, not merely the shadow, of education for Gaelic-speaking children in their own language. Furthermore, it has secured the cooperation of the Scottish Education Department in a project designed to 'make good the deficiencies of the absence of Gaelic school literature' (Rae, 1976:7). It is also intended that, in due course, all primary school teachers in the Isles should be Gaelic-speaking.

The mass media are, of course, highly influential and perhaps decisive in our age in determining the future of any minority language. Whereas, at the beginning of this century, English, for example, was to be heard in the Celtic-speaking parts of Scotland and Wales only when English-speakers were physically present, it has since pervaded the very homes of Celtic-speakers through the medium first of radio and, more recently, of television. Radio provision for Gaelic, though still far from adequate, has improved substantially in recent years, with some fourteen hours a week being provided in the Gaelic heartland, and the BBC's aim is gradually to increase this substantially.[8]

Television poses a major problem. Present provision of an average of half-an-hour a week in Gaelic on the BBC and one weekly twenty-five-minute programme on Independent Television, is far below anything that could be regarded as even minimally acceptable. In 1982, the Broadcasting Council for Scotland endorsed as an aim a recommendation that 'there should be steady expansion of television output for transmission throughout Scotland, especially children's programmes, during the coming five years, . . . designed to increase transmissions to two hours a week', and further endorsed a recommendation that high priority should be given to the

[8] For the report and recommendations of a BBC Study Group on the Future of Gaelic Broadcasting, see Broadcasting Council for Scotland, 1982.

installation of simple studio facilities at Stornoway, making possible a limited daily Gaelic presence on television in the Gaelic-speaking north-west (Broadcasting Council for Scotland, 1982:16–17).

The situation in the field of printed media is also woeful. Since the bilingual fortnightly magazine, *Struth*, founded in April 1967 and published by The Highland Association, An Comunn Gàidhealach, was forced by increasing financial losses to close early in 1971, the only remaining periodical in Gaelic has been the quarterly *Gairm*, a literary and current affairs periodical of high standard but, inevitably, limited appeal. *Crùisgean*, which ran as a three-weekly all-Gaelic paper for twenty-five issues from 1977 onwards, has been published since 1981 as a four-page monthly insert in the *West Highland Free Press*. The Church of Scotland's journal, *Life and Work*, also includes a monthly Celtic supplement, the Highlands and Islands Development Board's bi-monthly *Today* is bilingual, the *Stornoway Gazette* has a weekly Gaelic column (and occasional other features), and there are occasional Gaelic articles in the *Oban Times* and various church magazines.

In the field of book-publishing, Gairm Publications have brought out some seventy Gaelic books since the late 1960s and various other companies have recently entered the field, in particular Acair of Stornoway which is controlled by the Highlands and Islands Development Board, An Comunn Gàidhealach, Comhairle nan Eilean (see next paragraph) and the Highland Regional Council, and has published some thirty Gaelic books since its foundation in 1977. Activity in this field has been encouraged by the setting up of the Joint Committee on Gaelic Text-books in 1967, and of the Gaelic Books Council (founded to advise the University of Glasgow on the administration of its grant from the Scottish Education Department for the purpose of publishing Gaelic books) in 1968. However, as Professor Derick Thomson has recently pointed out (1981:16), 'despite these advances, the position of Gaelic publishing is still precarious, for the reading public is limited, and making books has become very expensive'.

If Gaelic is to survive, available resources and energies must be directed first to maintaining and then to strengthening its position in those areas where it can still be said to flourish. Kenneth MacKinnon has shown (1978:27), on the basis of an analysis of the figures for the 1971 census, that there were certain communities 'where . . . Gaelic had been acquired by the younger generation in very full measure: more than sufficiently to maintain the local intensity-factor for Gaelic in a stable situation'. These areas consist, broadly speaking, of the Western Isles (in parts of which Gaelic is more strongly maintained than Welsh is in any part of Wales) and parts of the Isle of Skye.

A hopeful development was the early decision of Comhairle nan Eilean, the Council of the new Western Isles Island District, set up after the reorganization of local government in Scotland in 1975, to adopt a policy of bilingualism.[9] The new authority brings together the Isle of Lewis and Harris and the islands of North Uist, Benbecula, South Uist, and Barra, and is not

---

[9] The full significance of this decision can only be grasped when one realizes that, previously, Gaelic had little or no place in any public activity associated with national or local government (see Thomson, 1981:11–12).

subject to the authority of any of the mainland regional councils. It therefore exercises real authority over the greater part of the area where Gaelic is still at all widely spoken. Clearly, this presents a fine opportunity for strengthening and consolidating the position of Gaelic. The first practical step in that direction was taken in November, 1977, when the Council issued a consultative document, *The Bilingual Policy* (Comhairle nan Eilean, 1977), and invited comments from members of the public and interested organizations. In March, 1978, the Council approved a statement of certain basic principles to be followed and a range of specific measures to be taken. Recognizing that, though Gaelic is the language of most homes in the Western Isles, English dominates in many other situations, the Council stressed the importance of achieving a better balance by developing opportunities for the use of Gaelic. This, to be realistic, could not mean that all speeches should be translated, or that all documents (such as minutes of committee meetings or reports) should be produced in both languages. The Council therefore preferred to set out aims that it might reasonably expect to achieve and also to express its active support for other organizations working for the encouragement of Gaelic. It was recommended that, wherever possible, personal contacts and correspondence by Council members and staff with members of the public should be in Gaelic, that efforts should be made to recruit Gaelic-speakers to the Council's staff, and that those of its employees who wished to learn Gaelic should be given the opportunity to attend suitable courses. The provision of bilingual forms, public notices, street names and so on, would be actively pursued.

It is too early to assess the success or failure of the Comhairle's policy. On the one hand, a start has been made on putting parts of the programme into effect. On the other hand, there have been major problems, particularly when it came to finding Gaelic-speaking senior administrative staff. There are also financial implications, all the graver at a time of general economic recession. But at least, now, a body with considerable authority behind it is aware that urgent steps must be taken if the language is to survive.

Perhaps a real chance to save Gaelic now exists. Certainly, if Gaelic *is* to be saved as a living language, with more than a very limited future ahead of it, then it will be saved in the Western Isles. But it would be unrealistic not to recognize that, even here, and particularly with the influence of English spreading out to the rural districts from Stornoway and Tarbert, and the dominance of English in the press and the broadcasting media, a major, and perhaps an irresistible, threat exists.

Postscript

At this book was about to go to press, early in 1983, a lengthy report (dated November, 1982) prepared for the Highlands and Islands Development Board was issued under the title *Cor na Gaidhlig. Language, Community and Development: The Gaelic Situation*. In addition to surveying the situation of Gaelic in such fields as the mass media, education, the churches, the arts and entertainment, local government and public life generally, the report sets the problem of the decline of Gaelic in its wider social and economic context, and stresses (p. 78) that 'if the aim of allowing Gaelic-speakers the opportunity of using their own language in as many situations as possible is to be attained, then action is required on a wide front, at several levels, and by a variety of agencies'. Recognizing that various bodies are at present 'floundering forward on the basis of ad hoc decisions and piecemeal initiatives' (*ibid.*), the authors of the report recommend the setting up of a new agency, which they propose to call *Comhairle na Gaidhlig* (Gaelic Council). This Council, to be composed of representatives of the Highlands and Islands Development Board, An Comunn Gàidhealach, Comhairle nan Eilean, and the Highland and Strathclyde Regional Councils, would be responsible for identifying opportunities, initiating or supporting (both financially and by offering expert advice and guidance) projects beneficial to the Gaelic community, and providing a 'common framework of approach'. At the time of writing it is not known whether or not such an agency will in fact be set up.[10]

References

An Comunn Gàidhealach (1936). *Report of Special Committee on the Teaching of Gaelic in Schools and Colleges.* Glasgow: An Comunn Gàidhealach.

Bannerman, John (1971), 'The Scots of Dalriada', in Gordon Menzies (ed.), *Who are the Scots?* London: BBC, pp. 66–79.

—(1977). 'The Lordship of the Isles', in Jennifer M. Brown (ed.), *Scottish Society in the Fifteenth Century*, London: Arnold, pp. 209–40.

Borgstrøm, C. Hj. (1940). *The Dialects of the Outer Hebrides.* Oslo: H. Aschehoug & Co.

Broadcasting Council for Scotland (1982). *Report of the Study Group on the Future of Gaelic Broadcasting*, June 1982. Glasgow: BBC.

Campbell, John Lorne (1950). *Gaelic in Scottish Education and Life. Past, Present and Future*, 2nd ed. Edinburgh: W. & A.K. Johnston for the Saltire Society.

[General Register Office, Edinburgh]. *Census 1971: Scotland, Gaelic Report.* Edinburgh: HMSO, 1975.

Comhairle nan Eilean (1977). *The Bilingual Policy: A Consultative Document.* Stornoway: Comhairle nan Eilean.

Donaldson, Gordon (1971). *Scotland: James V to James VII.* Edinburgh: Oliver & Boyd.

Donn, Thomas Mackenzie (1963). 'The Scots Gaelic Bible and its historical background.' *Transactions of the Gaelic Society of Inverness*, 43(1960–63):335–56.

Dorian, Nancy C. (1981). *Language Death. The Life Cycle of a Scottish Gaelic Dialect.* Philadelphia: University of Pennsylvania Press.

---

[10] V.E. Durkacz's recent book, *The Decline of the Celtic Languages*, Edinburgh: John Donald, 1983, appeared too late for me to take account of it in writing this chapter. In fact, despite the title, the focus of interest throughout is Scottish Gaelic, on which it is highly informative, particularly in respect of the role of Gaelic in the religious and educational life of Scotland. It is much less informative on Irish and Welsh, which are discussed mainly by way of comparison with Scottish Gaelic, and, as the subtitle (*A Study of Linguistic and Cultural Conflict in Scotland, Wales and Ireland from the Reformation to the Twentieth Century*) very fairly indicates, Cornish and Manx are left almost entirely out of account.

Durkacz, V.E. (1981). 'The Church of Scotland's eighteenth-century attitudes to Gaelic preaching.' *Scottish Gaelic Studies*, 13:145–58.

—(1983). *The Decline of the Celtic Languages*. Edinburgh: John Donald.

Gordon, Seton (1951). *Highlands of Scotland*. London: Robert Hale.

Holmer, Nils M. (1957). *The Gaelic of Arran*. Dublin: Dublin Institute for Advanced Studies.

—(1962). *The Gaelic of Kintyre*. Dublin: Dublin Institute for Advanced Studies.

Jackson, Kenneth (1951). 'Common Gaelic.' *Proceedings of the British Academy*, 37:71–97.

—(1958). 'The situation of the Scottish Gaelic language, and the work of the linguistic survey of Scotland.' *Lochlann*, 1:228–34.

—(1972). *The Gaelic Notes in the Book of Deer*. Cambridge: University Press.

James VI (1599). *Basilikon Doron*. Reissued in James, Bishop of Winton (ed.), *The Workes of the Most High and Mightie Prince, James*. London. (Facsimile reprint, Hildesheim and New York: Georg Olms Verlag, 1971.)

Lorimer, W.L. (1949). 'The persistence of Gaelic in Galloway and Carrick.' *Scottish Gaelic Studies*, 6:113–36.

—(1953). 'The persistence of Gaelic in Galloway and Carrick (*continued*)'. *Scottish Gaelic Studies*, 7:26–46.

MacKinnon, Kenneth (1974). *The Lion's Tongue*. Inverness: Club Leabhar.

—(1977). *Language, Education and Social Processes in a Gaelic Community*. London: Routledge & Kegan Paul.

—(1978). *Gaelic in Scotland, 1971. Some Sociological and Demographic Considerations of the Census Report for Gaelic*. Hatfield Polytechnic.

MacLeod, Murdo (1963). 'Gaelic in Highland education.' *Transactions of the Gaelic Society of Inverness*, 43(1960–63):305–34.

—(1978). 'Scottish Gaelic. Gàidhlig,' in C.V. James (ed.), *The Older Mother Tongues of the United Kingdom*, London: Centre for Information on Language Teaching and Research, pp. 39–53.

Murchison, Thomas M. (1960). 'Introduction', pp. xiii–xxxii, to *Prose Writings of Donald Lamont, 1874–1958*. Edinburgh: Oliver & Boyd, for the Scottish Gaelic Texts Society.

Murison, D.D. (1974). 'Linguistic relationships in medieval Scotland', in G.W.S. Barrow (ed.), *The Scottish Tradition: Essays in Honour of Ronald Gordon Cant*, Edinburgh: Scottish Academic Press, pp. 71–83.

Murray, James A.H. (1870–72). 'The dialect of the southern counties of Scotland.' *Transactions of the Philological Society*, Part II, 1–251. (Appendix, 'Present limits of the Celtic in Scotland,' 231–37.)

The New Statistical Account of Scotland (1834–45). 15 vols. Edinburgh and London: Blackwood.

Oftedal, Magne (1956). *The Gaelic of Leurbost, Isle of Lewis*. Oslo: Aschehoug & Co.

Price, Glanville (1966). 'The decline of Scottish Gaelic in the twentieth century.' *Orbis*, 15:365–87.

—(1978–79). 'Gaelic in Scotland at the end of the eighteenth century. (The evidence of the Statistical Account of Scotland [1791–9]).' *Bulletin of the Board of Celtic Studies*, 27(1976–78): 561–8, and 28 (1978–80): 234–47.

Rae, Steven (1976). 'Gaelic and Comhairle nan Eilean.' *New Edinburgh Review*, No. 33:4–10.

'The reply of School Boards to the circular of the Scotch Education Department on the subject of teaching Gaelic' (1877). *An Gàidheal*, 6:155–60.

Scottish Council for Research in Education (1961). *Gaelic-speaking Children in Highland Schools*. London: University of London Press.

Sinclair, Sir John (1791–99). *Statistical Account of Scotland*. Edinburgh, 21 volumes. (Reissue, ed. Donald J. Withrington and Ian R. Grant, 20 volumes, in course of publication, East Ardsley: E.P. Publishing Ltd, 1973–)

Smith, John A. (1968). 'The position of Gaelic and Gaelic culture in Scottish education,' in Derick S. Thomson and Ian Grimble (eds.), *The Future of the Highlands*, London: Routledge & Kegan Paul, pp. 59–91.

Smout, T.C. (1969). *A History of the Scottish People, 1560–1830*. London: Collins.

Thomson, Derick (1976). 'Gaelic in Scotland: the background', in Derick Thomson (ed.), *Gaelic in Scotland: Gàidhlig ann an Albainn*, Glasgow: Gairm, pp. 1–11.

—(1979). 'Gaelic: its range of uses', in A.J. Aitken and Tom MacArthur (eds.), *Languages of Scotland*, [Glasgow]: Chambers, pp. 14–25.

—(1981). 'Gaelic in Scotland: assessment and prognosis', in Einar Haugen, J.D. McClure and D.S. Thomson (eds.), *Minority Languages Today*, Edinburgh: University Press, pp. 10–20.

Watson, W.J. (1914). 'The position of Gaelic in Scotland.' *The Celtic Review*, 10(1914–16):69–84.

6 Manx

Manx became extinct when the last remaining native speaker, Ned Maddrell, died in 1974 at the age of 97. The last European language before Manx to die out was Dalmatian, a Romance language once spoken along parts of the coast of what is now Yugoslavia, the last speaker of which died in 1898. But whereas no-one will ever again hear the sound of Dalmatian, Manx survived into the age of the tape-recorder and, in the mid-1950s, the Manx Language Society, *Yn Cheshaght Ghailckagh*, having discovered that only fourteen native speakers, all of them elderly, could be traced, managed to acquire an early tape-recorder and was able to make some twenty hours of recordings. They worked to a carefully devised programme designed to bring in a wide range of vocabulary on a great diversity of subjects. So, though the language no longer survives as a normal living tongue, at least it remains in a form not envisaged by the eminent French Celticist, Joseph Vendryes, when he wrote in 1927 that 'in a few years Manx will be only a memory'. These recordings can serve as a firm foundation for efforts to encourage Manxmen to learn the language, whereas the 'revival' of Cornish, our knowledge of which is based almost entirely on a few medieval texts, is a highly artificial exercise.

Manx is one of the Goidelic or Gaelic group of Celtic languages, and is closer to Scottish Gaelic than to Irish. The inhabitants are not however of pure Gaelic origin − far from it. Before the Gaels arrived from Ireland in the fourth or fifth century AD,[1] the islands had been occupied by British-speakers and by others before them.[2]

The most important post-Celtic influence (other than large-scale immigration from England and elsewhere in recent centuries) to leave its mark on the ethnic make-up of the population was the Viking invasions. It is known from the Annals of Ulster that Viking raids occurred in the area of the Irish Sea as early as AD 798, but effective Viking rule of Man probably dates from the latter half of the ninth century, and lasted until 1266 when the Norwegians surrendered Man, together with the Western Isles of Scotland, by treaty to the Kingdom of Scotland.

---

[1] 'We know that Gaelic was spoken in Man at least as early as the fifth century AD, because several Ogam inscriptions of this period are found there, and the language was probably brought to Man in the fourth century, just as it was probably brought at this time to the Highlands and Islands of Scotland and the western peninsulas of Wales' (Dillon and Chadwick, 1972:66).

[2] It has been clearly demonstrated that in the extreme south of the island the dominant physical type is that of relatively short people with dark hair and eyes and sometimes darkish skin, representing an early, pre-Celtic stratum (see Fleure and Davies, 1937).

It may on the face of it seem curious that, in spite of this long period of Viking rule, the Norse speech − which, after all, remained in Orkney and Shetland until comparatively recently (see pp. 202−4) − should have left little trace (other than a few runic inscriptions) in Man. The reason may well be that the invaders brought few women with them and took wives amongst the local population, with the result that succeeding generations tended to be brought up Celtic-speaking. The Northern Isles, on the other hand, were probably only sparsely populated when the Vikings arrived, in which case the Norsemen would have brought their own womenfolk with them. However, a few Norse words penetrated the Manx language, e.g. *spret* 'start', *grinney* 'a gate', *oalsum* 'a rope from the head to the foreleg of a cow', from Old Norse *spretta, grind, hálsmen* respectively (see O'Rahilly, 1932:119−20). A considerable number of Scandinavian elements also remain in Manx place-names, e.g. *berg* 'rock, cliff' (as in *Walberry* from *Valaberg* 'hawks' cliff') *fjall* 'fell, mountain' (*Snaefell* 'snow mountain'), *dalr* 'dale, glen' (as in *Narrandale*), *nes* 'headland' (*Langness* 'long headland'), *vik* 'creek' (*Sandwick* 'sandy creek').

Gaelic, as we have seen, reached Man from Ireland, probably in the fourth century AD. It survived the period of Scandinavian domination[3] and, one may safely assume, from 1266 onwards was again the only language in general use on the island. The next seventy years or so were a time of struggle between Scotland and England for control of the island which, thereafter, was to come increasingly within the English sphere of influence and was never again to be linked politically with Scotland.

From 1334, Man was ruled by a succession of Anglo-Norman noblemen of various families and in 1405 sovereignty of the island was vested by Henry IV in Sir John Stanley. The Stanleys (from 1455 as Earls of Derby) ruled, through resident governors, until 1736 when the lordship passed to the Dukes of Atholl. In 1765, the then Duke was pressed into selling his rights in the island to the British government and, by the Isle of Man Revesting Act, sovereignty reverted to the English Crown. The island has however never been absorbed administratively into England nor, indeed, is it part of the United Kingdom (it has never been represented in the House of Commons), and under the present constitution, which in its essentials dates from 1866, it enjoys a considerable degree of self-government.

Apart from a few native names mentioned in inscriptions or documents, we have no knowledge of Manx before the sixteenth century. It is however certain that, though anglicizing influences must have been at work at least from the time of the early Stanleys, when English became the language of government and its administrators, the speech of the mass of the people must have been Manx for some centuries thereafter. That this was probably still true in the early seventeenth century is evidenced both by the translation at that time (in 1610 or thereabouts) of the Book of Common Prayer, and by

---

[3] One possibility is that the position of Gaelic was much weakened during the period of the Viking occupation but reinforced afterwards by outside influence, and it has been plausibly suggested (Gelling, 1977:81), on the basis of the close resemblance between Manx and Scottish Gaelic, that this influence came from Scotland.

contemporary comments, the earliest being from Speed's *Theatre of the Empire of Great Britaine* (1627), where we read (folio 91, r°):

> The wealthier sort, and such as hold the fairest possessions, do imitate the people of *Lancashire*, both in their honest carriage and good house-keeping. Howbeit the common sort of people both in their language and manners, come nighest unto the *Irish*, although they somewhat rellish and favour of the qualities of the *Norwegians*.

This comment of course also provides evidence that English already enjoyed greater social prestige and so found favour among the privileged classes, but it should not be taken to mean that they were ignorant of Manx: that they were not is implied by the statement in Edmund Gibson's additions to his 1695 edition of Camden's *Britannia* that:

> their Gentry are very courteous and affable, and are more willing to discourse with one in English than their own language (Gibson, 1695, col. 1063).[4]

James Chaloner, in his *Short Treatise of the Isle of Man* (1656), comments both that Bishop John Phillips, a Welshman, 'out of Zeal, to the propagating of the Gospel in these parts, attained the knowledge thereof [i.e. of the Manx language] so exactly, that he did ordinarily preach in it' and that 'few speak the English Tongue' (quoted after Cumming, 1864:9).

Whether or not the last-quoted comment was true in the middle of the seventeenth century, it appears that by the end of the century English had made substantial progress in the towns, for Gibson also claimed (1695, col. 1064) that:

> not only the Gentry, but likewise such of the Peasants as live in the towns, or frequent the town-markets, do both understand and speak the English language.

A comment made in 1690 by William Sacheverell, a former governor of the island, that 'in the Northern part of the Island they speak a deeper Manx, as they call it, than in the South' (quoted after Jenner, 1876:188), is perhaps to be interpreted as an indication that the language was maintained in a purer state, less corrupted by English influence, in the north (as being further from the centre of government at Castletown) than in the south.

It was in the seventeenth century that, so far as is known, Manx first became a written medium, with the translation of the Book of Common Prayer, made at the instigation of John Phillips, Bishop of Sodor and Man, and completed about 1610. It is possible that the translation was largely Phillip's own work. Unfortunately, this translation was not published until 1893–94 when it appeared not, of course, as a volume for use in connection with church services (in any case, a different translation was by then in use, which had been published in 1765 with later reprints), but primarily as a work of scholarly interest. R.L. Thomson raises, but is inclined to discount, the

---

[4] A curious comment, since they could not of course have conversed with outsiders (other than Gaelic-speakers) in Manx.

possibility that the one surviving manuscript (dating from about 1630) of Phillips's translation was one of a number of such copies provided for use in churches in the absence of a printed edition. He considers it more likely that it was 'a fair copy made for the press near the end of the bishop's life', and argues plausibly (1969:182) that the reasons why it was not printed were probably financial:

> In view of the smallness of the edition required − there were then only seventeen parishes in the Island, and few laymen could have been expected to have afforded a personal copy − the cost of so large a book would have been very high indeed.

Later bishops and other clergy continued to show an active interest in the Manx language. First and foremost among these was Thomas Wilson, an Englishman who was Bishop of Sodor and Man from 1698 to 1755. The first printed book in Manx was a translation by some of the clergy, published in 1707, of Wilson's *Principles and Duties of Christianity.*[5] Thomson (1969:184) commends the style of the translation which is, he says, 'quite a free and idiomatic one'. It was also during Wilson's episcopate that a start was made (according to tradition, by the bishop himself and two of his clergy) on translating the New Testament and the Book of Common Prayer.[6]

A comment on the orthography of Manx is called for at this point. Although closely related to the other Gaelic languages, Manx, in its usual orthography, which is largely based on that of English, looks very different, as the following few examples of words that are pronounced much the same in all three languages will illustrate:

	Irish	Scottish Gaelic	Manx
'dead'	marbh	marbh	marroo
'peace'	síth	sìth	shee
'egg'	ubh	ugh	ooh
'knife'	scian	sgian	skynn
'red'	dearg	dearg	jiarg
'head'	ceann	ceann	kione
'country'	tír	tìr	cheer
'summer'	samhradh	samhradh	sourey
'wine'	fíon	fìon	feeyn
'man'	duine	duine	dooinney

There can be no doubt that Manx was still very much alive in the mid-eighteenth century. Isaac Barrow (who was bishop from 1663 to 1671) had introduced schools for the teaching of English, but they seem to have been generally ineffective as an anglicizing medium. The fact that Manx translations of the Bible and the Book of Common Prayer were published in the period 1748−73 is a sure indication that the language was then still in widespread use, and this is confirmed by an SPCK paper of 1764 which

[5] A list of everything published in and on Manx up to 1931 is given in Kneen, 1931:10−14.
[6] On the history of the Manx translation of the Prayer Book and the Bible, see Thomson, 1979.

comments that 'the population of the Isle is 20,000, of whom the far greater number are ignorant of English'[7] (quoted after Jenner, 1876:189).

However, though it is reported that various parishes 'protested strongly in the seventeenth and eighteenth centuries against the use of English instead of Manx in the Church service' (Craine, 1955:101), it would be completely anachronistic to suppose that there was at that time any 'Manx language movement' having the explicit aim of defending the language as something worth preserving in its own right. R.L. Thomson, when drawing attention to the policy adopted by Bishop Hildesley (1755–72) of providing for the majority of the population, for whom Manx was the only effective means of communication, comments (1969:207) that this was because 'Hildesley accepted the fact of the language (it would probably be too much to expect that anyone in that rational century or in the materialist one following should regard the existence of Manx as a positive good)'. It would nevertheless appear, from another of Hildesley's letters quoted by Thomson, that the Bishop felt some responsibility towards the language itself and disapproved of the attitude of those who would willingly see it disappear. Writing in 1763 to one of the clergy about a young curate, he asks:

Has he made a Manks sermon yet? if he has not, ' 'tis fit he should: unless he is one of those geniuses of the South, who think the cultivation of the language *unnecessary*. If I were not fraught with full conviction of its utility, and with resolution to pursue my undertaking [to provide the Bible in Manx], what with the coolness of its reception by some, and the actual disapprobation of it by others, I should be so discouraged as to give it up. This, I believe, is the only country in the world, that is ashamed of, and even inclined to extirpate, if it could, its own native tongue (quoted after Thomson, 1969:208).

And he comments with some acerbity on 'the native railers against Manks-printing' who, he feels, regard him, with his scheme for providing the gospels and the liturgy in Manx, as a 'poor wrong-headed bishop'. Hildesley got his way and the Manx translation of the Gospels and the Acts of the Apostles appeared in 1763, the remainder of the New Testament in 1767, and the Old Testament (in two volumes) in 1771 and 1773. Also, as we have seen, the Book of Common Prayer was published in 1765 and went into five further editions, the last in 1842.

Before the end of the eighteenth century, a number of volumes of piety appeared in translation, including the *Christian Monitor* (1763) of which Thomson says (1969:185) that it is 'written in my opinion in the best Manx of the century', a volume of Bishop Wilson's sermons (1783), an adaption of *Paradise Lost* (1794), and a volume of John Wesley's hymns (1795, with a new and enlarged edition in 1799).[8] The Methodists were to continue to use

[7] Earlier in the century, Thomas Wilson (bishop from 1698 to 1755) had commented that 'the English is not understood by two-thirds at least of the island, though there is an English school in every parish; so hard is it to change the language of a whole country' (quoted after Craine, 1955:115).

[8] This last item is somewhat surprising, as Wesley himself, in a letter of 1789 to one of his preachers on the island, George Holder, had expressed not only strong objection to the

the language for some time afterwards, publishing not only the 1795 and 1799 hymn-books but also, in 1800, a translation of Wesley's *Rule of the people called Methodists* and, over a quarter of a century later, a volume of hymns by Wesley, Watts and others (1830, with a second edition in 1846). Meanwhile, the Anglicans, in addition to bringing out successive editions of the Book of Common Prayer with a selection of metrical psalms, published a Manx spelling book and reader for use in Sunday Schools (1818), a translation of the 39 Articles (1822), and a number of Catechisms.

So far, the only writings in Manx we have referred to have been religious works, virtually all of them translations or adaptations of English originals. The range of material printed in Manx was to be slightly extended during the nineteenth and early twentieth centuries with the production on the one hand of the first grammars and dictionaries (to which we shall return later) and on the other of a few non-religious texts, including a translation of some of Aesop's fables (1901), a volume of recipes (1908) and J. Clague's bilingual *Manx Reminiscences* (1911). The most significant – indeed, virtually the only – original literature that Manx possesses is its *carvels* ('carols'), mainly but not exclusively on religious themes. Jenner (1876:182) describes as follows the role they played in traditional Manx society:

> On Christmas Eve the churches are decorated, and the whole building generally filled with a large congregation, each bearing a lighted candle, and services take place which consist entirely of carol singing. Any member of the congregation who pleases gets up and sings one, and some of the country folk have an almost unlimited supply, collected in MS volumes, which, for fear of their being sung by some one else, the possessors keep most carefully to themselves.

He reported that 'I was unable to procure even a sight of these carvels, but I heard of several old people who possessed large volumes containing them'. A major contribution to Manx scholarship was to be the publication in 1891, under the title *Carvalyn Gailckagh*, of eighty-five religious carols, and in 1896 of a collection of secular verse, *Manx Ballads*. R.L. Thomson (1969:193) estimates that about ninety poems are still unpublished and that the total bulk of known poems amounts to some 20,000 lines.

The first person to embark on a systematic (if amateurish and, inevitably, imperfect) study of the Manx language was John Kelly who in 1766, as a boy of about sixteen, had been brought into the team of workers on the Bible translation as a copyist and, later, as a proof-reader. He later became a clergyman and achieved prominence with the publication in 1804 of his *Practical Grammar of the Antient Gaelic; or, Language of the Isle of Man,*[9] which

latter's proposal to publish a Manx hymnal but exceptionally hostile views towards the language itself:

I exceedingly disapprove of your publishing anything in the Manx language. On the contrary, we should do everything in our power to abolish it from the earth, and persuade every member of our Society to learn and talk English. This would be much hindered by providing them with hymns in their own language (see Telford, 1931, Vol. VIII, p. 189).

Only six years earlier, however, in 1783, Wesley had told another of his preachers in the Isle of Man: 'If you would learn the Manx language, I should commend you' (*ibid.*, Vol. VII, p. 178).

[9] For a critical study of Kelly's grammar, see R.L. Thomson, 1969:187–201.

was reprinted in 1859 and again in 1870. Kelly also composed a Manx –
English dictionary, which however was not published until 1866 (long after
his death, which occurred in 1809), and a 'Triglott' dictionary of Manx, Irish
and Scottish Gaelic, which never appeared in that form (a start was in fact
made on printing it in 1808, i.e. before his death, but all the sheets were
destroyed by fire; the manuscript later served as the basis for the Manx
Society's English–Manx dictionary of 1866). The only other nineteenth-
century dictionary – and the first to be published – is Archibald Cregeen's
Dictionary of the Manx Language (1835), which also contains, by way of
introduction, ten pages of remarks on Manx grammar.

But at this same period, the language had entered upon its decline, as
emerges from the evidence of various contemporary commentators. The
beginning of the end is perhaps to be dated to the period when bilingualism
was widespread, a stage that was probably reached in the early nineteenth
century, to judge by comments such as the following dating from the middle
of the century:

> 1848: The Manx is spoken generally in the mountain districts of the Isle
> of Man, and in the north-western parishes. There are however few
> persons (perhaps none of the young) who know no English (Cumming,
> 1848:325).

> 1849: Most or all of the parish clergymen preach in Manx as well as
> English; but the probability is that in a few years it will become nearly
> extinct (Rosser, 1849:16–17).

Rosser comments however (*ibid.*, 198) on Methodist local preachers of the
time that:

> Many of these valuable men still preach in Manx, and considerable
> numbers in our congregations, especially the aged, are very partial to it.
> And some of them are deeply affected when one begins to speak or pray
> in that language.

> 1859: The decline of the spoken Manx, within the memory of the pre-
> sent generation, has been marked. The language is no longer heard in
> our courts of law, either from the bench or the bar, and seldom from the
> witness-box . . . In our churches the language was used by many of the
> present generation of clergy three Sundays in the month. It was after-
> wards restricted to every other Sunday; and is now entirely discontinued
> in most of the churches. In the schools throughout the Island the Manx
> has ceased to be taught; and the introduction of the Government system
> of education has done much to displace the language. It is rarely now
> heard in conversation, except among the peasantry. It is a doomed
> language, – an iceberg floating into southern latitudes.
>
> Let it not, however, be thought that its end is immediate. Among the
> peasantry it still retains a strong hold. It is the language of their affec-
> tions and their choice, – the language to which they habitually resort in
> their communications with each other. And no wonder; for it is the

[9] For a critical study of Kelly's grammar, see R.L. Thomson, 1969:187–201.

language which they find most congenial to their habits of thought and feeling. In English, even where they have a fair knowledge of the tongue, they speak with hesitation and under restraint. In Manx they are fluent, and at ease. There is little probability, therefore, of their soon forgetting their *chengey-ny-mayrey* (mother-tongue) (Gill, 1859:v).

1861: As a spoken language the Manx appears not unlikely to die out in another generation. In most of the parish churches twenty-five years ago it was used on three Sundays out of four, but is now altogether discontinued (Cumming, 1861:10).

Some of these comments appear however to have been unduly pessimistic in their forecast of the imminent demise of Manx. The first careful, reasonably objective and apparently tolerably reliable survey of the state of Manx was made by Henry Jenner who, in 1874, addressed a questionnaire to all the parish clergy and later, in April 1875, visited the island. We shall return shortly to the results obtained by his questionnaire. On the use of Manx in church services he comments as follows (1876:189–90):

At the beginning of this century, in many parishes, on three Sundays a month, services were held in it, then two, and later only one, and at last, about thirty years ago, it ceased to be taught in schools, and gradually the number of churches where it was found necessarily dropped off, until at last only three or four still kept it up, and now only one does so. The introduction of Englishmen as clergy, and their ignorance of the language, may have something to do with this, and though several have learnt it sufficiently for conversational purposes, that is very different from being able to take a service in it. I am inclined to think that if Thomas Wilson were Bishop of Sodor and Man now, he would not be content to allow Kirk Arbory to be the only Church where a Manx service could be heard, and I believe there are several of the clergy who would hold Manx services if they could trust their own power to do it; meanwhile the Wesleyans in many instances use Manx in their meeting-houses, and make considerable way in consequence. This last bit may seem rather irrelevant, but I wish to show that the disuse of the Manx services is not necessarily the result of their being no longer needed.

He is careful however to avoid giving an unduly optimistic impression of the vitality of the language. Having reported that the congregation (mainly aged over 50) at a service in Manx he had attended at Kirk Arbory in 1875 had joined in it very heartily, he continues (*ibid.*, 192):

Still I noticed that before and after service, such of the congregation as remained talking together in the churchyard and near it, almost always spoke in English. Indeed, I heard but little Manx talked during my stay in the Island, excepting when done for my edification, though the English of many of the old people showed plainly that they must be more at home in Manx.

He later comments:

During the whole of my tour I only met with one person who could not speak English, though I went into a good many cottages on various pretexts of resting, asking the way, etc., so as to find some such person if possible (*ibid.*, 194).

His general conclusions are worth quoting in full:

From the shape and situation of the Island, the phenomenon of a gradual receding of the boundary line between the two languages, so clearly to be seen in the case of Cornish, Welsh or Scotch, is totally absent in Manx. One cannot speak of any district as the *Manx-speaking* part of the Island, though it prevails in some districts more than in others, and those furthest from the four towns of Douglas, Ramsay, Peel and Castletown have preserved more of it than the rest. Still there is but little difference on that account, since no place in the Island is more than ten or twelve miles at the most from one or other of these towns. On the whole, the 'Manxest' parts of the Isle are Dalby, a hamlet in the parish of Kirk Patrick; Cregneesh, and the neighbourhood of Spanish Head; in Kirk Rushen; the parish of Kirk Bride; and the north part of Kirk Andreas; and the hill country at about the junction of the three parishes of Lezayre, Maughold and Lonan. If there ever comes to be such a thing as a single Manx district, it will probably be the west coast from Peel to Spanish Head.

The language certainly received its death-blow when it ceased to be taught in schools and its use was discontinued in most of the churches. Those who speak it now are all of them old people, and when the present generation has grown up and the older folk have died off, it will cease to be the mother tongue of any Manxmen. It is now almost exactly in the same state that Cornish was in at the time at which Edward Lhuyd wrote his *Archaeologia Britannica* (1709), and though that survived in a sort of way for another century, for all purposes of conversation it was dead in less than half that time. The only public or official recognitions of Manx at present are the solitary monthly services at Kirk Arbory: the promulgation of the 'Acts of Tynwald' in Manx and English, without which they do not become law: and the carol singing of 'Oie'l Vorrey'. How long these will last it is hard to say; but there is a decided feeling on the part of the people, especially among the Manx speakers themselves, that the language is only an obstruction, and that the sooner it is removed the better (*ibid*, 194—5).

We now turn to the private census of Manx undertaken by Jenner in 1874 He sent the rector or vicar of each parish a questionnaire designed to elicit information about the prevailing language in each parish, the numbers, age-group and social class of monoglot Manx-speakers, the language or languages spoken by the children, the extent to which Manx was used in church services and parish work, and the quality of the Manx spoken.[10] The results showed that, out of a total population of 41,084 (excluding the town of Douglas), the estimated number of those speaking Manx habitually was 12,340, i.e. 30 per cent, of whom 190, i.e. less than 0.5 per cent, spoke Manx

[10]See Jenner's account of his survey, 1876:190—92. A brief account of Jenner's survey is also given in Kneen, 1931:16—20.

only. This global figure conceals an apparently significant discrepancy between the north and the south of the island. In the eight northern parishes, 48.5 per cent of the population (8040 out of 16,577) were recorded as Manx-speaking as compared with only 17.5 per cent (4300 out of 24,507) in the nine southern parishes.

At first sight, these figures would seem to indicate that Manx was in a reasonably healthy state, particularly in the north. The answers to the other questions however paint a much blacker picture. Jenner's summary of the answers to the question on the languages spoken by children provides the following information:

English and Manx: 3 parishes
English and a little Manx: 3 parishes
English only: 11 parishes

As we have seen, Kirk Arbory was the only parish in which Manx was still used for religious services, and even there only once a month, and only there and at Kirk Lonan did the vicar report that a knowledge of Manx was necessary to parish work (the vicar of Lonan, where no services were held in the language, commenting that 'Manx is preferred by the country people (in parochial ministrations), as they can understand *every* word, which they cannot in English'). A further six parishes reported that a knowledge of Manx was 'useful' or 'desirable'. Among other relevant comments recorded is that of the rector of Kirk Andreas that 'servants like to keep it up as a class language not understood by their master'.

To trace the progressive decline of Manx since Jenner's survey of 1874, leading to its extinction exactly a century later with the death of Ned Maddrell in 1974, we depend on two types of evidence, namely the assessments made by various individuals who, at one time or another, have investigated the situation on the spot, and the figures provided by the official census returns. As we shall see, the two do not always tally, particularly in the most recent decades.

The eminent Celticist, Sir John Rhŷs, visited the island on various occasions from 1886 to 1893. Native speakers at that time were still numerous enough for him to claim (1894:ix) that he had been 'fortunate enough to find opportunities of studying the pronunciation of every parish and of most of the villages in the Island'. He found little evidence however of any desire on the part of the Manx-speakers to preserve their language. On the contrary, he was driven to 'contemplating with sadness' the seemingly inevitable extinction of Manx. His pessimism, and the evident justification for it, are expressed in the following paragraph (*ibid.*, xi):

It is to me a cause of grief and profound sadness to see how rapidly the men and women who can talk and read Manx are disappearing. With regard to the prospects of Manx as a living language, one has frankly to confess that it has none. So far as my acquaintance with the Island goes, there are very few people in it now who habitually talk more Manx than English. Among those few one may perhaps mention the fishermen living in the little village of Bradda, in Rushen, some of whom I have surprised conversing together in Manx. Such is their wont, I learn, when they are out of doors, but when they enter their houses they talk

English to their wives and children, and in this conflict of tongues it is safe to say, that the wives and children have it. Perhaps Manx might be said to be more living in the village of Cregneish, on the Howe still further south; but even there I knew of only one family where Manx appeared to be more talked than English, and that was Mrs Keggin's. She was an octogenarian who had two sons living with her, together with a granddaughter in her teens. That girl was the only Manx-speaking child that I recollect meeting with in the whole Island.

Further evidence for the same period, i.e. the 1880s, is given in a letter by J.J. Keen (1927:467):

When I was a boy, between 40 and 50 years ago, I was acquainted with several old people, who were not 'at home' – as one might say – in English and spoke Manx much better. And quite a few spoke a broken English dialect interspersed with Manx words and idioms. In the house where I was reared, about 6 spoke Manx fluently, and at least 2 of them spoke English very haltingly. 30 years ago I have passed the Quarter Bridge, outside of Douglas, and have seen about a dozen men sitting on the bridge-wall and conversing in Manx only. I have gone into a country inn, – and on Saturday, market day, into a Douglas inn, – and heard nothing but Manx. But now it is all gone, and one has to search a great deal to find a Manx speaker.

A question on the Manx language was first included on the official census form in 1901, and produced the information that, out of a population (aged three or over) of 51,409, a total of 4657 (i.e. 9.1 per cent) claimed to speak Manx, of whom 59 spoke Manx only. No break-down by age-groups is given, but the fact that by 1921, when a similar question was next put, the number of Manx-speakers had declined to a mere 1.1 per cent, i.e. 896 (including nineteen claiming to speak Manx only) out of a total of 57,849, suggests that the great majority of Manx-speakers enumerated in 1901 must have belonged to the oldest generation and had since died. The twenty years in question can be clearly seen to represent the period of the final catastrophic collapse of the Manx language. Of the 915 speakers enumerated in 1921, some 60 per cent, viz. 550, were aged sixty-five or over and a further 237 fell within the age-group forty-five to sixty-four, leaving only 128 aged less than forty-five.

There were three more censuses to come (none was held in 1941 owing to the war, and by 1971 a question on the Manx language had ceased to have any significance), and the figures are as follows:

	Population aged 3 or over	Manx-speakers
1931	47,408	529
1951	52,897	355
1961	46,321	165

By 1931, no monoglot Manx-speakers were left, and even the figures for bilinguals enumerated at these last censuses cannot be taken at their face value. In particular, the figure of 355 speakers given for 1951 is wildly at variance with the testimony of scholars who had tried to list the last remaining speakers of Manx.

An article published in Welsh in 1948 states (Davies, 1947–48:89) that in August 1946 only twenty people could be found who had been brought up to speak Manx. When Kenneth Jackson visited the island at the end of 1950,[11] there were only ten speakers left, most of them in their eighties or nineties, and by the time Jackson's book appeared in 1955, four of the ten had died. In November 1957, the secretary of *Yn Cheshaght Ghailckagh* (The Manx Gaelic Society), Mr Walter Clarke, informed me in a letter that 'at present there are on the Island 4 native speakers still alive, one a woman'. Three years later, in June 1962, he wrote that 'only one of our old native speakers remains, Mr Ned Maddrell of Glen Chiass, Port St Mary, he is eighty-five years of age and is still hale and hearty', and that the last remining woman who was fluent in the language, Mrs Kinvig, had died a month before. As we saw at the beginning of this chapter, Mr Maddrell died in 1974 and, with him, the Manx language itself.

References

Carmody, F.J. (1954). 'Spoken Manx.' *Zeitschrift für celtische Philologie,* 24:58–80.

Craine, David (1955). *Manannan's Isle. A Collection of Manx Historical Essays.* Douglas: Manx Museum and National Trust.

Cumming, J.G. (1848). *The Isle of Man. Its History, Physical, Ecclesiastical, Civil, and Legendary.* London: John Van Voorst.

—(1861). *A Guide to the Isle of Man.* London: Edward Stanford.

—(ed.) (1864). J. Chaloner, *A Short Treatise of the Isle of Man* (1656). Douglas: Manx Society.

Davies, A.S.B. (1947–48). 'Cyflwr presennol iaith Geltaidd Ynys Manaw ["The present state of the Celtic language of the Isle of Man"].' *Bulletin of the Board of Celtic Studies,* 12:89–91.

Dillon, Myles and Nora K. Chadwick (1972). *The Celtic Realms,* 2nd ed. London: Weidenfeld & Nicolson. (1st ed., 1967).

Fleure, H.J. and Elwyn Davies (1937). 'The Manx people and their origins.' *Journal of the Manx Museum,* 3:172–7, 187–9.

Gelling, Peter S. (1977). 'Celtic continuity in the Isle of Man', in Lloyd Laing (ed.), *Studies in Celtic Survival* (British Archaeological Reports, 37), pp. 77–82.

Gibson, Edmund (1695). Camden's *Britannia,* newly translated into English with large additions and improvements. Published by Edmund Gibson. London, 1695. (Facsimile reprint, Newton Abbot: David & Charles, 1971.)

Gill, W. (ed.) (1859). John Kelly, *A Practical Grammar of the Antient Gaelic, or Language of the Isle of Man, usually called Manks.* Douglas: Manx Society.

Jackson, K.H. (1955). *Contributions to the Study of Manx Phonology.* Edinburgh: Nelson.

Jenner, Henry (1876). 'The Manx language: its grammar, literature and present state.' *Transactions of the Philological Society,* 1875–1876:172–97.

---

[11] Wagner, 1956, provides a brief but useful account of investigations with the last native speakers made by himself from 1948 onwards, by F.J. Carmody in 1949 (see Carmody, 1954), and by Jackson.

Kinvig, R.H. (1975). *The Isle of Man. A Social, Cultural and Political History.* 3rd ed. Liverpool: Liverpool University Press.

Kneen, J.J. (1927). [Letter]. *Revue celtique*, 44:467.

—(1931). *A Grammar of the Manx Language.* London: Oxford University Press.

O'Rahilly, T.F. (1932). *Irish Dialects Past and Present.* Dublin: Browne & Nolan.

Rhŷs, John (1894). *The Outlines of the Phonology of Manx Gaelic.* Douglas: Manx Society.

Rosser, James (1849). *The History of Wesleyan Methodism in the Isle of Man.* Douglas.

Telford, John (1931). *The Letters of the Rev. John Wesley*, 8 vols. London: Epworth Press.

Thomson, R.L. (1969). 'The Study of Manx Gaelic' (Sir John Rhŷs Memorial Lecture). *Proceedings of the British Academy*, 55:177–210.

—(1979). 'Introduction' to the reprint of *Bible Chasherick yn Lught Thie: The Manx Family Bible.* Onchan: Shearwater Press.

Wagner, Heinrich (1956). Review of Jackson (1955). *Modern Language Review,* 51:107–9.

7 British

We saw in Chapter 1 that, some time before the Christian era, various waves of Celtic-speaking peoples had invaded the island of Britain and settled here. We also saw that a distinction can be made between the Gaels or Goidels or Q-Celts on the one hand, and, on the other, the P-Celts who included (together with the Gauls and perhaps also the Picts) the peoples known collectively as Britons or Brythons. The language spoken by the Britons in the early period is variously known as Brittonic, Brythonic or British. In this book, we shall use the term 'Brittonic' (rather than 'Brythonic') as a general classifier for the languages descended from that branch of Celtic, viz. Cumbric, Welsh, Cornish and Breton, and 'British' as a name for the language of the pre-literary period, which is the subject of this chapter.

It cannot reasonably be doubted that, by the time of the Roman invasion of AD 43, most or all of Britain south of the Forth – Clyde valley was occupied by British-speaking tribes. The names of many of these tribes are known to us from Roman sources, among them the Damnonii, the Votadini, the Novantae and the Selgovae in Scotland, the powerful tribes of the Brigantes occupying much of the northern England, the Parisi in eastern Yorkshire, the Deceangli and the Ordovices in North Wales, the Demetae (whose name remains in that of the county of Dyfed) and the Silures in South Wales, the Cornovii and the Coritani and south of them the Dobunni and the Catuvellauni in the English Midlands, the Iceni (Boudicca's tribe) in East Anglia and, to the south of them, the Trinovantes, and, in the south of England, from west to east, the Dumnonii, the Durotriges, the Belgae, the Atrebates, the Regnenses and the Cantii (whose name remains in that of the county of Kent).

Of the British language of this early period, very little is known. No written texts of any kind, not even the briefest of inscriptions, are known to have existed. Certainly none have survived. At most, we have, as contemporary material evidence, a few names, in the Latin alphabet and often in abbreviated form, on coins struck for British chieftains, in some cases even before the Roman invasion of AD 43 but on the model of Roman coins. The names of Tasciovanus, king of the Catuvellauni, who died about AD 15, and his son Cunobelinus, for example, are found on their coins in the abridged forms *Tascio* and *Cuno*. Otherwise, such direct knowledge as we have of the British language of the Roman period derives entirely from the names of places, peoples and individuals quoted in Latin or, occasionally, Greek texts of one kind or another (and often preserved in a manifestly corrupt form).[1]

---

[1] For a comprehensive and authoritative survey and discussion of the British and other names attested in Roman Britain, see Rivet and Smith, 1979.

Tacitus's *Life of Agricola*, published in AD 98, mentions, among others, such names as *Boudicca, Clota* (the Clyde), *Cogidumnus* (a British king), *Mona* (Anglesey − modern Welsh *Môn*), *Orcades* (Orkney), and the tribes of the *Brigantes*, the *Ordovices* and the *Silures*. The Greek writer Ptolemy (second century AD, but much of his material derives from earlier Latin sources), gives very many names including *Dounion* (Maiden Castle, in Dorset), *Eborakon* (York), *Katouraktonion* (Catterick), *Londinion* (London), *Maridounon* (which should be *Moridounon*) (Carmarthen), *Otadinoi* (the tribe of the Votadini in Southern Scotland), *Ouirokonion* (Wroxeter), *Rigodounon* (an unidentified place in the north of England), and *Vectis* (Isle of Wight). The 'Antonine Itinerary', which is a gazetteer, dating perhaps from about AD 300, of Roman roads throughout the empire, listing the main towns and the distances between them, gives us, for example, the forms *Calleva* (Silchester), *Danum* (Doncaster), *Derventione* (the Yorkshire Derwent), *Durovernon* (Canterbury), *Letoceto* and *Pennocrucio* which, much changed, survive in the names of Lich(field) and Penkridge (Staffs) respectively, *Mamucio* (Manchester), *Sorbiodunum* (Salisbury), and *Viroconium* (Wroxeter). The *Notitia Dignitatum*, a collection of lists, possibly dating from the late fourth or the fifth century, of military and civil administrative posts in various parts of the empire, gives a number of British place-names, including, in the south-east, *Branodunum* (Brancaster), *Othona* (Bradwell-juxta-Mare), *Regulbium* (Reculver), *Dubrae* (Dover), *Lemannae* (Lympne) and other forts along the 'Saxon Shore', *Bremetennacum* (Ribchester), *Derventio* (Malton, Yorks), *Braboniacum* (Kirkby Thore), and a number of forts on Hadrian's Wall, including *Axelodunum* (which, as we know from other sources, is an error for *Uxelodunum*) (Castlesteads), *Borcovicium* (Housesteads), *Cilurnum* (Chesters), *Segedunum* (Wallsend), *Vindobala* (Rudchester) and *Vindolan(d)a* (Chesterholm).

Many of the elements contained in these names are readily identifiable, and have corresponding forms in modern Welsh. The widely distributed element *-dunum, -dounon* 'fort' is cognate with Welsh *din(as)* 'fort' (now, 'city'); the *mori-* and *rigo-* of *Moridounon* and *Rigodounon* are connected with Welsh *môr* 'sea' and (obsolete) *rhi* *'king'* respectively, so the names mean 'sea fort' and 'royal fort'; *Durovernum* probably contains an element *duro-*, also meaning 'fort', and *verno-* (Welsh *gwern*) 'swamp' or 'alder-trees'; *Derventio* has to do with oak-trees (Welsh *derwen* 'oak'); the two elements of *Letoceto* correspond to Welsh *llwyd* 'grey' and *coed* 'wood', and those of *Pennocrucio* to Welsh *pen* 'head, top, end' and *crug* 'hillock, heap, mound'; *Dubrae* and *Lemannae* can be shown to contain the same Celtic roots as Welsh *dwfr, dŵr* 'water' and *llwyfen* 'elm'; and *Uxelo-* survives in Welsh *uchel* 'high'.

From the first century AD onwards, British was in competition with other languages. From the date of the Roman invasion of AD 43 until Roman domination came to an end early in the fifth century, its principal rival was Latin, at least in the towns and probably to some extent in the low-lying rural parts of central and south-east England. These are topics that are discussed at some length in Chapter 12, 'Latin'. But even before the Romans left, the earliest manifestations of what was later to become a new and major threat had appeared, with the coming of the first of the Anglo-Saxons. Little is certain about this period, but it appears that, some time before they left, the Romans had hired Anglo-Saxon mercenaries or *foederati* and installed them in parts of the south-east of England, in what was soon to become known as the *Litus Saxonicum* or 'Saxon shore', stretching roughly from the Wash to Portsmouth. There had also been sporadic raids by Germanic tribes on the east and south coasts of the island from third century AD onwards. The first Anglo-Saxon invasions and settlements however, which marked the beginning of the process by which the island was to become in due course almost wholly English-speaking, date from the middle of the fifth century. According to the British chronicler, Gildas, writing in the sixth century, the Britons scored a great victory over the Saxons in or about the year 500 at the battle of Mons Badonis, a so-far unidentified site that must, however, have been somewhere in the south of England. This seems to have halted the advance of the invaders for about forty years. However that may be, the various Germanic tribes − traditionally, the Angles, Saxons and Jutes − who had landed at various times at various points on the coasts of what is now England gradually worked their way westwards and northwards and in due course split the territory still held by the Britons in the west and north of the island into three geographically separate areas. In AD 577, the Saxons of Wessex made a new thrust forward, defeating the Britons at the Battle of Dyrham (near Bath). By their subsequent occupation of territory in the Cotswolds and up to the lower Severn valley, by about AD 600 they had divided the Britons of the south-west from those of what is now Wales. The later story of the British tongue in those areas is the subject of our chapters on Cornish and Welsh respectively.

It is by no means clear when the Welsh were likewise cut off by land from the Britons of the north as a result of the expansion into Cheshire and south Lancashire of the Angles of Mercia, who had probably first entered England via the Humber estuary. Traditionally, a significance similar to that of the battle of Dyrham has been assigned to the defeat of the Britons at the battle of Chester in AD 616 or thereabouts, but it is far from certain that this led to permanent occupation of the area. However there seems little doubt that a substantial wedge had been driven between the Welsh and their northern kinsmen by the middle of the seventh century or not much later. The language of these northern Britons, or 'Cumbric' as it has come to be known, is, as we shall see, almost entirely lost, but enough is known about it to justify our devoting a brief chapter to it. Meanwhile, we shall return to the topic of the British language in those areas of England that, within a couple of hundred years of the first incursions in the mid-fifth-century, had been brought under the effective domination of the Anglo-Saxons.

Although there could in any case have been no good reason, even in the absence of any positive evidence, to doubt that the areas now known as England and Wales together with southern Scotland were British-speaking in the period before the Romans came and, to some extent (perhaps even to a considerable extent in the case of the Highland Zone), throughout the three and a half centuries of the Roman occupation, we are not in fact totally deprived of supporting evidence. We have already seen that names of undoubted British origin are attested in Greek and Latin texts and that they are widely distributed over the whole island. There are in fact many more names of natural features (hills, rivers) and human settlements (towns, villages) in England whose British origin has been clearly demonstrated (see Ekwall, 1928, 1960; Reaney, 1964; Nicolaisen, Gelling and Richards, 1970; in what follows, I shall not make specific reference to these works, on which I have drawn extensively, except when quoting directly from them).

It is hardly surprising that names of Brittonic origin should survive in those parts of England that were not anglicized until the Middle Ages or later, such as Devon, western parts of Herefordshire (where some Welsh survived up to the eighteenth century) and of Shropshire (where some Welsh is still spoken in one or two villages just across the border from Wales), and Cumbria. What is much more significant is the fact that there is at least a sprinkling of names of Brittonic origin over the whole of England, and that they occur even in areas like Essex, Surrey and Kent. The study of place-names and their origin is a notoriously difficult field, fraught with problems, full of traps for the unwary,[2] and, in particular, those place-names in England that seem not to be of English origin must be handled with care:

> Little wonder is it . . . that scholars differ and that we are often concerned with possibilities or probabilities rather than with definite etymologies. This is particularly unfortunate, as an agreed solution of many of these problems would be invaluable in discussing the extent of the survival of a British population after the Anglo-Saxon conquest (Reaney, 1964:72–3).

To take just one example, three totally different etymologies, all of them Brittonic as it happens, have been proposed for the name of the city of Leeds:

> Leeds has been derived by Max Förster from a Celtic river-name *Lotissa*, from **luto-* 'mud'. Jackson disputes this and does not fully accept Ekwall's explanation from a [British] root *plód 'flowing', an assumed early name of the Aire. He considers the name is more likely to be a tribe-name than a river-name, from a Brit *Latenses* which may well contain a river-name *Lāta* 'the boiling or violent one' and that Leeds 'very likely' means 'the Folk living round the Lāta' (Reaney, 1964:83).

Names of undisputed or generally accepted British origin are however so numerous and, though less thick on the ground in the east than in the west, so widely distributed, that one must conclude that most or all of the Lowland Zone must at one time have been British-speaking. Forms cognate with Welsh *mynydd* 'mountain', for example, occur not only in *Myndtown*, *Minton* and *Longmynd* (all in Shropshire) and *The Mynde* and *Meend's Wood* (Herefordshire), but much further east, as in *Mendip* (the second element is perhaps Old English *hop* 'valley') and *Mindrum* (Northumberland), whose second element corresponds to Welsh *trum* 'ridge'. As we have seen (p. 85), the first syllable of *Lichfield* comes from *Letoceto* 'grey wood' (Welsh *llwyd* + *coed*), and the same form gives *Lytchett* (Dorset). Welsh *moel*

---

[2] On the problems and pitfalls of place-name study, particularly in relation to Britain, see Wainwright's book (1962) on the interrelationship of history, archaeology and onomastics.

'bare' is akin to the first syllable of *Malvern* ('bare hill' = Welsh *Moelfryn*), *Mellor* (Derbyshire, Lancashire), (also 'bare hill' = Welsh *Moelfre*), and possibly *Melchet* (Hampshire), of which the second element is again *cet-* 'wood'. British *cet-* also turns up as the first element of *Cheetham* (Lancs), *Chicklade* and *Chitterne* (both in Wiltshire), *Chetwode* (Bucks) and *Chatham* (Essex), all of which have an English second element, and of *Kesteven* (Lincs), whose second element is Scandinavian, and also in *Penge* (Surrey), a much reduced derivative of the roots *penn-* 'top' and *cet-* (it occurs in 1067 in the form *Penceat*). *Liscard* (Cheshire) is cognate with Welsh *llys* 'court' + *carreg* 'rock' (so perhaps 'hall on the rock'), *Wenlock* (eastern Shropshire) with Welsh *gwyn* 'white' and (obsolete) *llog* 'monastery', *Berk-*(*shire*) with (obsolete) Welsh *bar* 'top, summit, crest', *Pant* (Hampshire) with Welsh *pant* 'valley, depression', *Crewe* with Welsh *cryw* 'weir, stepping-stones', and *Ross* (Herefordshire, Northumberland), *Roose* (Lancashire) and *Roos* (Yorkshire) with Welsh *rhos* 'moor'. The root *cruco-* (Welsh *crug* 'hillock, heap, mound'), which we saw in the 'Antonine Itinerary' in the name *Pennocrucio* (Penkridge), also survives in *Creech* (Dorset, Somerset), *Crutch* (Worcester), and *Crich* (Derbyshire). *Chevening* (Kent) and *Chevin* (Yorkshire) probably correspond to Welsh *cefn* 'back, ridge' (indeed, Chevin appears in Old English as *Scefinc*, in which the initial *S-* may well correspond to Welsh *is* 'below', so the whole name, like Welsh *is y cefn*, would mean 'below the ridge'), The name of the *Andred* forest (Kent and Sussex) contains a British prefix and the root *ritu-* (Welsh *rhyd*) 'ford'.

The various rivers *Avon* (six of them in all) preserve the British word *abona* 'river' that survives with the same meaning in Welsh *afon*, while the word for water, *dubro-* (Welsh *dwfr, dŵr*), occurs in the names of the river *Dour* (and the town of *Dover*, which stands on it), *Doverdale* (Worcestershire), *Dover-burn* (Warwickshire), *Dover Beck* (Notts), *Dovercourt* (Essex), and as the second element of the names (now of towns but originally of streams) *Andover* and *Micheldever* (both in Hampshire) (the first element in each case is obscure), *Candover* (Hampshire) (first element = Welsh *cain* 'fair, beautiful'), *Wendover* (Bucks) (first element = Welsh *gwyn* 'white'), and of the various streams in Lancashire and Yorkshire called *Calder* (Welsh *caled* 'hard' and *dwfr, dŵr*, so the meaning is perhaps 'violent rapid stream'), and probably, in the same area, in the name of the *Hodder*, whose first element may correspond to Welsh *hawdd* 'pleasant' (now 'easy'). *Winford* (Somerset) takes its name from that of a stream, and corresponds to Welsh *Gwenffrwd* 'white stream'. The names of the numerous rivers *Derwent*, the *Darwen* (Lancs), the *Darent* (Kent), and the *Dart* (Devon), all go back to a British *Derventio* (which is, as we have seen, p. 85, attested in the 'Antonine Itinerary' for the Yorkshire Derwent) which includes the root **derva* (Welsh *derw(en)*) 'oak'. Among very many other river-names of British origin, *Cole* and *Leam* (both in Warwickshire) are related to Welsh *coll(en)* 'hazel' and *llwyf* (British **lem-*) 'elm' respectively, *Laughern* Book (Worcestershire), *Laver* (Yorkshire), and *Leadon* (Gloucestershire), to Welsh *llywarn* (obsolete) 'fox', *llafar* 'speech' (probably here in the sense of 'chattering'), and *llydan* (British **litano-*) 'broad' respectively, and *Yarrow* (Lancashire) is probably connected with Welsh *garw* 'rough'. As a final example, we can refer to the various rivers *Dove* (two in Yorkshire, one each in the Midlands and Suffolk), whose name contains reflexes of a root *dubo-* 'black' (Welsh *du*). This also occurs with an element connected with an obsolete Welsh word *glais* 'stream' in a number of river-names (some of them now also the names of towns or villages), including *Dalch* and *Dawlish* in Devon, and also, further afield, *Dowlish* (Somerset), *Dowles* (Worcestershire), *Douglas* (Lancashire) and *Devil's Water* (Northumberland).

These and other place-names provide a substantial amount of information on British nouns and adjectives, but it is worth noting that we know nothing of the verb-forms of British.

The very fact of the survival of a substantial number of British names in those parts of England that were occupied relatively early by the Anglo-Saxons raises the question of the relations that may have existed between the Britons and the invaders and, in particular, that of the fate of the Britons. Broadly speaking, there are three possibilities: either they were exterminated, or they fled to the west, or they remained. That some were killed is inevitable, and that some – perhaps substantial numbers – fled to the mountainous western parts of the island is certain. What is far from clear is how many, if indeed any, remained, and if so in what circumstances, under Anglo-Saxon domination in the eastern, southern and central parts of the island.

It is likely that no serious scholar would now contend that all or even the great majority of the Britons who had formerly inhabited the Lowland Zone were massacred or put to flight, though such a view was fashionable at one time. Not only does it seem on general grounds more likely that very many of them remained and survived, but Nora Chadwick, after a wide-ranging and penetrating survey of the linguistic, historical and archaeological evidence, found that it led her to the conclusion that 'Anglo-Saxon Occupation of England was a gradual process which involved no change of population on any large scale' (Chadwick, 1963:146). On the contrary, 'everything points to a *modus vivendi*, with the incoming Saxons as heirs to the Roman arms for defending the south-east, and the unchronicled Britons quietly carrying on their former way of life' (*ibid.*, 142).

To suggest that the Britons carried on under Anglo-Saxon domination with their way of life virtually unchanged strains belief somewhat. However, one can accept that, with or without significant interruption to their habits and customs, they – or at any rate large numbers of them – probably did remain in their former haunts. It is indeed possible, likely even, that here and there, particularly in the more inaccessible or economically less desirable areas, areas of moorland, swamp, or forest for example, enclaves of unassimilated Britons and their language remained for some considerable time after the areas around them had come under the sway of the English. This is suggested, though admittedly not proved, by the fact that the element *Wal-* in some English place-names is connected with the words *Wales* and *Welsh*.[3] It is generally accepted, for example, that forms of Old English

[3] See, for example, Faull, 1977:12–13. This is not however the origin of all English place-names in *Wal-*. In many such names it represents Old English *weald* 'forest', *weall* 'wall', or *waelle* 'well, spring'. Furthermore, in some names *w(e)alh* perhaps meant 'serf' rather than 'Welshman' (see Gelling, 1978:93–5). On other place names in northern England that also

W(e)alh, plural *W(e)alas*, 'Briton(s)', are at the origin of such names as *Walden* (Herts), (*Saffron*) *Walden* (Essex) 'valley of the Britons', *Walpole* (Suffolk) 'pool of the Britons' (but the Norfolk *Walpole* means 'pool by the wall'), *Walmer* (Kent) 'mere of the Welsh'. In the north-west, *Wallasey* appears in 1086 as *Walea* (with *ea* from *eg* 'island') 'island of the Britons'.

One area that almost certainly remained British for some time was the kingdom of Elmet (the name corresponds to that of Elfed in Wales) in south-west Yorkshire (the name survives in that of the villages of Barwick in Elmet and Sherburn in Elmet), which preserved its independence until the beginning of the reign of Edwin of Northumbria (617–32). J.N.L. Myres argued that, to the north of the Yorkshire wolds, there may well have been another enclave among 'the wind-swept moors of Hambleton and Cleveland [which] remained, as they had done throughout prehistoric time, a refuge of broken peoples, a home of lost cultural causes' (Collingwood and Myres, 1973:454).

There is even some reason for thinking, though the evidence is not conclusive, that there were also British enclaves in the south of England. In particular, the Anglo-Saxon chronicle records a victory won over the Britons by a Saxon chieftain, Cuthwulf, in 571 at a place named Bedcanford (perhaps Bedford), which was followed by the occupation of the towns of Aylesbury, Limbury, Bensington and Eynsham. This suggests that a substantial number of Britons survived at least until that date in an area just north of the Thames (see Collingwood and Myres, 1937:406, 408). Other enclaves may have persisted in the heath and forest country of West Suffolk and Essex (see Collingwood and Myres, 1937:446 453, and Jackson, 1953:236), and in the Fens, where, Jackson suggests (1953:236), British-speaking natives were perhaps still to be found as late as the beginning of the eighth century. Further west, Jackson is of the view that British was still spoken in Somerset and Dorset at the end of the seventh century. In support of this, he draws attention to a reference in an Anglo-Saxon charter of the year 682 to a place in Somerset having distinct British and English names, *Britannica lingua Cructan, apud nos Crycbeorh*[4], which proves 'not only that the [British] language was still alive here at the time but also that the English were adapting British place-names and that the two forms could exist side by side' (*ibid.*, 239). Whether British lasted into the eighth century in Somerset and Dorset he regards as uncertain. But in any case, we are now talking of a period by which the British of the south-west and the British of the west (i.e. of Wales) are to be considered as two separate languages which will be dicussed in the chapters on Cornish and Welsh respectively.

Our discussion so far has been largely confined to the fate of British in the Lowland Zone (see p. 159). This is because there is not a great deal to be said about its role in the Highland Zone except that there – or, more precisely, in

---

suggest a continuing British presence in Anglo-Saxon times, see Faull, 1977:13–20. I have unfortunately not been able to consult Margaret Faull's unpublished MA dissertation, 'Linguistic and archaeological sources for the survival of the Romano-Celts and their relationship with the Anglo-Saxons during and after the Settlement Period', Macquarie University, 1970.

4 'In the British language Cructan, among us Crycbeorh' – or, more freely rendered, 'In British they call it Cructan, we call it Crycbeorh'.

most of the Highland Zone south of the Forth and the Clyde − it not only survived but flourished, to emerge in due course as two closely related but distinct languages, viz. Welsh and Cornish, and to remain for some centuries further north in yet another form, Cumbric, of which, as we shall see in Chapter 10, regrettably little is known.

Before bringing this chapter to an end, we have to consider the question of the relationship between, on the one hand, British, and, on the other, the languages that have sprung from it. Leaving aside for the moment the problem of Cumbric, one could ask the question in two ways: At what period had British evolved to the point where one should consider that one is now dealing with the beginnings of Cornish and of Welsh? or, putting the emphasis rather differently: At what period had the language of the south-west and the language of Wales diverged to such an extent that one has to consider them as separate languages rather than as dialects, or regional varieties, of one and the same language?

The evidence on which any such conclusion can be based is strictly limited. There are no written texts of any kind in British,[5] not even the briefest of inscriptions on stone corresponding to the fifty or so Irish inscriptions dating from the fifth to the early seventh centuries that are found in various western parts of Britain and particularly in Wales (see pp. 28−30). Although the stones in question are located in areas where British as well as Irish can be assumed to have been spoken and though a number of them are in fact bilingual, the other language is in all cases Latin. There are also in Wales and the south-west of England, and dating from the same period, a number of comparable inscriptions − mainly on tombstones − in Latin only. The importance of these Latin inscriptions for our present preoccupation is that they contain Latinized versions of a number of British names and so constitute direct evidence for the language of the period. Among the British names that occur, usually in the Latin genitive case, are VOTEPORIGIS (that is also given on the same stone in its Irish form, VOTECORIGAS), MAGLOCVNI (which was later to become *Maelgwn*), CVNIGNI, CVNOTAMI, CVNO-CENNI. These fifth or early sixth century forms are to be regarded as British (rather than Welsh or Cornish) in a Latin garb. In the seventh century, one finds occasional Brittonic names occurring in Latin inscriptions in Wales without any case endings, e.g. VIRNIN, CUURIS (= Welsh *Cyrys*), CINI (= Welsh *Cyny*), and these forms are considered by Jackson to be already Primitive Welsh.

---

[5] Jackson had asserted (1953:100) that 'it would not occur to anyone to write in British, nor would they know how to do so'. Frere, on the other hand, points out (1978:350−1) that the closely related Celtic language of Gaul *was* used for inscriptions, and that the Belgae of southern Britain used Celtic names (in Roman characters) on their coins, whence he concludes that British not only could be but probably was both written and read. These arguments are taken up and amplified by Colin Smith, who adds (Rivet and Smith, 1979:15) that 'the Celtic languages did eventually become fully written languages, using the Latin alphabet' and that there is 'no inherent reason why it should not have been done much earlier, under Roman rule when the degree of literacy must have been much greater'. And he suggests that British may indeed have been written at that time, but only on cheap, perishable materials, such as may have been available to the poorer classes.

In brief, Jackson concludes that the phonetic changes that transformed British into Welsh, Cornish and Breton belong mainly to the period between the middle of the fifth and the end of the sixth century and that, therefore, 'from the middle of the sixth century we can begin to speak of these [i.e. Welsh, Cornish and Breton] as separating languages, and from the end of the century as separate' (1953:5).[6]

All this raises the question of the survival, perhaps until the eleventh or twelfth century, of a Brittonic language in the north-west of England and the south-west of Scotland. Are we to be content to continue to call it merely 'British', and discuss it in the present chapter, or could it be considered under the heading of Welsh, or is it to be looked upon as a separate language? Having defined 'British' as the British speech common to the whole of the island south of the Forth–Clyde valley, and having accepted that the term is no longer applicable, with reference to the period from about AD 600 onwards, to the south-western and western varieties which are thereafter to be referred to as 'Cornish' and 'Welsh' respectively, we cannot, to be consistent, regard any variety of Brittonic speech that continues in use well beyond the seventh century as merely 'British'. And since, from about the seventh century, this north-western speech-area was as completely divided from Wales as was the Cornish-speaking area, and since it can reasonably be supposed (even in the almost total absence of supporting evidence) that the language of the north-west continued to change and diverge from that of Wales, there is no justification for referring to it as 'Welsh'. Consequently, bizarre though it may seem to devote a chapter to a language of which only three words have survived (though much more can be learned, as we shall see, from other sources), that is the only logical solution.

References

Chadwick, N.K. (1963). 'The British or Celtic part in the population of England', in *Angles and Britons* (six O'Donnell Lectures by various scholars), Cardiff: University of Wales Press, pp. 111–47.

Collingwood, R.G., and Myres, J.N.L. (1937). *Roman Britain and the English Settlements*. 2nd ed. Oxford: Clarendon Press. (1st ed., 1936).

Ekwall, E. (1928). *English River-names*. Oxford: Clarendon Press.

—(1960). *The Concise Oxford Dictionary of English Place-names*. 4th ed. Oxford: Clarendon Press. (1st ed., 1936).

Faull, Margaret L. (1977). 'British survival in Anglo-Saxon Northumbria', in Lloyd Laing (ed.), *Studies in Celtic Survival* (British Archaeological Reports, 37) pp. 1–55.

Frere, Sheppard (1978). *Britannia. A History of Roman Britain*. 2nd ed. London: Routledge & Kegan Paul. (1st ed., 1967).

Gelling, Margaret (1978). *Signposts to the Past. Place-names and the History of England*. London: Dent.

---

[6] This is a much less vague answer, and a much more thoroughly documented and rigorously argued one, than that given by Ifor Williams to the question 'When did British become Welsh?' (Williams, 1939). Williams had gone no further than to claim that British had become Welsh certainly by the eighth century, probably by the seventh, and perhaps by the sixth or even the fifth century.

Jackson, Kenneth (1953). *Language and History in Early Britain. A Chronological Survey of the Brittonic Languages, 1st to 12th c. AD.*Edinburgh: University Press.

Nicolaisen, W.F.H., M. Gelling and M. Richards (1970). *The Names of Towns and Cities in Britain.* London: Batsford.

Reaney, P.H. (1964). *The Origin of English Place-names.* 3rd impression (with corrections and bibliographical additions). London: Routledge & Kegan Paul. (1st impression, 1960).

Rivet, A.L.F. and Colin Smith (1979). *The Place-names of Roman Britain.* London: Batsford.

Wainwright, F.T. (1962). *Archaeology and Place-names and History.* London: Routledge & Kegan Paul.

Williams, Ifor (1939). 'When did British become Welsh?' *Anglesey Antiquarian Society and Field Club: Transactions*, 27–39.

8 Welsh

Of the languages spoken at the present time in mainland Britain, Welsh has been here by far the longest. But since what period has the Welsh language as such, as distinct from the earlier British language from which it evolved, existed? Or, to put it differently: 'How old is the Welsh language?' The question can best be answered by attempting to define a stage in the evolution of the language at which its whole physiognomy, so to speak, in terms of its pronunciation, grammar and vocabulary, is so different from that of an earlier stage that one can feel justified in speaking of a different language rather than of merely a different stage in the history of the same language. All languages are constantly evolving but at some periods the rate of change is much quicker than at others, and it sometimes happens that, after a period of rapid and far-reaching change, a language reaches a stage at which its physiognomy *is* markedly different from what it was, and that it thereafter settles down for a period of centuries or millennia of more gradual evolution. Such a stage seems to have been reached in the history of the Brittonic speech of Western Britain in the late sixth century, and so it is from that time onwards that the language can be considered to be specifically Welsh (see Jackson, 1959).

Jackson had earlier suggested (1953:691) that 'if there is any one datable phonological change which marks the end of British and the beginning of Welsh, Cornish, and Breton, it is the loss of final syllables'. On this basis we can assume with reasonable confidence, when we find Latin inscriptions containing Brittonic names that have lost their final syllables, that these are Welsh rather than British. What is probably the earliest example is provided by the form IDNERT or IVDNERT (the inscription is damaged) that occurs in a seventh-century Latin inscription from Llanddewi-Brefi that begins [HI]C IACET [IV]DNERT FILIVS (etc.) 'Here lies Iudnert son of . . .' Another stone now in Llangaffo Church in Anglesey has an inscription that is likewise in Latin but contains Celtic names. According to Nash-Williams (who dates the stone '7th-9th century', 1950:65) the reading is . . . . . . VS . . . NIN . . . FILIU[S] CUURI[S?] CINI EREXIT HUNC LAPIDEM. The word *filius* and the last three words pose no problem, being straightforward Latin for 'son' and 'erected this stone'. But what of the rest? Jackson, who considers that the inscription dates from the mid-seventh century, has little doubt (1953:188) that the correct reading is VIRNIN FILIUS CUURIS CINI and that the three names, *Virnin, Cuuris* and *Cini* have lost their final syllables and so must be considered as Primitive Welsh.

The earliest surviving text wholly in Welsh is an inscription probably dating from the early eighth century, on a stone now in Tywyn Church. The reading of the inscription is not wholly certain, but it includes, together with various personal names, the phrase CINGEN CELEN TRICET NITANAM 'the body of Cingen dwells (i.e. lies) beneath' (*celen* corresponds to modern Welsh *celain* 'corpse', *tricet* is a part of the verb that in its modern form is *trigo* 'to dwell', and *nitanam* contains the preposition *tan, dan*, 'under'), and the word PETUAR (an earlier form of the modern *pedwar* 'four').

Apart from inscriptions on stone, the earliest surviving piece of written Welsh (with which we reach the Old Welsh period) is a brief text (an account of a lawsuit) inscribed on one of the pages of a Latin manuscript of the gospels, known as the Book of St Chad, now in the Cathedral Library at Lichfield. Opinions as to the date of this text vary widely. Jackson (1953: 43–6) surveys the arguments for and against the various views and concludes that, though it *may* be a copy of a sixth- or seventh-century text, what we have is an eight-century (and probably late eighth-century) version modernized according to the language of the time.

A number of other names, glosses and brief texts from the eighth, ninth and tenth centuries occur in the Book of St Chad and other manuscripts. Of particular interest is the Juvencus manuscript in the Cambridge University Library which includes two short poems that probably date from the ninth century and so, in one sense, count as the earliest surviving literary texts in Welsh (but see below). Another manuscript in the same library contains the longest continuous piece (twenty three lines) of Old Welsh, the so-called Computus Fragment, probably dating from the tenth century. Other fragments of Old Welsh, mainly names, occur in a few later (eleventh- and twelfth-century) manuscripts, in Latin inscriptions set up from the eighth to the twelfth century, and occasionally in the Anglo-Saxon Chronicle and other contemporary Anglo-Saxon documents.[1]

Although there are no pre-tenth-century literary manuscripts, other than the Juvencus poems, the origins of Welsh literature probably go back to the sixth century and some scholars have argued that some material, though not in its original form, survives from that period. The Latin *Historia Brittonum* or 'History of the Britons', perhaps composed around the year AD 800 and attributed (perhaps wrongly) to Nennius, refers to five poets who are said to have flourished in the time of the Anglian King Ida of Bernicia (547–559). As translated by Professor Caerwyn Williams (1959:44), the passage in question reads:

> Then Talhaearn Tad Awen [i.e. Father of Inspiration] gained renown in poetry and Neirin and Taliessin and Bluchbard and Cian who is called Gueinth Guaut [perhaps an error for Guenith Guaut, 'the wheat of song'], gained renown together at the same time in British poetry.

We know nothing of Talhaearn, Bluchbard and Cian, but a substantial amount of poetry attributed to Aneirin and Taliesin (to give the modern forms of their names) remains in thirteenth-century manuscripts. Some of the poems in question are certainly not their authentic work, but, when all this

---

[1] All the known sources for Old Welsh are surveyed and evaluated by Jackson (1953:42–59).

doubtful material has been stripped away, there remains in each case a nucleus that, though it had been modernized and otherwise modified in the period before it was written down, very probably does date in its essentials from the time of Aneirin and Taliesin and can be plausibly assumed to be their work. Both of these poets wrote in praise of the kings and heroes not of Wales but of the northern British kingdoms of Gododdin and Rheged, and, though Taliesin's homeland may have been in Wales, there is no reason to suppose that Aneirin was anything other than a northerner. For this reason, we discuss these early texts at some length in our chapter on Cumbric (see pp. 52–4), though there is no doubt that the language of the versions that remain to us is Welsh and not Cumbric.

Another name traditionally associated with the poetry of early Wales (particularly Powys) and Rheged is that Llywarch Hen, 'Llywarch the Old'. It used to be thought that some of his work too had survived. However, some fifty years ago Sir Ifor Williams put forward the view, which is now generally accepted, that the poems attributed to Llywarch are not in fact by him at all. They are, he suggests, verse passages that had formed part of two tales, one of them *about* not *by* Llywarch, that were mainly in prose and of which the prose passages have not survived. Williams (1935:lxxiv) tentatively dates the composition of these texts to about AD 850. If this is so, then the Llywarch material can be claimed as the earliest surviving literary text that is indisputably Welsh in every sense of the word.[2]

It is no part of our purpose to attempt even the briefest sketch of a history of Welsh literature.[3] What is strictly relevant to the theme of this book, however, is the fact that Welsh has one of the longest literary traditions of any European language and that that tradition has remained vital and unbroken to the present day. We must in particular mention two of the outstanding highlights of Welsh medieval literature, namely the prose romances collectively known as the Mabinogi or Mabinogion, and the poetry of Dafydd ap Gwilym. The term 'Mabinogi', in its strictest sense, relates to four tales whose origins must go very far back, probably to the pre-Welsh period, but which are known to us from two late medieval manuscripts (though in a version that dates perhaps from the eleventh century). These are the so-called 'Four branches of the Mabinogi'. namely 'Pwyll Lord of Dyfed', 'Branwen Daughter of Llŷr', 'Manawydan Son of Llŷr' and 'Math Son of Mathonwy'. Also grouped under the term 'Mabinogi' in its loose sense are seven other tales,[4] four of which are of native origin, namely 'The Dream

[2] A lengthy study and a full translation are afforded by Patrick K. Ford, *The Poetry of Llywarch Hen*, Berkeley, Los Angeles: University of California Press, 1974. Translations of parts of the Llywarch material can be found in Conran (1967), Gurney (1969), Clancy (1970), and Gwyn Jones (1977).

[3] The reader who is interested in knowing more will find a series of studies by distinguished scholars in Jarman–Hughes (1976, 1979) and a general survey in Thomas Parry's history of Welsh literature, translated into English (Parry–Bell, 1955) by Idris Bell, who had earlier produced a survey of the development of Welsh poetry (Bell, 1936). Selections of Welsh literature in translation are available in Clancy (1965, 1970), Conran (1967), Gurney (1969), Gwyn Williams (1973), and Gwyn Jones (1977).

[4] Modern translations of all 11 tales are provided by Gwyn Jones and Thomas Jones, *The Mabinogion*, London: Dent, 1949; Jeffrey Gantz. *The Mabinogion*, Harmondsworth:

of Macsen', 'Lludd and Llefelys', 'Culhwch and Olwen', and 'The Dream of Rhonabwy', while the other three are Arthurian romances, 'Owain and Luned' (or 'The Lady of the Fountain'), 'Geraint and Enid', and 'Peredur Son of Efrawg'.[5]

Taking up and echoing Gwyn Jones's description (1959:139) of the Mabinogion as 'Wales's own distinctive contribution to medieval prose literature', Sir Thomas Parry, to whom we owe the standard edition of the poems of Dafydd ap Gwilym (Parry, 1952), refers to Dafydd's work as 'our real contribution to medieval poetry' (Parry, 1959:168). He is, says Rachel Bromwich (1979:112), 'a poetic genius who is acknowledged to have been the greatest that Wales has known'. His main themes are love and nature, and his poetry, which has something in common with that of the troubadours, is characterized, in Parry's words, by an 'extremely fertile imagination', an 'exhuberant inventiveness', and an 'amazing mastery of word and idiom' (*ibid.*, 169 and 174).[6]

Though Wales has never since produced a poet of the stature of Dafydd ap Gwilym, poets have flourished in every generation from his day to our own. The same is not true of prose. From the thirteenth to the mid-sixteenth centuries, there was little by way of creative writing in prose. There were, indeed, numerous prose translations of other romances, particularly from French, and many other translations, mainly from Latin, and some at least partly original writing (religious and historical or semi-historical works, based on Latin sources, and a book of herbal and other remedies attributed to a thirteenth-century family of physicians, *Meddygon Myddfai* 'the physicians of Myddfai').[7] But though the literary value of most of these works is slight, they served an invaluable purpose by maintaining the practice of prose writing, which was to lead in the sixteenth century, with the Reformation, to the beginnings of modern prose literature in Welsh.

It was in 1536, merely two years after the Act of Supremacy declared Henry VIII to be the head of the Church of England and made the breach with Rome absolute, that the Act of Union, which in effect incorporated Wales in England, was passed. One consequence of the break with Rome was the

Penguin Books, 1976; and Patrick K. Ford, *The Mabinogi*, Berkeley: University of California Press, 1977; each of these volumes has a substantial introduction and a bibliography. See also the study by Proinsias Mac Cana, *The Mabinogi*, Cardiff: University of Wales Press, 1977.

[5] These last three correspond respectively to the twelfth-century French romances by Chrétien de Troyes, 'Yvain', 'Érec et Énide' and 'Perceval', and ultimately they must derive from the same source or sources, but the relationship between the two sets, and in particular which owes what, if anything, to the other is something that has not yet been satisfactorily explained in spite of all the attention that many eminent scholars have devoted to the problem.

[6] Translations of some of Dafydd's poems are to be found in H. Idris Bell and David Bell, *Dafydd ap Gwilym: Fifty Poems*, London: Cymmrodorion, 1942 (with a substantial introduction), in Clancy (1965), Conran (1969), Gurney (1969), Gwyn William (1973) and Gwyn Jones (1977). A translation of the complete works (based on Parry's edition), with introduction and notes, has now been provided by Richard Morgan Loomis, *Dafydd ap Gwilym: The Poems*, Binghampton, NY: Center for Medieval and Early Renaissance Studies, 1982.

[7] For a comprehensive listing of Middle Welsh texts, both verse and prose, including unpublished manuscripts as well as printed editions, see D. Simon Evans, *A Grammar of Middle Welsh*, Dublin: The Dublin Institute for Advance Studies, 1964, pp. xxi–xliii.

replacement of Latin by the vernacular, i.e. in England, English, as the language of public worship. But the vast majority of the people of Wales — which was now technically part of England — had little or no English, and this fact constituted a serious obstacle to the progress of the reformed religion in Wales. The Act of Union, however, while drawing attention in somewhat disparaging terms to the existence of the Welsh language, contained no provisions for doing away with it. The spirit of the age, in relation to Welsh, seems to have been dominated by a high degree of pragmatism — the Welsh language was there, it was a (perhaps regrettable) factor that had to be reckoned with, and so steps would have be to taken to put it to good use in the service of the reformed religion in those areas where English could not serve. Only thirteen years after the Act of Supremacy, i.e. in 1547, what is probably the first book printed in Welsh (dated in fact 1546) appeared, containing among other things the Creed, the Lord's Prayer and the Ten Commandments. It had no title, and so has come to be known by its opening words, *Yn y lhyvyr hwnn* ('In this book . . .') (illustration 3.) Also in 1547 there appeared

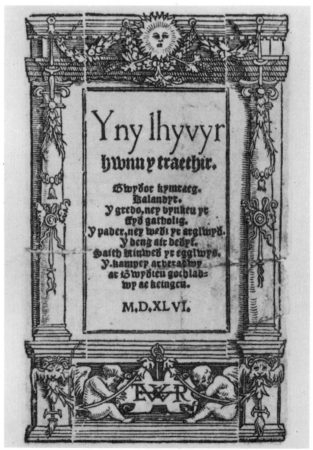

Illustration 3   First page of the earliest printed book in Welsh.

a book of proverbs with a preface by William Salesbury (to whom we shall return shortly), entitled *Oll Synnwyr Pen Kembero ygyd* ('All the common sense of a Welshman together'), and another by Salesbury, viz. *A Dictionary of Englyshe and Welshe . . .*, the first Welsh dictionary (it is in fact a Welsh-English dictionary). In 1551, yet another work by Salesbury came off the press, namely a translation, under the title *Kynniver Llith a Ban*, of the Epistles and Gospels appointed to be read in the Church of England on Sundays and Holy Days throughout the year.

By, or at any rate shortly after, the death of Henry VIII in January 1547, a significant beginning had, then, been made on the task of providing the people of Wales with the means of worshipping, according to the practices of the Church of England, in their own language. In 1563, an Act was passed providing for the translation into Welsh of the Book of Common Prayer and the Bible, and making the Welsh bishops responsible for seeing that this was done. The effective initiative for carrying out the provisions of the Act seems to have been taken by Richard Davies, Bishop of St David's, who himself translated the Book of Common Prayer which appeared in 1567. Later in the same year appeared the translation of the New Testament, to which Davies himself contributed five of the epistles while most of the rest was the work of William Salesbury, whom Davies had had the shrewdness to call in as his principal collaborator. The translation has been called 'a fine piece of work in the matter of style, idiom, and dignity of language' (Parry–Bell, 1955:194).

The third name particularly associated with the Welsh Bible is that of Bishop William Morgan. His translation of the Old Testament together with his revision of Salesbury's New Testament appeared in 1588, providing for the first time a complete Welsh version of the Bible, twenty-three years before the English 'Authorized Version' or 'King James Version'. Morgan based his language on that of traditional Welsh poetry as maintained in the bardic schools, and thereby achieved a greater dignity than might have been the case had he attempted to conform to the unstandardized spoken tongue of his day.

In 1620, a second edition of the complete Bible, revised by Dr John Davies, was published. This version, with few modifications, has been reprinted hundreds of times and still offers the only available Welsh version of the Old Testament.[8] Its influence not only on the religious life of Wales but on the literary Welsh language (and, so, on Welsh literature and culture in general) is incalculable:

> Perhaps the greatest service of the Bible to Welsh Literature was that it gave the nation a standard tongue superior to any dialect. In a country which lacked a university or any cultural institution to act as a centre for its literary vitality and to foster that enlightened conservatism which is indispensable to the continuance of a tradition, there would have been a risk that the language might degenerate into a number of disconnected dialects, as happened in Brittany, and the speech of one part of the country would have been so awkward to another part as to make it

[8] A new translation of the New Testament was published in 1975 and it is aimed to produce a new translation of the complete Bible for the fourth centenary in 1988 of William Morgan's Bible.

impossible to get a means of expression dignified and acceptable enough for the requirements of fine poetry (Parry – Bell, 1955:195 – 6).

The fact that Welsh acquired at this time a literary language that was both firmly based and generally accepted was to prove of inestimable benefit. There is certainly room for debate about the extent to which literary Welsh might be brought closer to the spoken language, but Wales and the Welsh language are spared the bitter quarrels that have all too often sprung up among the partisans of rival systems in the case of such languages as Breton, Occitan or Basque, where there is no common literary language and no agreement as to the principles (orthography, dialectal or inter-dialectal basis, and so on) according to which such a common language might be established.

Much of the specifically linguistic work on Welsh in the sixteenth century originated with Salesbury. As we have seen, he compiled the first Welsh dictionary[9] and in 1556 he published the first book on Welsh pronunciation, *A briefe and a playne introduction teaching how to pronounce the letters in the British Tong (now com'enly called Welsh)*. For the first work which could truly be described as a grammar of Welsh, however, we have to turn to Milan, where, in 1567, Gruffydd Robert, one of the Catholics who fled the country after the accession of Elizabeth I in 1558, published the first part of his Welsh grammar, the remainder of which appeared some time after 1584. Other grammars were published by Siôn Dafydd Rhys and Henry Salesbury in 1592 and 1593 respectively, and, in particular, by John Davies of Mallwyd, whose *Antiquae Linguae Britannicae . . . Rudimenta* ('Rudiments of the Ancient British Language') of 1621 is referred to by Thomas Parry as 'a masterpiece of grammar' (Parry – Bell, 1955:203).

The fact that standard Welsh was first codified for solemn purposes (the translation of the Bible and of the Anglican Book of Common Prayer) gave it an appreciably archaic flavour. It retains a number of morphological and syntactic features that are no longer in use in the spoken language and the orthography often reflects an obsolete pronunciation. Consequently, since the Second World War in particular, there has been a growing tendency to modify literary usage in the direction of the spoken language. This is to be welcomed, but is is noticeable – and probably inevitable – that it has led to a certain 'destandardization' in that a whole variety of regional variants are penetrating the written language. Whether this is a temporary phase and whether some of these forms will come to be preferred to others as standard forms, and, if so, when and why, is a subject on which it would be futile to speculate. The one point I would make is that the standard written language exists and that the task that confronts us in Wales is not that of creating a standard language but of modernizing the one we have.

---

[9] It was to be eighty-five years before another Welsh dictionary was to appear, namely the Welsh – Latin and Latin – Welsh dictionary by John Davies of Mallwyd, the reviser of the 1620 version of the Bible. This was the famous *Antiquae Linguae Brittanicae . . . Dictionarium Duplex* ('Two-way Dictionary of the Ancient British Language') of 1632; the Welsh – Latin part was Davies's own work but the Latin – Welsh part he abridged from a still unpublished manuscript by Thomas Wiliems.

[10] For an admirable survey of early printing in Welsh, see A. Crawford and A.P. Jones, 'The early typography of printed Welsh', *The Library*, 6th series, 3(1981):217 – 31.

Wales, then, embarked on the age of the printed word with a standardized language to hand.[10] The first Welsh printed book dates from (probably) 1547, but it was not until 1719 that the first press (apart from a clandestine Catholic press that is thought to have functioned in a cave on the North Wales coast in or about 1585) was set up in Wales. Meanwhile, however, some 300 Welsh books had been published in England (mainly in London and just across the border in Shrewsbury). Thereafter the pace quickened and it is estimated that well over 1000 Welsh books were published in the remainder of the eighteenth century and well over 8000 in the nineteenth (Humphreys, 1979:56). Altogether, a total of perhaps 15,000 to 20,000 Welsh books (depending on what one decides to count as a book rather than as, say, a pamphlet or an issue of a periodical) have been published since 1546 (see G. Morgan, 1966:123 — who also points out however that this is no more than the total of titles of books now published *in one year* in English). The annual total of Welsh books published (excluding reprints), which had long stood at between 100 and 125, was consistently over 200 from 1973 (239 titles) to 1978 (262 titles).[11] This increase is welcome, but it is still regrettably true that anyone who attempted to subsist on a diet of Welsh books alone would inevitably be seriously undernourished.

Book publishing in Welsh is not, in general, an economic proposition.[12] In practice, public subsidies for Welsh books are now available from a variety of sources. The Welsh Joint Education Committee has been active since 1950, and in a more ambitious way since 1966 (see Eric Evans, 1978:16), in promoting some hundreds of titles for children (including learners). A government Welsh Books Grant was instituted in 1956, for the purpose of making grants to publishers for producing Welsh books for adults, and in 1961 the Welsh Books Council (founded in 1958) was officially recognized for the purpose of promoting books and periodicals (mainly but not exclusively in Welsh) that serve the needs of Wales. The Council receives its own grants from the State and from the Welsh county councils, and now administers the Welsh Books Grant referred to above. The Welsh Arts Council also makes *ad hoc* grants to publishers and awards bursaries and prizes to authors.

There has been a long-standing complaint that there is too much poetry and 'high-brow' literature in Welsh, and not enough for the ordinary man or woman who just wants 'a good read'. The medieval and later classics in prose and poetry establish the credentials of Welsh as a literary language, but a

[11] A classified analysis of Welsh books published in 1899 (96 titles), 1925 (74), 1935 (123), 1945 (119), 1950 (100), 1957 (119), 1963 (107), and annually from 1971 to 1978 is provided in *Llais Llyfrau/Book News*, Winter 1977:24–25, and Spring 1979:4. For a general (but in my view over-optimistic) survey of the state of Welsh publishing in the early 1970s, see R. Gerallt Jones, 1973.

[12] An official report (Home Office, *Report of the Committee on Welsh Publishing*, London: HMSO) stated in 1952 that the average print-run of a Welsh edition was 2500 copies, and the average sale about 1200 copies in two years, and that it was a rare event for a Welsh book to go into a second edition. More recently, the Assistant Director of the Welsh Arts Council, Meic Stephens, has claimed (*Llais Llyfrau*, No. 18, Winter 1972, pp. 22–3) that the number of those who regularly buy Welsh books or periodicals is no greater than 3000, and that the sales of a popular novel or of a volume of poetry alike are around 800 (of which about 500 are bought by libraries). See also the report of the Council for the Welsh Language, *Publishing in the Welsh Language*, Cardiff: HMSO, 1978.

ready supply of throw-away thrillers, science fiction, romances and the like would do more to keep the language alive, and in recent years more and more such work has been appearing.

The heyday of Welsh periodicals was the nineteenth century. By 1870 there were some thirty periodicals (quarterlies, monthlies, weeklies, most of them of a religious nature) and weekly or monthly newspapers (there has never been a regular daily paper in Welsh). Now, there are two 'national' weeklies, some local weeklies, some religious weeklies, a few monthlies or quarterlies catering for various other specialized interests, and a number of local monthlies produced by voluntary cooperative effort (see B.L. Jones, 1981:48).

We have seen that, from the beginnings of the Protestant Reformation onwards, Welsh was the language of religion in Wales. This was to have important consequences, reaching far beyond the field of religion itself. Indeed, 'it may well have done more than anything else to safeguard the continued existence of the language. Quite definitely it ensured its survival as literary language' (Glanmor Williams, 1971:6). And the field of religion was long to remain one of the strongholds of Welsh in the public domain (see R. Tudur Jones, 1973). The Puritan movement of the seventeenth century and the Methodist revival of the eighteenth both used the vernacular in their preaching and their teaching, thereby ensuring for the language a respected status in at least one important sphere. The positive influence of the various non-conformist churches has been exercised not merely through their use of the language for public service, prayer meetings and Sunday schools, but also through their publications, including not only books but a number of newspapers and magazines. The attitude of the Anglican church, too, has been much more favourable towards Welsh than is sometimes acknowledged. Until the Act of Parliament severing the Welsh dioceses from the Church of England and setting up the Church in Wales as a separate body under its own archbishop came into effect in 1920, Wales formed part of the Province of Canterbury. Nevertheless, and in spite of the fact that throughout the eighteenth and nineteenth centuries the majority of the bishops appointed to Welsh sees were Englishmen, the language or languages used in Anglican Church services probably corresponded closely to the linguistic situation in individual parishes (see Pryce, 1978:3).

The churches and associated bodies have had a crucial role to play, too, in fostering literacy in Welsh. The (Anglican) Society for Promoting Christian Knowledge, founded in 1698 for the purpose, *inter alia*, of establishing charity schools in all parts of England and Wales, quickly spread throughout Wales and, though it was intended in principle to teach English in the schools, the fact that in many areas the only language spoken by all but a few was Welsh led to the setting up of Welsh schools in some parts of North Wales and, incidentally, to the publication by the SPCK of a number of books in Welsh. Much more significant, however, than the activity of the SPCK itself was what was to grow out of it. In the 1730s, the Rector of Llanddowror (Carmarthenshire), Griffith Jones, conceived the idea of teaching large numbers of his compatriots to read Welsh through 'circulating schools'. An itinerant teacher would stay in the same place for not more than three months teaching children and adults to read the Scriptures in Welsh and then move on to another locality. By the time Griffith Jones died in 1761, over 150,000 children and scores of thousands of adults had been taught in some 3325 schools (Glanmor Williams, 1979:207–8), and the work continued successfully for nearly twenty years thereafter. Throughout the nineteenth century, the various nonconformist denominations in particular carried on the work of maintaining a high level of literacy in Welsh through the medium of their Sunday schools, and surviving registers from the latter part of the century 'indicate that it was not unusual for more than 90% of households in Welsh-speaking areas to be associated with a Sunday school . . . By the end of the century, however, the movement had reached its peak and a steady declined followed as this voluntary Welsh-medium system of popular education was undermined by the growth of a state-sponsored, English medium system' (Jac. L. Williams, 1973:94).

The role of State education when it came was indeed much less creditable.[13] The report of an official Commission of Enquiry into the State of Education in Wales, published in 1874 in three volumes, in the usual 'blue book' format of such reports, and ever since known as 'Brad y Llyfrau Gleision' ('The Blue Books Betrayal') indulged in a deal of ill-informed and offensive criticism of various aspects of Welsh life (including the nonconformist churches and the Sunday schools) and, in particular, came to conclusions hostile to the Welsh language (for an account of the 1847 report, see the report of the Central Advisory Council for Education, 1953:7–9, from which the following quotations from the 'Blue Books' are taken):

> Whether in the country or among the furnaces the Welsh element is never found at the top of the social scale . . . His language keeps him under the hatches, being one in which he can neither acquire nor communicate the necessary information (I, 3).

> The Welsh language is a vast drawback to Wales, and a manifold barrier to the moral progress and commercial prosperity of the people . . . It dissevers the people from intercourse which would greatly advance their civilization, and bars the access of improving knowledge to their minds (II, 66).

Not surprisingly, a report containing comments such as this provoked a variety of reactions. On the one hand, anger and resentment – but on the other, an accentuation of the inferiority complex many Welsh-speakers had about their language (a complex that has still not entirely disappeared).

In fact, the Commissioners recommended that Welsh *should* be used in schools – not however for its own sake but because the best way of teaching the pupils English was to use Welsh for the purpose ('for as long as the children are familiar with none other [language than Welsh] they must be educated to a considerable extent through the medium of it', I, 7). This, the teaching of Welsh as a means to an end (viz. the better acquisition of English) rather than as an end in itself, was to be the key-note of activity on behalf of

---

[13] For fuller historical discussion that is possible here of the role of Welsh in the schools of Wales, see Central Advisory Council for Education, 1953:3–31; W.R. Jones, 1966; Morgan, 1966:97–115; Le Calvez, 1970:87–112; Jac L. Williams, 1973.

Welsh in education for some time to come. It is significant, for example, that a prize was offered at the Caernarfon eisteddfod in 1861 for an essay on 'The best mode of teaching the English language to Welsh children', and that the full title of a society popularly known as Cymdeithas yr Iaith Gymraeg, 'The Welsh Language Society', set up in 1885 with the support of a number of prominent Welsh educationalists, was 'The Society for the Utilization of the Welsh Language in Education for the Purpose of Serving a Better and More Intelligent Knowledge of English'.

It is not surprising that the Elementary Education Act of 1870, which laid the foundations of the whole system of State education in England and Wales, took no account whatsoever of the existence of the Welsh language which, consequently, had no place in the schools that came into being as a result of the Act.

Progress was however made, though very slowly, in the last quarter of the nineteenth century. In 1875, the Code of Regulations for Public Elementary Schools at least recognized the existence of the language by stipulating that 'in districts where Welsh is spoken the intelligence of the children may be tested by requiring them to explain in Welsh the meaning of passages read'. Provision for Welsh to be used as a medium of instruction was first made in 1890 when an official circular stated that 'bilingual books may be used for the purpose of instructing the scholars'. Welsh was introduced into the curriculum in 1891 as an optional subject that could be taken by individual pupils in the upper classes, and in 1893 as a subject that could be taken by whole classes. Secondary education in Wales under the aegis of the state began in 1889 with the Welsh Intermediate Education Act, but little encouragement was given to the teaching of Welsh and by 1906 only a little over a fifth of the 10,000 pupils in the Intermediate Schools were receiving any instruction in the language (and no such instruction at all was provided in forty-two schools out of ninety-five).

In 1907, a separate Welsh Department of the Board of Education was set up and soon expressed the wish 'that every Welsh teacher should realize the educational value of the Welsh language' and advised that 'where local needs make it desirable' any subject in the secondary curriculum could be taught in Welsh. These were modest statements indeed, and their practical effect may not have been very great. But they were indicative of a much needed sympathetic attitude on the part of those in authority and set the seal of approval on the policy of those local education authorities (among them Cardiff) that had introduced the teaching of Welsh as a subject. By 1914, Welsh was being widely if still insufficiently taught, not only in rural and largely Welsh-speaking areas like Carmarthenshire and Cardiganshire but also in some of the already relatively anglicized areas of the industrial south such as Llanelli, Swansea, the Rhondda valleys and Newport (Central Advisory Council, 1953:17–18). On the other hand, at that time there was, as R.I. Aaron says, 'no sense of urgency about the language', and it can safely be assumed that many Welsh-speaking people, even those who were anxious that their children should speak Welsh, shared the view of his parents that the purpose of the school was to provide a good education in English and that 'Welsh would be looked after in the home, the church and the playground' (Aaron, 1970:238).

A significant advance came with the publication of the official report, *Welsh in Education and Life* (Board of Education, 1927), which affirmed that the Board of Education fully accepted that 'the administration of education in the Principality should be sympathetic towards the utilization of the Welsh language to the full extent demanded by educational considerations' (pp. 85–6). In the course of the 1930s, the use of Welsh as a medium of instruction became much more widespread in primary schools (though not – except in teaching Welsh as subject and possibly religious knowledge – in secondary schools). The use of Welsh in such circumstances, and the extent to which it was used, were however matters of practice, and therefore liable to variation, rather than procedures formally laid down. The feasibility of Welsh-medium education in a partially anglicized area was first demonstrated by an independent (fee-paying) school opened in Aberystwyth in 1939 under the auspices of the national youth movement, Urdd Gobaith Cymru, in face of the possibility that an influx of English evacuees might result in the complete anglicization of local primary schools. The first primary school to be officially established in the State system as a Welsh-medium school was opened in Llanelli in 1947, and since the early 1950s some scores of such schools have been set up by local education authorities both in the Welsh-speaking areas and, in cases where Welsh-speaking parents have pressed for it, in many mainly English-speaking areas too. A further development has been the growth in recent years of a number of Welsh-language nursery schools, some under the aegis of local authorities, many more sponsored by *Mudiad Ysgolion Meithrin Cymraeg* (The Welsh Nursery School Movement) founded in 1971. The role of such nursery and primary schools in maintaining the Welsh language is crucial. They can justly lay claim to considerable success not only in ensuring that Welsh-speaking children retain their language but in leading some English-speaking children to achieve a good command of Welsh. They may or may not be able to arrest the decline in Welsh among the younger generations, but they, more than any other factor perhaps, may at least succeed in slowing down the rate of decline.

Though there are no secondary schools in which the sole medium of instruction is Welsh, eleven bilingual schools have come into existence. The Flintshire Education Authority set up the first (at Rhyl) in 1956 and a second (at Mold) in 1961, with Glamorgan and Denbighshire quickly following suit at Pontypridd and Wrexham in 1962 and 1963 respectively. The usual practice in such schools is that some or all science subjects are taught through the medium of English but that other subjects are taught through Welsh, and Welsh is the official and working language for administrative purposes. By 1980, a total of 7860 pupils were attending the eleven schools in question.

A policy of bilingualism (which in the context means teaching Welsh to English-speaking children and English to Welsh-speaking children) was recommended by the Central Advisory Council for Education (Wales) in its reports, *The Place of Welsh and English in the Schools of Wales* (1953) and *Primary Education in Wales* (1967). This may therefore be considered now to be official policy, and it is indeed implemented by most education authorities in Wales.

The fact that some thousands of pupils are now receiving much of their secondary education through the medium of Welsh has led to demands that similar provision should be made within the University of Wales (where, in fact, Welsh has long served as the medium of instruction in the departments of Welsh, and, in some Colleges of the University, in such other departments as Welsh History and Biblical Studies). Consequently, in the late 1960s and 1970s a small number of staff were appointed to teach through the medium of Welsh in various departments at the University College of Wales, Aberystwyth and the University College of North Wales, Bangor. A prominent place is also given to Welsh in two of the training colleges, viz. the Normal College at Bangor and Trinity College at Carmarthen.

The importance of the schools in maintaining Welsh is considerable (see Khleif, 1980:100–219, 'The schools as an agency of regeneration'). Whether they can act as a strong enough barrier to resist the encroaching tide of anglicization in the world outside is another matter. Comments such as the following, made in 1978 on the basis of a survey of the use of Welsh in various domains by some 3000 children, all fluent bilinguals, make depressing reading:

> In the thoroughly Welsh-speaking areas at age 10 + a great deal of Welsh was used in church and chapel and in talking to teachers in school. Less Welsh was used in running errands and in talking to people outside school though the bias was still towards Welsh. English was the dominant language in playing with friends, in private reading, and in listening to the radio and television (G. Lewis, 1978:327).

The use of English, particularly in communicating with teachers and for private reading, was even more widespread among older children. But particularly disturbing is the fact that children from schools established for the specific purpose of encouraging Welsh 'used English almost exclusively in running errands and used more English than Welsh in playing with friends, talking to adults outside school, and in reading':

> This is an indication of the overwhelming influence of population change, among other factors, in creating an environment where, whatever the intentions of the parents and the efforts of the schools, English is clearly dominant in nearly all domains of use (*ibid.*).

If the role of Welsh in the religious life of the country has long been well established and even dominant, and its role in education has improved steadily in the course of the last hundred years, it is only very recently that it has been accorded anything approaching a satisfactory position in public and official life generally.

The Act of Union of England and Wales of 1536, while not proscribing the Welsh language, did specify that 'from hensforth no personne or personnes that use the Welsshe speche or langage shall have or enjoy any maner office or fees within the Realme of Englonde Wales or other the Kinges dominions upon peyn of forfaiting the same offices or fees onles he or they use and exercise the speche or langage of Englisshe' (quoted after Rees, 1948:70) − in other words, a command of English was an essential qualification for public life.

In reality, however, though it had no legal or official status, Welsh continued − inevitably, since the majority of Welshmen knew little or no English − to be used in courts of law, and it appears that throughout the three centuries of the existence of the Court of Great Sessions (set up in Wales by Henry VIII and abolished in 1830), there are instances of the use of Welsh by monoglot Welsh-speaking parties and witnesses (see Robyn Lewis, 1974:3). Thereafter, and perhaps as a direct consequence of the increase in the numbers of those who had at least a working knowledge of English, the situation changed and it appears that by the end of the nineteenth century Welsh was used only when there was no alternative.

In response to a nation-wide petition organized on the eve of the Second World War and bearing nearly 400,000 signatures, Parliament in 1942 passed the Welsh Courts Act which, though apparently intended to confer a measure of official recognition on Welsh, had little practical effect. In particular, though it specifically repealed that section of the Act of Union which was held to restrict unduly 'the right of Welsh speaking persons to use the Welsh language in courts of justice in Wales', its only positive provision (apart from allowing the oath to be administered in Welsh and recognizing the need for interpreters to be appointed and paid) was the following:

> It is hereby enacted that the Welsh language may be used in any court in Wales by any party or witness who considers that he would otherwise be at any disadvantage by reason of his natural language of communication being Welsh.

It should be noted that this falls far short of allowing a party or witness to speak in Welsh merely out of preference − he may do so only if he considers he would otherwise be at a disadvantage.

It was not until the 1960s that a substantial improvement in the official and legal status of Welsh was achieved. The movement that led to the change had comparatively small beginnings. In the 1950s a Carmarthenshire family who, year after year for eight years, had declined to pay their rates because the Llanelli Rural Council did not provide rates demand forms in Welsh as well as in English, had each year had items of furniture seized and sold by order of the magistrates' court, until finally in 1960 the Council agreed to issue bilingual forms. The following year, also in Carmarthenshire, a candidate at a local government election had his nomination papers declared invalid because they were in Welsh, but in 1962 two judges of the Queen's Bench Division of the High Court of Justice ruled that the nomination papers in question were valid. The situation was regularized by the Election (Welsh Forms) Act of 1964 which legalized the provision of Welsh versions of all forms used in connection with local or parliamentary elections.

Meanwhile, an official committee set up in 1960 to enquire into the situation of the Welsh language had reported (The Council for Wales and Monmouthshire, *Report on the Welsh Language Today*, 1963) and recommended that the Welsh language be given official status and, in particular, that anyone who preferred to use Welsh in a court of law, whether or not he would be put at a disadvantage by having to use English, should be allowed to do so.

In that same year, 1963, the Minister for Welsh Affairs set up a committee to enquire into the status of the Welsh language. This committee duly reported in 1965.[14] They concluded that, with the conspicuous exception of the field of education, 'the Welsh language has been in effect ignored by the British state machinery' (§161, p. 35). Rejecting on the one hand the 'principle of necessity' (i.e. the principle that Welsh be legally recognized only when an individual would otherwise be at a disadvantage) and on the other the 'principle of bilingualism' (according to which all legal and administrative business would be carried on, and all records and other documents kept, in both languages), the committee came down in favour of the 'principle of equal validity'. More specifically they recommended that:

> there should be a clear, positive, legislative declaration of general application to the effect that any act, writing or thing done in Welsh in Wales . . . should have the like legal force as if it had been done in English (§171, p. 39).

The report led to the passing in July, 1967 of the Welsh Language Act, 1967 (for the text thereof, see Robyn Lewis, 1969:122–5). The main provisions of this Act are that 'in any legal proceeding in Wales . . . the Welsh language may be spoken by any party, witness or other person who desires to use it', that 'the appropriate Minister may [NB "may" *not* "shall"] by order prescribed' a Welsh version of 'any document or any form of words which is to be used for an official or public purpose', and that 'anything done in Welsh' on the basis of any such document or form of words 'shall have the like effect as if done in English' (i.e., the 'principle of equal validity' is now officially enshrined in law).

A law, of course, is of little value if it is not implemented. The most one can say about the Welsh Language Act is that its success has been patchy (for a hostile view, see Betts, 1976:121–5). An extensive range of forms and documents, emanating from government departments, local government offices, the nationalized industries, and commercial concerns is now available. They include driving licences, television licences, rates demands (in many areas), telephone and electricity bills, bank paying-in slips, various electoral documents, the Department of the Environment's (motor) 'Test Certificate', information leaflets issued by the Post Office, British Telecom, the Office of Fair Trading, banks, building societies, the BBC, the Equal Opportunities Commission, the police, the National Trust, the Nature Conservancy Council, etc., etc. On the other hand, there has been much criticism, some of it reasoned, some of it not, of what has *not* yet been done, particularly in the

[14] Their report (Welsh Office, *Legal Status of the Welsh Language*) is well worth consulting for its historical survey of the role of Welsh in law and administration and for its comprehensive analysis of contemporary practice in relation to the use of Welsh in the administration of justice, in police administration, in public administration and in semi-public institutions (i.e. the nationalized industries, the Welsh Hospital Board and hospital management committees, and the BBC).

field of the administration of justice (see Moseley, 1969, Robyn Lewis, 1969, 1973, 1974, I.B. Rees, 1972).

Meanwhile, pressure had been building up from another direction. In February, 1962, the distinguished writer and critic, Saunders Lewis, delivered a radio lecture on the subject 'Tynged yr Iaith' ('The destiny of the language'). Surveying all the panoply of forces ranged against the Welsh language, he called for an organized and energetic campaign 'to make it impossible to conduct local authority or central government business without the Welsh language' (S. Lewis, 1962:29; translation, p. 26).

The call was soon heeded. In July 1962, in direct response to the Saunders Lewis lecture, a group of young nationalists founded Cymdeithas yr Iaith Gymraeg ('The Welsh Language Society'), which has since waged a number of campaigns in favour of such causes as Welsh or bilingual summonses for alleged lawbreakers, bilingual road-signs, due recognition of Welsh on the part of the Post Office, and greatly improved provision for Welsh on radio and television (see Ned Thomas, 1971:79–89; Fishlock, 1972;73–101; Cynog Davies, 1973; Colin H. Williams, 1976–77). The Society states that it 'uses non-violent democratic methods, wherever possible, but is prepared to break flagrantly unjust laws when all other methods fail' (Cymdeithas yr Iaith Gymraeg, 1966:4), and indeed many of its campaigns have involved not merely demonstrations but acts of civil disobedience and damage to property, such as daubing and, later, removing or destroying English-only road signs, occupying post offices and tearing down English-language posters, and, more seriously, damaging television studios and transmitter masts. As a result, many of its members have served terms of imprisonment. But the members of the Society are not mindless vandals:

> Many leading Welshmen, firmly believing that the Welsh language is the supreme expression of the uniqueness of the Welsh as a people, gave the society support and guidance. Most notably the late Professor J.R. Jones, a philosopher of great integrity and incomparable passion, somehow summoned up that tremendous courage that is born of grim despair — the despair that can overwhelm a person confronted by the suffocating death of his mother tongue and of everything that is associated with it; this was movingly recorded in the writings of the last few years of his life. The challenging militancy, the irrepressible campaign to increase the prestige of Welsh and to extend the use of the language on mass media and in administration and before the law, the resort to public violence, must be viewed in the light of that sort of anguish, allied to an understandably impatient desire to get things done in order to try to reverse the tide of recession (D. Ellis Evans, 1972:178).

There seems little doubt that, though this would probably not be admitted by the administrative authorities, many of the advances achieved for Welsh in recent years, such as the decision by the Secretary of State for Wales in 1974 to authorize bilingual road-signs, have come about at least partly in response to the Society's activities. On the other hand, 'militancy has already had the effect of sharpening and embittering the conflict in language loyalty in Wales' (*ibid.*, 178), and these same activities have stirred up considerable opposition among sections of the Welsh-speaking and non-Welsh-speaking communities alike, and, since the future of Welsh depends in no small measure on a sympathetic attitude on the part of both those communities, the Society could be in danger of finding that, in the long run, its successes are counter-productive.

It is only since 1891 that information on the distribution of the Welsh language has been given in the decennial census reports. Furthermore, because of the unsatisfactory wording of the relevant question and the way the information was presented, the report on the 1891 census is open to a number of objections and so our first acceptable statistics date from 1901.

The decline in Welsh-speaking this century is catastrophic, in terms both of absolute numbers and of the proportion of the population speaking either Welsh only or both Welsh and English. This emerges with terrifying starkness from the following data drawn from the reports on the decennial censuses[15] (no census was taken in 1941):

	Speaking Welsh only		Speaking English and Welsh		Total	
1901	280,905	15%	648,919	35%	929,824	50%
1911	190,292	8.5%	787,074	35%	977,366	43,5%
1921	155,989	6%	766,103	31%	922,092	37%
1931	97,932	4%	811,329	33%	909,261	37%
1951	41,155	2%	673,531	27%	714,686	29%
1961	26,223	1%	629,779	25%	656,002	26%
1971	32,725	1%	509,700	20%	542,425	21%
1981[16]	21,583	1%	486,624	18%	508,207	19%

These figures cannot be taken as representing absolute truth, for a number of reasons. First, many whose Welsh is less than fluent will hesitate as to whether or not to declare themselves as Welsh-speakers – some do, some do not. Then, the Census question has sometimes been a little obscure – in particular, in censuses up to 1921, the question referred to ability to speak 'English only',

---

[15] Excepting in the case of percentages in 0.5, I have rounded up or down the figures that, in the Census reports, are given to one decimal place.

[16] At the time of writing, detailed results of the 1981 census are not yet available. Figures for each county, and for the districts into which the counties are divided, have however been published (see Office of Population Censuses and Surveys, *Census 1981: County Report* [on each individual county], Part I, London: HMSO, 1982). These reveal that only one of the eight Welsh counties, viz. Gwynedd, had a majority (61 per cent) of Welsh-speakers, the next highest proportions being Dyfed (46 per cent) and Powys (20 per cent). Of the 37 districts, only eight (four of the five districts in Gwynedd and four out of six in Dyfed) had a majority of Welsh-speakers, and in only four of these did as many as two-thirds speak Welsh, namely Dwyfor (79 per cent), Arfon (75 per cent) and Meirionydd (68 per cent), in Gwynedd, and Dinefwr (71.5 per cent) in Dyfed. On the other hand, the fact that the rate of decline has slowed down (a drop of 2 per cent in 1971–81 as compared with 5 per cent in 1961–71) has been thought by some to provide grounds for optimism. How significant this slowing-down really is, however, is impossible to estimate. The average rate of decline of 3 per cent per ten years over the last sixty years (from 37 per cent of Welsh-speakers in 1921 to 19 per cent in 1981) has been far from constant, fluctuating from only 0.3 per cent in 1921–31, up to 8 per cent in the twenty year period 1931–51, down to 3 per cent in 1951–61, and, as we have seen, up to 5 per cent in 1961–71 and now down to 2 per cent in 1971–81.

and so did not strictly apply to persons speaking English and another language other than Welsh[17] (since 1931, the reference is to ability to speak 'Welsh only' or 'English and Welsh'). Finally, in 1971 (and probably also in 1981 and perhaps in earlier censuses) there was a deliberate move by some bilinguals to inflate the number of monoglots recorded by putting themselves down as speaking Welsh only (this must be the reason why the number of monoglots in Cardiff, for example, rose from 136 in 1951 to 975 in 1971).

The overall picture is distressingly clear: since 1901, the total number of Welsh-speakers has been almost halved (and the number of monoglots reduced to negligible proportions), while the *proportion* of Welsh-speakers has fallen from a half of the total population to less than a fifth. An analysis by age-groups is even more depressing, and bodes ill for the future: whereas 40.5 per cent of those aged 65 and over were recorded as Welsh-speaking in 1981, the proportion for the age-group 16−24 was down to 15 per cent and for the 3−4 age-group to a little over 13 per cent. Furthermore, a survey made over twenty years ago (Welsh Joint Education Committee, 1961, tables I and II) revealed that already then only 13.4 per cent of pupils in the 5−15 age-group in Welsh schools were able to express themselves 'with fair fluency' in Welsh (only 11.3 per cent had Welsh as their first language), and that only a further 4.2 per cent could 'conduct elementary conversation' in Welsh.

The decline in the proportion of Welsh-speakers is even more worrying than the decline in absolute numbers. In other words, the 'intensity factor' is more important to the survival of a language than the 'quantity factor'. (The long-term future of, say, Faroese, spoken by virtually all of the 30,000 inhabitants of the Faroe islands, including the capital, Torshávn, is perhaps more secure than that of Welsh.) The lower the proportion of Welsh-speakers in a given area, the more use they inevitably make of English, and the less likely they are to succeed in passing Welsh on, at any rate as a first language, to the next generation. In such conditions, 'a knowledge of English is essential, and the older language becomes atrophied and dies' (J.G. Thomas, 1956:76). A further important consideration is that, in the areas where the 'intensity factor' is high, i.e. the areas 'wherein geographical factors of inaccessibility and comparative lack of economic developments have operated to preserve the native language' (*ibid.*, 77), the 'quantity factor' is low − we are dealing with sparsely populated areas (and areas which, moreover, are among those most adversely affected by the problem of rural depopulation) which cannot be expected to exert any linguistic influence on other areas where anglicization is already at a more advanced stage.

The result of this steady decline in the proportion of Welsh-speakers is, of course, that areas that were quite recently almost totally bilingual have become mixed (bilingual/monoglot English), while others that, just as recently, used to be mixed have now gone over completely to English.

The beginnings of the geographical recession of Welsh go back at least as far as the thirteenth century, when the southern part of Pembrokeshire and parts of the Gower peninsula and the Vale of Glamorgan became the domains

---

[17] The report on the 1951 census suggests that this may have been the reason why, at the 1921 census, 98,000 people failed to answer the language question. On the difficulties of interpreting census statistics for Welsh, see Khleif, 1980:54−63.

of Anglo-Norman lords and Welsh was in due course replaced by English (and not, it is interesting to observe, given the view of some scholars – see p. 221 – that French was a well-established vernacular, by French.)[18]

Thereafter, Welsh seems to have maintained its position well for several hundred years. W.H. Rees's unfortunately unpublished PhD thesis quotes (1947:38) contemporary evidence to show that in the mid-seventeenth century it was still spoken in some fifteen parishes in the English counties of Hereford and Shropshire (see also Charles, 1963). As we have seen, census figures for the distribution of the Welsh language are not available until 1891. However, a particularly informative source for evidence on the period from about 1750 onwards, and one that has recently been tapped to good effect, is provided by the returns made by parochial clergy of the Anglican Church in response to specific questions from their bishops as to the language or languages used in their churches. In a well documented account, W.T.R. Pryce argues (1978:10) that 'with the notable exception of a few northern towns – Beaumaris, Caernarfon, Conwy, and Rhuthun – Welsh was the sole language used regularly in the services of the Anglican Church over most of the country in 1750', though English seemed to have been introduced in a few parishes in the south-west. The accompanying map reveals also that English was used in Gower (and presumably, though no information was available, in south Pembrokeshire), eastern Monmouthshire and Radnor, and the eastern fringe of Denbigh and Flint. There is no good reason to suppose that the Church would continue to use Welsh as its medium of public worship after it had ceased to be the language of at least a substantial proportion of the parishioners, and so we may agree with Pryce that 'rural Wales in the mid eighteenth century was essentially Welsh in speech' (*ibid.*).

By about 1850, the bilingual zone had moved further west. In some parishes that had been bilingual a century earlier, the services were now conducted solely in English. The most noticeable area of retreat was in the south, where 'the bilingual zone had expanded considerably in west Glamorganshire, in the Vale of Neath and up the Swansea and Lougher (*sic*) valleys. Moreover, it had clearly established itself in the parishes surrounding the Tywi estuary', and there were 'undoubted signs of northward penetrations [from south Pembrokeshire] towards Fishguard and into the low Teifi valley' (*ibid.*, 17). Furthermore, a number of parishes in the rural Welsh-speaking heartland had begun to introduce some English into their services.

Pryce's overall conclusion however is that, both numerically and in territorial terms, Wales was 'overwhelmingly Welsh in speech' at the beginning of the nineteenth century and that, in territorial terms at least, it remained so until the middle of the century. But by the end of the century there are indications that 'a cultural invasion of the Welsh heartland was taking place' (*ibid.*, 24). English speech had penetrated right along the north coast as far as the Menai Strait and was spreading southwards into the Vale of Clwyd and the Conwy valley, and, all along the west coast from Holyhead to Fishguard, a number of towns (including Pwllheli and Aberystwyth) were going over to English.

[18] On the anglicization of southern Pembrokeshire, see John, 1972, and on Gower, D.T. Williams, 1934, and Michael Williams, 1972.

In the course of the nineteenth and twentieth centuries then, for reasons we shall discuss later, English, which had already (probably between 1750 and 1820) ousted Welsh from the greater part if not the whole of Radnorshire and some other parts of the eastern borders, overwhelmed the southern counties of Monmouth (now Gwent) and Glamorgan and much of the north coast of Wales (map **2**). At the same time, behind the lines as it were, anglicization also

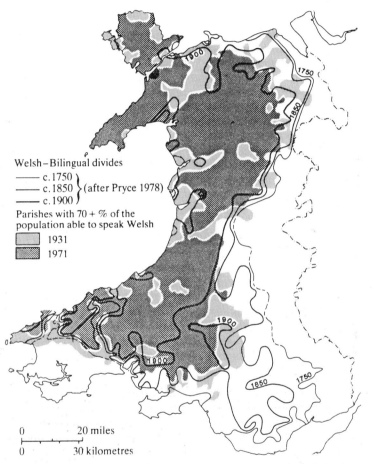

Map **2**. The territorial retreat of Welsh since 1750 (after J.E. Ambrose and C.H. Williams, 1981:54).

began to spread out like an ink-blot from partially English-speaking towns like Holyhead, Bangor, Aberystwyth and Carmarthen into the hitherto almost totally Welsh-speaking hinterland. A particularly disturbing feature of this process emerged from the report on the 1961 census, which revealed by comparison with the picture as presented by the 1951 report the existence of:

an expansion of English-speaking inland from the north coast and south Cardiganshire resorts, others along the Dee in Denbighshire and along the upper Severn in mid-Wales. It begins to look as if this last change is pinching the former waist between north and south, splitting Welsh-speaking Wales into two parts (Jones and Griffiths, 1963:195).

This threat became all the more real when, between 1961 and 1971, five parishes in northern Ceredigion, all within a few miles of the heavily anglicized university town and tourist centre of Aberystwyth, suffered a decrease of more than three times the national average in the proportion of Welsh speakers (the reasons for this we shall return to later). Professors E.G. Bowen and Harold Carter (1975:6; see also 1974:434−5) stress the significance of this 'anglicized corridor', which they see as 'the spearhead of a long established anglicizing drive through the Severn−Dyfi routeway into mid-Wales':

> From the point of view of those concerned with the preservation of the language this corridor is a geographical feature of great concern, for there are clear indications that its extension will leave the country in the near future with its Welsh-speaking area irrevocably divided into two separate sections, the north-west and the south-west.

And, in a vivid comparison, they conclude (1974:439):

> It would seem that . . . the decline and eventual disappearance of the language can be compared with the drying up of a lake. The continuous expanse of water has disappeared and there remains a series of separate pools, patchy and uneven, slowly drying out.

This spreading out of English from Aberystwyth and other coastal towns of Cardigan Bay they see as 'another linguistic frontier which has taken off from the west coast and is now pressing inland' (*ibid.*, 440). If they are right, then, they say (and it would be difficult not to agree), 'two frontiers, one from the east and one from the west, are moving together, pushing with greater rapidity up the valleyways and surrounding the last isolated fastnesses of the Welsh language' (*ibid.*).[19] (For the territorial distribution of Welsh according to the 1971 Census, see map **3**.)

One of the causes of the territorial recession of Welsh at various periods has been an influx, for one reason or another, of English-speaking immigrants. We have already mentioned the linguistic influence of Anglo-Norman settlements in Gower and south Pembrokeshire, and the same was

[19] For discussion of the evidence for the territorial decline of Welsh presented by earlier census reports, see Emrys Jones, 1967 (on the period up to 1961), T. Lewis, 1926 (on the census of 1921), D.T. Williams, 1953, and J. Gareth Thomas, 1956 (both on the change between 1931 and 1951), and Emrys Jones and Ieuan L. Griffiths, 1963 (on the 1961 report). For an admirable general survey of the territorial regression of Welsh, see Mathias, 1973. For historical surveys of the situation of Welsh in particular areas, see Ellis, 1882 (on Pembroke, Glamorgan and the borders from Flint to Monmouth), W.H. Rees, 1947 (covering Flint, Denbigh, Montgomery, Radnor, Brecknock, Monmouth, and Glamorgan), D.T. Williams, 1936 (on North Wales), Pryce, 1972, 1974−75, 1975 (on north-east Wales), Dodd, 1940 (on east Denbighshire), G.J. Lewis, 1979−80 (on east Wales), D.T. Williams, 1935 (on South Wales), J.P. Lewis, 1969, and B.Ll. James, 1972 (both on Glamorgan). There are also unpublished theses by L. Hooson Owen (1954) and R. Hindley (1952) on Radnorshire and south-east Wales respectively.

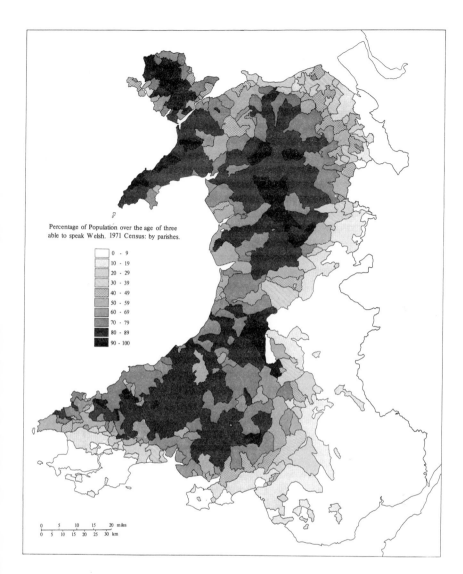

Percentage of Population over the age of three
able to speak Welsh. 1971 Census: by parishes.

	0 - 9
	10 - 19
	20 - 29
	30 - 39
	40 - 49
	50 - 59
	60 - 69
	70 - 79
	80 - 89
	90 - 100

```
0    5    10   15   20 miles
0   5  10  15  20  25  30 km
```

Map **3**. The distribution of Welsh-speakers according to the 1971 Census (after Harold and Mari Carter, 1974:207, and Bowen and Carter, 1975:5).

doubtless also true to some extent of the Norman lordships in the borders and the Vale of Glamorgan. (Linguistic assimilation was not however entirely a one-way process: the result of intermarriage between Anglo-Norman nobles and Welsh women was sometimes that their descendants were Welsh-speaking.) A new type of threat was posed by the far-reaching anglicization of the socially and politically dominant strata in the community from the sixteenth century onwards:

> State policy from the Tudor period onwards . . . installed English in
> public affairs and administration; it created an upper ruling class which
> grew increasingly Anglicized as it was increasingly attracted by the

widening opportunities of an expanding social, economic and cultural London-based sphere. A pattern of diglossia without bilingualism was established, with the governing classes belonging to one linguistic community and the mass of the population to another. It was a situation not unlike that which prevailed in Ireland, and had it lasted the progressive sociopolitical drift in favour of English might well have undermined the position of the Welsh language and led to its virtual demise in the course of the last century (B.Ll. Jones, 1981:41).

The factor that was to prevent this from happening was the Methodist revival of the eighteenth century which, as we have seen (p. 102), led to widespread literacy in Welsh and enhanced the prestige of the language. There is also evidence that, under the influence of the Methodist revival, the tide was even turned for a while in the Vale of Glamorgan in the late eighteenth century, and that 'by the early years of the nineteenth century Welsh was the normal language in use by all but the highest social strata throughout that district' (James, 1972:24).

The industrialization of much of south-east Wales and part of the north-east in the late eighteenth and nineteenth centuries, and particularly the development of the coal industry, brought about a far-reaching demographic change in the south-east of Wales (Monmouthshire and Glamorgan) and, to some extent, in the north-east by attracting large numbers of workers both from other parts of Wales and from outside (England and Ireland). It has been accepted as self-evident that this seriously undermined the Welsh language, particularly in the second half of the nineteenth century. Professor Brinley Thomas, however, has argued that, on the contrary, 'the Welsh language was saved by the redistribution of a growing population brought about by industrialism' (1962:26). He estimates that, in the period 1861–1911, some 160,000 people migrated to Glamorgan alone from other Welsh counties, and that the vast majority of the 556,000 Welsh-speakers (57 per cent of the total for the whole of Wales) enumerated in south Wales in 1911 'would not have been there but for the pull of industrialism', and that, had Wales been an agricultural country like Ireland, they would have emigrated to England or overseas, which would have been 'a major disaster for the Welsh language' (*ibid.*).

The prosperity brought about by industry and trade may have helped to increase the absolute numbers (but not necessarily the proportion) of Welsh-speakers in the regions affected:

> For the first time there existed a sufficiently large Welsh-speaking *urban* population and a wide enough margin of prosperity to support flourishing societies and institutions; most important of all to sustain a really vigorous publishing industry for Welsh books and periodicals (Glanmor Williams, 1971:11).

W.T.R. Pryce, on the other hand, has recently demonstrated convincingly that industrialization (accompanied by immigration both from England and from Welsh-speaking Wales) was a potent factor in the anglicization of north-east Wales at least:

> By the mid-nineteenth-century the bilingual zone [of north-east Wales] corresponded geographically with the extent of the exposed coal-field: in this language zone, as the population increased, there was a clear tendency for bilingual communities to become more English than Welsh (Pryce, 1974–75:339).

The bilingual zone both served to anglicize incoming Welsh-speakers from the rural areas further west, and itself extended progressively westwards. A further period of industrial expansion in the South Wales coalfield in the first two decades of the twentieth century brought in more workers from outside, particularly from the neighbouring Forest of Dean and the Bristol area, and so further hastened the anglicization of that part of Wales.

A major surge of English influence followed the opening up of hitherto relatively remote and inaccessible parts of Wales with the development in the mid-nineteenth century of the railways and the later evolution of towns and villages all round the coast into seaside resorts. Much more recently, the process of anglicization in consequence of the physical moving-in to Welsh-speaking areas of English-speaking people has been aggravated by such factors as, on the one hand, tourism and second-home ownership and, on the other, suburbanization. Many coastal and rural areas of Wales have become attractive to people from the big cities and industrialized areas of England who, in the last twenty years or so, have been in the habit of acquiring country cottages or houses in small Welsh towns and villages, for use as week-end holiday residences and/or as permanent homes for their retirement (see Betts, 1976:62–4). It has to be recognized that, in many cases, the properties concerned had long been empty and might otherwise have become derelict. But in other cases the effect has been to push up prices beyond the reach of local residents (young married couples, for example) who, in normal circumstances, might have been expected to buy them. This in itself has caused considerable resentment, the more so since those who use their properties as second residences contribute little to the economy of the area and those who settle permanently often have little in common with the local inhabitants. But in either case, the result is to bring in a new and damaging English linguistic presence. The resentment provoked by this led in the late 1970s and early 80s to a campaign of arson in which some scores of holiday cottages were damaged or destroyed in the absence of their owners. For an example of the extent to which the make-up of the population has been affected by this kind of immigration (one might almost say colonization), one need only look at the island of Anglesey: the dramatic fall in the proportion of the population speaking Welsh from 75.5 per cent in 1961 to 61 per cent in 1981 must be due in large measure to the fact that, in the same period, the proportion of the population born outside Wales rose from 21 per cent to 31 per cent.

This is a problem Wales shares with other parts of western Europe where the same factor, namely relative isolation from large centres of population, that in the past has kept a minority language alive now attracts those who want to get away from the urban sprawl to the relatively calm, unspoiled and often scenically beautiful areas where minority languages survive. The highlands and islands of Scotland (once the stronghold of Gaelic), Brittany, and the Basque country are cases in point, and one could apply to Wales such comments as the following made with reference to the Romansh-speaking Engadine (where, in 1978, I was told that the only hope for the survival of Romansh was to put an end to tourism — and that in an area that includes St Moritz!):

> It is reasonable to suggest that the disruptive effect of tourism [on the local language] lies as much in its stimulation of economic change and the encouragement of immigration as in any direct social interaction (White, 1974:31).

> It is largely the increase in the number of roles played by non-local people — their invasion of more sociolinguistic domains — that changes the sociocultural make-up of the whole community and the dominance of the original language (*ibid.*, 36).

The effect of suburbanization is felt when, as is increasingly the case, private or council-owned housing estates are incongruously tacked on to previously small and predominantly Welsh-speaking villages within easy travelling distance of a (typically more anglicized) resort or market town:

> The impact of urban commuters on the cultural and social patterns of the villages is immediate and the Anglicization which traditionally characterized the towns of Wales is by this mean extended into, and occasionally far into, the surrounding countryside . . . . If urbanization in the nineteenth century did much to destroy the Welsh language, then it is possible that suburbanization will do the same in the twentieth (Bowen and Carter, 1974:439).

It is not difficult to map, on the basis of census returns, either the proportion of Welsh-speakers in a given area or the density of population. A more subtle and more informative approach is to map the distribution of Welsh taking account of both of these factors, and this has been done by E.G. Bowen for the 1951 census (Bowen, 1959). Taking the French term 'le pays de Galles' in the new and restricted sense of 'the land of the people who speak the Welsh language' with an implication also that there is a very real correlation between Welsh language and Welsh culture, he defines it as having 'a core area (with over 80 per cent Welsh speakers and a population density above 50 persons per square mile), and a peripheral area (over 80 per cent Welsh speakers and less than 50 persons per square mile)' (*ibid.*, 5). On this basis, the core area includes, in the north-west, most of Anglesey and Caernarfonshire, a few pockets further east, and, in the south-west, central and southern Cardiganshire and much of Carmarthenshire. The peripheral area is largely accounted for by a band of territory stretching down the centre of Wales almost all the way from north to south (see map, *ibid.*, 4). The map also shows clearly the ominous significance, referred to above, of the central coastal zone: the area stretching from Tywyn and Aberdyfi to Aberystwyth is not even included in the peripheral area (though it *is* in the area having a density of over 50 persons per square mile and 40–80 per cent of Welsh-speakers).

A related factor is that of mixed marriages. If one parent is monoglot English-speaking, the chances that the other, Welsh-speaking, parent will succeed in bringing the children up to speak Welsh are slight. A survey taken in Flintshire in 1950, for example, revealed that of over 3500 children from linguistically mixed marriages, only 115 (i.e. about 3 per cent) were bilingual (see Jac L. Williams, 1958:257). A national survey of the language of school-children in the 5–15 age-group taken in 1961 revealed (Welsh Joint Education Committee, 1961:10) that, whereas 73 per cent (itself a surprisingly low proportion) of those from homes where both parents spoke Welsh had Welsh as their first language, this was true of only 12 per cent of those whose mother alone spoke Welsh and of only 7 per cent of those whose father alone spoke Welsh. The reason, of course, is that unless the Welsh-speaking parent makes a conscious and continuous effort to speak Welsh to the children, then almost inevitably the children will speak English only. It has to be recognized that, if intolerable strains are not to be placed on a marriage, it may be difficult or impossible for one parent and the children to speak together in a language the other parent does not understand. This is of course particularly so for fathers, who are less likely than mothers to be alone with their small children for any length of time. A recent survey has demonstrated that the great majority of Welsh-speaking mothers of non-Welsh-speaking children are sympathetically disposed towards Welsh, and that, while other factors of course also come into play, the attitude of their non-Welsh-speaking husbands is crucial:

> Their influence when against Welsh is overwhelming: none [of those in the families surveyed] had bilingual children . . . . When they are for Welsh there is a good chance that their children will be bilingual (Harrison *et al.*, 1981:63).

In the past, the process of anglicization has been furthered by direct contact between people, by the association of Welsh-speakers in one way or another (education, immigration of English-speakers, the influence of anglicized towns on Welsh-speaking rural districts, mixed marriages) with English-speakers. The coming of radio and, more recently, of television has changed all that. Now, over the air, a constant stream of English penetrates the very homes of Welsh-speakers, even in the remotest parts of the Welsh-speaking heartland.

When broadcasting started in the 1920s, there was little place for Welsh and it was not until 1936 that a separate Welsh region of the BBC was established. (Previously, Wales had been grouped together with the West of England.) Thereafter, and particularly since the Second World War, provision for Welsh on radio improved steadily and there is now a Welsh-medium channel, Radio Cymru, providing a regular and varied service for several hours every day of the week.

The position as regards television is less satisfactory. The BBC first transmitted Welsh programmes in 1952 and the independent television companies in 1957. By 1981, something over fourteen hours a week, on average, of Welsh language programmes were being provided (rather more than half of them by the BBC) – as compared with some 200 hours a week of English-language programmes. But even this modest provision for Welsh caused considerable tension as a result of the resentment among many non-Welsh-speaking (and, sadly, some Welsh-speaking) viewers who felt that they were being 'deprived' of certain English programmes that were being replaced (or displaced to another time) by Welsh programmes. The following extracts from a letter published in the *Western Mail* on 18 April 1980 are not untypical of the quite absurd intolerance towards Welsh often expressed:

> I am Welsh born and bred but, fortunately, do not speak the language. I consider myself as Welsh as any Welsh-speaker, yet I am subjected to a stream of foreign language every evening on BBC Wales . . . . If the BBC is looking for ways to economise, I would suggest that BBC Wales be closed down and the majority of Welshmen could then receive and watch television programmes they understand.

The only way to satisfy the demands for more Welsh programmes while at the same time avoiding antagonizing those who consider the loss of a few hours a week of English programmes as a deprivation is, of course, to provide a Welsh-language TV channel in addition to the various English-language channels. It is agreed on all sides that, in present circumstances, this is not feasible. It was therefore decided, after years of discussion and acrimony, that when the fourth television channel (which, in England, is a second independent channel) was inaugurated in November 1982, all programmes in Welsh, both those provided by BBC and those provided by the independent contractor for Wales (at present Harlech Television) or by independent producers should be transferred to it. At the same time, the amount of Welsh-language programmes was increased to 22 hours a week. It remains to be seen how well this will work and whether it will satisfy either Welsh-speakers or non-Welsh-speakers. Certainly, if, by the quality of its programmes, the new channel can win the allegiance of a substantial proportion of Welsh-speaking viewers (many of whom will not watch Welsh programmes merely out of language loyalty, i.e. merely because they are in Welsh), it can be a potent influence in strengthening the position of the Welsh language and perhaps acting as a brake on its decline (or even, in the most optimistic view, saving it). First indications are that the new channel is being watched by an encouragingly high proportion of the Welsh-speaking population.

For many years there has been extensive study and debate in Wales about the problem of bilingualism, and in particular about the possibility − or, in the view of many, the probability − that bilingualism is merely a transitional stage on the road to complete anglicization. But there has been relatively little discussion of a related but distinct, and certainly, as far as the survival of Welsh is concerned, much more important topic, namely that of diglossia.

'Bilingualism' is a term that can relate either to an individual or to a community. A bilingual individual is one who has more or less equal command of two languages. A bilingual community is one in which two languages fulfil more or less the same functions though they may be distinguished on a geographical basis (as in, say, Belgium, which is bilingual in Dutch and French, or Canada, which is bilingual in English and French). Individuals belonging to a bilingual community may or may not themselves be bilingual (in Belgium, for example, those whose first language is Dutch are much more likely to speak French than the other way round.) 'Diglossia', on the other hand, refers to a situation in which two languages fulfil different roles in society. Typically, one is a 'high variety' (it may be, for example, the language of administration, education, religion or serious literature), the other a 'low variety', used in more informal contexts.

For a period of over three hundred years, Welsh coexisted with English in what were, when compared either with its present situation or with the situation of most other 'minority' or 'regional' languages in Western Europe, relatively favourable circumstances *both* of bilingualism *and* of diglossia.

Take first the bilingual situation. As recently as 1911 there were whole counties where a third of the population declared themselves to be monoglot Welsh-speakers (Merioneth, 37 per cent; Anglesey, 36 per cent; Caernarfonshire, 36 per cent; Cardiganshire, 34 per cent), and even as late as 1931 there were areas where over one in five of the population claimed to speak Welsh only (Anglesey, 24 per cent; Merioneth, 22 per cent; Caernarfonshire, 21 per cent; Cardiganshire, 20 per cent). But by 1951, only Anglesey had as many as 10 per cent monoglots (more precisely, 9.6 per cent, followed by Merioneth with 9.2 per cent). By 1981,[20] Anglesey had only 2 per cent, Merioneth 4.5 per cent, Caernarfonshire 4 per cent, and Cardiganshire 3.5 per cent. It is clear, therefore, not only that the total number of monoglot Welsh-speakers is now so low as to be virtually insignificant (21,583, or 0.8 per cent, in 1981, and, as we have seen, p. 111, even this figure may have been artificially inflated), but that nowhere in the whole country do they constitute more than a very small minority. During the same period, 1911–81, the proportion of the inhabitants of Wales declaring themselves as speaking only English rose from 56.5 per cent to 81 per cent. Very roughly then, whereas in 1911 the linguistic make-up of the population of Wales was just over a half 'English only', just over a third bilingual, and one-twelfth 'Welsh only', in 1981 it was over four-fifths 'English only', slightly under one-fifth bilingual, with the 'Welsh only' counting for less than one in a hundred. Such a situation, in which the odds are weighted heavily against Welsh and in favour of English, is likely to be unstable and, from the point of view of Welsh, is most unhealthy. As Iorwerth Peate put it (1965:429), 'there can be no true bilingualism where millions speak English only but where none speaks Welsh only'.

But Welsh also stood in a diglossic relation to English, though by no means in all respects as a 'low variety'. In particular, Welsh maintained an unbroken tradition as a vehicle of 'serious' literature, in both prose and verse, and, in all parts of Wales where it was at all widely spoken, it served more widely than English as a language of public religious worship. On the other hand, English was, until very recently, the only language recognized for any purposes to do with administration and the law, and, apart from unofficial use sometimes made of it in some primary schools in strongly Welsh areas, in the field of education. The position of Welsh has however improved considerably, even

[20] Since the local government reorganization of 1974, the former counties no longer exist as such. However, apart from some minor adjustments of borders of little consequence for our present purpose, the districts of Aberconwy, Arfon and Dwyfor correspond to Caernarfonshire, and Meirionydd to Merioneth, whereas the Isle of Anglesey district is identical with the former county.

dramatically, in the last twenty or thirty years, first with the marked increase in Welsh-medium teaching in nursery, primary, and secondary schools and in some departments of the University of Wales, and then, more recently, with the passing of the Welsh Language Act in 1967 and the significant, if still inadequate, increase in the use of Welsh in public life that has followed from it.

The situation is constantly changing, and anything I write now will be out of date by the time this book is published. Speculation as to the future is inevitably highly subjective, and hazardous. What follows can only be my own moderately well informed guess as to how the situation *may* develop.

Let us begin with what is more or less common ground. It seems to be generally accepted both that the language is rapidly declining and that the number of monoglot speakers of Welsh has declined almost to the point of extinction. Broadly speaking, however, there are three different types of reaction.[21] On the one hand there are those (among them some Welsh-speakers) for whom the language is at best a nuisance and at worst a socially divisive factor that should be allowed to die. On the other hand, there are those for whom the language (whether or not they speak it themselves) is at least something to which they have a sentimentally indulgent attitude and whose loss they would regret or, in extreme cases, a cause to which they are prepared to devote all their energies, to the extent if necessary of engaging in illegal and possibly violent action and suffering the consequences. In between there are those − the great, silent, apathetic majority − who really do not care whether the language lives or dies and cannot understand what all the fuss is about. This group includes first, monoglot English-speakers who are quite happy to let those who want to speak Welsh continue to do so. It also includes bilinguals who use Welsh perfectly naturally with relatives and acquaintances but would normally speak English to a stranger or in any kind of 'official' context, and never read a Welsh newspaper (let alone a book), rarely watch Welsh television programmes, and may or may not speak Welsh to their children.

This last category tends to be overlooked, but it could be argued that, as there are so many of them, it is they who will determine the future of the language. The relatively small number of outright opponents of Welsh may do their worst, their hostility will remain largely ineffectual if there is a substantial body of people who are determined to hand on the language to the next generation. The pro-language 'extremists', on the other hand, whatever their successes in enhancing the public status of Welsh, can do little to ensure the long-term survival of the language, and may indeed find their actions counter-productive, if, as happens, they antagonize not only the indifferent majority but many of those who are sympathetic to the language.

There seem to be only three even theoretically possible solutions, other than the eventual disappearance of Welsh.

First, there is the much canvassed 'bilingual' solution. The case for this was put forcefully by the 1967 report, *Primary Education in Wales* (Central

---

[21] On attitudes towards Welsh, see Khleif, 1980:38−54.

Advisory Council for Education, 1967). Chapter 11 of the report, 'Welsh in the primary schools of Wales', recommends a continuation and a strengthening of the existing policy of teaching Welsh as a second language in the anglicized areas. Chapter 13, 'English as the second language', begins quite uncompromisingly thus (p. 281):

> We cannot accept that it is any longer possible or desirable for a Welsh child to speak Welsh only . . . . Every child in Wales must be enabled not only to communicate with the wider community and have access to a wide field of learning, but be able to enter his wider heritage as a citizen of these islands.

It then goes on to enunciate the claim that 'Welsh-speaking children not only can, but need to, achieve a standard of English comparable with that of the native English speaker' (*ibid.*).

The intention is that, if − as is certain − those whose first language is Welsh are also going to be competent in English, efforts should be made to ensure also that a substantial number of those whose only native language is English should acquire a comparable competence in Welsh. This would be done not only through the schools and in further-education establishments, but also by providing crash-courses for adult learners and encouraging the staff of public and commercial offices and the like to follow them. Certainly, language-classes for adult learners of Welsh are much in demand and are well attended. It is also true that a number of individuals have acquired a more or less adequate mastery of the language, and that many are now fluent in it. These however are the exceptions − and in any case, the motivation is usually 'personal' (e.g. the desire to find their lost roots) rather than 'official' (a response to pressure to achieve a certain competence in Welsh because it is a requirement for or an advantage in their work). Indeed, this 'personal' motivation is the only one that is likely to lead to any great measure of success. I share entirely the view of Professor Ellis Evans (1972:178) that 'the compulsory implementation of a *thorough-going* bilingualism in the schools of Wales is, alas, neither practicable nor acceptable at present. The attempt to impose the minority language would probably not overcome the disinclination to learn it.' I would go even further and say that no one learns a language well merely through coercion, and compulsion (whether at school or in one's job) is likely to breed resentment.

But not only is an educational policy aimed at bilingualism unlikely to strengthen the situation of the language to any great extent in the only way that counts, namely by increasing the numbers of those who have a full and fluent command of it, it appears, on the contrary, to dilute the Welsh of those for whom it already is a first language. This point has been made time and time again and I will quote from only two of those who have stressed it:

> As the Welsh-speaking Welshman has a knowledge of English, linguistically mixed social groups tend to adopt English as a medium of social intercourse and this often results in a Welsh-speaker making little use of his mother tongue. Lack of practice in speaking the language usually leads to less command over its resources and the Welsh-speaker's

command of his second language, English, is often greater than his command over his mother tongue (Jac L. Williams, 1958:251).

The growth of bilingualism has had a remarkable effect upon the development of the Welsh language. This effect is less a question of a gradually shifting language frontier than of the linguistic penetration of a weaker language by a stronger one. It is as if the battle between Welsh and English has been transferred from the geographical field to the mind of each individual Welsh speaker (Watkins, 1962:43).

This is seen principally in the vocabulary ('words are now borrowed with almost complete abandon even where there are familiar Welsh words that could be used', Watkins, 1962:44) and idiom (almost any English idiom may be literally translated, e.g. *rhoi i fyny* 'to give up', *rhedeg i lawr* 'to run down', i.e. to detract'), but also, even if only to a limited extent, in grammar (e.g. in the use of prepositions as postpositions as in English − *Beth wyt ti'n chwilio am?* 'What are you looking for?'). The consequence of this impact of anglicization on the language itself, of what Ned Thomas (1971:35) calls 'the slovenliness of much spoken Welsh', is that 'it may hold its ground territorially, but it is now losing it linguistically' (Jones and Griffiths, 1963:196).

There is worse. Not only is a bilingualism of the type envisaged most unlikely to save the language, it could on the contrary hasten its decline. Most people are pragmatists and tend not to be interested in maintaining, merely for their own sake, what they see as out-dated and pointess conventions. In a society in which all members know language 'A' and a minority also know language 'B', and in which 'A' serves all purposes at least as well as 'B', if not better, 'B' *will* quickly come to be regarded as an out-dated and pointless convention. For this reason, bilingualism of the kind we have to envisage for Welsh is almost inevitably no more than 'a transitory bilingualism leading to a new English monolingualism' (Peate, 1972:148). There is nothing new in this view − it had already been stated as long ago as 1962 by Saunders Lewis in his broadcast lecture, when he proclaimed that he was one of the minority who saw in a policy of bilingual education 'a respectable and easy death and tearless funeral for the Welsh language' (Lewis, 1962:22; translation, p. 22). This is a more realistic assessment than that of Jac L. Williams, who thought (1958:256) that the bilingual society to be found in Wales seemed to be 'in the process of developing norms, behaviour patterns and goals that may enable a state of linguistic equilibrium to be achieved in a stable bilingualism and so enable the national language of Wales and the culture that is associated with it to survive'.

The threat to the Welsh language that is constituted by bilingualism of the type envisaged is also recognized by others who are concerned not merely to proclaim as an ideal the cause of the language but to look present realities squarely in the face. Periodically, therefore, the idea of a 'Welsh heartland' or 'Bro Gymraeg' ('Welsh-speaking region') is floated, a region in which Welsh would be the dominant or, in some versions, the only officially recognized language. As early as the 1930s, Saunders Lewis had argued (1938:60) that 'creating a monolingual Welsh-speaking Wales is the sure way to build a country immune from the oppression of international capitalism'. Similarly,

Iorwerth Peate argued (1965:428) not only that the only certain result of a thorough-going bilingual educational policy would be 'to eliminate completely within a generation or so the remaining . . . monoglot Welsh speakers' but that 'a monoglot core is as essential to the spiritual health of the Welsh nation as it is to the English or the French':

> It is our duty in Wales to maintain a Welsh-speaking community not by a universal policy of complete bilingualism but possibly by first delimiting an area . . . where Welsh shall be the one official language and prove (to those who need such proof) that civilization and culture can be as completely achieved through the medium of Welsh as of any other language (*ibid.*, 429).

A much more fully developed version of the same project was given in 1976 by Clive Betts in his book *Culture in Crisis*. His recommendation for the Heartland (defined as those areas that are at least 70 per cent Welsh-speaking) is that Welsh will be 'the official language, the primary language used by all organs of government both for public relations and internal work. English will be an also-ran, used only as much as it has to be' (1976:195), and that 'the basic education system will be Welsh-medium. Only in the Anglicized Heartland towns [i.e. Holyhead, Bangor, Aberystwyth, Carmarthen and Llandovery] will there be a legal right to English-medium primary education' (*ibid.*, 199).

There seem to me to be three decisive objections to any such scheme. First, it would almost inevitably raise insuperable financial and practical difficulties. Second, it would encounter the determined opposition not only of those in the Heartland who speak only English but of very many of the Welsh-speakers too. Third, there is also a serious moral problem. In today's world, a life lived solely through the medium of Welsh is bound to be much more restricted than the life of a person who has access to all the literature (in the widest possible sense of the word) that is available in a major world language such as English. There can be no realistic hope that anything remotely comparable could be made available in Welsh. That being so, who, in a democratic society, could be given the authority to deny to a substantial minority of the population of Wales the right of access to opportunities of economic advancement and sources of information and cultural enrichment that would otherwise be open to them? Not that the advocates of Welsh monolingualism are unaware of this – but they seek an escape from the dilemma by trying to have it both ways. Iorwerth Peate, for example, in a speech reported in the weekly newspaper *Baner ac Amserau Cymru* on 15 August 1956, urged that, in the Welsh-speaking areas, Welsh should be the only official language and the only language of instruction in schools, but that English should be taught as a second language. But this is trying at one and the same time to keep the door firmly shut while carefully holding it half open. And English cannot be kept out by a half-open door. If it is allowed in at all, its presence will become increasingly felt, and we shall soon be back in the kind of situation that the advocates of a monoglot Welsh-speaking heartland seek to avoid.

The inescapable conclusion seems to be that Welsh cannot compete on equal terms with English but that English is here to stay. This does not, however, lead to the further conclusion that Welsh is necessarily doomed. The lesson to be drawn is, rather, that if Welsh is to be saved, it has to be saved in a situation of coexistence not of competition with English. In other words, there *is* a third possibility, but one that depends upon coming to terms with the presence of English.

This third possibility is to settle for a diglossic relationship between the two languages. This could well be more advantageous to Welsh than a 'bilingual' situation in which the two languages were theoretically equivalent but manifestly not so in practice. It would of course mean facing up to the fact that Welsh cannot compete on equal terms with English. (It might entail, for example, abandoning campaigns for the provision of the whole range of government services in Welsh, or for the establishment of a Welsh-medium College within the University of Wales.) It would, in consequence, mean accepting that, for certain purposes, the use of English is unavoidable. On the other hand, among other functions, Welsh would serve as the medium of instruction in primary and secondary schools where demand justified this, it would enjoy full recognition in courts of law, and public signs and notices would continue to be bilingual.

In such a situation, those who chose to do so could live their lives very largely, though not entirely, though the medium of Welsh. Furthermore, the concentration of available energies and resources on strengthening the position of Welsh in those fields in which it is still relatively well maintained would be more beneficial to the language than a policy of dissipating them over a whole range of activities. And the damaging hostility aroused among many Welsh-speakers as well as others by militant campaigns for the adoption of Welsh in *all* spheres of activity might well be disarmed by such an approach and this too could only be in the best interests of Welsh. In such circumstances, Welsh would be in a stronger position than in a bilingual situation that, it is widely agreed, would in all likelihood serve to undermine it.

Now that Welsh has achieved a considerable measure of official recognition and − much more importantly − of respect on the part of Welsh-speakers and non-Welsh-speaking Welshmen alike, the chances of survival in a diglossic situation are greater than they would have been only twenty years ago. And the fact that a 'low variety' (the term is an unfortunate one) can flourish even when it occupies far fewer 'prestige' roles than Welsh does is very clearly shown by, for example, Swiss German (one of the examples taken by C.A. Ferguson in the article, 1959, which both launched the word 'diglossia' in English and stimulated widespread interest in this particular sociolinguistic phenomenon). The point is that, although Swiss Germans regularly employ High German as a 'high variety', they feel no sense of inferiority about using one of a multiplicity of local dialects of Swiss German as a 'low variety'. And there is no reason why the same should not be true when 'high' and 'low' varieties are *not* forms of the same language.[22] The

---

[22] The term 'diglossia', used by Ferguson solely with reference to varieties of the same language, has since been extended to cover situations in which two different languages − e.g. French and Breton − are in presence.

important thing is that speakers of the 'low' variety need not feel that it is in any qualitative sense inferior. On the contrary, there is every reason why (like the Swiss-Germans) they may be proud of it.

The 'diglossic' approach, then, could perhaps be more effective in keeping Welsh alive than either a policy of bilingualism which is likely to be merely a stage on the road to total anglicization or an unrealistic policy of striving against insuperable odds to maintain a sizable monoglot Welsh community. But it could only be effective if it were fully realized that, in such a situation, Welsh retains an honourable position. This is *not* a return to the old situation in which Welsh was looked down on. Any chance of success such an approach may have depends entirely on the retention of a positive attitude by a large number of Welsh-speakers, for the fate of the language will be determined not by government, not by education, not by the mass media, but by the Welsh-speakers themselves.

What has been called 'The Dilemma of the Vernacular' (see the chapter under that title in R. Brinley Jones, 1970) is no new phenomenon. There have always been those Welsh-speakers who have been not merely indifferent towards the language but ashamed of it, and shame has bred hostility.[23] There is evidence from the sixteenth and seventeenth centuries of 'a strong desire on the part of many Welshmen for the extinction of the language which had served for years as a sign of subjection' (James, 1887:7). And as time went on, this kind of reaction was to become more and more widespread. The example of Dylan Thomas's family is not untypical of the attitude of many in the partly-anglicized regions of Wales between the wars:

> Dylan spoke no Welsh . . . . His father, who did speak Welsh, refused to teach his son the language, and even felt a certain contempt for those who did speak and write it. There was no question but that speaking Welsh in Swansea was a sign of not having quite arrived yet from the valleys or the mountains. It was somehow a little common (Sinclair, 1975:17).

This attitude, though it has not disappeared, is now much less widespread than it used to be. There *is* a good deal of goodwill towards the language among Welsh-speakers and non-Welsh-speakers alike, but it is precariously balanced and, if it is alienated by the ill-considered actions of an 'extremist' minority, then the language is lost. Indifference on the part of the mass of Welsh-speakers could be as disastrous in this respect as outright hostility. For if they opt for what is now undoubtedly the easy way out and do not take a conscious decision to ensure that their children have not just a smattering or a mere passive knowledge of Welsh but are fully fluent in it, then all that has been done in recent years to encourage the use of Welsh in the fields of education, the mass media and public life generally, will do no more than prolong by a few decades the agony of the dying language.

If, on the other hand, even at this late stage, the great majority of those who still speak it, and their descendants, are sufficiently interested in its

---

[23] For the view of a foreign observer, who concluded that the average Welsh-speaker was often ashamed of his language, see Pilch, 1957.

survival to pass it on to succeeding generations, then, despite all the anglicizing influences ranged against it, there is no reason why it should not flourish, in a diglossic situation, for many generations to come. But one has to recognize that this will not come about easily. As Ned Thomas has put it (1971:36), 'to maintain one's own language, to bring up one's children to speak the language, requires a positive act of will in present-day Wales'.

Professor Ellis Evans has expressed cogently in a single sentence (1972:179) the message that must be heeded if Welsh is not to go the way of Cornish and Manx:

> The genuine and zestful desire among people of all ages to use Welsh naturally and freely is the only hope for the healthy survival and revival of the language.

References

Aaron, R.I. (1970). 'The struggle for the Welsh language: some pre-Census reflections.' *The Transactions of the Honourable Society of Cymmrodorian*, Session 1969 [1970]:229–49.

Ambrose, J.E. and C.H. Williams (1981). 'On the spatial definition of minority: scale as an influence on the geolinguistic analysis of Welsh', in E. Haugen, J.D. McClure and D.S. Thomson (eds.), *Minority Languages Today*, Edinburgh: University Press, pp. 53–71.

Bell, H. Idris (1936). *The Development of Welsh Poetry*. Oxford: Clarendon Press.

Betts, Clive (1976). *Culture in Crisis. The Future of the Welsh Language*. Upton, Merseyside: The Ffynnon Press.

Board of Education (1927). *Welsh in Education and Life*. London: HMSO.

Bowen, E.G. (1959). 'Le Pays de Galles.' The Institute of British Geographers, *Transactions and Papers*, 1959:1–23.

Bowen, E.G. and H. Carter (1974). 'Preliminary observations on the distribution of the Welsh language at the 1971 Census.' *Geographical Journal*, 140:432–40.

—(1975). 'The distribution of the Welsh language in 1971: an analysis.' *Geography*, 60:1–15.

Bromwich, Rachel (1979). 'Dafydd ap Gwilym', in Jarman–Hughes (1979), pp. 112–43.

Carter, Harold and Mari (1974). 'Cyfrifiad 1971: Adroddiad ar yr iaith Gymraeg yng Nghymru.' *Barn*, 137 (March, 1974):206–11.

Central Advisory Council for Education (Wales) (1953). *The Place of Welsh and English in the Schools of Wales*. London: HMSO.

—(1967). *Primary Education in Wales*. London: HMSO.

Charles, B.G. (1963). 'The Welsh, their language and place-names in Archenfield and Oswestry', in *Angles and Britons* [six O'Donnell lectures by various scholars], Cardiff: University of Wales Press, pp. 85–110.

Clancy, Joseph P. (1965). *Mediaeval Welsh Lyrics*. London: Macmillan; New York: St Martin's Press.

—(1970). *The Earliest Welsh Poetry*. London: Macmillan.

Conran, Anthony (1967). *The Penguin Book of Welsh Verse*. Harmondsworth: Penguin Books.

Council for Wales and Monmouthshire (1963). *Report on the Welsh Language Today*. London: HMSO.

Cymdeithas yr Iaith Gymraeg (1966). *The Welsh Language Society: What it's All About* [Aberystwyth:] Cymdeithas yr Iaith Gymraeg.

—(1974). *Bywyd i'r Iaith/Welsh Must Live.* [n.p.]: Cymdeithas yr Iaith Gymraeg.

Davies, Cynog (1972). *Maniffesto Cymdeithas yr Iaith Gymraeg.* Aberystwyth: Cymdeithas yr Iaith Gymraeg. [Translation by Harri Webb, 'Cymdeithas yr Iaith – the Manifesto', *Planet*, 26/27, Winter 1974/75:77–136.]

—(1973). 'Cymdeithas yr Iaith Gymraeg' [in English], in Meic Stephens (ed.), 1973:248–63.

Dodd, A.H. (1940). 'Welsh and English in east Denbighshire: a historical retrospect.' *Transactions of the Honourable Society of Cymmrodorion*, Session 1940:34–65.

Ellis, A.J. (1882). 'On the delimitation of the English and Welsh languages.' *Y Cymmrodor*, 4:173–208.

Evans. D. Ellis (1972). 'The language and literature of Wales', in R. Brinley Jones (ed.), *Anatomy of Wales*, Peterston-super-Ely: Gwerin Publications, pp. 171–86.

Evans, Eric (1978). 'Welsh', in C.V. James (ed.), *The Older Mother Tongues of the United Kingdom.* London: Centre for Information on Language Teaching and Research.

Ferguson, C.A. (1959). 'Diglossia.' *Word*, 15:325–40. (Reprinted in D. Hymes, ed., *Language in Culture and Society*, New York: Harper & Row, 1964, pp. 429–39, and P.P. Giglioli, ed., *Language and Social Context,* Harmondsworth: Penguin, 1972, pp. 232–51.)

Fishlock, Trevor (1972). *Wales and the Welsh.* London: Cassell.

General Register Office (1955). *Census 1951. Report on Welsh Speaking Population.* London: HMSO.

—(1962). *Census 1961. Report on Welsh Speaking Population.* London: HMSO.

Gurney, Robert (1969). *Bardic Heritage. A Selection of Welsh Poetry in Free English Translation.* London: Chatto and Windus.

Harrison, Godfrey, Wynford Bellin and Brec'hed Piette (1981). *Bilingual Mothers in Wales and the Language of their Children.* Cardiff: University of Wales Press.

Hechter, Michael (1975). *Internal Colonialism. The Celtic Fringe in British National Development, 1536–1966.* London: Routledge & Kegan Paul. (Especially 'The decline of Celtic language speaking in the British Isles', pp. 191–206.)

Hindley, R. (1952). 'Linguistic distributions in southeast Wales: a study in trends over the last century.' Unpublished MA thesis, University of Leeds.

Humphreys, Humphrey Ll. (1979). *La Langue galloise. Une Présentation.* 2 vols. Brest: Université de Bretagne Occidentale, Section de celtique.

Jackson, Kenneth (1953). *Language and History in Early Britain.* Edinburgh: University Press.

—(1959). 'The dawn of the Welsh language', in Roderick, A.J. (ed.) (1959–60), I, pp. 34–41.

—(1971). *A Celtic Miscellany. Translations from the Celtic Literatures.* Harmondsworth: Penguin Books. (Original edition, London: Routledge & Kegan Paul, 1951.)

James, B.Ll. (1972). 'The Welsh Language in the Vale of Glamorgan.' *Morgannwg*, 16:16–36.

James, Carl (1977–78). 'Welsh bilingualism – fact and friction.' *Language Problems and Language Planning*, 1:73–81.

James, Ivor (1887). *The Welsh Language in the Sixteenth and Seventeenth Centuries.* Cardiff: D. Owen.

Jarman – Hughes (1976). Jarman, A.O.H. and Gwilym Rees Hughes, *A Guide to*

Welsh Literature, Vol. I [up to the end of the thirteenth century]. Swansea: Christopher Davies.

—(1979). Jarman, A.O.H. and Gwilym Rees Hughes, *A Guide to Welsh Literature,* Vol. II [fourteenth to early sixteenth centuries]. Swansea: Christopher Davies.

John, B.S. (1972). 'The linguistic significance of the Pembrokeshire landsker.' *Pembrokeshire Historian*, 4:7–29.

Jones, Bedwyr Ll. (1981). 'Welsh: linguistic conservation and shifting bilingualism', in Einar Haugen, J.D. McClure and D.S. Thomson (eds.) *Minority Languages Today*, Ediburgh: University Press, pp. 40–52.

Jones, Emrys (1967). 'The changing distribution of the Celtic languages in the British Isles.' *Transactions of the Honourable Society of Cymmrodorion,* Session 1967:22–38.

Jones, Emrys and Ieuan L. Griffiths (1963). 'A linguistic map of Wales: 1961.' *Geographical Journal*, 129:192–6.

Jones, Gwyn (1977). *The Oxford Book of Welsh Verse in English.* Oxford: Oxford University Press.

—(1959). 'The prose romances of medieval Wales', in Roderick, A.J. (ed.) (1959–60), I, 138–44.

Jones, Morris (1973). 'The present condition of the Welsh language', in Meic Stephens (ed.), 1973:110–26.

Jones, R. Brinley (1970). *The Old British Tongue. The Vernacular in Wales, 1540–1640.* Cardiff: Avalon Books.

Jones, R. Gerallt (1973). 'The Welsh writer and his books', in Meic Stephens (ed.), 1973:127–47.

Jones, R. Tudur (1973). 'The Welsh language and religion', in Meic Stephens (ed.), 1973:64–91.

Jones, W.R. (1966). *Bilingualism in Welsh Education.* Cardiff: University of Wales Press.

Khleif, Bud B. (1980). *Language, Ethnicity and Education in Wales.* The Hague – Paris – New York: Mouton.

Le Calvez, Armand (1970). *Un Cas de bilinguisme: le Pays de Galles.* Lannion: "Skol".

Lewis, Glyn (1978). 'Migration and the decline of the Welsh language', in Joshua A. Fishman (ed.), *Advances in the Study of Societal Multilingualism*, The Hague: Mouton, pp. 263–351.

Lewis, G.J. (1979–80). 'The geography of cultural transition: the Welsh borderland, 1750–1850.' *National Library of Wales Journal*, 21:131–44.

Lewis, Henry (1946). *Datblygiad yr Iaith Gymraeg* ('The Development of the Welsh Language'). 2nd ed. Cardiff: University of Wales Press. (1st ed., 1931.)

Lewis J.P. (1969). 'The anglicization of Glamorgan.' *Morgannwg*, 4:28–49.

Lewis, Robyn (1969). *Second-Class Citizen.* Llandysul: Gomer Press.

—(1973). 'The Welsh language and the law', in Meic Stephens (ed.), 1973:195–210.

—(1974). *Magistrates' Courts Procedure and the Welsh Language.* Aberystwyth: University College of Wales.

Lewis, Saunders (1938). *Canlyn Arthur.* Aberystwyth: Gwasg Aberystwyth. ('Un iaith i Gymru' ['One language for Wales'], first published as an article in 1933, pp. 57–61.)

—(1962). *Tynged yr Iaith.* London: BBC. (Translation, 'The fate of the language', *Planet*, 4, Feb.–March, 1971, 13–27.)

Lewis, T. (1926). 'Sur la distribution du parler gallois dans le Pays de Galles, d'après le recensement de 1921.' *Annales de géographie*, 35:413–18.

Mathias, Roland (1973). 'The Welsh language and the English language', in Meic Stephens (ed.), 1973:32–63.

Mayo, Patricia Elton (1974). *The Roots of Identity*. London: Allen Lane.

Morgan, Gerald (1966). *The Dragon's Tongue. The Fortunes of the Welsh Language*. Cardiff: Triskel Press.

Morgan, Kenneth O. (1981). *Rebirth of a Nation: Wales, 1880–1980*. Oxford: Clarendon Press; Cardiff: University of Wales Press.

Moseley, Hywel (1969). 'Forensic Welsh.' *The Solicitor's Journal*, 27 June 1969, pp. 498–500.

Office of Population Censuses and Surveys (1973). *Census 1971. Report on the Welsh Language in Wales*. Cardiff: HMSO.

Owen, L. Hooson (1954). 'A history of the Welsh language in Radnorshire.' Unpublished MA thesis, University of Liverpool.

Parry, Thomas (1959). 'Dafydd ap Gwilym', in Roderick, A.J. (ed.) (1959–60), pp. 169–72.

—(ed.) (1962). *The Oxford Book of Welsh Verse*. Oxford: Clarendon Press.

—(ed.) (1963). *Gwaith Dafydd ap Gwilym*. 2nd ed. Cardiff: University of Wales Press. (First ed., 1952.)

Parry–Bell (1955). Parry, Thomas, translated by H. Idris Bell, *A History of Welsh Literature*. Oxford: Clarendon Press. (N.B. Parry's original Welsh version, *Hanes Llenyddiaeth Gymraeg hyd 1900*, Cardiff: University of Wales Press, 1944, stopped, as the title indicates, at the end of the nineteenth century; Bell provided for his translation an appendix, pp. 374–498, 'The twentieth century'.)

Peate, Iorwerth C. (1965). 'The present state of the Welsh Language.' *Lochlann*, 3:420–31.

—(1972). 'Bilingualism and the Welsh society', in H. Pilch and J. Thurow (eds), *Indo-Celtica: Gedächtnisschrift für Alf Sommerfelt*, Munich: Hueber, pp. 143–9.

Pilch, Herbert (1957). 'Bilinguisme au Pays de Galles', in *Miscelánea Homenaje a André Martinet*, Tenerife: University of La Laguna, Vol. I, pp. 223–41.

Pryce, W.T.R. (1972). 'Approaches to the linguistic geography of northeast Wales, 1750–1846.' *National Library of Wales Journal*, 17:324–63.

—(1974–75). 'Industrialization, urbanization and the maintenance of culture areas: north-east Wales in the mid-nineteenth-century.' *Welsh History Review*, 7:307–40.

—(1975). 'Migration and the evolution of culture areas: cultural and linguistic frontiers in northeast Wales, 1750 and 1851.' *Transactions of the Institute of British Geographers*, 65:79–108.

—(1978). 'Welsh and English in Wales, 1750–1971: a spatial analysis based on the linguistic affiliation of parochial communities.' *Bulletin of the Board of Celtic Studies*, 28:1–36.

Rees, I. Bowen (1972). 'Land of the White Gloves.' *The New Law Journal*, 122 (no. 5528):38–40. (Reprinted, under the title 'The Welsh Language and the Courts', *Planet*, no. 12, June/July 1972, 20–6).

Rees, William (1948). *The Union of England and Wales*. Cardiff: University of Wales Press.

Rees, W.H. (1947). 'The Vicissitudes of the Welsh Language in the Marches of Wales, with Special Reference to its Territorial Distribution in Modern Times.' Unpublished PhD thesis, University of Wales.

Roderick, A.J. (ed.) (1959–60). *Wales through the Ages*. I, *From the Earliest Times to 1485*. II, *From 1485 to the Beginning of the 20th Century*. Llandybie: Christopher Davies.

Sinclair, Andrew (1975). *Dylan Thomas: Poet of his People*. London: Joseph.

Stephens, Meic (ed.) (1973). *The Welsh Language Today*. Llandysul: Gomer Press.

Thomas, Brinley (1962). 'Wales and the Atlantic economy', in Brinley Thomas (ed.), *The Welsh Economy: Studies in Expansion*, Cardiff: University of Wales Press, pp. 1–29 (especially 'Industrialization and the Welsh Language'. pp. 26–9). [Originally published in *The Scottish Journal of Political Economy*, 6(1959):181–92.]

Thomas, J. Gareth (1956). 'The geographical distribution of the Welsh language.' *Geographical Journal*, 122:71–9.

—(1957). 'The Welsh language', in E.G. Bowen (ed.), *Wales: a Physical, Historical and Regional Geography*, London: Methuen, pp. 247–63.

Thomas, Ned (1971). *The Welsh Extremist*. London: Gollancz.

Watkins, T. Arwyn (1962). 'Background to the Welsh dialect survey.' *Lochlann*, 2: 38–49.

Welsh Joint Education Committee (1961). *Language Survey, 1961*. [Cardiff]: WJEC.

Welsh Office (1965). *Legal Status of the Welsh Language*. London: HMSO.

—(1980). *The Welsh Language: A Commitment and a Challenge. The Government's Policy for the Welsh Language*. Cardiff: HMSO.

White, P.E. (1974). *The Social Impact of Tourism on Host Communities: A Study of Language Change in Switzerland*. School of Geography, University of Oxford.

Williams, A.H. (1941–48). *An Introduction to the History of Wales*. I, *Prehistoric Times to 1063 A.D.* II, *The Middle Ages,* Part I, *1063–1284*. Cardiff: University of Wales Press.

Williams, Colin H. (1976–77). 'Non-violence and the development of the Welsh Language Society, 1962–c. 1974.' *Welsh History Review*, 8:426–55.

—(1980–81). 'Language contact and language change in Wales, 1901–1971: a study in historical geolinguistics.' *Welsh History Review*, 10:207–38.

Williams, D. Trevor (1934). 'Gower: a study in linguistic movements and historical geography.' *Archaeologia Cambrensis*, 89:302–27.

—(1935). 'Linguistic divides in South Wales: a historico-geographical study.' *Archaeologia Cambrensis*, 90:239–66.

—(1936). 'Linguistic divides in North Wales: a study in historical geography.' *Archaeologia Cambrensis*, 91:194–209.

—(1937). 'A linguistic map of Wales according to the 1931 census, with observations on its historical and geographical setting.' *Geographical Journal*, 89:146–51.

—(1953). 'The distribution of the Welsh Language, 1931–1951.' *Geographical Journal*, 119:331–5.

Williams, Glanmor (1979). *Religion, Language and Nationality in Wales*. Cardiff: University of Wales Press.

Williams, Gwyn (1953). *An Introduction to Welsh Poetry. From the Beginnings to the Sixteenth Century*. London: Faber. (Also published New York: Books for Libraries Press, 1970.)

—(1959). *Presenting Welsh Poetry. An Anthology of Welsh Verse in Translation and of English Verse by Welsh Poets*. London: Faber.

—(1973). *Welsh Poems, Sixth Century to 1600*. London: Faber. (Originally published 1976, with Welsh as well as English texts, under the title *The Burning Tree*, London: Faber.)

Williams, Ifor (1935). *Canu Llywarch Hen*. Cardiff: University of Wales Press. (Reprinted 1953.)

—(1944). *Lectures on Early Welsh Poetry*. Dublin: Dublin Institute for Advanced Studies.

Williams, Jac L. (1958). 'The national language in the social pattern in Wales.' *Studies*, 47:247–58.

—(1973). 'The Welsh language in education', in Meic Stephens (ed.), 1973:92–109.

Williams, J.E. Caerwyn (1959). 'Early Welsh literature', in Roderick, A.J. (ed.) (1959–60), I, pp. 42–9.

Williams, Michael (1972). 'The linguistic and cultural frontier in Gower.' *Archaeologia Cambrensis*, 121:61–9.

Williams, W.O. (1964). 'The survival of the Welsh language after the union of England and Wales: the first phase, 1536–1642.' *Welsh History Review*, 2:67–93.

9　Cornish

The old Celtic speech of Cornwall died out two centuries ago. It is still dead, and will evermore remain so. It is true that the present century has seen the propagation by a small band of enthusiasts of a type of language that is partially derived from the old Celtic speech of Cornwall, but it is also partially invented and to claim that it represents a 'revival' of authentic Cornish is to misrepresent the situation. We shall return to this so-called 'revival' at the end of this chapter, but it has to be mentioned at this stage so as to enable us to make an important distinction in terminology. In the past, the term 'Cornish' has been used with reference both to the traditional and authentic language of Cornwall and to modern pseudo-Cornish, but I shall reserve the term for genuine Cornish and shall refer to pseudo-Cornish as 'Cornic'.[1]

Cornish is what British (see Chapter 7) became in the extreme south-west of the island. The gradual retreat of Cornish in the face of the advance of English, to the point where it was restricted to a small area in the extreme west of the peninsula, cannot however be traced with any great precision. In the absence of any direct references to the state of the language before the fourteenth century, we are dependent upon indirect evidence. One particularly valuable source is the form taken by place-names at various periods, on the basis of which it is sometimes possible to come to an informed view (though one must in such cases allow for a wide margin of error) as to whether the language spoken in a particular locality was Cornish or English. Much of this evidence is collected together in an unpublished work, 'The Place-Names of Cornwall', by J.E.B. Gover, on the basis of which Martyn Wakelin deduces (1975:76−7) that, by the year 1100, 'English was vastly predominant as far west as Bodmin' and that Cornish had even ceased to be spoken in some places west of Bodmin. Applying similar criteria to the evidence available for a period four centuries later, Wakelin concludes (*ibid.*, 77) that, by 1500, the linguistic border passed west of Truro and was not far removed from Falmouth, Camborne and Redruth. It could be, however, that Wakelin's suggested dates are too early by, say, a century, i.e. that English was not dominant everywhere east of Bodmin until about 1200 and that the line he suggests for 1500 is perhaps more appropriate for around the year 1600.

From the fourteenth century, we begin to find fragments of direct evidence on the state of the language.[2] For example, in 1336 some of the parishioners of St Buryan (near Land's End), petitioning the Bishop of Exeter over the

[1] There is sufficient justification for this term in the fact that *lingua cornica* has been used in Latin and that the French term for 'Cornish' is *cornique*.

[2] Much of what follows is taken from Wakelin, 1975:88−93.

status of a college of secular canons in the parish, made their submission in Cornish (though others did so in English or French), and a document of 1339 reveals that one of the duties of the curate of St Merryn (near Padstow, i.e. relatively far to the north-west) was to preach in Cornish.

There is no contemporary evidence for the fifteenth century, and little for the sixteenth other than Andrew Borde's comment in his *First Boke of the Introduction of Knowledge* (1547) that in Cornwall 'there be many men and women the which cannot speake one worde of Englyshe, but all Cornyshe'.

In the seventeenth century, there are numerous references to the grievously weakened state of Cornish. The first of these is from Richard Carew's *Survey of Cornwall* (1602, but perhaps written as early as 1594), where we read that English had driven Cornish 'into the uttermost skirts of the shire' and that 'most of the inhabitants can speak no word of Cornish, but very few are ignorant of the English'. Shortly afterwards, in 1610, John Norden (whose visit to Cornwall may have taken place in 1584), reported that 'of late the Cornishe men have muche conformed themselves to the use of the Englishe tounge' and that, though Cornish was much in use in the west of the county, i.e. in the hundreds of Penwith and Kerrier, between husband and wife, parents and children, masters and servants, 'yet there is none of them in manner but is able to conuers with a *Straunger* in the Englishe tounge, vnless it be some obscure people, that seldome conferr with the better sorte'. And he concludes that 'it seemeth that in few yeares the Cornishe Language wilbe by litle and litle abandoned'. In view of statements such as these, the observation made in his diary in 1644 by one of Charles I's officers, Richard Symonds, that 'all beyond Truro they speak the Cornish language', must be interpreted as meaning only that *some* Cornish speakers are to be found anywhere west of Truro, not that Cornish was in general use, and even his comment that 'at Land's-end they speake no English' is perhaps not wholly reliable. However, in the mid-seventeenth century, the vicar of a parish as far east as Feock still had some elderly parishioners who did not understand English, and so administered Holy Communion in Cornish.

Thereafter, apart from William Scawen who commented c. 1680 that a few old people still did not understand a word of English and that the parson of Landewednack 'had preached a sermon not long since in the Cornish tongue, only well understood by his auditory', nearly all those who comment on the language forecast its imminent demise. John Ray's *Itinerary*, dating from the 1660s, expresses the view that 'the language is like in a short time to be quite lost', and Gibson's additions to his 1695 translation of Camden's *Britannia* state that 'the old Cornish is almost quite driven out of the Country, being spoken only by the vulgar in two or three Parishes at the Lands-end; and they too understand the English. In other parts, the inhabitants know little or nothing of it: so that in all likelihood, a short time will destroy the small remains that are left of it.' Nicholas Boson reported, c. 1700, that, though some Cornish was spoken in parts of the area to the west of Redruth and Falmouth, even there 'there is more of English spoken than Cornish, for here may be some found that can hardly speak or understand Cornish, but scarce any but both understand and speak English . . . . We find the young Men to speak it less and less, and worse and worse.' At about the same time, Edward

Lhuyd, in his *Archaeologia Britannica* (1707), while listing a number of parishes where Cornish was still spoken, mainly in the extreme west, i.e. beyond St Ives and Penzance, but also 'all along the Seashoar from the Land's end to St Kevern's, near the Lizard point', comments that 'there's no Cornish Man but speaks good English'.

That a few speakers of Cornish survived until the late eighteenth century seems certain. In 1768, the antiquary Daines Barrington[3] made what he calls 'a very complete tour of Cornwall', in the course of which he made determined efforts to discover whether any speakers of the language remained. Undeterred by the advice of 'several persons of that county' who 'considered it as entirely lost', he eventually tracked down in the village of Mousehole, on the western shore of Mount's Bay, an old woman named Dolly Pentreath who, so he had been informed, 'could speak Cornish very fluently'. He managed to persuade her to speak 'for two or three minutes, and in a language which sounded very like Welsh'. (Barrington was of course aware of the relationship of Cornish to Welsh and this may well have led him to express the view that what he heard sounded 'very like Welsh', which seems a little improbable.) It would appear the Dolly's Cornish was at any rate fluent, though how good or, on the other hand, how corrupt it was is a different matter. Certainly, she can have had little opportunity of speaking it for many years previously. Two other women, ten or twelve years younger than Dolly, told Barrington that they could not speak the language 'readily', but that they understood it. When, in 1775, Barrington made further enquiries about Dolly, he received a reply from 'a gentleman whose house is within three miles of Mousehole', who asserted that, if she was to be believed, she could not 'talk a word of English before she was past twenty years of age' but that she was 'positive' that, by then, 'there is neither in Mousehole, nor in any other part of the country, any person who knows any thing of it, or at least can converse in it'.

Dolly Pentreath, who died in 1777, probably in her very late eighties, is the last known native speaker of Cornish. It has sometimes been suggested that another claimant to the title could be a fisherman named William Bodinar, also of Mousehole, who wrote to Barrington in 1776, in both English and Cornish, a letter which 'is of great interest as being the last passage of authentic Cornish writing to survive' (Pool, 1975:27). It must be remembered, however, that Bodinar, who died in 1789, i.e. twelve years after Dolly, 'was not a native speaker like her; he had first learnt Cornish when going to sea with old fishermen, whereas she had learnt it in earliest childhood' (*ibid*., 28). But whether one considers Dolly Pentreath or William Bodinar to have been the last speaker of Cornish, what is certain is that 'after the death of Bodinar, there is no evidence of the survival of anyone who could speak Cornish fluently, and no reliable witness claims to have met such a person' (*ibid*.). An assiduous search for Cornish-speakers made around Land's End in 1808 by the Revd Richard Warner of Bath met with a total lack of success (see Pool, 1975:28).

[3] See his account, 'On the expiration of the Cornish language', in the journal of the Society of Antiquaries, *Archaeologia*, 3(1776):279–84.

There is evidence that, well into the nineteenth century, scraps of Cornish − odd words and phrases, the basic numerals, the Lord's Prayer − were still known to a few people who, presumably, had acquired them in childhood from members of their grand-parents' generation (who may themselves have known little more). But these are at best relics, and, as in an ecclesiastical sense, relics imply that the body they belonged to is dead. It seems impossible to dissent, with any good reason, from Nance's view (1973) that 'even in its last strongholds, Cornish by 1800 was no longer used in daily speech by anyone, old or young, but remembered only occasionally and in fragments' and that, as even those who knew a few words or phrases 'would have been quite unable to take their words and form new sentences with them', we must 'accept 1800 as being about the very latest date at which anyone really spoke Cornish traditionally, as even the remnant of a living language, all traditional Cornish since then having been learned parrot-wise in greater or less quantity from those of an earlier generation'.

A few Cornish words remain in the spoken English of parts of Cornwall − e.g. *banal* 'broom [plant]' (from *banallen*, cf. Welsh *banadl*), *dram* 'swathe' (from *dram*), *fuggan* 'pastry dinner-cake' (from *fugen*), *groshaus* 'dregs' (from *growjyon*), *muryans* 'ants' (from *muryon*, cf. Welsh *morion*), *scaw* 'elder [tree]' (from *scawen*, cf. Welsh *ysgawen*). And of course there are the thousands of place-names (including names of hills, fields and other small features) that are of Cornish origin. In particular, there are the numerous names in *Lan-* 'enclosure, church' + saint's name (e.g. *Landewednack, Laneast, Lanhydrock, Lanivet, Lansallos*), *Pen-* 'head, top, end' (e.g. *Pentire* 'end of the land' < *tir* 'land', *Penzance* 'holy headland' < *sans* 'holy' < Latin *sanctum*), *Pol-* 'pool' (e.g. *Polglaze* 'blue pool' < *glas* 'blue', *Polscoe* 'boat pool' < *scath* 'boat'), *Porth-* 'harbour' (e.g. *Porthallow* 'harbour on the river Allow'), *Ros-* 'hill, moor' (e.g. *Roseglos* 'hill of the church' < *eglos* 'church', *Rosewarne* 'alder hill' < *(g)wern* 'alder'), and *Tre-* 'farmstead, estate' (e.g. *Tremaine* 'farmstead of the rock' < *men* 'rock, stone', *Treneglos* < *tre an eglos* 'township of the church', *Trenowth* 'new township' < *noweth* 'new'). Other names of clear Cornish origin are *Boscawen* 'dwelling of the elder tree' < *bos* 'dwelling' + *scawen* 'elder [tree]', *Kelynack* < *celin* 'holly', *Landrake* < *lanherch* 'glade, clearing', *Lizard* 'high court' < *lis* 'court' + *ard* 'high', < *Prisk* < *prysk* 'bushes'.

We have not yet suggested any reasons why Cornish should have faded away to the point where it could no longer be considered to exist as a living language in any valid sense of the term. Up to, perhaps, the twelfth century, English had been spreading because English-speakers had been physically moving westwards. In later centuries, we face a different phenomenon. There was certainly some continuing immigration of English -speakers into the restricted area where Cornish was still spoken. Professor D. Simon Evans reminds us (1969:305) that 'in the sixteenth century the centre of the tin industry steadily shifted within Cornwall from east to west, with the result that hundreds of English speakers from the east moved to the west. During the same period we have the rise in importance of the Cornish ports and the growth of commerce. Furthermore, Cornwall became of strategic importance in England's military enterprises.

These were powerful factors in the decline of Cornish'.

The growing importance of English as a trading language from the Tudor period onwards can only have worked to the disadvantage of Cornish, which came to be more and more associated with the lower classes. 'Even as early as 1336, it was the principal parishioners of St Buryan [a village only three or four miles from Land's End] who spoke English or French, while the last speakers of Cornish in the eighteenth century were fishermen and the like' (Wakelin, 1975). If the analogy of other minority languages in the recent past is anything to go by, this is likely to have led not only English-speakers but many Cornish-speakers to consider a command of English as a mark of social superiority and to regard Cornish as a badge of social, and indeed cultural and perhaps intellectual, inferiority.

Though Jenner goes too far in saying (1904:12) that 'the Reformation did much to kill Cornish', it certainly struck a further blow to the grievously ailing language. Had the Bible or the Book of Common Prayer been translated into Cornish, this might perhaps have slowed down the decline of the language. (Jenner again exaggerates in suggesting that, if this had been done, 'the whole language might have been preserved to us', but at least we should not have been dependent for our knowledge of Cornish on a few fifteenth-century plays and little else.)

This brings us to the question of the written remains of Cornish and, fortunately, limited though they are, there is enough to give us a generally adequate view of the language, though an incomplete one (in respect of pronunciation, grammar and vocabulary alike). Indeed, the significance of what is left to us in written Cornish is largely linguistic rather than literary. As D. Simon Evans puts it (1969:293–4), 'the miserable literary remains of Cornish . . . throw much light on the state and use of the language, although they would hardly interest the student of literature'.

The history of Cornish as a written language falls very clearly into three periods, viz. Old Cornish (tenth to twelfth centuries), Middle Cornish (thirteenth to sixteenth centuries), and Late Cornish (seventeenth and eighteenth centuries).

Our knowledge of Old Cornish comes largely from the 961 entries (of which a few however are Anglo-Saxon or Anglo-Norman) included in a Latin − Cornish glossary (now known as the *Vocabularium Cornicum*) that exists only in one manuscript, dating probably from the late twelfth century but almost certainly copied from an earlier manuscript that may date from around the year 1100.[4] Examples from this glossary are *scouarnoc* ('hare'), *oin* ('lamb'), *ki* ('dog'), *avallen* ('apple-tree'), *guernen* ('alder') (cf. modern Welsh *ysgyfarnog, oen, ci, afallen, gwernen*). Even earlier fragments include a few Cornish glosses from the ninth and tenth centuries, and a number of Cornish personal names mentioned in tenth- and eleventh-century Latin and Anglo-Saxon notes in a manuscript of the gospels.

We have, therefore, not a single complete sentence in Old Cornish. And apart from one single phrase, *In Polsethow ywhylyr anethou* 'In Polsethow [i.e. Glasney] shall be seen dwellings (*or* marvels)', dating perhaps from the

[4] On this and the other sources for Old Cornish, see Jackson, 1953:59–62.

thirteenth century, there is a gap of over two hundred years in the history of written Cornish.

Cornish literature, properly so-called, dates largely from the Middle Cornish period and consists of the following items:[5]

1   A poem of 41 lines (perhaps part of a play), probably dating from about the year 1400.

2   The *Poem of Mount Calvary* or *The Passion*, a poem of over 2000 seven-syllabled lines (so running to about 10,000 words in all). It was probably composed in the fourteenth century, but the earliest of the five manuscripts dates from the fifteenth century.

3   The *Ordinalia*, the one major item of Cornish literature, consisting of 8734 lines (say approximately 40,000 words) in all. The *Ordinalia* is a trilogy of verse dramas on biblical and apocryphal themes, viz. *Origo Mundi* ('the Origin of the World', following the biblical account of events from the Creation to Solomon), *Passio Domini* ('The Passion of Christ'), and *Resurrectio Domini* ('The Resurrection of Christ'). These too may well have been composed in the late fourteenth century, though again the oldest manuscript dates from the fifteenth century.

4   Another verse drama, *Beunans Meriasek* or the *Life of St Meriasek*, a text of 4568 lines, or some 20,000 words, the sole manuscript of which dates from 1504 (illustration **4**).

Thereafter, we have another major gap until we come to two Late Cornish texts which are of negligible literary interest and are 'marked only by a further deterioration of the language. Writers of the period knew it only very imperfectly' (Evans, 1969:296). These are:

5   William Jordan[6] of Helston's *Creacion an Bys* ('The Creation of the World'), of 1611, based in part on the first section of the *Origo Mundi*; it runs to 2548 lines or some 12,000 words;

6   A folk-tale of some 1500 words, 'The Story of John of *Chy-an-Hur*', the only piece of original Cornish prose literature, of which various copies exist, the earliest being that given in his *Archaeologia Britannica* (1707) by Edward Lhuyd who says it was written down 'about forty years since', i.e. in the mid-seventeenth-century.[7]

That, then, is the sum total of extant Cornish literature (though some, perhaps much, has almost certainly been lost), amounting in all to less than 100,000 words, or the length of one modern novel. One further text, of no literary interest, is a translation from English, probably dating from 1555–58, by one John Tregear, of whom nothing is known, of thirteen homilies, twelve of them from Bishop Edmund Bonner's *A Profitable and Necessary Doctrine* (1555). The manuscript of this text came to light only in 1949 and it has not so far been published. As it is the only substantial text we have in mid-sixteenth-century Cornish, it might have been of considerable linguistic interest, but unfortunately, though it contains some new words, a

---

[5] The following comments on Middle and Late Cornish texts are in general based on Wakelin, 1975:78–80, and on Jenner, 1904:25–34.

[6] It is not known whether Jordan composed the work or whether he was merely the transcriber.

[7] The text has been recently edited, with a translation and notes, by Oliver Padel (1975:14–23).

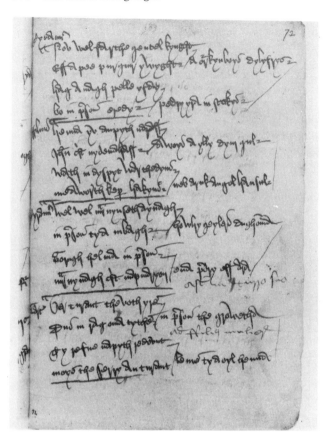

Illustration **4**   A page of the manuscript of the Cornish *Life of St Meriasek* (1504).

few variants of words already known and some plural forms and infinitive endings not otherwise known (see Nance, 1954), in general both the vocabulary and the grammar bristle with anglicisms, which suggests that Tregear was perhaps not a native speaker of Cornish. From slightly earlier, in Andrew Borde's *Booke of the Introduction of Knowledge* (1542), we have the numerals and, in a corrupt form, twenty-four sentences. Carew's *Survey of Cornwall* (1602) also includes the numerals and a handful of other words, names and phrases. From the eighteenth century, i.e. from the dying years of the language, there remain a short work, *Nebbaz Gerriau dro tho Carnoack* ('A Few Words about Cornish'), by Nicholas Boson of Newlyn (who appears not to have been a native speaker of Cornish), and a number of miscellaneous fragments including songs, proverbs, letters, conversational phrases, and translations of brief passages of Scripture.[8]

---

[8] These exist mainly in various eighteenth-century manuscript collections that are described in some detail by Jenner, 1904:34–46. The text of *Nebbaz Gerriau* and of a number of the fragments (including various letters and translations of passages of Scripture), with translations and notes, can be found in Padel (1975).

This chapter could well end here, perhaps with a final quotation from a lecture delivered by Henry Jenner in 1876 (1877:145):

> But, though Cornish is dead, its ghost still haunts its old dwelling, in the form of idioms, provincialisms, words, and phrases, and still more apparently in the names of every hill, farm, river, rock, stream, or well, and of the descendants of those who once spoke it.

But there is the matter of the 'revival' to which we alluded at the beginning of this chapter. In general, the extent to which even the living languages of this island, and in particular Scottish Gaelic and Welsh, are taught and used as 'acquired' languages (as distinct from their use as native languages) is beyond the scope of this book. But something must be said about this alleged 'revival' of Cornish, if only because ill-informed journalists sometimes give the impression that Cornish is now once more a living language. One is tempted merely to say that if the nineteenth-century remains of the language are, in Jenner's words, a 'ghost that still haunts its old dwelling', the 'Cornish' that is now being 'revived' is perhaps best described as a 'phantom' (defined in Webster's dictionary, second edition, as 'one that is something in appearance but not in reality'). That there is a considerable amount of active interest in the 'revival' and the language associated with it is undeniable, but we suggested at the beginning of this chapter that the language in question is not the same thing as the traditional and authentic Celtic speech of Cornwall and that some terminological distinction was necessary. As we said there, having reserved the term 'Cornish' for the traditional language, we shall refer to the 'revived' language as 'Cornic'.

The origins of the 'revival' go back to the turn of the century and are associated particularly with the name of Henry Jenner (1848–1934). As a very young man, Jenner, a Cornishman on the staff of the Manuscripts Department of the British Museum, drew attention to the Cornish language and its literature in two lectures delivered respectively to the Philological Society in 1873 (i.e. when Jenner was only 25) but not published until twenty years later (see Jenner, 1893), and to the British Archaeological Association in 1876 (Jenner, 1877).

For the next quarter of a century, Jenner kept up his interest in Cornish and in 1903 attended a congress of the *Union Régionaliste Bretonne* at Lesneven, in Brittany, making a speech in the language and claiming (1904:7, n.1) (with perhaps some permissible exaggeration or over-optimism) that 'rather to his astonishment he was fairly well understood by the Bretons'. The first step that was to have major consequences, however, and the one that can be considered really to have initiated the 'revival' of Cornic, was the publication in 1904 of Jenner's book, *A Handbook of the Cornish Language*. 'This book', he wrote (1904:ix), 'is principally intended for those persons of Cornish nationality who wish to acquire some knowledge of their ancient tongue, and to read, write, and perhaps even to speak it.'

One of those who immediately started learning Cornic from Jenner's *Handbook* was Robert Morton Nance (1873–1958), who throughout his life was to labour indefatigably on behalf of the Cornic 'revival'. Among his many publications are his influential primer, *Cornish for All: A Guide to*

Unified Cornish,[9] and a series of dictionaries, all of them published by the Federation of Old Cornwall Societies, beginning with an English–Cornic dictionary[10] that he produced in 1934 with A.S.D. Smith (also known by his bardic name of Caradar). This was followed four years later by a Cornic–English dictionary.[11] By the 1950s, both dictionaries were out of print and new versions were brought out.[12] Nance also wrote extensively on the language and literature of Cornwall, composed tales and other original work in Cornic, and edited the journal *Old Cornwall*. Meanwhile, the third main figure at the 'revival', A.S.D. Smith (1883–1950), published what is, apart perhaps from *Cornish for All*, the most successful grammar of Cornic, viz. *Cornish Simplified*,[13] and a pamphlet, *The Story of the Cornish Language*,[14] produced a Cornic version in verse of the Tristan and Isolt story and a translation of the medieval Welsh Mabinogi, and collaborated with Nance in producing in 'Unified Cornish' editions of parts of the Middle Cornish texts and a translation of the Gospel according to St Mark.

The activities of the 'revival' are nowadays largely guided by a body known as *Kesva an Tavas Kernewek* (The Cornish Language Board), set up in 1967, its stated function (which it has carried out energetically) being 'to promote the study and revival of the Cornish language'. This is has done in particular by reprinting grammars and dictionaries and publishing texts. Other bodies and individuals have also published short texts in Cornic, there have been various attempts (some more successful than others) at launching Cornic magazines, gramophone records and tape-recordings of readings in Cornic have been issued, every now and then on special occasions there are religious services and theatrical performances in Cornic, and Cornic is taught in evening classes in various parts of the county.[15]

But what *is* it that is being 'revived'? In fact, 'revived' is a barely appropriate term as Cornic is to no inconsiderable extent a nineteenth- and, more especially, a twentieth-century invention, in its orthography, its pronunciation, its vocabulary, and even its grammar.

The orthography of Middle Cornish (like that of other medieval vernaculars) was far from being completely standardized, and the 'Unified Spelling' now in use among those who write Cornic represents 'the reduction of the highly confused spelling of the existing texts and manuscripts to an

---

9 1st ed., St Ives, 1929; revised [= 2nd] ed., St Ives, 1949; 3rd ed., Penzance, 1958.

10 R.M. Nance and A.S.D. Smith, *An English–Cornish Dictionary*, 1934.

11 R.M. Nance, *Gerlyvver Noweth Kernewek a Sawsnek/A New Cornish–English Dictionary*, 1938.

12 R.M. Nance, *An English–Cornish Dictionary*, 1952 (reprinted 1965 and 1973); *A Cornish–English Dictionary*, 1955 (reprinted 1971).

13 Caradar (A.S.D. Smith), *Cornish Simplified, Short Lessons for Self-Tuition*, St Ives, 1939; 2nd ed., Camborne, 1965.

14 *The Story of the Cornish Language, its Extinction and Revival*, Camborne, 1947; 2nd ed., revised by E.G.R. Hooper, Camborne, 1969.

15 A detailed survey of the 'revival' is beyond our scope. For further information, see Ellis, 1974, especially the last two chapters, 'The revivalists' and 'The growth and future of the revival'. However, this book contains numerous errors (see reviews by A.L. Rowse, *Times Literary Supplement*, 22 Nov. 1974, and by G. Price, *Studia Celtica*, 12–13 (1977–78):474–5). J.J. Parry (1946) is also informative, if over-optimistic about the extent to which the 'revival' had progressed.

artificial system of orthography which R. Morton Nance invented' (Thomas, 1963:197). The fact that Middle Cornish texts are now available in a standardized, if modern, orthography is certainly a great advantage for those who wish to read them in a version approximating to the original. It is nevertheless a fact that this standardized orthography, at least insofar as it is entirely 'regular', is a twentieth-century construct, and those to whom it is offered should be made fully aware that that is what it is.

It is − or ought to be − self-evident that there is no way by which the pronunciation of a language that no one now living has ever heard spoken can be recovered in anything more than an approximate form, if that. It has however been argued that the way English is now pronounced in West Cornwall can enlighten us as to both the sounds and the intonation of spoken Cornish, as it was in its last days. E.G.R. Hooper, in particular, claimed (1931) that the present-day English dialect of west Cornwall was 'a key to Cornish' in that it retained, among other features, 'practically all the sounds of Cornish as last spoken' and its intonation. This may well be so of intonation, but it is very doubtful whether the authentic Cornish pronunciation of vowels and consonants survives − and even if it does, what is preserved is the sounds of Cornish *in its last stages* (by which time it was heavily influenced by English), whereas written Cornic is based on Middle Cornish. (In any case, a language based on its own fifteenth-century written form and the twentieth-century spoken form of another language is indeed a curious animal.)

The most easily recognized, and the most readily acknowledged, area of invention in Cornic is that of vocabulary. In principle, Nance's dictionaries distinguish between what is authentic, i.e. words that actually occur in the Cornish texts, and what is invented. In practice, it is not always clear what the status of a given word is. In his *English–Cornish Dictionary* of 1952, for example, Nance marks with an asterisk words borrowed from Breton and/or Welsh (e.g. *eos* 'nightingale' [Welsh], *selsygen* 'sausage' [Breton]), *kelgh* 'circle' [Welsh, Breton]) but does not distinguish between authentic Cornish words and those that he has made up but on the basis of attested Cornish elements. So, for example, as *jyn* 'machine' and *nyja* 'to fly' are genuine Cornish words, *jyn-nyja* 'aeroplane' is left completely unmarked. While it is patently obvious that this and certain other unmarked words − such as *dywever* 'wireless', *forth-horn* 'railway', *gwaya-myr* 'cinema', *pellwolok* 'television' − cannot have occurred at the time when Cornish was a living language, there is no way at all of determining whether or not words like *arethva* 'rostrum', *arghansek* 'financial', *cornwhylen* 'lap-wing', *cuntellyans* 'congress', *dyscüdha* 'to unveil', *dyvroa* 'to emigrate', *gwastattyr* 'plateau', *ombrofyer* 'candidate', *pennoeth* 'bare-headed', *scryvynas* 'secretary', and very many others are or are not genuine.

Most serious of all, even the grammar of Cornic is not entirely authentic. Given that the whole corpus of Cornish writing is so limited, it is not surprising that not only many words but many grammatical forms never occur. For this reason, the only usable grammar of Cornish, viz. Henry Lewis's *Llawlyfr Cernyweg Canol*[16] ('Handbook of Middle Cornish', in Welsh), which is

---

[16] 2nd ed., Cardiff: University of Wales Press, 1946; this completely supersedes the much less satisfactory 1st ed. of 1923.

concerned only with what is actually attested and not with reconstructed or hypothetical forms, has, inevitably, many gaps. Edward Lhuyd, in his chapter 'A Cornish Grammar', in his *Archaeologia Britannica* of 1707, had already started inventing forms, on the basis of existing forms or by analogy with Welsh and Breton, and Jenner makes it clear on occasion that forms given in his *Handbook* are not attested[17] but are invented on the basis of Breton (which is closer to Cornish than Welsh is) (see Jenner, 1904:xi). In his *New Cornish–English Dictionary* of 1938, Nance explicitly recognizes (p. xiii) the need to supply missing forms in the grammar, as well as missing words:

> In the necessary replacement of so many missing genders, plurals, infinitive-endings and inflected parts of verbs, too, the suggestions of Breton have usually been taken as preferable to those of the more distant Welsh,

but, although his *Cornish for All* (3rd ed., 1958) refers to the adoption of 'a systematic spelling and grammar', nowhere is there the slightest hint that the grammar is partly made-up.[18] It is of course very likely that many of the forms supplied by the 'revivalists' did in fact exist – but they cannot be proved to have existed and so are indisputably invented. And in the view of Professor Charles Thomas (1963:202) 'the reconstructed language is full of assumptions, accretions and inaccuracies'.

So, Cornic is not Cornish – or, to use traditional terminology, 'revived' Cornish is not real Cornish. It could perhaps be compared to a painting so heavily restored as no longer to qualify as an authentic work by the artist who originally painted it, or to a piece of music found in fragmentary form and arranged some centuries later by another composer. To envisage the nature and scale of the task facing those who seek to restore it as a living language, one need only think that it is rather as if one were to attempt in our present century to create a form of spoken English on the basis of the fifteenth-century York mystery plays and very little else.

References

Ellis, P. Berresford (1974). *The Cornish Language and its Literature.* London: Routledge & Kegan Paul.

[17] For example, when giving for the 'pluperfect or conditional' of the verb *mos* 'to go' the forms:
singular : I, elsen, 2, elses, 3, elsa
plural : I, elsen, 2, elseugh, 3, elsens
he adds the comment (1904:143) that they are 'probable, but not found', and for *dôs* 'to come', he quotes two forms for each person with the comment 'Pluperfect not found, except third person singular, *dothye* or *dethye*, and third plural *dothyans*' (*ibid.*, 145).

[18] The difference between Lewis's authentic Cornish and Nance's invented Cornic is particularly noticeable in respect of verbs. One of the more startling examples is provided by the imperfect indicative of the verb *dos* 'to come', for which Lewis finds only 2nd person singular *dves*, whereas Nance provides a full paradigm, *dēn, dēs, do, dēn, deugh, dens*. Identical forms to Nance's are also given, again without any indication that some of them are artificially created, in A.S.D. Smith's *Cornish Simplified*.

Evans, D. Simon (1969). 'The story of Cornish', *Studies*, 58:293–308.

Hooper, E.G.R. (1931), 'Dialect as a gateway to Cornish.' *Old Cornwall*, II, 2:34–5.

Jackson, Kenneth (1953). *Language and History in Early Britain*. Edinburgh: Edinburgh University Press.

Jenner, Henry (1877). 'The history and literature of the ancient Cornish language.' *The Journal of the British Archaeological Association*, June, 1877:137–57.

—(1893). 'The Cornish language.' *Transactions of the Philological Society*, 165–86.

—(1904). *A Handbook of the Cornish Language, chiefly in its Latest Stages with some Account of its History and Literature*. London: Nutt.

Nance, R. Morton (1954). 'Cornish words in the Tregear MS.' *Zeitschrift für celtische Philologie*, 24:1–5.

—(1973). 'When was Cornish last spoken traditionally?' *Journal of the Royal Institution of Cornwall*, new series, 7:76–82.

Padel, O.J. (1975). *The Cornish Writings of the Boson Family*. Redruth: Institute of Cornish Studies.

Parry, J.J. (1946). 'The revival of Cornish: An Dasserghyans Kernewek.' *Publications of the Modern Language Association of America*, 61:258–68.

Pool, P.A.S. (1975). *The Death of Cornish (1600–1800)*. Penzance: the author.

Thomas, Charles (1963). 'An Dasserghyans Kernewek.' *Old Cornwall,* VI, 5 (Autumn, 1963):196–205.

Wakelin, Martyn F. (1975). *Language and History in Cornwall*. Leicester: Leicester University Press.

10 Cumbric

Before the Roman invasion, most or all of Britain south of the Forth and the Clyde was settled by British-speaking tribes whose language survived in the Highland Zone of Britain (see p. 159) (and probably very extensively in the Lowland Zone as well) throughout the period of the Roman occupation, i.e. until the early fifth century AD. The fifth century, however, was also the period when the Anglo-Saxon occupation of the Lowland Zone was beginning in earnest and so British speech once again found itself in competition with that of invaders.

Within perhaps a couple of centuries, the various Germanic dialects of the Anglo-Saxons had ousted British from all of the Lowland Zone with the exception of a few enclaves here and there (see pp. 89–90), and British was henceforward confined to the Highland Zone. Even here, the onward thrust of the Saxons in the south-west and the Angles in the north-west divided the British-speaking territory into three geographically separated areas, which broadly speaking correspond respectively to Devon and Cornwall, Wales, and an area in south-west Scotland and north-west England that we shall refer to as Cumbria. Although the term 'Cumbria' now generally applies solely to the English, as distinct from the Scottish, part of the area in question, there is ample historical justification for using it in this wider sense. As Kenneth Jackson has pointed out (1955:77), the Brittones of southern Scotland 'called themselves in Latin *Cumbri* and *Cumbrenses*, which is a Latinization of the native word *Cymry*, meaning "fellow-countrymen", which both they and the Welsh used of themselves in common'.

In the late sixth century, much of the north of England and of Scotland south of the Clyde and Forth was still British territory, consisting principally of the three kingdoms of Gododdin, Strathclyde and Rheged. Gododdin – the name derives from that of the pre-Roman tribe of the Votadini – took in the area between the Forth and the Tyne and had its capital at Din Eidyn, i.e. Edinburgh. To the west of Gododdin, occupying much of south-west Scotland, was Strathclyde, 'with its capital at Dumbarton [i.e. "the fort of the Britons"], its religious centre at Glasgow, and its heartland the valley of the Clyde, but reaching probably from Upper Loch Lomond and Cunningham to Peebles and the source of the Tweed' (Jackson, 1969:64). The area covered by Rheged is even less certain, but 'it seems fairly clear that it included the Solway basin (and perhaps Galloway), and the Eden valley up to the crest of the Pennines and possibly across them into Swaledale. The capital may have been Carlisle' (Jackson, 1963:68).

Some time in the seventh century the Angles of Mercia spread into the

Cheshire plain and the area between the Mersey and the Ribble, and there is no evidence for the survival of the British-speaking population in that area thereafter. Meanwhile, the Northumbrian Angles were pressing forward along the east coast, taking over Gododdin from the Britons and probably capturing Edinburgh in 638. They had probably occupied the whole of south-east Scotland by the middle of the seventh century.

The two western kingdoms survived somewhat longer. It is not certain when the Northumbrians moved into Rheged, but it may have been during the reign of Oswy who was king of Northumbria from 642 to 671. Jackson suggests (1955:84) that 'the English occupation of these widespread western districts was more in the nature of a scattered upper crust of landlords rather than a really thick settlement of peasants' and that there is reason to suppose that the Cumbric language did not entirely die out in the lands taken by the English. He also points out however (*ibid.*) that the result of losing control of this territory to the Northumbrians was that the independent Britons of north-west England and southern Scotland were confined to little more than the valley of the Clyde and the surrounding uplands.

Events were to take a different turn when the Northumbrians came under pressure from the Vikings, both in the east, when they lost Yorkshire to the Danes in 867, and some time later in the west when much of Galloway and, later still, in the early tenth century, the whole of north-western England were occupied by incomers of mixed Viking and Gaelic origin. One important effect of this breaking of the Northumbrian grip on the former territory of Rheged was that the Britons of Strathclyde reoccupied south-west Scotland and north-west England as far south as the Derwent and Penrith. They held these areas until the early eleventh century when their kingdom was finally absorbed into Scotland – an event which, as we shall see, is important in relation to the few words of Cumbric that remain.

Like much else in the history of this period, our knowledge of the course of events during the last period of the kingdom of Strathclyde is both fragmentary and uncertain. It appears however that 'the native·ruling family of Strathclyde may not even have survived the death, between 900 and 943, of Donald, king of the Britons' and that 'Strathclyde passed under the control of an off-shoot of the Scottish dynasty' (Kirby, 1971:87). A tradition developed whereby the heir apparent to the Scottish kingdom was given British territory to govern and when, in 1015, Owen the Bald, king of Strathclyde, died, apparently without direct heir, the reigning king of Scots, Malcolm II, granted Strathclyde (which, it will be recalled, extended as far south as the Derwent) to his grandson and heir, Duncan, who in 1034 succeeded him as king of Scots. Strathclyde was now definitively incorporated in the kingdom of Scotland. 'It was now at last', comments Jackson (1963:72), 'that Cumbria and the Cumbrians finally lost their individuality as a Brittonic nation.' The boundary between England and Scotland was pushed north from the Derwent to its present line when William Rufus annexed the southern part of the area in question in 1092.

The linguistic consequences of the tenth-century reoccupation by the Britons of what had been parts of Rheged are summarized by Jackson, who argues (1963:72−3) that Cumbric 'must have been reintroduced into

Dumfriesshire and Cumberland, or at any rate greatly strengthened there if it had not previously quite died out, by the reoccupation from Strathclyde in the tenth century', but that it 'faded away throughout Cumbria in the course of the eleventh century, perhaps to disappear finally in the early twelfth'.

The first problem we have to face in dealing with the Cumbric language itself is that we have virtually no written records of it. This contrasts markedly not only with Welsh which has a long and rich literary tradition but also with Cornish, whose few literary remains are adequate enough to reveal to us, if not the whole language (far from it), at least the essentials of its phonetic and grammatical structure and a substantial part of its vocabulary.

Our only direct knowledge of Cumbric from more or less contemporary documents (but late ones which could even date from a period after Cumbric had ceased to be a spoken language) is limited to three words and a few personal names. The three words occur in a Latin legal text, probably dating from the eleventh century, namely the *Leges inter Brettos et Scottos* 'Laws between the Britons and the Scots' (see Jackson, 1953:9–10, and 1955:88), which were presumably drawn up to regulate relations between the two communities when Strathclyde was absorbed into the kingdom of Scotland. They are *galnes* or *galnys*, which corresponds to Middle Welsh *galanas* 'blood-fine', and *mercheta* and *kelchyn*, connected with Welsh *merch* 'daughter' and *cylch* 'circuit' respectively. The second of these Jackson interprets (1955:88) as denoting 'a tax paid by a father to his lord on the marriage of his daughter', while the third refers to some sort of fine 'but perhaps originally a contribution paid when the king went on royal progress through his lands'. These legal terms were perhaps incorporated in a Latin text because they stood for concepts that had no precise equivalent in Scots law or in the Latin language. Such terms could of course have survived after the Cumbric language itself had become extinct, just as Anglo-Norman words survive as legal technical terms in English.

A couple of British names from what was to become the Cumbric area, viz. those of two princes, Nudus and Dumnogenus, appear in a Latinized form in a Latin inscription, probably of the early sixth century, from Yarrowkirk. More authentically Cumbric are names given in the Latin *Life of St Kentigern* which survives only in a twelfth-century version but draws on earlier sources. One such name is that of a king of Strathclyde, Rhydderch (Old Welsh *Riderch*), which here appears as *Rederech*.

It is however the place names that tell us most about Cumbric. They fall broadly speaking into three groups. The first group comprises the names of British origin that are known – and in many cases still survive – from that part of Scotland, the south-east, the old kingdom of Gododdin, that fell to the Angles in the first third of the seventh century, an area in which the great majority of place-names are in fact English. Some of the names of undoubted Cumbric origin are based on roots corresponding to Welsh *coed* 'wood', *moel* 'bare', *rhos* 'moor', *pen* 'head, summit, end', *tre(f)* 'township', that frequently occur in Welsh place-names and which we have already come across in British names from the Lowland Zone of England (see pp. 87–89). The British root *cet-*'wood' (= Welsh *coed*) provides the second element of *Bathgate* and *Dalkeith* (the first elements correspond respectively to Welsh *baedd* 'boar' and, probably, *dol*, 'meadow'). *Melrose* corresponds to Welsh *Moel+rhos*. *Pen* occurs in *Penicuik* (= Welsh *Pen y gog* 'cuckoo's summit') and *Pencaitland* (cf. Welsh *coedlan* 'copse'), and cognates of *tre(f)* occur in *Tranent* (found in the twelfth-century in the form *Treuernent* = Welsh *tref + yr* 'the' +*neint*, an archaic plural of *nant* 'valley, stream'), *Traprain* (Welsh *pren* 'tree') and *Trabrown* (Welsh *bryn* 'hill'), and, preceded by an element meaning 'new', in *Niddry*, *Niddrie* and *Longniddry* in the Lothians. A number of the principal towns in the area also have Cumbric names, including *Linlithgow* (= Welsh *llyn* 'lake' +*llaith* 'damp' + *cau* 'hollow', so the name means something like 'the lake in the damp hollow') and *Lanark* (= Welsh *llannerch* 'glade'). A widely distributed element in the Scottish border counties is the word *pren* 'tree' that occurs, nowadays usually in a much mangled form, in the names of two localities called *Pirn* (in the former counties of Peebles and Midlothian respectively), with an unidentified suffix in *Pirnie* and *Pirny*, with colour adjectives in *Prinlaws* (Welsh *(g)las* 'blue, green') and *Primside* (earlier *Prenwensete*, in which *wen* is 'white' and *sete* is English *seat*), and in a variety of other names including *Primrose* and *Barnbougle* (whose second elements correspond respectively to Welsh *rhos* 'moor' and *bugail* 'shepherd') (see Nicolaisen, 1964:146−8).

In south-west Scotland we have other Cumbric names from the kingdoms of Strathclyde and Rheged (see Jackson, 1955, 1963, and Nicolaisen, 1964). The root *tre* 'township' turns up again in *Trerregles* (= Welsh *tre'r eglwys* 'church town'), *Trostrie* (corresponding to the Welsh place-name *Trostre*, whose first element derives from *traws* 'across, athwart') and *Ochiltree* (Welsh *uchel* 'high'), while forms equivalent to Welsh *caer.* 'fort' (but perhaps here having taken on the meaning 'hamlet', cf. Breton *kêr* 'town') occur in *Caerlanrig* (Welsh *llannerch* 'glade', which as we have seen, also gives *Lanark*), *Carfrae* (Welsh *fre* for *bre* 'hill'), and *Cathcart* and *Cramond* (found in the twelfth century as *Kerkert* and *Karramunt* respectively) 'the fort or hamlet on the river Cart/Almond'. *Pennersax* (Dumfriesshire) would in Welsh be *Pen y Sais* 'Englishman's summit', and *Leswalt* in Galloway corresponds to Welsh *llys* 'court' + *(g)wellt* 'grass', so the meaning is presumably 'grassy courtyard'. The Latin words *pontem* 'bridge' and *ecclesia* 'church' (originally a Greek word) have come down into modern Welsh as *pont* and *eglwys*, and are also found in the names of *Penpont* 'bridge-end' and *Ecclefechan* (Welsh *eglwys fechan*) 'little church'.

When we turn to the English part of Cumbria, we find that there is a particularly high proportion of names of Brittonic origin, and not only names of natural features such as rivers and hills, which are often taken over by an incoming community from those who were there before them, but also names of villages and other settlements which, in general, survive less frequently. Professor Jackson shows (1963:74) that, out of some 210 village names in the former county of Cumberland, about sixty, i.e. roughly 29 per cent, are of Brittonic origin, and that over fifty of these 'occur in the area north of the Derwent, that is to say in the part of Cumberland reoccupied by Strathclyde in the tenth century, and that there is a particularly close concentration in the north, east and north of Carlisle'. It seems more than likely therefore that many of these names — though there is no means of telling which — date from the time of the reoccupation rather than from the pre-Northumbrian period.

Among the Cumbric names of north-west England are many that contain elements we have already come across. The seemingly ubiquitous roots that have given Welsh *tre(f)* 'township', *pen* 'head, to, end', *coed* 'wood' and *blaen* 'summit', appear again in *Triermain* 'village by the rock' (Welsh *tre'r maen*), *Penrith* 'end of the ford' (Welsh *rhyd* 'ford'), *Culgaith* 'backwood' (Welsh *cil* 'recess, corner') (cf. *Culcheth* in Lancashire), *Blencarn* 'summit with a cairn' (Welsh *carn*), *Blaencogo* 'summit of the cuckoos' (Welsh *cog* 'cuckoo', plural *cogau*). Roots we found in *Lanark* and *Caerlanrig* (Welsh *llannerch* 'glade, clearing' and *caer* 'fort') occur again in *Lanercost* (with an uncertain second element) and *Cardew* (Welsh *du* 'black'). *Lamplugh* (found as *Lamplou*, *Lanplo* in the twelfth century) corresponds to Welsh *llan* 'church' and *plwy (f)* 'parish' and so means 'parish church'. *Carrock* (Fell) is Welsh *carreg* 'rock', and *Calder, Cumrew* and *Glendhu* correspond respectively to Welsh *Calettwr* (*caled* 'hard' + *dŵr* 'water', see p. 88 above), *cwm* 'valley' + *rhiw* 'slope', and *glyn* 'valley' + *du* 'black'. *Tallentire* 'end of the land' (probably a headland in ploughing, Jackson suggests) corresponds to Welsh *tâl* 'brow, front' and *tir* 'land'.

What evidence place-names provide for Cumbric is, of course, largely to do with its vocabulary. However, the fact that many of the names in question reflect not isolated words but words used in combination opens up the possibility that they may tell us something, if only a very little, about pronunciation and grammar. For example, a feature of the Celtic languages is that, in certain constructions, initial consonants may change or, in the case of Welsh and Cornish *g*, disappear — so, Welsh *gwen* (feminine of *gwyn* 'white') and *glas* 'blue, green' become *wen*, *las* after a feminine noun. The word *pren* 'tree' in Welsh is masculine, so one has *pren gwyn*, *pren glas*, but the medieval names *Prenwen(sete)* (Roxburghshire) (now *Primside*) and *Prinlaws* (Fife) lead us to suppose that the original forms were something like *pren wen* and *pren las*. and therefore that in Cumbric the word *pren* was feminine (see Nicolaisen, 1964:146).

There is one possible remnant of Cumbric that we have not yet mentioned, and that is the set of numerals up to twenty, the so-called 'Cumbric score', characterized by Jackson (1955:88) as 'the old Cumbric numerals [which] have survived very extraordinarily to modern times among the Pennine shepherds of Cumberland and the West Riding, for the purpose of counting sheep'. These, he accepts, are none other than 'a garbled version of something which must have been identical with the numerals in Welsh'. A.J. Ellis, who a century ago published fifty-three versions of them (some of them incomplete), tells us that, although the use of the score for counting sheep already seemed to have become obsolete, it was apparently still used by old women to count their stitches in knitting, and continues (1877–79:321):

Most people . . . merely recollect it as a strange piece of gibberish, which they retail from memory, extending sometimes more than fifty years back, and in the process necessarily either forget or alter the words, to which they attach no value or importance, regarding them as an idle curiosity. The Score in fact seems to have descended to be a plaything, especially of girls and boys at school, used for the purposes of 'counting-out', that is, of determining who is to take an objectionable part in a game, or to be excluded from something desirable when the admissible number is limited.

Much more recently, the Score has been subjected to thorough scrutiny by Michael Barry, who publishes (1969) some 70 versions (many of them incomplete) reported to hail mainly from Cumbria, Yorkshire and other parts of the north of England, with a few from south-west Scotland and elsewhere. The various versions often differ considerably, but the following specimens (from Barry's article) will give an idea of how closely or otherwise some fairly representative sets approximate to Welsh:

	Welsh	Borrowdale (Cumberland)	Kirkby Stephen (Westmorland)	High Furness (Lancs)	Nidderdale (W. Yorks)
1	un	yan	yan	yan	yain
2	dau	tyan	tahn	taen	tain
3	tri	tethera	teddera	tedderte	eddero
4	pedwar	methera	meddera	medderte	peddero
5	pump	pimp	pimp	pimp	pitts
6	chwech	sethera	settera	haata	tayter
7	saith	lethera	littera	slaata	layter
8	wyth	hevera	hovera	lowra	overo
9	naw	devera	dovera	dowra	covero
10	deg	dick	dick	dick	dix
15	pymtheg	bumfit	bumfit	mimph	bumfit
20	ugain	giggot	jiggot	gigget	jiggit

If anything at all is certain about these numerals, it is that no-one seems to have come across them actually being used, whether for counting sheep or for any other purpose. Ellis had already commented on this over a hundred years ago and, as Barry says (1964:75), 'those who have investigated the counting system since his day have always come up against the same persistent difficulty that they are available only at second-hand, – one can never run to earth an informant who really *uses* them'. It is noteworthy that sixteen of the sets recorded from the north of England were reported to be used either for counting-out (like 'eeny, meeny, miney, mo'), or in children's games, or in nursery rhymes. This of course explains the fact that, apart from 'five' and 'ten', the numerals usually fall into rhyming pairs (*yan/tyan, teddera/meddera, haata/slaata, overo/covero*, etc.). Not that this is an argument of much significance against their possible Cumbric origins:

> Such a strong tradition must have some foundation and it may well be that the numerals were once used by shepherds and perhaps others, probably in conjunction with a tally-stick or similar device for marking off each twenty and that they have gradually fallen out of use or been 'down-graded' into a meaningless jingle (Barry, 1964:75).

Indeed, that they are in some way connected with the Welsh numerals cannot be doubted. This is particularly true of those forms that have not been affected by the tendency to group the numbers in rhyming or alliterative pairs, namely 'five', 'ten', 'fifteen' and perhaps 'twenty': *pimp* is exactly the Welsh *pump* (-*u*- being pronounced 'i'), and *dick* and *bumfit* are too close to Welsh *deg* and *pymtheg* (the first syllable being pronounced 'pum') for the resemblance to be purely fortuitous. There is also the fact that 'eleven' and 'sixteen' in the Cumbric Score are most frequently formed on the pattern of Welsh *un-ar-ddeg* (lit. 'one on ten') and *un-ar-bymtheg* ('one on fifteen'), e.g. Borrowdale *yan-a-dick, yan-a-bumfit*.

But *is* the Score really a relic of the Cumbric speech of the area, which, though becoming progressively corrupt, has survived for some seven or eight centuries after the death of the language itself? The answer seems to be 'possibly, but not necessarily'. Jackson, as we have seen, accepts that is what it is. Ellis however had taken the view (1877−79:322) that to regard them as part of the 'original British speech' of the old Cumbrian kingdom would call for 'great theoretical boldness' and inclined to regard them 'as a comparatively recent importation'. Barry surveys the evidence and comes to the conclusion (1969:82) that 'if the numerals are a survival, it will, unfortunately, probably never be conclusively demonstrated'.

The other hypothesis, namely that the numerals were imported to Cumberland and neighbouring areas at a relatively late date, exists in two versions. According to the first, they could have been imported from southern Scotland − but this really barely modifies the situation: in that case the numerals would still be Cumbric, though originating in a different area. In other words, Barry's comment (*ibid.*, 83) that 'importation from Scotland . . . presents many of the same problems as the survival hypothesis since it implies survival in the border counties' does not go far enough: this *is* the survival hypothesis in a slightly different form. The only real 'importation hypothesis' is represented by the second version, which argues that 'somehow the numerals were imported from Wales into north-west England at a period subsequent to the Saxon [*sic* − read 'Anglian'] Conquest, probably during the medieval or immediately post-medieval era' (Barry, 1969:84). But, as Barry points out (*ibid.*), no substantial evidence in favour of this view has ever been presented. Other versions of the hypothesis suggest that the numerals may have been imported through the agency of Cistercian monks who had houses in Wales and the north-country and an interest in sheep-rearing (a feature of both areas), or of natives of the Welsh lead-mining areas employed in the lead-mines of Cumbria.

The only defensible conclusion one can come to in the present state of our knowledge is that the numerals must be of Brittonic origin but that there is no hard evidence of any kind to show where they came from.

While it is true on the one hand that not one single complete phrase of Cumbric has come down to us, there is evidence to suggest on the other hand that Cumbric had a strong literary tradition − which must have been a tradition of oral rather than written literature − and that some of these very early texts are known to us in a Welsh version.

The earliest Welsh literary texts, traditionally ascribed to two sixth-century poets, Taliesin and Aneirin, have Cumbrian associations. The fifty-seven Taliesin poems, singing the praises of kings and princes of Rheged, are preserved in only one manuscript, dating from the thirteenth century, and the majority of them are certainly of relatively late composition. Sir Ifor Williams however argues in his authoritative edition (1960) that about a dozen of them could well have been, in their original form (which is not identical with the form in which we have them), the authentic work of Taliesin. Aneirin's long poem, *The Gododdin*, consists of a series of elegies on a band of three hundred warriors sent south from Eidyn (Edinburgh), capital of the kingdom of Gododdin (situated, as we have seen, in south-east Scotland between the Forth and the Tweed), on a disastrous expedition against the Angles of Bernicia and Deira (later to be joined together as Northumbria). A battle took place at Catraeth (almost certainly to be identified with Catterick in northern Yorkshire) in which the force from Gododdin was wiped out almost to the last man. To fit in with what we know of the history of Bernicia and Deira, this must have taken place between 586 and 605, and perhaps in the period 588–90 (see Jackson, 1969:12), and Kenneth Jackson states (*ibid.*, 63) his 'firm conviction' that *The Gododdin* in its original form was composed 'quite soon after the battle'. Sir Ifor Williams, to whom we owe the authoritative edition (1938) of this text too, had also argued that the earliest version of the poem was composed in the sixth century. On the other hand, there are those[1] who point out that the arguments for a sixth-century dating for these two works are by no means conclusive and that a dating as late as the ninth century cannot be excluded.

If one accepts the early dating, then, to be consistent, one must also accept that Taliesin and Aneirin composed their poems in the kingdoms of the northern Britons (Rheged in the case of Taliesin, Gododdin in the case of Aneirin[2]), and that the language they wrote in was not, in the strictest sense of the word, Welsh, but Cumbric. What we now have, of course, is not the poems in their original state: not only do the manuscripts date from several centuries after the alleged date of composition, but the text is indisputably in Welsh, not in Cumbric. This however presents no real problem. It can be assumed that, like much poetry of the Dark Ages, these poems were composed not to be read but to be recited publicly or declaimed by bards, and that they were transmitted orally from one generation of bards to another for some hundreds of years. In the course of time, the language would be to some extent modernized and, if necessary, adapted to Welsh rather than Cumbric conventions, and the text itself would be modified, not only by the substitution here and there of one word or phrase for another but by the omission of some passages and the interpolation of others.

The most we can say, then, is that some – certainly not all – of the poetry attributed to Taliesin and Aneirin *may* have been composed in the sixth century, and in Cumbric. Be that as it may, there is a certain irony in the possibility that the two earliest known literary works emanating from Britain

---

[1] See in particular David Greene, 'Linguistic considerations in the dating of early Welsh verse', *Studia Celtica*, 6 (1971):1–11, and Proinsias MacCana's review of Jackson (1969), *Celtica*, 9 (1971):316–29.

[2] The subtitle of Kenneth Jackson's book on *The Gododdin* (1969) is 'The Oldest Scottish Poem'.

were composed in one of the least-known languages to have been spoken in this island in historical times.

References

Barry, Michael (1964). 'Traditional enumeration in the North Country.' *Folk Life,* 7:75–91 (+ tables).

Ellis, Alexander J. (1877–79). 'The Anglo-Cumbric Score.' *Transactions of the Philological society*, 316–72.

Jackson, Kenneth (1953). *Language and History in Early Britain*. Edinburgh: Edinburgh University Press.

—(1955). 'The Britons in southern Scotland.' *Antiquity*, 29:77–88

—(1963). 'Angles and Britons in Northumbria and Cumbria' in *Angles and Britons* (six O'Donnell Lectures by various scholars), Cardiff: University of Wales Press, pp. 60–84.

—(1969). *The Gododdin. The Oldest Scottish Poem*. Edinburgh: Edinburgh University Press.

Kirby, D.P. (1971). 'Britons and Angles', in *Who are the Scots*? (ed. Gordon Menzies), London: BBC, pp. 80–9.

Nicolaisen, W.F.H. (1964). 'Celts and Anglo-Saxons in the Scottish border counties.' *Scottish Studies*, 8:141–71.

Williams, Ifor (ed.) (1938). *Canu Aneirin*. Cardiff: University of Wales Press.

—(ed.) (1960). *Canu Taliesin*. Cardiff: University of Wales Press.

11 Celtic Pictish

We saw in Chapter 2 that the language of the Pictish inscriptions of northern Scotland is, in the view of most scholars, both unintelligible and unidentifiable. The most one can say with any certainty is that it is not only not Celtic but not even Indo-European. We also saw, however, that there is evidence for the existence in more or less the same area of another language, which *was* Celtic, and we now turn to survey the little that is known of this 'Celtic Pictish' and its relations, if any, with other varieties of Celtic that are known to have existed in Scotland.

The evidence for this language is of two kinds.

First, there are names of places and people that occur in classical writers (see Jackson, 1955:134–8). Kenneth Jackson considers that sixteen names in northern Scotland occurring in Ptolemy's map (second century AD) are Celtic, and that all of these *could* be P-Celtic and two of them, *Bannatia* ('probably the Roman fort at Dalingross, Perthshire' – Rivet and Smith, 1979:262) and *Decantae* (the name of a tribe), certainly are. Of the occasional Celtic names occurring in other texts, some (e.g. *Uepogenus*, a personal name that occurs in a third-century inscription) are certainly P-Celtic, while the remainder (e.g. *Calgacus*, whose name appears in Tacitus, and *Argentocoxos* 'Silver Leg', a third-century AD chief mentioned by Dio Cassius) could be either P-Celtic or Q-Celtic: none are *necessarily* Q-Celtic. Much later, the *Annals of Ulster* for AD 726 refer to a Pict by the name of *Tolarggan Maphan*, a name that in Jackson's view (*ibid.*, 145) certainly contains the P-Celtic word for 'son', *map*. Finally, though some of the names given in the list of Pictish kings (the earliest and most reliable version of which is found in a manuscript dating probably from the tenth century) are certainly not Celtic, others, such as *Drostan, Uuen, Tarain, Lutrin* and *Onuist* just as certainly *are* Celtic, and P-Celtic at that.

The other source of evidence for P-Celtic in northern Scotland is place-names. These provide such P-Celtic elements as *carden* (e.g. *Pluscarden, Kincardine*) (cognate with Welsh *cardden* 'thicket'), *pert* (*Perth, Larbert*, etc. – cf. Welsh *perth* 'hedge'), *lanerc* (*Lanrick, Lendrick*, etc. – cf. Welsh *llannerch* 'glade, clearing'), *pevr* (*Peffery, Strathpeffer*, etc. – cf. Welsh *pefr* 'shining'), *aber* (e.g. *Aberdeen* – cf. Welsh *aber* 'river mouth, confluence').[7]

Fragmentary though the evidence is, it is nevertheless enough to establish that, at some stage, a form of P-Celtic was in use throughout much of the area associated with the Picts. One might easily assume that one more or less

---

[1] For further examples of these elements, see Nicolaisen, 1976:158–65.

homogeneous form of P-Celtic was spoken all over Scotland, and that it remained longest in the south-west, as Cumbric (see Chapter 10). There is some evidence however for a differential distribution of certain P-Celtic place-name elements in Pictland on the one hand and in the Cumbric area on the other. In particular, in the area stretching from the Firth of Forth to Sutherland, there are many instances of such names beginning in an element that occurs only four times further south, namely *Pit-* (*Pittenweem, Pitlochry, Pitbladdo, Pitcaple*, etc.).[2] This, it is generally agreed, is cognate with Welsh and Cornish *peth* 'thing', but seems to have had the meaning of 'a piece (of land)'. Interestingly, there is evidence that the P-Celtic speech of Gaul had a cognate word, **petia*, also meaning 'a piece of land'.[3] This semantic parallel between the Celtic of Pictland and Gaulish, which is not shared by Brittonic, leads Jackson to suggest (1955:148) that this particular element was 'part of the vocabulary of a P-Celtic people who were distinct from the Brittonic tribes south of the wall,[4] and it may perhaps hint that their connexions were with the Gauls at least as much as with the Britons'. In support of this interpretation, Jackson points (*ibid.*, 149) to the fact that, whereas some P-Celtic features are found in both northern and southern Scotland, others, such as *din* 'fort', *penn* 'head, hill', and *moel* 'bare hill', that occur widely in the Cumbric area (and in Welsh), are unknown in Pictland, which suggests that they were not characteristic of the Celtic speech of that area.[5]

Jackson is careful not to overestimate the strength of the evidence. He does however go so far as to suggest that the 'slight indications' of possible affinities with Gaulish rather than Brittonic (from which, in most respects, 'Pictish Celtic' was perhaps indistinguishable) could lead us to recognize the language in question as 'a third dialect of the P-Celtic family, parallel to the other two, neither Gaulish nor Brittonic, though Gallo-Brittonic in descent and closely related to both' (*ibid.*, 152).

Even this cautiously expressed view has not, however, gone unchallenged. In particular, Professor Nicolaisen (1975:164–71) has stressed the fact that, as Jackson had already pointed out, a number of P-Celtic elements such as *carden, pert, lanerc, pevr* and *aber* (see above) occur both north and south

---

[2] The second element of these names is nearly always Gaelic, which suggests that 'the Pictish word *pett* was borrowed and applied by the incoming Gaelic population as a convenient toponymic generic while seemingly also current for a while in everyday speech' (Nicolaisen, 1976:154).

[3] Our knowledge of Gaulish is strictly limited and the word *petia* does not occur in any of the Gaulish inscriptions that we have. It does however occur in the Low Latin expression *petia* (*terrae*) 'piece of land', which is certainly a borrowing from Gaulish, and which is the origin of the French word *pièce*.

[4] i.e. the Roman Antonine Wall running from the Firth of Clyde to the Firth of Forth.

[5] Further hints that 'Celtic Pictish' may have had closer affinites with Gaulish than with Brittonic are provided by a couple of possible phonetic features. The fact that the river-name *Loxa* (in Ptolemy) has become *Lossie* recalls the fact that *x* also became *s* in Gaulish (but the *ch* sound of *loch* in Brittonic) (Jackson, 1955:137). And the name that elsewhere appears as *Nechton* or *Nehhton* is given by Bede as *Naiton*: the development of *-echt-*to *-ait-* (or perhaps *-eit-*) is not what one would expect either in Gaelic (which has *Nechtan*) or in Brittonic (Old Welsh has *Neithon*, with *-th-*) but recalls the development of the group *-cht-* in Gaulish (*ibid.*, 145).

of the Forth–Clyde line, i.e. in both Pictish and Cumbric territory (and indeed also in Welsh). So, while by no means rejecting Jackson's view that some features may seem to associate Pictish with Gaulish, he suggests that the separateness of Pictish from Brittonic may have been overstressed and that 'Pictish, although not simply a northern extension of British (or Cumbric), should rather be called a dialect of Northern Brittonic or of Brittonic in general, and not a separate language' (*ibid.*, 171).

The evidence, as we have seen, is very slight. That some form of P-Celtic *was* indeed spoken in Pictland before the coming of the Gaels is certain. Its precise relationship to Brittonic and Gaulish is, and will probably always remain, problematic, as will the extent and nature of its coexistence with the non-Celtic language of the Pictish inscriptions.

References

Jackson, Kenneth (1955). 'The Pictish language', in F.T. Wainwright (ed.), *The Problem of the Picts*, Edinburgh: Nelson, pp. 129–66.

Nicolaisen, W.F.H. (1976). *Scottish Place-names. Their Study and Significance.* London: Batsford.

Rivet, A.L.E. and Colin Smith (1979). *The Place-names of Roman Britain*. London: Batsford.

Part III   Latin

12   Latin

British history properly so called begins with Caesar's two expeditions to Britain, in 55 BC and 54 BC respectively. However, each of these lasted only a few weeks and they had no direct and enduring effects on the linguistic situation in the island. The long-term Roman presence here began with the invasion of AD 43, in the reign of the Emperor Claudius. The northern frontier of Roman Britain was constituted, for most of the period of the occupation, by Hadrian's Wall which was first built about AD 122–7. For two brief periods, however, the frontier was much further to the north, along the Antonine Wall (so named after Hadrian's successor as emperor, Antoninus Pius) that ran between the Clyde and the Forth. First constructed *c.* 139–42, the Wall was abandoned for a few years in the 150s, reoccupied for a while, and then again abandoned for good at some date well before the end of the century, probably as early as 163.[1]

Roman Britain, in the sense of 'Britain as a part of the Roman Empire', lasted until 410, or perhaps a little longer though the balance of the evidence is against this. It is known that part of the army was withdrawn in 401 to campaign against the Goths who had invaded Italy and were threatening Rome itself. In 407, the army in Britain proclaimed a usurping emperor, Constantine III, in opposition to the legitimate emperor Honorius, and in the same year Constantine crossed to Gaul to ward off a threat from Germanic tribes that had crossed the Rhine, and took with him most of the forces, leaving Britain virtually unprotected. This history of the last years of Roman Britain is by no means clear, but it appears that in 408 there was a major Saxon raid on Britain to which the Britons reacted by rising in their own defence, expelling the Roman administrators of the island, and defeating the barbarians. It also appears that in 410 the Britons appealed to Honorius for protection, but that he was unable to afford them any assistance and urged them to see to their own defence. Rome no longer exercised any control in Britain.

This was not however the end of Roman influence in Britain. In some respects, life for the romanized population perhaps continued for a while much as before. In particular, the Latin language may well have continued in use, and our consideration of the position of Latin as a spoken language in Britain must take in not only the period of the Roman occupation but also the period immediately following.

---

[1] Until recently, it was generally accepted that the final withdrawal from the Wall took place in 184 or 185. However, research by B.R. Hartley (1972) has led to the conclusion, that has now been widely accepted, that occupation of the Wall probably ended over twenty years earlier.

From certain points of view, the most important division within Roman Britain is not administrative (the division into provinces), but geographical. The island falls fairly clearly into two geographical zones, a Lowland Zone, consisting more or less of England (other than the south-west) south of the Pennines, and a Highland Zone, consisting roughly of Devon and Cornwall, Wales, and the north. Of the two, the Lowland Zone was in Roman times the more prosperous, the more densely populated (few villas and civilian settlements were to be found outside the Lowland Zone), and the more extensively romanized.

The Romans were in Britain for well over three and a half centuries – that is, for a period longer than that from the accession of Charles I to the present day. Indeed, the influence of Rome was felt even before Claudius's invasion of AD 43,[2] and it was not long after the occupation of much of the Lowland Zone became effective that the process of romanization was seriously put in hand. The historian, Tacitus, for example, in his biography of his father-in-law, Agricola, who was governor of Britain from AD 77 to 84, i.e. only about forty years after the Claudian invasion, tells us that, in order to accustom the scattered and uncivilized Britons to peace and a settled existence, Agricola encouraged the building of temples, market-places and houses. He also educated the sons of British chieftains, with the result that those who had previously rejected the Latin language were now anxious to achieve a mastery of it (*ut qui modo linguam Romanam abnuebant, eloquentiam concupiscerent*) (Tacitus, *Agricola*, Chap. 21).

This is not the place to discuss the non-linguistic aspects of the romanization of Britain.[3] However, it is important for our purposes to stress that romanization did affect many aspects of the life of the island profoundly[4] and that this must inevitably have had far-reaching linguistic consequences.

That Latin was in widespread use as a *written* language in Roman Britain is beyond question. Our concern however is with its role as a *spoken* language, and the extent to which Latin was spoken, and in particular the circles and circumstances in which it was spoken, are far from clear. That Latin *was* used to some extent is, of course, not only inevitable in the circumstances of a prolonged Roman military and civil occupation, but can be proved on the basis of a variety of evidence that has come down to us.

[2] We have firm evidence for such influence in the fact that pre-Claudian British kings issued coins with inscriptions (usually abbreviated forms of their own name) in the Latin alphabet. For example, the name of Tasciovanus, who ruled over the Catuvellauni from about 20 BC to about AD 15, with his capital at Verulamium (St Albans), figures on his coins in the form TASCIO, and that of his son, Cunobelinus (Cymbeline), who died in AD 40 or 41, as CVNO. Pre-Claudian coins of the south-coast tribe of the Atrebates included, in addition to a name, the Latin word REX 'king'.

[3] For this, see Collingwood and Myres (1937), Liversidge (1968), Frere (1978), Johnson (1980), and also I.A. Richmond, *Roman Britain* (London: Cape, Harmondsworth: Penguin, 1963), John Wacher, *Roman Britain* (London: Dent, 1979), and H.H. Scullard, *Roman Britain: Outpost of the Empire* (London: Thames & Hudson, 1979).

[4] One thinks, for example, of the romanization of Celtic religious cults, the 'clothing of Celtic deities with the attributes, appearance and personality of the Roman gods' (Frere, 1978:366) (what is known as the *interpretatio Romana*) (see, for example, Frere, 1978:366–71, and Colin Smith in Rivet and Smith, 1979:12).

First of all, we have the observations of contemporary writers, foremost among them Tacitus whose comments on Agricola's policy of furthering the education in Latin of the sons of British chieftains we have already mentioned. In the early second century AD, the poet Juvenal tells us that Britons were trained by Gauls to plead (in Latin, of course) in the law-courts (*Gallia causidicos docuit facunda Brittanos*) (Juvenal, *Satire XV*, 112 – written in or after AD 127).

Then we have the numerous Latin inscriptions of various kinds that can plausibly be assumed to have been composed in Britain. Volume I of *The Roman Inscriptions of Britain* (Collingwood and Wright, 1965) gives over 2300 'public' inscriptions, mainly on stone but some on metal, to which must be added some thousands of 'domestic' inscriptions on wall-plaster, tiles and pottery known to have been made in Britain, wood, bone, metal, and so on, that are to form the matter of a second volume, some of which can meanwhile be found in A.R. Burn's anthology of inscriptions (Burn, 1969; see also Collingwood and Richmond, 1969, Chapter XI, 'Inscriptions'). Many of these, particularly the 'public' ones, are in good classical Latin and do not differ significantly from comparable inscriptions from other parts of the Empire. Others, however, particularly the more informal ones, reveal features that are characteristic of everyday spoke Latin (what is normally known as 'Vulgar Latin' – 'vulgar' being used in the sense of 'pertaining to the people').

The evidence for Latin as a spoken language in Britain as illustrated by deviations from Classical Latin has recently been set out by Dr J.C. Mann in an article (1971) in which he classifies the attested examples of each such feature. On this basis, Professor Eric Hamp has argued (1975:151)[5] that, although 'some features were characteristic of folk spoken Latin throughout most of the Empire', others were characteristic specifically of the spoken Latin of Britain. Furthermore, they are not to be attributed to the faulty pronunciation of those whose first language was not Latin but are truly representative of regional, i.e. British, Latin, and 'must have been transmitted across age-groups regardless of whether these speakers were bilingual or not' (*ibid.*). It should not be expected that features that must be considered as having arisen specifically within the spoken Latin of Britain will be either numerous or spectacular, but the fact that they exist at all is significant. In particular, Hamp draws attention to the form *defuntus* found in one inscription for *defunctus*, and a parallel form *santus* that (on the basis of Welsh and Breton *sant*) can be assumed to have existed instead of *sanctus*. These, he claims, are 'purely Latin', and British Latin at that, since such forms are not characteristic of the Vulgar Latin of other parts of the Empire. Other cases which, on the basis of highly technical arguments that it would be out of place to reproduce here, Hamp considers to be representative of British Latin are *sinum* for *signum* and *posuuit* for *posuit*.

Other inscriptions lead by their very existence to the conclusion that Latin was in everyday use. One that is often quoted is the following, scratched (while the clay was still wet) on a tile found at Newgate, London:

[5] The evidence and Hamp's conclusions are reproduced, with favourable comments, by Thomas, 1981:69–73.

AVSTALIS DIBUS XIII VAGATVR SIB COTIDIM

i.e. 'Austalis has been going off on his own every day for thirteen days', which is generally assumed to be a comment by a workman on another workman's absenteeism. A fragment of a tile from Silchester bears the one word PVELLAM 'girl', which has been interpreted, probably with reason, as 'part of an amatory sentence otherwise lost' (Haverfield, 1923:80). As a final example, we may refer to a couple of graffiti scribbled, in different hands, on the plaster of a room off the basilica at the tribal capital of the Silures at Venta Silurum (Caerwent, in Gwent). One of them, no longer wholly legible, perhaps read DOMITILLA VICTORI SVO, i.e. 'Domitilla to her Victor', and may have meant something like 'Domitilla sends her love to her sweetheart Victor'; below it, another hand has added the comment PVNIAMINI, 'For shame!' (Nash-Williams, 1952–4:162).

Finally, we have the evidence of the many words borrowed from Latin by the British language. About 800 of these survived in at least one, and in most cases more than one, of the three historical Brittonic languages (Welsh, Cornish, Breton), though not all are still in use, and it is more than likely that these do not represent the sum total of such words borrowed but that others have since disappeared.

Those that occur in Welsh have been studied in some detail by Henry Lewis (1943). The borrowings in question include a few that relate to basic, everyday objects, e.g. *barba* 'beard', *bracchium* 'arm', *caseum* 'cheese', *flamma* 'flame' (which have come down to Modern Welsh as *barf, braich, caws, fflam* respectively), and *piscis* 'fish' (which, having taken on a couple of suffixes, forms the first syllable of Welsh *pysgodyn*), and one wonders why it was that such words as these were borrowed. It emerges however from a classification made by Professor Kenneth Jackson (1953:78–80; see also Haarmann, 1970) that the great majority of the words fall into such categories as:

'Agriculture' (e.g. *brassicae* 'cabbage', *fructus* 'fruit', *molina* 'mill', *oleum* 'oil', giving Welsh *bresych, ffrwyth, melin, olew* respectively),

'Arts and Crafts' (*aurum* 'gold', *durus* 'hard', *plumbum* 'lead'; Welsh *aur, dur* 'steel', *plwm*),

'Building' (*columna* 'column', *fenestra* 'window', *pontem* 'bridge'; Welsh *colofn, ffenestr, pont*),

'Calendar and Time' (*hora* 'hour', *dies Mercurii* 'Wednesday' and the names of the other days of the week, *Aprilis* 'April' and the names of certain other months; Welsh *awr, Dydd Mercher, Ebrill*),

'Clothing' (*manica* 'sleeve'; Welsh *maneg* 'glove'),

'Daily Life' (*catena* 'chain', *frenum* 'brake', *rete* 'net', *solidus* [type of coin]; Welsh *cadwyn, ffrwyn, rhwyd, swllt* 'shilling'),

'Education and Intellectual Life' (*auctor* 'author', *liber* 'book', *schola* 'school'; Welsh *awdur, llyfr, ysgol*),

'Household, Kitchen, Food and Furniture' (*cathedra* 'chair', *coquina* 'kitchen', *cultellus* knife', *vinum* 'wine'; Welsh *cadair, cegin, cyllell, gwin*),

'Military Life' (*arma* 'weapons', *legionem* 'legion', *sagitta* 'arrow', *vagina* 'sheath'; Welsh *arf, lleng, saeth, gwain*),

'Officialdom, Administration, and Communal Life' (*carcerem* 'prison', *medicus* 'doctor', *plebem* '[common] people', *testis* 'witness'; Welsh *car-char, meddyg, plwyf* 'parish', *tyst*),

'Religion' (*altare* 'altar', *episcopus* 'bishop', *infernum* 'hell', *maledictio* 'curse', *peccatum* 'sin', *sanctus* 'holy', *spiritus* 'spirit'; Welsh *allor, esgob, uffern, melltith, pechod, sant, ysbryd*),

'Seafaring' (*anchora* 'anchor', *remus* 'oar'; Welsh *angor, rhwyf*).

As Professor Frere has put it (1978:350), these words 'derive in the main from experience of the middle and upper classes rather than from the agricultural peasantry'. Professor Colin Smith has, however, recently pointed out (Rivet and Smith, 1979:17, note 1) that many of the Latinisms in the Celtic languages are not recorded in writing until the twelfth century or later and suggests that they may in fact have been borrowed 'not during the imperial period, but later, from written Latin and from Church sources'.[6]

This admittedly fragmentary evidence has led to widely differing conclusions.

First of all, it cannot reasonably be doubted that Latin was, to use an anchronistic term, the 'official language' of Britain, the language of military and civil administration, of the law courts and of the schools. But how much further did it extend? In particular, to what extent was it spoken by the lower classes in the towns and by country-dwellers?

One major problem is that, although it is a reasonable assumption that the rural population was very largely, perhaps almost entirely, made up of Britons, we cannot be at all sure of the ethnic composition of the army of occupation and we cannot even make an informed guess as to that of the population of the towns. We know that units of the army were frequently moved around, sometimes quite literally from one end of the Empire (Britain) to the other (Dacia, corresponding approximately to present-day Romania), and 'the lingua franca of the great mass of the army must have been the general Vulgar Latin of the Empire' (Jackson, 1953:98). Jackson goes on to argue, however, that in the later stages of the occupation of Britain, there was a substantial amount both of local recruitment and of intermarriage with British women and that, in these ways, the rank and file may well have become to some degree British in speech, particularly in the Highland Zone.

As for the civilian administration, there can be little doubt that some officials were of Roman or at least of Italian origin or recent descent, but, on the other hand, 'the native upper classes came to play a part in local self-government and official life, and were encouraged to do so' (*ibid.*, 97). The language of administration and the law, however, can only have been Latin. But what of other sections of the community? As a recent work on Roman Britain puts in (Salway, 1981:506), 'there is some evidence that in Britain [Latin] remained a second language, but like English in India it was not only indispensable for public affairs but the only practical *lingua franca* in what was becoming a very mixed population'. Collingwood estimated that the Roman conquest itself brought into Britain at least 100,000 immigrants, of whom some 40,000 were soldiers, the rest being 'traders and camp-followers

---

[6] This point is developed in his recent article, 'Vulgar Latin in Britain: epigraphic and other evidence' (see 'References' to this chapter). I am grateful to Professor Smith for allowing me to see this article in typescript.

of every kind' and that 'during the generation that followed the landing of Claudius's army the influx of foreigners must have continued, though it probably declined and, by the end of the first century, was no longer very considerable' (Collingwood and Myres, 1937:181). The great majority of these early settlers, Collingwood considered, were either attached to the army or engaged in trade and so 'may be supposed to have taken up their abode for the most part in London, and to a lesser extent in Colchester, Verulam, Chichester, Silchester, and the other Roman or romanized towns of the south-east' (*ibid.*, 181–2). However, at a rough estimate (which is all that can be expected in the circumstances), the total population of 'more or less romanized inhabitants of Britain' (at some unspecified period) was about half a million, out of a total population of perhaps about a million (*ibid.*, 180). It follows therefore that, whatever language or languages they may have spoken, the greater part of the romanized town-dwellers were probably of British origin.

This brings us back to our main concern: what language or languages did they in fact speak? As has already been mentioned, opinions differ greatly.

Some of those who have dealt with the problem seem to have built far too much on the data provided by the inscriptions and in particular on the assumption that some of the words and phrases scratched on tiles and pottery were written by workers. But even if one accepts this assumption – which is not an unreasonable one – all it proves is that some workers were able to write some Latin. It does *not* prove that Latin was their normal everyday language. There is no justification for concluding, for example, on the basis of a few inscriptions (including the PVELLAM one mentioned above) from Calleva Atrebatum (Silchester) that 'we may be sure that the lower classes of Calleva used Latin alike at their work and in their more frivolous moments' (Haverfield, 1923:30), or for concluding, on the basis of the absence of Celtic inscriptions that, though we cannot prove that Celtic was *not* spoken at Silchester, 'all probabilities suggest that it was, at any rate, spoken very little' (*ibid.*, 31).

The interpretation to be placed on the fact that so many Latin words were borrowed by British is likewise open to contention. Arguing – but unconvincingly – that Latin influence penetrated even the phonetic and morphological structure of British, and drawing attention to the undisputed fact that even the names of some features (but, in reality, very few) of 'the elementary vocabulary of everyday life' were borrowed (e.g. *psyg*[*odyn*] 'fish', *braich* 'arm' – see p. 161 above) – David Greene claims (1968:76) that 'all this points to a vigorous Latin speech, both classical and vulgar, and massive bilingualism on the part of the speakers of British'. This does not follow at all. Earlier, Henry Lewis had gone much further and maintained (1946:22) that, in the course of time, Latin became the everyday speech of much of the south and east of the island, probably totally displacing British by the fourth century AD up to a line running, broadly speaking, from Exeter to York. At the other extreme, Myles Dillon and Nora Chadwick expressed the view (1972:34) that 'Latin never gained wide currency in Britain'.

Enough has already been said to indicate that our knowledge of the place occupied by Latin in various aspects of public and private life in Britain during the centuries of the Roman occupation is limited and uncertain. We can, at best, consider, on the basis of the fragmentary and incomplete evidence at our disposal and of reasonable assumptions, what the situation was *likely* to have been. This can be done most satisfactorily by considering in turn the towns (and villas outside the towns), the rural parts of the Lowland Zone, and the Highland Zone.

In the towns and villas, there can be no reasonable doubt that Latin was the language of administration and, at least for 'elevated' purposes, of all literate sections of the community. This does not necessarily mean that their first language was Latin. It is quite possible that not only the artisans who, as we have seen, sometimes scratched a few words in Latin on tiles, pottery or wall plaster,[7] but also many of the middle and upper classes acquired Latin only as a second language. Jackson plausibly suggests (1953:110) that it was via this stratum of society that Latin words penetrated into the British speech first of the house serfs and labourers of the villas and them more generally into the speech of the rural lower classes. The following comments probably represent as good an assessment as we can hope for of the situation in the towns and villas:

> Most educated Romano-Britons were no doubt bilingual, Latin being the language of law, government, business and cultured life, British that of the intimate family circle and of intercourse with the lower orders (Frere, 1978:350).

> In the rural areas, the villas were centres of romanised taste in many (but far from all) cases, and it is likely that their owners spoke Latin regularly, enjoyed literary culture . . . but had to maintain Celtic speech for communication with servants and estate workers (Colin Smith, in Rivet and Smith, 1979:13).

In other words, there existed a situation of what has recently come to be known as 'diglossia', i.e. a situation in which two languages in a given community are distinguished primarily by function, one acting as a 'high language' for use in such contexts as administration, education, religion, the literary arts, and the other serving as a 'low language' for informal everyday use. How far this situation descended down the social scale in Roman Britain we can only guess. Collingwood may well be going too far in maintaining (Collingwood and Myres, 1937:194) that 'the townfolk, even the poorest and lowest in the social scale, learnt Latin'.

Though there is room for difference of opinion about the extent to which Latin was spoken in the towns, we cannot doubt that it *was* spoken. But what kind of Latin was it? Certainly not the highly codified Classical Latin that we know from literary texts. It would perhaps be a reasonable assumption that the spoken Latin of Britain was much the same as the Vulgar Latin spoken in other parts of the Empire. In the first years of the occupation, this must have been so. However, after analysing the phonetic characteristics of the numerous Latin loan-words in the British language, Jackson argues

---

[7] For a description and discussion of some of these, see Liversidge, 1968:315–18.

(1953:108) that they reflect a more conservative type of Latin than the Vulgar Latin of other parts of the empire. The reason, he suggests, is that those Latin-speakers who were the channel through which loan-words were transmitted to British were neither 'the members of the army, nor the merchants, nor the middle and lower classes in the towns, all of whom no doubt spoke various types of the ordinary standard Vulgar Latin just as their counterparts did on the Continent', but rather 'the well-to-do landowners of the Lowland Zone, the native upper classes of town and country' (*ibid*., 109). And for them Latin would be a language acquired in the schools, a Latin characterized by features of pronunciation (and perhaps also of grammar and vocabulary) that would strike less well educated speakers as archaic and pedantic. However, in a recent paper (1982) in which he subjects the evidence to painstaking scrutiny, Dr A.S. Gratwick argues forcefully and persuasively that it does not support the view that the Latin of Britain was any more archaic in either its phonology or its word-stock than that of Gaul or Spain. So perhaps even the term 'British Latin' is an inappropriate one.

So much for the at least partially romanized population of the towns and villas. But what of the rural population of the Lowland Zone, and those who dwelt in the Highland Zone?

Some of the peasants of the Lowland Zone, many of whom would have come into contact with the romanized landowners and their families in the villas and, by way of trade, with the Latin-speaking town-dwellers, may well have acquired a fair amount of Latin, and many more may have had a smattering of it. There seems little reason however to suppose that Latin was in widespread use among them for any purpose whatsoever and Nora Chadwick's comment (1963:22) that 'the Roman Conquest did not change the population or the Celtic tribal units, nor the language of the people as a whole', insofar as it applies to the country districts, must surely be well founded. In this connection, it is significant that, as Colin Smith puts it (Rivet and Smith, 1979:18), 'when we turn to toponymy the balance is heavily tilted towards Celtic' – only some forty British place-names (excluding the names of provinces and seas) are wholly Latin.

If British remained the first, and probably for very many the only, language in the rural parts of the Lowland Zone, this was even more true of the Highland Zone. Remote from the possible romanizing influence of the towns, with no villas set in their midst, with a military presence but little Roman civilian presence of any kind among them, the inhabitants of this area can but rarely, if ever, have heard Latin spoken during the whole time of the Roman occupation. Their British speech remained, intact and unassailed.

Archaeological evidence from a number of sites shows that, for some considerable time before the end of the Roman period, the standard of living in the towns had declined significantly and even catastrophically. Even the inhabitants of the best houses seem to have lived in squalor, and private and public buildings were allowed to decay or were not repaired when damaged by fire or structural weakness. All this seems to have dated from the middle of the third century AD, and is paralleled all over the empire. The reasons for this economic collapse are obscure, in all likelihood it was brought about by misguided financial policies that led to massive inflation, coupled perhaps with growing hostility towards the towns on the part of officialdom and peasantry alike.[8] On the other hand:

> we have a picture of country life and the villa economy flourishing and even expanding slowly in the third and fourth centuries. One may reasonably conclude that the decline of the towns, those centres of romanization, must have lessened the proportion of Latin to British spoken in the province by the end of the fourth century (Jackson, 1953:112).

Neither this, however, nor the end of Roman administration in or around AD 410, meant an end to all traces of romanization or even the immediate disappearance of Latin as a spoken language. In the first place, some kind of public administration inherited from the Roman period, and with it the use of Latin, persisted for some time. The Church, too, exercised a latinizing influence – as Professor Charles Thomas has recently put it (1981:73), with reference to fifth-century Britain, 'at the very least, Latin was around wherever and whenever any Christians were around'.[9]

After 450, we enter 'a region where the light is dim' (Collingwood and Myres, 1937:313):

> As the Saxon settlements grew in strength, the Roman civilization of the Lowland zone was declining into a Celto-Roman civilization whose Celtic elements were more and more prevailing over Roman. Latin must have been less and less used. Rome was becoming a memory (*ibid.*, 316).

Or, as Jackson puts it, more positively (1953:117):

> It would be wrong, however, to go on to suppose that Latin was suddenly forgotten at this stage. Celtic though they were, the Highland chiefs at the end of the Roman period, or some of them, were nevertheless identified with Rome.

But the reference here, it will be noted, is, paradoxically, to the Highland Zone, the zone which was but lightly affected by Roman cultural influences (as distinct from the Roman military presence, which was well established in parts at least of the zone) throughout the period of the occupation. There is indeed good reason to believe that, in the fifth and sixth centuries AD, there was, for a variety of reasons, a considerable strengthening in the Highland Zone of cultural influences derived from what had been in earlier centuries the more decisively romanized Lowland Zone. 'We must', says Professor D. Simon Evans (1979:28)

> accept the view, based on valid evidence, that Roman culture and also probably the Latin language thrived anew in the so-called Highland

---

[8] The decline of town life and its possible causes are discussed at some length by Collingwood (Collingwood and Myres, 1937:195–207).

[9] For a wide-ranging discussion of the role and possible influence of Latin as the language of Christianity in late Roman and early post-Roman Britain, see Thomas's chapter 'Languages, literature and art' (1981:61–95).

Zone of Britain . . . during the two centuries after the ending of Roman rule, at the time when it was severely disrupted and in parts eradicated in the Lowland Zone.

Tangible evidence for the continued use of Latin is provided by the fact that the funerary inscriptions on the monuments that local British chieftains in Wales set up in the fifth and sixth centuries are all either in Latin (if on occasion a somewhat defective Latin) alone or else in Latin and Irish (i.e. in Ogams – see pp. 28–30). It must however be recognized that this does *not* necessarily imply that their first language was Latin, which would be highly unlikely. Furthermore, the custom of erecting such monuments may have derived not from the romanized Lowland Zone but rather from Gaul, whence it is known that missionaries set out for Britain in the fifth century. Nevertheless, the very fact that such inscriptions are found only in the Highland Zone is one of great significance. It tends to confirm the view that, at this period, there were more traces of Roman influence there than in the Lowland Zone. And the reason can only have been that, in the face of the advancing Angles and Saxons, romanized or partly romanized Britons from the Lowland Zone had fled to the comparative safety of the Highland Zone, taking with them some of their romanized customs, a knowledge of the Latin language, and a form of British speech that had been much more deeply penetrated by Latin than that of the highlanders.

All in all, then, the evidence seems to point to the conclusion that some knowledge and use of Latin persisted in the Highland Zone of Britain, or at the very least in western parts, in what is now Wales, for perhaps a couple of hundred years after the island ceased to be a part of the Roman empire. But it is a fair assumption – though only an assumption, as there is no firm evidence either for or against it – that this knowledge was more or less limited to the educated and the aristocracy, and that even for them it was a second language, a prestige language, and that their first language, like that of the mass of those around them, was British. Even among the ruling class, the use of Latin for any kind of secular purposes seems to have ceased in the early seventh century (see Jackson, 1953:120).

The role of Latin as a spoken language in Britain seems, then, to have gone through three fairly clearly defined, but overlapping, stages.

First, Latin was brought to this island as the all-purpose language of an invading army which was soon to become an army of occupation, and of the associated administration and traders, and, in due course, of the urban civilization that quickly became established. The next stage was the at least partial romanization of those Britons who dwelt in the towns and villas, and perhaps, though certainly not to the same extent, of the rural parts of the Lowland Zone. In time, perhaps after two or three generations, some of these romanized Britons may well have spoken Latin as their first language, but, for the community as a whole, it is likely that, in a diglossic situation, Latin occupied the role of a 'high language' and British that of a 'low language'. Finally, during the later years of the Roman occupation and for some considerable time, perhaps as long as two centuries, afterwards, the role of Latin even as a 'high language' became more and more artificial, Latin no longer had any real roots in the ordinary life of the community, and, around the year

AD 600, perhaps even earlier, British re-established itself, in those areas not yet taken over by invading Germanic tribes, as the only language in use for secular purposes.

References

Burn, A.R. (1969). *The Romans in Britain. An Anthology of Inscriptions.* 2nd ed. Oxford: Blackwell. (1st ed., 1930).

Chadwick, Nora K. (1963). *Celtic Britain.* London: Thames & Hudson.

Collingwood, R.G., and J.N.L. Myres (1937). *Roman Britain and the English Settlements.* 2nd ed. Oxford: Clarendon Press. (1st ed., 1936).

Collingwood, R.G. and I.A. Richmond (1969). *The Archaeology of Roman Britain.* 2nd ed. London: Methuen. (1st ed., 1930).

Collingwood, R.G. and R.P. Wright (1965). *The Roman Inscriptions of Britain,* I, *Inscriptions on Stone.* Oxford: Clarendon Press.

Dillon, Myles and Nora K. Chadwick (1972). *The Celtic Realms.* London: Weidenfeld and Nicolson. (1st ed., 1967).

Evans, D. Simon (1979). 'Irish and the languages of post-Roman Wales.' *Studies,* 68:19–32.

Frere, Sheppard (1978). *Britannia. A History of Roman Britain.* 2nd ed. London: Routledge & Kegan Paul. (1st ed., 1967).

Gratwick, A.S. (1982). 'Latinitas Britannica: was British Latin archaic?', in *Latin and the Vernacular Languages in Early Medieval Britain* (ed. Nicholas Brooks), Leicester: University Press, pp. 1–79.

Greene, D. (1968). 'Some linguistic evidence relating to the British Church', in *Christianity in Britain, 300–700* (ed. M.W. Barley and R.P.C. Hanson), Leicester: University Press, pp. 75–86.

Haarmann, H. (1970). *Der lateinische Lehnwortschatz im Kymrischen.* Bonn: Romanisches Seminar der Universität.

Hamp, E.P. (1975). 'Social gradience in British spoken Latin.' *Britannia,* 5:150–62.

Hartley, B.R. (1972). 'The Roman occupation of Scotland: the evidence of Samian ware.' *Britannia,* 2:1–55.

Haverfield, F. (1923). *The Romanization of Roman Britain.* 4th ed. Oxford: Clarendon Press. (1st ed., 1906).

Jackson, Kenneth (1953). *Language and History in Early Britain.* Edinburgh: University Press.

Johnson, Stephen (1980). *Later Roman Britain.* London: Routledge & Kegan Paul.

Lewis, H. (1943). *Yr Elfen Ladin yn yr Iaith Gymraeg* ('The Latin Element in the Welsh Language'). Cardiff: University of Wales Press.

—(1946). *Datblygiad yr Iaith Gymraeg* ('The Development of the Welsh Language'). 2nd ed. Cardiff: University of Wales Press. (1st ed., 1931).

Liversidge, Joan (1968). *Britain in the Roman Empire.* London: Routledge & Kegan Paul.

Mann, J.C. (1971). 'Spoken Latin in Britain, as evidenced in the inscriptions.' *Britannia,* 2:218–24.

Nash-Williams, V.E. (1952–54). 'The Forum-and-Basilica and public baths of the Roman town of Venta Silurum at Caerwent in Monmouthshire.' *Bulletin of the Board of Celtic Studies,* 15:159–67.

Rivet, A.L.F. and Colin Smith (1979). *The Place-names of Roman Britain.* London: Batsford.

Salway, Peter (1981). *Roman Britain.* Oxford: Clarendon Press.

Smith, Colin (1983). 'Vulgar Latin in Roman Britain: epigraphic and other evidence', in H. Temporini and W. Haase (eds.), *Aufstieg und Niedergang der Römischen Welt*, II, *Principat*, Berlin and New York: Walter de Gruyter, Vol. 29.2, pp. 893–948.

Thomas, Charles (1981). *Christianity in Roman Britain to AD 500.* London: Batsford.

Thompson, E.A. (1977). 'Britain, AD 406–410.' *Britannia*, 8:303–18.

13   English

English is central to the theme of this book. In nearly every other chapter, we refer again and again to English, to the relations between, say, Welsh, or Norse, or Anglo-Norman on the one hand and English on the other. Of all the languages dealt with in other chapters (and allowing for the fact that British is just an earlier stage of Welsh, Cumbric and Cornish, and that early Irish is continued as Scottish Gaelic), the only ones to which English is completely irrelevant are Pictish and Celtic Pictish, which died out in northern Scotland before English penetrated thus far.

For English is a killer. If there are still parts of the United Kingdom, in Wales, Scotland and the Channel Islands, where sizeable communities speak languages that were there before English, sometimes as their first language, nowhere in these islands is English not in everyday use and understood by all or virtually all. It is English that has killed off Cumbric, Cornish, Norn and Manx. It is English that has now totally replaced Irish as a first language in Northern Ireland. And it is English that constitutes such a major threat to Welsh and to Scottish Gaelic, and to French in the Channel Islands, that their long-term future must be considered to be very greatly at risk.

One could of course seek a more optimistic standpoint, and argue that, a millennium and a half after the English came to these islands, and many centuries after they had established themselves as the numerically, militarily, politically, economically, socially and culturally dominant community, there *are* still, within a day's travel, and in some cases within only a few hours' distance, of London, areas where other languages survive as the preferred medium of everyday life. Such a view is by no means indefensible. But one must remember too that, recently enough for tape-recordings to be made, the last speakers of Manx were still alive, that at the beginning of this century there were still some thousands of Irish-speakers in Northern Ireland, and that half a century or so earlier one might still have found a few people who spoke Norn and, less than a hundred years before that, Cornish still survived.

Who were the original English, where did they come from, and when? One of the best known 'facts' of English history − perhaps the best known apart from the date of the Norman invasion − is that Britain was invaded by the 'Angles, Saxons and Jutes'. And this belief has good documentary justification, since that is precisely what we are told by the Venerable Bede in his *Historia Ecclesiastica Gentis Anglorum* ('Ecclesiastical History of the English Nation'), which he completed in the year 731. But, unfortunately, Bede's account has to be treated with caution. In the first place it has to be remembered that he was writing not much less than three hundred years after the event. Furthermore, there are discrepancies between his account of the origins of the invaders[1] and two briefer accounts, dating from the sixth century. The Byzantine historian, Procopius[2], mentions Angles and Frisians, but not Saxons or Jutes, whereas his Welsh contemporary, Gildas, in his *De excidio et conquestu Britanniae* ('On the ruin and conquest of Britain'), which is believed to have been written no later than 550, i.e. only a hundred years after the events referred to, calls all the invaders Saxons. As if that were not enough, 'another clue is provided by evidence such as the place-name Swaffham in Norfolk which suggests that at least one group of Suebians arrived. Archaeology also attests the Franks' (Laing, 1979:23). A further problem is that, though the names 'Jutes' and 'Jutland' must surely be connected, there is no archaeological evidence that the Jutes (if indeed there ever *were* any Jutes among the invaders) came from modern Jutland, i.e. mainland Denmark. Nor is there any certainty that the Angles came from present day Angeln (in German Schleswig), though these names too are presumably connected.

The most plausible conclusion one can arrive at in the face of the uncertain evidence is that the terms 'Angles', 'Saxons', 'Jutes' and 'Frisians' do not denote clearly differentiated tribes, but are somewhat vague and possibly synonymous or partly overlapping terms for the Germanic-speaking peoples who crossed the North Sea to Britain from an area corresponding more or less to modern Friesland (divided between the Netherlands and Germany) and the Frisian Islands (stretching from the Netherlands to Denmark), and from the coastal areas of Saxony in north-west Germany.

The origins of the invaders are not the only problem in a period that has been called 'the most difficult and obscure in the history of our country' (Myres, 1937:325). Not only do we not know precisely who the original 'English' were or whence they came, we do not know for certain why they came, or in what strength. Germanic-speaking raiders had been attacking the coasts of Britain since long before the end of the Roman occupation, which is why the Commander of the chain of coastal defences erected in the third century from the Wash to the Isle of Wight bore the title of *Comes litoris saxonici* 'Count of the Saxon Shore'. But the later and somewhat shadowy event that is traditionally termed *Adventus Saxonum*, 'the coming of the Saxons', did not, it appears, partake of the nature of a raid. The Romans sometimes adopted a policy in frontier areas of enlisting the help of one barbarian tribe, as mercenaries or *foederati* ('allies'), against attack from other tribes from without the Empire. It would appear that, after the Imperial authority had been withdrawn from Britain, the romanized Britains followed a similar policy. According to the somewhat obscure account given by Gildas, and the later more circumstantial one by Bede (to whom we owe the names of the leaders concerned), the first Saxons to settle in Britain under their leaders

---

[1] For the full text of his account (Book I, Chapter XV), see the edition and translation of the *Ecclesiastical History* by Bertram Colgrave and R.A.B. Mynors, Oxford: Clarendon Press, 1969, pp. 48–51.

[2] A Byzantine historian may seem a strange source for English history, but Myres points out (1937:337) that Procopius 'probably derived his information from Angles who are known to have accompanied a Frankish embassy to Constantinople in his day'.

Hengist and Horsa came at the invitation of a powerful British leader, Vortigern, as mercenaries (against, it seems, their former allies, the Picts and the Scots). Having once established themselves, the Saxons (and, for the moment, the term must serve to denote all and any of the incomers) declined to leave when their services were no longer required. Over a period of perhaps about a hundred years, other groups settled along various sections of the east and south coasts and, in due course, made themselves masters of the greater part of the island south of the Forth.

We shall not attempt to trace even in the broadest outline the stages by which the English occupied the island (see, for example, Blair, 1956:27–49). By way of indication of the speed with which they spread out, we need only mention that by the time Augustine arrived in the year 597, they controlled most of southern England east of Dorset and the lower Severn, together with much of Yorkshire and parts of Northumberland and Durham. By the mid-seventh century, the Northumbrians has probably reached the Forth, and by 722 Ine, king of Wessex, had reached Cornwall, though it was to be more than another hundred years before the Britons of Cornwall were finally subdued.

Nor shall we attempt to follow the shifting, kaleidoscopic pattern of the early English kingdoms, which by the eighth century had been reduced to three, namely, Northumbria, Mercia and Wessex.

Where the English went, their language went with them. As we have seen (pp. 89–90), British-speaking enclaves may well have remained here and there, far removed from the main British-speaking territories of Cornwall, Wales and Cumbria, but, in general, England (with the exception of the extreme south-west and north-west) together with south-east Scotland was English-speaking well before the Norse raids began in the eighth century (see Chapter 15).

The English language of the period up to the early 12th century, i.e. until some fifty years after the Norman Conquest, is conventionally known as 'Old English'. Though there is no disagreement among scholars that, from the Forth to the Tamar, the language spoken was English – i.e., it was one language and not several – it is also beyond dispute that there were dialectal differences within Old English. It is not possible to draw clear lines on a map marking off dialectal divisions, but, provided we do not seek to be too rigorous in defining the zones in question, we can identify four main dialects of Old English. The northernmost, Northumbrian, was the dialect of England north of the Humber and of south-east Scotland. Further south, there is the Mercian or Midland dialect – with two main subdialects, West Midland and East Midland. (Northumbrian and Mercian are sometimes grouped together as 'Anglian'.) In the south-east we have the Kentish dialect, the dialect not only of the modern county of Kent but also of an area corresponding more or less to Surrey. The fourth dialect – i.e. that of the remainder of England south of the Thames, from Sussex to Devon, but excluding the Cornish-speaking area – is usually known as West Saxon.

The origins of the different dialects are far from clear. The most obvious explanation, and one that used to be widely accepted, is that they correspond to linguistic differences among the various groups that migrated to England, i.e. that these dialectal differences were already there before the Angles,

Saxons and others left the Continent. But this is merely an assumption, albeit not an implausible one. As we have seen, however, it is by no means certain that the terms 'Angles', 'Saxons' and so on in fact corresponded to tribal (and, consequently, linguistic) divisions among the incomers. It has therefore been argued (DeCamp, 1958) that the dialectal divisions of Old English could have developed in England itself as a result of various political, social and economic factors and relationships. In particular, it is suggested that Kent maintained trade and cultural links with continental England, that Frisian influence was therefore strong on the English of that area, and that the varying extent to which features of Kentish-Frisian pronunciation spread to other parts of England accounts in part for the dialectal divisions of Old English.

A substantial amount of pre-Conquest − i.e. Old English − material has come down to us. By far the greater part of it is in the West Saxon dialect, in which we have − to mention only a few of the more important texts − the Anglo-Saxon Chronicle, the writings of Abbot Ælfric (including many homilies and a grammar of Old English) and of Archbishop Wulfstan, and translations of a number of Late Latin texts (including St Augustine's *Soliloquies*, Boethius's *On the Consolations of Philosophy*, and Pope Gregory I's *Pastoral Care*, all of them translated by King Alfred). One of the major works of Western European medieval literature, the epic poem *Beowulf*, is also preserved for us in a predominantly West-Saxon dress, in a manuscript dating from around the year 1000, though both the area in which and the period when it was originally written are unknown.

The other Old English dialects are, in comparison, poorly represented. In Northumbrian we have four fragmentary poems and some interlinear glosses (word-for-word translations) of parts of the gospels added to Latin manuscripts thereof. Mercian is represented by similar glosses to a psalter and to parts of a gospel manuscript, by some alphabetical glossaries giving (as in a bilingual dictionary) the English equivalents of Latin words, and by a short prayer, while in Kentish there is little other than a paraphrase of one of the psalms and a number of charters (i.e. legal documents).

The distance that separates Old English from modern English can be illustrated by a couple of brief extracts (note that the characters þ and ð are both the equivalent of modern *th*):

(a) The Lord's Prayer

> Fæder ūre, þ ū þ e eart on heofonum, sī þ īn nama gehālgod. Tōbecume
> þ īn rīce. Gewurþe ðīn willa on eorðan swā swā on heofonum. Ūrne
> gedæghwāmlīcan hlāf syle ūs tō dæg. And forgyf ūs ūre gyltas, swā swā
> wē forgyfað ūrum gyltendum. And ne gelæd   ū ūs on costnunge, ac ālȳs
> ūs of yfele. Sōþlīce.

(b) *Beowulf*, lines 1383−5 (quoted after Whitelock, 196:106−7):

> Bēowulf maþelode, bearn Ecgþeowes:
> 'Ne sorga, snotor guma! Selre bið æghwǣm
>   aet hē his frēond wrece þonne hē fela murne.'

'Beowulf spoke, the son of Ecgtheow: "Do not grieve, wise man. It is better for each one that he avenge his friend than that he greatly mourn."'

As we shall see in the chapter on Norse (see especially p. 199), contact from the ninth century on with the Danes and with their language, which was closely related to Old English, was to leave a permanent mark on the vocabulary of English, giving it not only a large number of everyday nouns, adjectives and verbs but even the pronouns *they* and *them* and the possessive *their*. An even more extensive influence was to be exercised by French, in particular after the Norman Conquest, as we shall see in the chapter on Anglo-Norman. Since French is a Romance language, rather than a language closely related to English as Norse was, borrowings from French were less easily assimilated and the presence of large numbers of them on a page of English − and it was, at first, the written language that was principally affected − has the effect of changing markedly the appearance and, indeed, the character of the language. Anglo-Norman also served as a channel for large numbers of Latin loan-words to pass into English, and once the practice of borrowing Latin words through French had become established, then, inevitably, others were taken directly from Latin.

Among the hundreds of Latin words borrowed into English directly, not through French, in the Middle English period, i.e. the period from the early twelfth century to the mid-fifteenth century, are *conspiracy, contempt, distract, frustrate, gesture, history, include, index, individual, infancy, inferior, intellect, interrupt, legal, lucrative, magnify, mechanical, minor, moderate, necessary, nervous, picture, polite, popular, prevent, private, quiet, reject, solitary, submit, summary, suppress, temperate, tract, tributary, ulcer* (see Baugh and Cable, 1978:184−5).

It is largely because of the effect of this massive French and Latin element that English no longer gives the impression of being as closely related to its sister Germanic languages, German, Dutch and the Scandinavian languages, as they are to one another.

The effect exercised by Anglo-Norman on vocabulary was not however the only way, or even perhaps the most significant way, in which it influenced the fortunes of the English language. As we have seen, before the Conquest the West-Saxon dialect had established itself as the principal written variety of English:

> The history of the country caused this West-Saxon to become by the tenth century the accepted language for most vernacular literary purposes. Even the literature of other dialects, such as was most of the poetry, was re-copied into the 'standard' West-Saxon which, with local modifications, had become a sort of common literary language all over the country (Wrenn, 1949:24).

But the fact that English was replaced for a time by French as the dominant vernacular in the cultural field dealt a death-blow to literary West Saxon:

> The use of Latin for learned work, and of Norman French for aristo-cratic entertainment, reduced the English vernacular to a set of spoken dialects with little common impetus towards a norm or standard, and West-Saxon had no successor as a common literary vehicle (*ibid.*, 1949:26).

When in the late Middle English period a standard was gradually to emerge, it was to be on the basis of a different dialect. But which? Strangely, there is some uncertainty about this.

The first point to be made is that, if it is legitimate to refer to West Saxon as having represented, to some extent at least, a 'standard' language, then, in the early Middle English period, the language suffered, among other set-backs, that of going through a time of 'destandardization':

> One of the striking characteristics of Middle English is its great variety in the different parts of England. This variety was not confined to the forms of the spoken language, as it is to a great extent today, but appears equally in the written literature. In the absence of any recognized literary standard before the close of the period, writers naturally wrote in the dialect of that part of the country to which they belonged (Baugh and Cable, 1978:188).

Not only was there no standard, but even the 'idea of a kind of standard or common literary dialect which had been a feature of later Old English' had been lost (Wrenn, 1949:26).

The main Middle English dialectal areas did not differ greatly from those of the Old English period, except perhaps that West Midland and East Midland are often regarded not as subdialects of Mercian but as distinct dialects on a par with Northumbrian, West Saxon and Kentish (or Northern, South Western and South Eastern as they are often termed in relation to Middle English).

When English first re-emerged from the shadow of French as a literary language (though it had never entirely ceased to be written), no one dialect enjoyed supremacy. There are important Middle English texts in every one of the five main dialects.

The best known Middle English works in the Southern dialect are the poem *The Owl and the Nightingale* (*c.* 1250), attributed (perhaps wrongly) to Nicholas of Guildford, from Portisham in Dorset, and John of Trevisa's translation (1387) into a Gloucestershire dialect of Higden's *Polychronicon* (a history of Britain and the world), after which there is virtually nothing in Southern English. Kentish is best represented by *The Ayenbite of Inwyt*, 'Remorse of Conscience', translated from French by Michael of Northgate (Canterbury).

The various Midland dialects are well represented. West Midland has such major texts as the *Brut* (a poem of over 32,000 lines) by Layamon, and the *Ancrene Riwle* or *Ancrene Wisse* (a manual of devotion for anchorite nuns), both from the early thirteenth century. There is also one of the most important Middle English texts, *Piers Plowman*, probably written by William Langland, who hailed from near Malvern, in the second half of the fourteenth century, and the verse Romance *Sir Gawain and the Green Knight* and other poems, also from the late fourteenth century. In the East Midland dialect we have the later parts of the *Anglo-Saxon Chronicle*, which was continued at Peterborough until 1154, and, as early as 1200 if not before, a lengthy poem by one Orm, known (from its author's name) as *The Ormulum*, which, though of little literary significance, is of particular linguistic interest in that Orm uses a phonetic spelling of his own devising. Among later East

Midland texts are, from the early fourteenth century, *The Lay of Havelock the Dane*, and, from later in the century, the important works of John Gower (in particular, his *Confessio Amantis*) and Chaucer, both of whom wrote in what is basically the dialect of London, but who did not hesitate to adopt Kentish forms when these could provide a useful rhyme – Chaucer, for example, uses Kentish *ken* and *kesse*, instead of *kin* and *kisse*, when he wants rhymes for *ten* and *stedfastnesse*.

The following lines from the 'Prologue' to the *Canterbury Tales* illustrate the gulf that separates Middle English from pre-Conquest Old English:

> Bifil that in that seson on a day,
> In Southwerk at the Tabard as I lay
> Redy to wenden on my pilgrymage
> To Caunterbury with ful devout corage,
> At nyght was come into that hostelrye
> Wel nyne and twenty in a compaignye,
> Of sondry folk, by aventure yfalle
> In felaweshipe, and pilgrimes were they alle,
> That towards Caunterbury wolden ryde.

The language is by now recognizably English – and indeed, one suspects that the language of *Beowulf* would be as unintelligible to a man of Chaucer's time as it is to the modern reader who has not studied Old English.

There is practically nothing in the Northern dialect before about 1300, after which, even leaving aside for a moment the early works in the dialect now referred to as Scots (see Chapter 14), there are a number of important texts. Among the earliest of these are the *Cursor Mundi*, a poem probably from the Durham area, surveying the history of the world in some 30,000 lines, and a Yorkshire translation of the psalms. Also from Yorkshire are the poem *The Prick of Conscience* (c. 1340), by Richard Rolle of Hampole, near Doncaster, and, somewhat later, the cycles of religious plays known as 'Miracles' or 'Mystery Plays' from York and Wakefield. It is worth stressing that, though it was spoken over such a wide area (including much of Scotland), the Northern dialect at this time was remarkably homogeneous. Writing of the texts we have from before 1400, Skeat for example says (1911:33) that 'the Durham dialect of the *Cursor Mundi* and the Aberdeen Scotch of Barbour are hardly distinguishable by grammatical or orthographical tests; and both bear a remarkable resemblance to the Yorkshire dialect as found in Hampole'. However, there are still enough minor differences to make distinction possible.

In the course of the fifteenth century, we see the emergence of a fairly uniform or 'standard' kind of English that gradually comes to be used all over the kingdom for both official and literary purposes. (The terms 'standard language', 'literary language' and 'official language', though often used as if they were virtually interchangeable, in fact express different concepts. Since however, in the case of English, the 'standard language' also serves as a literary and as an official language, we shall here use that term without further qualification.)

It used to be held that modern standard English is based on the East

Midlands dialect, and in particular on the East Midlands dialect as spoken in London (for it stretched that far south), Oxford and Cambridge. Three main and, indeed, plausible reasons are usually given for this. One is that it enjoyed a special prestige as the language of the capital and the two university cities. Another is that, as a geographically central dialect, it was well placed to serve as the basis of a common means of communication for the entire country, being less unfamiliar and hence more acceptable to speakers of southern dialects than a northern form of English would be and vice versa. Thirdly, there was the influence of Chaucer (1340? – 1400?) and perhaps also of Wyclif (whose translation of the Bible dates from the 1380s) and his followers.

However, all this was perhaps something of an oversimplification. Professor M.L. Samuels drew attention some years ago to the likelihood that the survey of Middle English dialects, begun in 1952 under the direction of Professor Angus McIntosh, could 'cast light on the probable sources of the written standard English that appears in the fifteenth century' (Samuels, 1963:84). Having first shown that the written language of Wyclif and his followers (which used to be regarded as the language of Oxford, and then of London) is 'obviously . . . not "Wyclif's dialect" ', he demonstrates, on the basis of various linguistic features (such as *sich* 'such', *ony* 'any', *stide* 'stead'), 'that this is a standard literary language based on the dialects of the Central Midland counties, especially Northamptonshire, Huntingdonshire and Bedfordshire' (*ibid.*, 85) and that it was copied in areas as far removed from the Central Midlands as Somerset and Devon. Though Wyclif's followers, the Lollards, did not invent this 'literary standard', they were, he argues, 'a powerful influence in spreading it, in their bibles, sermons and tracts'. Samuels goes on to assert, plausibly, that the spread of a standard written English depends primarily on the *quantity* written. He stresses in this connection the fact that, whereas up to 1430 – 35 English is the exception rather than the rule in the administrative documents preserved in the Public Record Office, thereafter there is a sudden change 'from a mere trickle of English documents among thousands in Latin and French, to a spate of English documents' (*ibid.*, 87). And this written language is significantly different from that of Chaucer's London (i.e. East Midlands) English (for example, whereas Chaucer writes *yaf* 'gave', *nat* 'not', *hir* 'their', *swich* 'such', etc., the 'Chancery Standard', as Samuels terms it, usually has *gaf, not, theyre, such*, etc. – *ibid.*, p. 89, n. 10). So, if this is a form of London English at all, then it is 'a stage of London English changed beyond all recognition from that of a century previous' (*ibid.*, 89). Samuels goes on to argue that the previously popular theory East Midland influence is not supported by what we know of the dialect in question, and that the source of new influences on London English is the Central Midlands dialect which was 'the only one that achieved the status of literary standard' (*ibid.*).[3] The plausibility of this case is strengthened when Samuels is able to show that, whereas in the thirteenth and early fourteenth centuries, immigration to London had mainly been from East Anglia and neighbouring counties, thereafter immigration

[3] On the evolution of London English up to the fifteenth century and the decisive influence of the changing pattern of immigration, see Samuels, 1972:165 – 70.

from Northamptonshire and Bedfordshire increased. The immigrants would bring with them a form of English that, being geographically central, was more widely accessible than peripheral dialects (including that of the capital itself). The standard language, therefore, developed 'from a combination of spoken London English and central Centre Midland elements, which themselves would be transmitted in the spoken, not the written language. But the result was a written, not a spoken, standard, which was to spread considerably in use by 1470' (*ibid.*, 93).

The case for a 'Chancery Standard' has been taken up and persuasively argued by John H. Fisher who points out (1977:872) that, until the end of the fifteenth century, 'Chancery comprised virtually all of the national bureaucracy of England except for the closely allied Exchequer' and that, by 1400:

> the use of English in speaking and Latin and French in administrative writing had established a clear dichotomy between the colloquial language and the official written language, which must have made it easier to create an artificial written standard independent of the spoken dialects when the clerks in Chancery began to use English in their official writing after 1420 (*ibid.*, 874).

The estimated 120 or so civil servants of whom Chancery was composed were therefore responsible for introducing English as an official language of central administration in the mid-fifteenth century and so played a major part in the evolution of standard written English.

This variety of 'fairly modern, fairly standard prose' (*ibid.*, 887) was in fairly wide use at Westminster by the 1430s, and 'in view of the enormous prestige and ubiquitous presence of Chancery writing, it is not surprising that Chancery set the fashion for business and private correspondence' (*ibid.*, 891). The success of this particular variety of written English was assured when Caxton set up his press in 1476 at Westminster, close to the government offices, and, almost inevitably, adopted in his publications the type of English that was in normal use in official circles. It is true that printers gradually introduced a few London features for Chancery features (e.g. *are* for *be*, verb forms in -*s* instead of -*th*), and that 'Modern English is not Chancery English', and has continued to evolve. Nevertheless

> Chancery English of the early fifteenth century is the starting point for this evolution, and has left an indelible impression upon the spelling, grammar, and idiom of Modern English (*ibid.*, 899).

Spelling has changed little in the last four or five hundred years, failing to keep up with the evolution of pronunciation. The following extract is from Tyndale's translation of the Bible (1525):

> Ye can nott serve God and mammon. Therefore I saye vnto you, be not carefull for youre lyfe, what ye shall eate, or what ye shall dryncke, nor yet for youre boddy, what rayment ye shall weare. Ys not the lyfe, more worth then meate?[4]

---

[4] For the whole of this parable, Matthew 6, 24–34, in various English versions, beginning with one dating from the tenth century, see Bolton, 1972:68–77.

By the early eighteenth century, the orthography was virtually completely stabilized, since when there have been no more than a few minor changes (see Scragg, 1974:80–1).

The grammar has evolved in some respects. Among the most immediately striking differences when one compares the language of, say, the Authorized Version of the Bible (1611) with contemporary English are the abandonment of the second person singular (*thou, thee, thy*), the replacement of the subject pronoun *ye* by *you* and of the possessive determine *mine* (which was already restricted to pre-vocalic positions, e.g. *mine eyes*) by *my*, the substitution of the (originally northern) verb ending *-s* (*comes*) for the southern *-th* (*cometh*), the generalization of the auxiliary 'do' in questions ('When did we see you sick?' for 'When saw we thee sick?') and negative constructions ('I do not know you', 'Do not fear' for 'I know you not', 'Fear not'), and an increasing tendency to avoid inversion of the subject (i.e. putting it after the verb), as in 'Then came she and worshipped him'.[5]

And there have inevitably been far-reaching changes in the wordstock as civilization and life-style have evolved. Every year we all acquire new words, or new meanings for old words. Among the many recent innovations given in Strang's chapter 'Changes within living memory' (1970:23–69), are *apartheid, chromatography, collage, couchette, entrepreneurial, fail-safe, gimmickry, to hospitalize, marijuana, to monopolize, motorway, non-event, ombudsman, pizza, quasar, stop-go, teenager, terylene, voyeur, with-it;* other, older, words that have acquired additional meanings include *to commute, to escalate, gear* (= 'clothing'), *nucleus, redundancy,* and *square.*

The 'standard' we have just been discussing is primarily a *written* standard. But the written language and the spoken language, though not identical, are not by any means independent of one another, rather each influences the other, and so many of the conventions, and particularly the grammatical conventions, of the written language may well act as constraints upon the spoken language, at least of educated speakers when they are at pains to express themselves carefully. (However, speech that models itself too closely on the written standard is apt to sound stiff or pretentious – most of us, for example, would say 'Who did you see?' even if we were sufficiently observant of written standards to write 'Whom did you see?'.)

Although the term 'standard English' is sometimes applied to pronunciation as well as to aspects of the written language, it is perhaps not strictly applicable, or at least not in the way in which it is applied to written English. For example, we can say without contradiction that forms like *I seen it*, or spellings like *accomodate* are 'wrong'. This does not mean that they are any less efficient than the 'correct' *I saw it* and *accommodate*, but merely that they are excluded by the accepted conventions of standard English grammar and spelling. While it is also sometimes possible to label certain pronunciation features as 'wrong' (as when, for example, a foreigner pronounces the

<hr>

[5] On changes in the grammar of English in the last four hundred years, see Barbara Strang's *A History of English*, 1970, which adopts the strikingly original procedure of tracing the history of the language backwards, by two-century periods, from '1970–1770' to 'Before 370'; see especially, on '1970–1770', pp. 96–101, and on '1770–1570', pp. 136–53.

-*u*-of *guard* as a *w*), a considerable degree of latitude in pronunciation is tolerated, particularly in respect of regional varieties. We shall return to this point.

What *is* beyond dispute is that, as far as British English is concerned, one particular type of pronunciation enjoys a certain special prestige. This is what is generally known by the somewhat vague term 'Received Pronunciation' or 'RP' ('received' by whom? by those who adopt it?) and we must now briefly trace its origins and development. With the reservations expressed above, we can, provisionally and for convenience, refer to it as a 'standard'.

The existence of a *spoken* standard seems to be first recognized in the sixteenth century. Professor E.J. Dobson, the author of a thorough study of English pronunciation in the sixteenth and seventeenth centuries (Dobson, 1968), draws attention (1955:27) to comments such as those made by Sir Thomas Elyot, who urged in his treatise, *The Boke named the Governor* (1531), that the children of noblemen should be taught only the type of English 'which is cleane, polite, perfectly and articulately pronounced'. This recommendation and others like it from other sources allow us to draw the conclusion that 'by Henry VIII's reign there was already a clear idea that there was a correct way of pronouncing English, that some form of speech had already become a criterion of good birth and education, and that it was deliberately fostered and taught' (Dobson, 1955:27). The spoken standard in question was defined not merely geographically but socially, as being the language of the highest social classes and of those who had studied at the universities of Oxford and Cambridge: in brief, the language 'in use among well-bred and well-educated people in the Home Counties' (*ibid.*, 30). It is not clear, however, how widely (in either a geographical or a social sense) this standard was spoken in the sixteenth and seventeenth centuries, but Professor Dobson concludes (*ibid.*, 33) that a reasonable interpretation of the evidence is that:

> the common people everywhere spoke dialect and the standard language was the possession only of the well-born and the well-educated, that in the Court and the Home Counties one might expect all well-born and well-educated people to use this standard language, but beyond those limits, though one might still find men who spoke pure standard English, the greater part of the gentry and scholars were influenced by the speech of the common people (i.e. they spoke 'modified Standard'), and finally that in the far West and the North the standard did not apply at all.

Although regional accents were by no means excluded from the Court (it is related, for example, that Sir Walter Raleigh spoke with a Devon accent), nevertheless, for the reasons mentioned above, the pronunciation of the Court, based on that of the London area (though in the course of time it shed some features of London pronunciation), acquired the status of a prestige variety:

> it may be said to have been finally fixed, as the speech of the ruling class, through the conformist influence of the public schools of the nineteenth century. Moreover, its dissemination as a class pronunciation through-

out the country caused it to be recognized as characteristic not so much of a region as of a social stratum. With the spread of education, the situation arose in which an educated man might not belong to the upper classes and might retain his regional characteristics; on the other hand, those eager for social advancement felt obliged to modify their accent in the direction of the social standard. Pronunciation was, therefore, a marker of position in society (Gimson, 1980:89).

This prestige it retains. Its role however is that of a yardstick against which other varieties of pronunciation may be measured rather than that of a standard, all deviations from which are to be considered as incorrect. The eminent authority on English pronunciation, Daniel Jones, while stating his intention of basing his description of English pronunciation on RP which he regards as 'useful' and having the advantage of being perhaps more widely understood than any other type throughout the English-speaking world, is careful to make it clear that he does not 'consider it possible at the present time to regard any special type as "standard" or as intrinsically "better" than other types' (Jones, 1960:12).

There seem, in fact, to be two contrary tendencies at work at the present time. It is true, on the one hand, that 'the more marked characteristics of regional speech and, in the London region, the popular forms of pronunciation, are tending to be modified in the direction of RP, which is equated with the "correct" pronunciation of English' (Gimson, 1980:89). On the other hand, it seems to be increasingly accepted that, provided intelligibility is not impaired, regional pronunciations are neither 'inferior' (or indicative of a lack of education) nor 'ugly'. It is worth mentioning in this context that Daniel Jones, in both of his authoritative works on the pronunciation of English (1958, 1960) not only makes this specific point but, though giving priority of attention to RP, refers throughout to 'some of the more outstanding [British and other] divergences commonly heard in various localities' (Jones, 1958:4). Indeed, the demotion of RP from its privileged position seems to be already in train. Not only is it indisputably true that 'RP no longer has the unique authority it had in the first half of the twentieth century' (Quirk *et al.*, 1972:20, 1973:6), but, as Gimson points out (1980:90):

some members of the present younger generation reject RP because of its association with the 'Establishment' in the same way that they question the validity of other forms of traditional authority. For them a real or assumed regional or popular accent has a greater (and less committed) prestige.

This leads him to speculate (*ibid*.) on the possiblity that:

if this tendency were to become more widespread and permanent, the result could be that, within the next century, RP might be so diluted that it could lose its historic identity and that a new standard with a wider popular and regional base would emerge.

In reality, there are as many varieties of English (and of all other languages) as there are speakers − each of us has his own idiolect − and any attempt to reduce the varieties even of British English to a small number of categories is bound to be an over-simplification. Even if we restrict ourselves to dialects rather than to idiolects, we have to agree with Quirk *et al.* (1972:15, 1973:2) that 'it is pointless to ask how many dialects of English there are: there are indefinitely many, depending solely on how detailed we wish to be in our observations.' Fortunately, however, within the innumerable varieties of English there is what Quirk *et al.* call (1972:13 – 14, 1973:1) 'a common core or nucleus' which 'dominates all the varieties' and means that 'however esoteric or remote a variety may be, it has running through it a set of grammatical and other characteristics that are common to all', and this 'justifies the application of the name "English" to all the varieties'.

However, if any manageable account of pronunciation is to be given, an attempt must be made to reduce the literally countless varieties to a small number of well-defined categories, taking account of at least two main dimensions, namely the social and the geographical. The problem is that there is no simple correlation between the two: an individual's pronunciation is determined *both* by his regional origins *and* by his level of education and his social position (see Quirk *et al.*, 1972:15 – 16, 1973:3). One of the most successful categorizations is that made by Gimson who (1980:91 – 2) distinguishes three grades of RP, namely 'conservative' (characteristic of the elderly and of certain professions or social groups), 'general' (typified by what is generally considered to be 'BBC pronunciation'), and 'advanced' (or 'affected'), and three grades of regional pronunciation, namely 'educated', 'popular' (or less educated), and 'modified' (i.e., a basically regional pronunciation modified by the adoption of certain RP characteristics).[6]

Although many, or most, people speak with a regional accent (and it has been estimated that only about 3 per cent even of English people – 'English', not 'English-speaking' – speak RP, Hughes and Trudgill, 1979:3), very few nowadays speak what can properly be termed 'dialect' (the distinction being that the term 'dialect' covers much more than the term 'accent' – a dialect has not only its own characteristic pronunciation but also, to a greater or less extent, its own grammar and its own vocabulary):

> the English of most English (and English-speaking Welsh) people is neither RP Standard English nor a rural dialect. The vast mass of urban working-class and lower-middle-class speakers use a pronunciation nearer to RP, and lexical and grammatical forms much nearer to Standard English, than the archaic rural dialects recorded by the dialectologists (Wells, 1970:231).

As we have seen above, the regional dialects of English virtually ceased to be written after the fifteenth century. The exceptions are all the more noticeable because they *are* so highly exceptional – like, for example, William Barnes's *Poems of Rural Life in the Dorset Dialect* (1844), the language of which can be illustrated by the following extract:

---

[6] A useful and readable introduction to social and regional varieties of contemporary English is provided by Hughes and Trudgill, 1979. See also Petyt, 1980, Chap. 7, 'Social and urban dialectology: Britain'.

The gre't woak tree that's in the dell!
There's noo tree I do love so well;
Vor times an' times when I wer young
I there've a-climb'd, an' there've a-zwung
An' pick'd the eäcorns green, a-shed
In wrestlèn storms from his broad head.

Dialectal studies in England can perhaps be said to have begun as far back as 1674 when John Ray published his *Collection of Words not Generally Used*. The late eighteenth century saw the appearance of Francis Grose's *Provincial Glossary* (1787), followed in the nineteenth century by others (none of which however stand comparison with Jameson's *Etymological Dictionary of the Scottish Language* (1808–25)). An important advance came with the foundation of the English Dialect Society by William Skeat in 1873. This led to the publication of some eighty dialectal glossaries, but unfortunately, 'by 1896, when the *English Dialect Dictionary* was commenced, it was considered that the Society's function had been fulfilled and it was wound up' (Wakelin, 1972:46). Joseph Wright's *English Dialect Dictionary*, published in 6 volumes, 1898–1905, and including (in Vol. 6) an 'English Dialect Grammar' (also published separately), contained some 100,000 entries and was to remain for over half a century the principal monument of English dialectological research. Thereafter, serious work on the dialects of England lagged far behind what was going on in many other European countries. Skeat's comment (1911:105) that 'certainly no other country can give so good an account [as England] of its dialects' may perhaps have been true when it was written, but it was already out-of-date when it appeared in print, since publication of Jules Gilliéron's monumental *Atlas linguistique de la France*, the first great linguistic atlas of any area in the world, was completed in 1910. Recent years have seen the appearance of a number of French regional linguistic atlases, and meanwhile every major linguistic area and many minor ones on the mainland of Europe had been provided with a linguistic atlas. That of England (to which we shall return) did not appear until 1978, and, admirable though it is, it cannot compare in scope with many of the continental atlases. And, regrettably, it is now too late. The steady decline of dialects in the course of the present century and the escalating costs of dialectological research (not least in the costs of printing) must mean that there will never be a really major atlas of the English dialects.

A number of dialectal monographs, many of them of great value (see Wakelin, 1972:173), have indeed appeared since the early years of this century. But there was no worthy successor to the work of the English Dialect Society and Wright's dictionary until the *Survey of English Dialects* (*SED*) (see Orton, 1960 and 1962, and Petyt, 1980:88–93), based at the University of Leeds, was initiated in 1946 by Professors Harold Orton and Eugen Dieth (Dieth, who was Professor of English Language at Zurich, died in 1956, and the bulk of the work was directed by Orton). The ultimate aim of the *SED* was the compilation of a linguistic atlas of England, on the basis of direct investigation carried on between 1950 and 1961 by trained field-workers, using a questionnaire designed for the purpose by Orton and Dieth (and reproduced in Orton, 1962:39–113). Lack of 'the vitally necessary editorial and financial assistance' (Orton, 1962:22) has unfortunately meant that the plans for the atlas, which was to have provided 'interpretative maps of the whole country' showing 'important lexical, phonologial and grammatical distributions' (Wakelin, 1972:56), have had to be drastically revised. It has not proved necessary to abandon the idea entirely, but, as we saw above, what was eventually produced (Orton, Sanderson and Widdowson, 1978) was, by comparison with other linguistic atlases, a relatively modest volume: 406 small-scale maps, of which the great majority (249) are of phonological interest, while 65 relate to vocabulary and 92 to grammar (83 to morphology, 9 to syntax). It is a tragedy that it has not been possible to achieve Orton and Dieth's ambition – for, as one of Orton's associates has put it, 'although this work is styled "Linguistic Atlas of England", it is not . . . the full linguistic atlas planned as the crowning achievement of the *SED*' (Wakelin, 1972:57).

A subsidiary but nevertheless important aim of the *SED* has however been fully attained with the publication in tabular form of the 'basic materials' obtained by means of the questionnaire and on which the projected atlas was to have been based. This has appeared in four volumes, each in three parts, covering respectively the North of England and the Isle of Man (Orton and Halliday, 1962–63), the West Midlands (Orton and Barry, 1960–71), the East Midlands and East Anglia (Orton and Tilling, 1969–71), and the South of England (Orton and Wakelin, 1967–68).

We began this chapter by referring to the role that English has played in killing off other languages with which it has shared these islands. It is ironic to have to end with a discussion of the efforts made to rescue from oblivion the remnants of the dialects of English itself before they too decline to the point of extinction.

References

Baugh, Albert C. and Thomas Cable (1978). *A History of the English Language*. 3rd ed. Englewood Cliffs: Prentice Hall; London: Routledge & Kegan Paul. (1st ed. by Albert C. Baugh, 1935.)

Blair, Peter Hunter (1956). *An Introduction to Anglo-Saxon England*. Cambridge: University Press.

Bolton, W.F. (1972). *A Short History of Literary English*. 2nd ed. London: Arnold.

DeCamp, David (1958). 'The genesis of the Old English dialects. A new hypothesis.' *Language*, 34:232–44.

Dobson, E.J. (1955). 'Early modern standard English.' *Transactions of the Philological Society*, 25–54.

—(1968). *English Pronunciation, 1500–1700*. 2nd ed. Oxford: Clarendon Press. (1st ed., 1957).

Fisher, John H. (1977). 'Chancery and the emergence of standard written English in the fifteenth century.' *Speculum*, 52:870–99.

Gimson, A.C. (1980). *An Introduction to the Pronunciation of English*. 3rd ed. London: Arnold.

Hughes, Arthur and Peter Trudgill (1979). *English Accents and Dialects. An Introduction to Social and Regional Varieties of British English*. London: Arnold.

Jones, Daniel (1958). *The Pronunciation of English*. Cambridge: University Press.

—(1960). *An Outline of English Phonetics*. 9th ed. Cambridge: Heffer.

Laing, Lloyd and Jennifer (1979). *Anglo-Saxon England*. London: Routledge & Kegan Paul.

Myres, J.N.L. (1937). 'The English settlements', Book V of R.G. Collingwood and J.N.L. Myres, *Roman Britain and the English Settlements*, 2nd ed., Oxford: Clarendon Press, pp. 325–461.

Orton, Harold (1960). 'An English Dialect Survey: Linguistic Atlas of England', *Orbis*, 9:331–48.

—(1962). *Survey of English Dialects*. (A) *Introduction*. Leeds: E.J. Arnold for the University of Leeds.

Orton, Harold and Wilfred J. Halliday (1962–63). *Survey of English Dialects*. (B) *The Basic Material*. Vol. 1, *The Six Northern Counties and the Isle of Man*, Parts 1–3. Leeds: E.J. Arnold for the University of Leeds.

Orton, Harold and Michael V. Barry (1969–77). *The Survey of English Dialects*. (B) *The Basic Material*. Vol. 2, *The West Midland Counties*, Parts 1–3. Leeds: E.J. Arnold for the University of Leeds.

Orton, Harold and Philip M. Tilling (1969–71). *The Survey of English Dialects*. (B) *The Basic Material*. Vol. 3, *The East Midland Counties and East Anglia*, Parts 1–3. Leeds: E.J. Arnold for the University of Leeds.

Orton, Harold and Martyn F. Wakelin (1967–68). *The Survey of English Dialects*. (B) *The Basic Material*. Vol. 4, *The Southern Counties*, Parts 1–3. Leeds: E.J. Arnold for the University of Leeds.

Orton, Harold, Stewart Sanderson and John Widdowson (1978). *The Linguistic Atlas of England*. London: Croom Helm.

Petyt, K.M. (1980). *The Study of Dialect*. London: Deutsch.

Quirk, Randolph, Sidney Greenbaum, Geoffrey Leech and Jan Svartik (1972). *A Grammar of Contemporary English*. London: Longman.

Quirk, Randolph and Sidney Greenbaum (1973). *A University Grammar*. London: Longman.

Samuels, M.L. (1963). 'Some applications of Middle English dialectology.' *English Studies*, 44:81–94.

—(1972). *Linguistic Evolution with Special Reference to English*. London: Cambridge University Press.

Scragg, D.G. (1974). *A History of English Spelling*. Manchester: Manchester University Press; New York: Barnes & Noble.

Skeat, Walter W. (1911). *English Dialects from the Eighth Century to the Present Day*. Cambridge: University Press.

Strang, Barbara M.H. (1970). *A History of English*. London: Methuen.

Wakelin, Martyn F. (1972). *English Dialects: An Introduction*. London: Athlone Press.

Wells, J.C. (1970). 'Local accents in England and Wales.' *Journal of Linguistics*, 6:231–52.

Whitelock, Dorothy (1967). *Sweet's Anglo-Saxon Reader in Prose and Verse*, revised throughout by Dorothy Whitelock. Oxford: Clarendon Press.

Wrenn, C.L. (1949). *The English Language*. London: Methuen.

14   Scots

A problem faced by anyone seeking to discuss, or even merely identify, the languages of Britain is that of deciding how to cope with the form of speech and the written medium derived from it – for the moment I am deliberately avoiding using any such term as 'language' or 'dialect' – variously known as 'Scots', 'Braid (or Broad) Scots', or 'Lallans' (= 'Lowlands [Scots]'). The specific problem that confronts us is that of the linguistic status of Scots. In short, is it a distinct language from English, or is it merely a highly differentiated dialect of English?

It is not always easy to define what is a 'language' and what is merely one 'dialect' among others of a particular language. The distinction is not always based merely on strictly 'linguistic' criteria, on, for example, the degree of mutual intelligibility or otherwise of two linguistic varieties, or on a comparison of phonetic, grammatical or lexical features. On any such criteria, it would be difficult to argue that Danish, Norwegian and Swedish are separate languages – the fact that, though very largely mutually intelligible, they are acknowledged to be separate languages rests mainly on the fact that each has become the accepted and standardized language of a different nation-state. But when we come to consider Scots, there *is* no obvious answer, and the decision as to whether or not to accord to it the status of a 'language' is inevitably based to a considerable extent either on largely subjective criteria, or on practical considerations. The point has been very fairly made by J.D. McClure (who argues strongly for the recognition of Scots as a language) that the concept of Scots is 'extremely nebulous' and that 'it could easily be a matter of debate whether a given speaker was talking Scots or not, or whether a certain piece of writing was in Scots or not' (McClure, 1979:26). In planning and writing this book, I have changed my mind four times, and, in the end, I devote a separate chapter to Scots not because I necessarily accept that it is a 'language' rather than a 'dialect' but because it has proved to be more convenient to handle it thus rather than include some treatment of it in the chapter on English.[1]

---

[1] For a well-informed and balanced discussion of the linguistic status of Scots, which concludes that it is not possible to prove that 'actual Scots' (as distinct from the 'Ideal Scots' of MacDiarmid and others) has an identity that clearly distinguishes it as a different language from English, see Aitken, 1981. For a comprehensive general introduction to Scots, with sections on, *inter alia*, its spelling, pronunciation, and grammar, see Murison, 1972. See also Murison's summary account (1981:346–7) of the main distinctive phonetic and grammatical features of Scots. For a classification of the dialects of modern Scots, based on phonetic criteria, see Grant and Murison (1931–76), Vol. I, pp. xxiv–xli.

What is beyond dispute is that Scots, whatever its present status, is not a corrupt or debased form of Standard English.[2] It is derived from the North-umbrian or Northern dialect of English that, in the Old English period, was spoken with no major sub-divisions from the Humber to the Forth. During the later Middle Ages, this Northumbrian English was carried north and west by immigrant settlers and by the mid-fourteenth century it had replaced Gaelic throughout eastern Scotland as far north as the Moray Firth, and in most of the south-west. It thereafter spread further north, again primarily as the result of the migration of Lowlanders, to Caithness, Orkney and Shetland, in all of which it displaced Norn (see Catford, 1957) (map **4**).

There is no question but that, even after a written standard evolved in England, Scots was regarded by those who wrote it as a form of English. Not only Barbour, in the fourteenth century, but Dunbar, Lyndsay and others (see below) a century and more later refer to their language as 'Inglis' or 'Ing-lisch'. The word 'Scottis' was reserved (very properly, one might say, if one thinks in historical terms) for Gaelic, and it was not until the end of the fifteenth century that it was applied to Scots − the first recorded example of such a usage dates from 1494 (Templeton, 1973:6).

The fact remains, however, that a form of English other than that based on 'Chancery Standard' (see pp. 177−78) continued to be written in Scotland long after dialectal English had gone out of written use south of the border. The reasons are not linguistic but social and political. Until the Union of the Crowns in 1603, when James VI of Scots succeeded Elizabeth I on the English throne as James I, Scotland was a totally separate state, and it retained its own parliament and other political and administrative institutions until the Act of Union of 1707. So, whereas in the southern part of its territory, i.e. the north of England, the traditional Northumbrian dialect was ousted both as a standard and as a literary language from the mid-fifteenth century onwards, north of the border it was, for a while, neither in competition with other forms of English as a literary medium nor ousted from official and adminis-trative linguistic registers. J.C. Catford claims (1957:109) − probably without exaggeration − that 'from about the 14th to the 17th century a form of Scots (based on the "metropolitan" dialect of Fife and the Lothians) was the official and literary language of Scotland', a view supported by Charles Barber (1976:37):

> When Middle Scots was the standard literary language of Scotland, all written transactions (if they were not in Latin) were carried out in this language − official documents, private letters, contracts, sermons, pamphlets, works of scholarship.

The situation is well summed up by Skeat (1911:42):

> Hence it came about, by a natural but somewhat rapid process, that the only dialect which remained unaffected by the triumph of the Midland variety was that portion of the Northern dialect which still held its own

---

[2] McClure argues (1979:27) − in my view without good reason − that Scots cannot justifiably be described as a dialect of English because this 'conveys the misleading impression that Scots is derived from *modern* English'.

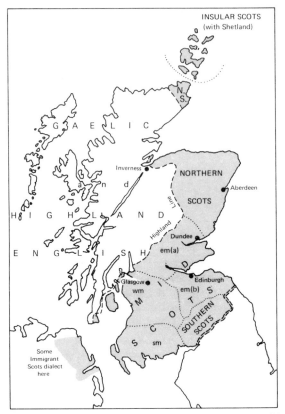

DIALECT MAP OF SCOTLAND

Dialect Criteria

	stone	who	he	dead	good	cow
N	steen	fa	he	deid	g(w)eed	coo
M	stane	wha ⎱ whae ⎰ (em.b)	he	deid ⎱ dead ⎰ (em.a)	guid	coo
S	stane ⎱ stien ⎰	whae (obsolete)	hei	died	guid	cow

Map **4**   Areas in which Northern (N), Mid (M) and Southern (SO) Scots dialect are spoken. East Mid (em) with sub-dialects (a) and (b), South Mid (sm) and West Mid (wm) are all subdivisions of Mid Scots. The Northern Scots dialect (N.S.) spoken in Caithness is basically the same as that of the Aberdeen area. (After Murison, 1981:346.)

in Scotland, where it was spoken by subjects of another king. As far as literature was concerned, only two dialects were available, the North-umbrian of Scotland and the East Midland in England.

Nevertheless, during the century preceding the Union of the Crowns, the influence of the southern standard on the spelling, grammar, vocabulary and idiom of Scots becomes increasingly noticeable: books and pamphlets printed in England circulated in Scotland, and Scottish writers and printers, anxious that their work should enjoy the wider circulation provided by the English market, tended to anglicize their products. On the other hand, the switch to English is not as sudden in manuscript documents: minor records and private letters and the like, although increasingly anglicized in the course of the seventeenth century, 'display a much wider overall range of characteristically Scottish spelling variation' (Aitken, 1971:199).

As a medium of literary expression, Scots was to survive, albeit primarily as a language of poetry. Before 1500, there was no Scots prose at all of any great consequence. There was a certain amount of Scots prose writing in the sixteenth century, mainly translations from French or Latin, but including also one important text, *The Complaynt of Scotland* (1549) that, though based in part on Alain Chartier's *Le Quadrilogue invectif*, is partly original. The language of the *Complaynt* can be illustrated by the following extract:

> There is nocht tua nations vnder the firmament that ar mair contrar and different fra vthers nor is inglis men and scottis men, quhoubeit that thai be vitht in ane ile and nychtbours, and of ane langage.

There was little to follow:

> Scots prose . . . was not seriously attempted any more. Scott, Galt, Susan Ferrier, Hogg and their successors in the novel restricted their Scots to dialogue between Scottish characters . . . The narrative of the novels is invariably in English, with the exception of Galt who experimented with a kind of Scotticized English in his narrative (Murison, 1979:11−12).

And in fields other than fiction, virtually nothing.

The verse tradition is much stronger. Here, we shall do no more than mention a few of the major figures. (For full-length surveys, see Wittig, 1958, Craig, 1961, Speirs, 1962, Lindsay, 1977.) The first figure of note was a slightly older contemporary of Chaucer's, John Barbour, whose epic poem 'The Bruce' dates from about 1375. The following (quoted from MacQueen and Scott, 1966:11−12) is a characteristic example of Barbour's Scots:

> The worthy kyng, quhen he has seyn
> His host assemblit all bedeyn ['at once'],
> And saw thame wilfull to fulfill
> His liking, with gud hert and will.

The Golden Age of Scots literature is the fifteenth and early sixteenth centuries, the period of the Great 'makars' (i.e. 'makers', 'poets') Robert Henryson, William Dunbar, Gavin Douglas, and Sir David Lyndsay of the Mount. Later, there is a succession of minor poets, and a variety of (often anonymous) ballads which 'have an unusually important place in Scottish literature' (Wittig, 1958:132), but no major figure until the eighteenth century when we have, among others, Allan Ramsay, Robert Ferguson and, foremost among all Scots writers, Robert Burns (1759−96). And thereafter there was, if not silence, little more than faint whispers, until 'the Scottish Renaissance' began after the First World War when Hugh MacDiarmid (the pen-name of C.M. Grieve) (1892−1978) − 'the man who really put Scottish poetry back on the map of Europe' (Wittig, 1958:281) − set out to create a medium for literary expression by drawing on all the resources of Scots, present and past, i.e. by taking his material wherever it was to be found, in the modern dialects, in the Scots writers of the past, or straight from the dictionary (see Murison, 1980). MacDiarmid himself used his language to fine effect. It was also taken up by others, including William Soutar, Douglas Young (who, in addition to writing original Scots verse, provided Scots translations of some of the plays of Euripides), Sydney Goodsir Smith, and Alexander Scott. But, if this is not an invented language in the sense that contemporary Cornic is, this latter-day Scots – which MacDiarmid himself referred to as 'synthetic Scots' and others have called 'plastic Scots' – is a highly artificial creation. If, on the one hand, 'C.M. Grieve had restored [to Scots] its dignity, largely by making it once more an adult language capable of expressing human experience in general' (Wittig, 1958:289), on the other hand 'the weakness of such of Grieve's work as.is in his "Synthetic Scots" can at once be traced back to the fact that he himself does not speak "Synthetic Scots", nor does anyone else. His medium is not a spoken medium' (Speirs, 1962:155). Speirs goes even further (*ibid.*, 15):

> A language consciously constructed or reconstructed by a few literary men, even though they may be potentially poets, out of earlier texts (however much loved) or by collecting words and idioms still in use in different parts of the country, or with the aid of national or dialect dictionaries, is not in any real sense a language. It is not the language that is spoken by themselves and the people around them, shaped by the experience of generations and out of which literature has been and can still be made.

This brings us back to Scots as a spoken language.

In Wales, as in other countries where it led to vernacular translations of the Bible and other texts, the Protestant Reformation served to maintain and perhaps even to save the traditional tongue. But in Scotland, where the Bible was not translated, the Reformation was to work against the preservation both of Gaelic and of Scots:

> By a Scottish law of 1579, every householder worth 300 marks had to possess 'a bible and psalme buke in vulgare language'. By the following year, a Bible printed in Scotland was on sale in the booths of Edinburgh, but it was not in Scots. It was a reprint of the English 'Geneva' Bible of 1561. Versions of Calvin's *Forme of Prayers* (in 1562) and *Catechism* (in 1564) had already brought the English language to the whole lowland population. The Scots were hearing English in church, and reading it in their homes – their children learned to read with an English Bible. English was not foreign any more (Templeton, 1973:7).

This was to have far-reaching repercussions. As the first editor of *The Scottish National Dictionary*, William Grant, pointed out, the inevitable consequence of the fact that 'the humblest Scot' was accustomed to hearing English in church, not only when the Bible was read aloud but also in prayers and sermons was that

> he came to regard it as the most suitable medium for religious expression. In the consciousness of the average Scotsman the feeling arose that his national speech was inferior to English, and he was apt to modify it

in the direction of Eng. or substitute for it the best English he could muster in addressing a superior or a stranger, or in touching upon elevated subjects of discourse. By the end of the 18th century English had supplanted Scots in fashionable circles, in the pulpit, the school, the University, the Law Courts and on the public platform (Grant and Murison, 1931–76, Vol. 1:xiii).

And his successor as editor of the *SND*, David Murison, was later to comment:

The decade on either side of that year [1700] may be said to mark also the last critical stage in the history of the Scots language. In 1707 the process which had been going on with increasing momentum for 150 years was finalized when the Union with England made the English of London the official language of Great Britain – and thenceforth Scots was relegated to the position of a dialect or series of dialects and there was a consequent shrinkage in the range of its usage and the scope of its vocabulary. It gradually became a mark of social prestige to speak English with an authentic accent and Scots was more and more restricted to the context of the domestic, the familiar, the sentimental, the comic – in fact to the ambit of folk-life (Murison, 1964:37).

And Murison has summed up as follows (1979:9) the historical process by which Scots was ousted from virtually all positions of prestige and influence:

Scots became more and more restricted in use and scope, having lost spiritual status at the Reformation, social status at the Union of the Crowns, and political status with the Parliamentary Union.

Yet, even if Scots is considered to be not a language but a dialect of English, it is not to be put on a level with other dialects. It may be true that, in terms of its status and role in society, spoken Scots has little more prestige than other dialects (those of the north of England, say, or of the south-west), and that, even as a written variety, it has a strictly limited range of functions – it is not, for example, used for technical prose, official documents, and other 'non-literary' purposes (see McClure, 1979). But it does have behind it an authentic and multi-secular, if in some respects restricted, literary tradition, whereas there is no such tradition in the case of the other dialects (even though they have occasionally served as the medium for 'serious' literature – one thinks in particular of William Barnes's poems in the Dorset dialect, see p. 183). Furthermore, these other dialects have not – or had not, until recently (see pp. 183–4) – been studied with anything like the same degree of intensity as Scots.

One important consequence of the maintenance of a Scots literary tradition and of the keen interest that went with it in recording its rich vocabulary and its specific grammatical features has been the production of a number of reference works that must be distinguished both, on the one hand, from the amateurish publications of local enthusiasts (some of them useful never-

---

[3] For an assessment of the methods adopted by MacDiarmid and others for extending the vocabulary of Scots, see McClure, 1981.

theless as sources of data) and, on the other hand, from technical dialectal monographs, intended only for the specialist.[4] Scots has at its disposal, and in manageable and generally accessible form, both a dictionary (Warrack, 1911 – frequently reprinted) and a manual containing a detailed phonetic description, a grammar, and a reader (Grant and Dixon, 1921). A century earlier, there had been John Jamieson's four-volume *Etymological Dictionary of the Scottish* Language (1808–25), now superseded by the end-product of two major lexicographical projects (see Aitken, 1964) designed to collect and record in their entirety the specifically Scottish lexical resources. The first of these two dictionaries to begin publication, and the first to reach completion, is *The Scottish National Dictionary*, work on which started in 1927 and which appeared between 1931 and 1976 in ten volumes (Grant and Murchison, 1931–76). The *SND* deals only with the period from 1700 onwards. The early period is covered by a complementary but entirely separate work, *A Dictionary of the Older Scottish Tongue*, of which Volumes 1 to 4 (letters A to N) and the first three parts of volume 5 have so far appeared (Craigie and Aitken, 1937–).

A systematic investigation of the present-day Scots dialects has recently been undertaken under the direction of Professor Angus McIntosh, as part of the Linguistic Survey of Scotland, set up at the University of Edinburgh in 1949 (see Catford, 1957). The first major result has been the publication of two volumes of the Scots section of a linguistic atlas of Scotland (Mather and Speitel, 1975–77).

The Linguistic Survey came, perhaps, just in time. Lacking prestige, long excluded from the services of the church, from the schools, from all public manifestations of officialdom, and, nowadays, from the mass media, except by way of local colour and character portrayal, open (to a degree that non-Germanic languages such as Gaelic and Welsh are not) to penetration of its phonology, grammar and, particularly, its lexicon by southern English, Scots has declined virtually everywhere. What one now hears over the greater part of the south or east of Scotland where Scots used to be spoken is merely a regional form of southern English, with a Scottish accent and a Scots element (greater or smaller according to the locality and according to the individual) in its vocabulary. Indeed, the editor of the *Scottish National Dictionary*, who is probably as well qualified as anyone to judge, has forecast that 'whatever the speech of this country [i.e. Scotland] at the beginning of next century, it is very doubtful whether it will be anything that is recognizably Scottish, at least in the ordinary historical meaning of that term' (Murison, 1964:47). Seven years later, he was if anything even more pessimistic, getting near to pronouncing the epitaph of Scots:

> The stark fact remains that the Scots language is in a bad state of decay and will assuredly pass into such a vestigial condition as to be virtually dead (Murison, 1971:179).

[4] Surveys of work on Scots are provided by David Murison, 'A survey of Scottish Language studies', *Forum for Modern Language Studies*, 3 (1967):276–85, and A.J. Aitken, 'Studies on Scots and Scottish standard English today', in A.J. Aitken and Tom MacArthur (eds.), 1979:137–60 (the latter has an extensive bibliography).

References

Aitken, A.J. (1964) 'Completing the record of Scots.' *Scottish Studies*, 8:129−40.

—(1971). 'Variation and variety in written Middle Scots', in A.J. Aitken, Angus McIntosh and Hermann Pálsson (eds.), *Edinburgh Studies in English and Scots*, London: Longman, pp. 177−209.

—(1981). 'The good old Scots tongue: does Scots have an identity?', in Haugen *et al.* (eds.), pp. 72−90.

Aitken, A.J. and Tom McArthur (eds.) (1979). *Languages of Scotland.* [Glasgow]: Chambers.

Catford, J.C. (1957). 'The Linguistic Survey of Scotland.' *Orbis*, 6:105−21.

Craig, David (1961). *Scottish Literature and the Scottish People, 1680−1830.* London: Chatto & Windus.

Craigie, Sir William and A.J. Aitken (eds.) (1937−   ). *A Dictionary of the Older Scottish Tongue from the Twelfth Century to the End of the Seventeenth.* Chicago: University of Chicago Press. (Vols. 1−3 also London: Oxford University Press.)

Grant, William and James Main Dixon (1921). *Manual of Modern Scots.* Cambridge: University Press.

Grant, William and David D. Murison (eds.) (1931−76). *The Scottish National Dictionary.* 10 vols. Edinburgh: The Scottish National Dictionary Association.

Haugen, Einar, J. Derrick McLure and Derick Thomson (eds.) (1981). *Minority Languages Today.* Edinburgh: University Press.

Lindsay, Maurice (1977). *History of Scottish Literature.* London: Robert Hale.

McClure, J.D. (1979). 'Scots: its range of uses', in A.J. Aitken and Tom McArthur (eds.), pp. 26−48.

—(1981). 'The synthesizers of Scots', in Haugen *et al.* (eds.), pp. 91−9.

MacQueen, John and Tom Scott (eds.) (1966). *The Oxford Book of Scottish Verse.* Oxford: Clarendon Press.

Mather, J.Y. and H.H. Speitel (1975−77). *The Linguistic Atlas of Scotland. Scots Section.* Vols. 1 and 2. London: Croom Helm.

Murison, David (1964). 'The Scots tongue − the folk-speech.' *Folklore*, 75:37−47.

—(1971). 'The future of Scots', in Duncan Glen (ed.), *Whither Scotland?* London: Gollancz, pp. 159−77.

—(1977). *The Guid Scots Tongue.* Edinburgh: Blackwood.

—(1979). 'The historical background', in A.J. Aitken and Tom McArthur (eds.), pp. 2−13.

—(1980). 'The language problem in Hugh MacDiarmid's work', in P.H. Scott and A.C. Davis (eds.), *The Age of MacDiarmid*, Edinburgh: Mainstream, pp. 83−99.

—(1981). 'The Scottish Language', in David Daiches (ed.), *A Companion to Scottish Culture*, London: Edward Arnold, pp. 345−7.

Skeat, Walter W. (1911). *English Dialects from the Eighth Century to the Present Day.* Cambridge: University Press.

Speirs, John (1962). *The Scots Literary Tradition.* 2nd ed. London: Faber. (1st ed., 1940).

Templeton, Janet M. (1973). 'Scots, an outline history', in A.J. Aitken (ed.), *Lowland Scots, Papers Presented to an Edinburgh Conference.* Edinburgh: Association for Scottish Literary Studies (occasional Paper, No. 2).

Warrack, Alexander (1911). *Chambers's Scots Dictionary.* Edinburgh: Chambers.

Wittig, Kurt (1958). *The Scottish Tradition in Literature.* Edinburgh and London: Oliver & Boyd.

15 Norse

Some two centuries ago, when Cornish was approaching the point of extinction in the south-western tip of Britain, another ancient tongue was dying out at the other extreme of the kingdom, in the Northern Isles of Scotland. A thousand years earlier, Norwegian Vikings had carried their Norse speech to the three groups of islands that lie between Norway, Iceland and Scotland, namely, the Faroes (which now belong to Denmark), Shetland and Orkney. In the Faroes, which lie some two hundred miles north-west of Shetland, it still survives and flourishes. Faroese is not only the first language of the inhabitants but has also been officially recognized, since 1948, as the chief language of the islands and is used in every sphere of official and cultural as well as family life, although Danish also retains its official status and both languages are taught in the schools.

The fate of the language in the other two groups of islands, which in the fifteenth century came under Scottish jurisdiction, has been very different. Though the inhabitants of Orkney and Shetland have by no means forgotten their historical ties with Norway, and on occasion draw attention to them, the language itself has disappeared − though not, as we shall see, without having left extensive traces in the toponymy and dialect of the islands.

It was in the eighth century that Vikings from Norway and Denmark began their expansion westwards and first appeared around the coasts of Britain. The earliest records of their coming are to be found in the *Anglo-Saxon Chronicle*, which remains in seven Old English manuscripts.[1] The first attested raid on England was made by three shiploads of Norwegians on the coasts of Dorset during the reign of Beorhtric (786−802). This however seems to have been an isolated incident, and the main brunt of Norwegian raids in the next few years was borne by areas further north. There was a ferocious raid on Lindisfarne in 793, and the following year an attack on another monastery in Northumberland, referred to in the Chronicle as *Donemutha* and probably to be identified with Jarrow, was resisted. The Norwegians are next recorded as raiding Iona and the island of Lambey (north of Dublin) in 795. It is highly probable that, earlier than this, they had begun raiding and perhaps even settling in the Northern Isles of Scotland, but Scotland has no equivalent of the *Anglo-Saxon Chronicle* and there are no contemporary written records to enlighten us. We must therefore depend on

[1] Our quotations are taken from the translation by G.N. Garmonsway, *The Anglo-Saxon Chronicle*, London: Dent, 1953. In some cases, the dating of events in one or more manuscripts can be shown to be erroneous, owing to a slip on the part of a copyist; in such cases, we quote the corrected date as given by Garmonsway.

the evidence of archaeology and place-names which, Professor H.R. Loyn considers (1977:45), enables us 'to argue in favour of a settlement in the North in the course of the late 8th and early 9th centuries'. From there, 'Scandinavians spread south to the mainland and west to the Western Isles in the course of the 9th and early tenth centuries' (*ibid.*, 48).

Before we turn to consider the Danish Vikings, we can briefly look at the later activities of the Norwegians. They probably colonized the Northern Isles not later than the early ninth century, completely dominating but probably not entirely expelling or physically exterminating the existing Pictish population of Orkney (it is uncertain to what extent the Shetlands were inhabited when the Vikings arrived). Some time thereafter, settlements were established in the Hebrides and other islands off the west coast (including the Isle of Man), and on the mainland — Caithness, Sutherland, and other parts as far south as the Moray Firth. In some of the islands of the west, which are now (or were until recently) Gaelic-speaking, Norse was probably the dominant language for a period, though how long is uncertain.

From the west of Scotland and the Isle of Man, the Norwegians reached Ireland, but, though settlements and kingdoms were set up, Ireland was not colonized as parts of Scotland were. It did however serve the Norwegians as a base for raids on Wales and other parts of Britain.

The most important of these moves eastward from Ireland was to the north-west of England. Whereas other parts of England were occupied by Danes, the evidence of place-names (which is particularly important in the absence of documentary sources) justifies the conclusion that, probably in the early tenth century, there was a substantial immigration of Norwegians from Ireland (and perhaps also from the Isle of Man and the islands of western Scotland) to Cumberland, Westmorland and neighbouring areas.

Danish Vikings also arrived in Ireland about 850 and were sometimes in conflict with the Norwegians. But the direct influence of the Vikings in Ireland itself is largely outside the scope of this book and we shall therefore merely record that Norse power in Ireland was effectively brought to an end in the early eleventh century. The Norse, however, though militarily defeated, remained a recognizable community, under their own kings, for a further century and a half.

After the early Norwegian raids on the north-east in the 790s, England was spared further harrying until a wave of attacks by Danish Vikings began in 835 when 'the heathen devastated Sheppey' (*Anglo-Saxon Chronicle*). There were further raids on southern England in the next twenty years or so, in 851 and 855 the Danes wintered in Kent, and then, in 865, what the *Chronicle* calls a 'great heathen host' arrived in East Anglia, with the aim it would appear not merely of raiding and plundering but of military conquest and permanent settlement. Within two years they had captured York and in the course of the next ten years they roamed as far as southern Scotland and Exeter.

Danish occupation of tracts of English territory later became not only institutionalized but in some degree recognized by treaty. King Alfred led the fight against the invaders with mixed fortunes until, in 886, an agreed boundary was drawn up between Danish-held territory (what was later, in the time of Canute, to become known as the Danelaw) and the lands that continued to be, in every sense of the word, English. The boundary ran roughly north-west from London, leaving Hertford, Buckingham and Lichfield to the English, and Bedford, Northampton and Derby to the Danes, and then from near Lichfield more or less due north to the Tees. West of this line, England north of the Mersey was to some extent, as we have seen, occupied by Norwegian Vikings while an area corresponding to the counties of Durham and Northumberland formed part of the English kingdom of Bernicia, and further north, again, stretching to the Forth, was northern Bernicia, which was to be ceded by King Edgar to the Scots in or about 973.

This early Danelaw (the use of the term with reference to this period is convenient if anachronistic) was 'a kind of Denmark overseas, conquered, occupied and organized by Danes, and clearly distinguishable from the rest of England by race, law, language, personal names and place-names, and not least by social custom' (Loyn, 1977:63). Had it lasted for any considerable length of time, it might have led to the perpetuation of the division of England into two distinct linguistic zones, one English-speaking, the other Norse-speaking. But this was not to be. Before his death in 924, Alfred's son, Edward the Elder, had wrested from the Danes all their territories south of the Humber. The next thirty years were a turbulent period, with the fortunes of war ebbing and flowing, and further complicated by an influx of Norwegians from Ireland who invaded and at times controlled Northumbria and its capital, York. In 954, the Norwegians were driven out of York and for more than a quarter of a century England was no longer under threat of Viking attack on sea or on land.

But there was to be yet a third stage of Viking assault. In the years 980–982, Danish raids began again, particularly in the south. These continued intermittently for some thirty years, becoming increasingly serious after 991, and by the end of 1013, virtually the whole of England had submitted to Sweyn Forkbeard, king of Denmark, and had accepted him as King of England in place of Ethelred the Unready, who fled temporarily to Normandy. In 1016 a compromise was reached, by which Ethelred's son, Edmund Ironside, was to take Wessex and Sweyn's son, Canute (Cnut), the remainder of the country. But later that same year, Edmund died and 'Cnut succeeded with common consent and through universal exhaustion to the whole kingdom' (Loyn, 1977:91). England under his rule enjoyed a much needed period of peace and prosperity, but the Danish hegemony was not to last. After his death in 1035, there was conflict between rival claimants and when, in 1042, his son and then king, Harthacnut (Hardicanute) died, Ethelred's son, Edward (the Confessor), was chosen as his successor and Dano-Norwegian involvement in the ruling of England was at an end.

Scandinavian linguistic influence can still be seen in place-names, in loanwords in English and to a limited extent in other languages, and in the runic inscriptions that have come down to us.

The study of place-names is a notoriously perilous enterprise. Many are not what they seem to be and it is essential to start, not from modern forms which may have been considerably distorted, but from the earliest forms that can be retrieved from documents and inscriptions (and even these must be used with caution). However, despite the problems and uncertainties, one *can* come to valid general conclusions about Scandinavian influence on place-names in Britain.[2]

Some of the most characteristic and widespread Scandinavian elements in British place-names are *-by* < *bý(r)*, 'town, village' (e.g. *Derby, Kirkby, Selby, Sowerby, Ormesby, Whitby*), *-thorp (e)* < *þorp* 'farmstead or outlying settlement dependent on a larger village' (this occurs in a great number of names of hamlets, e.g. *Northorpe, Southorpe, Easthorpe, Westhorpe, Kirkthorpe, Grassthorpe, Kettlethorpe, Oakthorpe, Painthorp, Thorpe by Water, Thorpe le Willows*), *-thwait* < *þveit* ' clearing' (e.g. *Braithwaite, Brackenthwaite, Smaithwaite, Kirkthwaite, Applethwaite, Ickenthwaite*), *-toft* < *toft* 'plot of ground, homestead' (e.g. *Brothertoft, Bruntoft, Lowestoft, Nortoft, Wigtoft*). Others include *-beck* < *bekkr* 'brook', *dale* < *dalr* 'dale', *ey* < *ey* 'island', *fell* < *fjall* 'hill', *garth* < *garðr* 'enclosure', *-holm/-hulme* < *holmr* 'island', *-ness* < *nes* 'promontory', *-scar/-sker/-skerry* < *skar* 'rock rising out the sea', *-wich* < *vík* (bay). In some cases it is possible to distinguish between the two main varieties of Scandinavian: names in *-thorp* are of Danish origin, while *-breck* < *brekka* 'hill, slope' (*Scarisbrick, Warbreck*, etc.), *-gill* < *gil* 'ravine' (*Reagill, Rossgill, Swarthgill*, etc.), *-scale* < *skáli* 'temporary shelter' (*Seascale, Scaleby, Winscales*) and *-slack* < *slakki* 'hollow' (*Hazelslack, Nettleslack, Witherslack*) are Norwegian. Evidence of this kind can sometimes throw important light on past history. Ekwall for example, points out (1925:76) that, whereas the Vikings who occupied the north-west of England were in general Norwegians, 'a small Danish colony must have existed near Manchester, on the northern bank of the Mersey, as indicated by the names *Flixton* and *Urmston* (*Flik, Urm* are Danish, not Norwegian), *Hulme, Oldham* (formerly *Aldehulm*) in Withington, *Levenshulme* and one or two others. The colony also embraced the adjoining part of Cheshire, where several *Hulmes* are to be found.' (It should be noted that, in Norwegian-speaking areas, *holmr* became *-holm*.)

The greatest concentrations of Scandinavian names in Britain are to be found, in chronological order of settlement, in the Northern and Western Isles of Scotland and neighbouring parts of the Scottish mainland, in the former Danelaw territories of the midlands and north-east of England, and in Cumbria.

Orkney and Shetland are of course full of Scandinavian names. In particular, there are the many names of islands ending in *-ay* < *ey* (*Whalsay, Bressay, Ronaldsay, Westray, Sanday, Stronsay, Ronsay, Eday, Egilsay, Shapinsay*), numerous examples of *-ness*, *Skerry* or *Skerries*, and *-wick* (including *Lerwick* < *leir vík* 'mud bay', *Otterswick, Hillswick, Erwick, Renwick, Braeswick* and *Rackwick*). Others include *Kirkwall* (< *kirkju-vágr* 'church bay'), *Foula* (< *fugl-ey* 'bird island'), *Fair* (Isle) (< *faar* 'sheep').

On the Scottish mainland we have, among many others, *Wick* (< *vík* 'bay') *Dingwall* 'the field (*völlr*) of the assembly (*þing*)' (cf. 'Tynwald', the name of the Manx parliament), *Golspie* (which includes the element *-by* 'town, farm' − the first part is either *guld* 'gold' or a personal name), and

---

[2] On the particular problems posed by the study of Norse place-names in England, see Gelling, 1978:215−36.

numerous names, particularly in Caithness, ending in *-dale* < *dalr* 'dale' (e.g. *Helmsdale, Berriedale, Westerdale*) or *-ster* < *staðr* 'place, settlement' (e.g. *Rumster, Stemster, Thrumster, Nybster, Brabstermire, Scrabster, Shebster*). In the west (see Henderson, 1910), including the Hebrides, there are numerous instances of *dalr, vík, ey*, such as *Eisceadal* < *eski* + *dalr* 'ash-dale', *Teamradal* < *timbr* + *dalr* 'timber-dale', *Alcaig* < *alka* + *vík* 'auk's bay', *Ramasaig* < *hrafns* + *vík* 'raven's bay', *Rosaidh* < *hross* + *ey* 'horse island', *Stornoway* is probably from *starnja* 'star' or *stjórn* 'rudder' + *vágr* 'bay', and, in names such as *Knoidart* ('Knut's fiord'), *Moidart, Suinart*, the *-art* represents *fjörðr* 'fiord'. Magne Oftedal (1962) draws attention to the difficulty of identifying with certainty Scandinavian elements in place-names in the Gaelic-speaking areas, but comments that, in general, the density of Scandinavian names is greater in Lewis (which he thinks may have been 'completely Norse-speaking during a limited period') than in the more southerly islands. Among the (unfortunately very few) examples he gives are *Tàbost* < *Hábólstaðr* 'high-farm', *Valtos* < *Vatnlausa* 'waterless place', *Hamairseadar* (the name of a croft in Lewis) < *Hamarsetr* 'rock farm'.

The extent of Scandinavian influence on place-names in the Danelaw emerges clearly from Kenneth Cameron's study (1975)[3] of names in *-by* and *-thorp* (see p. 197 above) in the territory of the Five Boroughs, i.e. the area of the north-east midlands settled by the Danes after 878 and corresponding more or less to the counties of Derby, Leicester, Nottingham and Lincoln. He shows that, in this area alone, there are over 360 names (303 of them attested in Domesday Book) in *-by*, and at least 109 in *-thorp*, including some parishes called merely *Thorpe, Thorpe on the Hill, Thorpe by Water*, etc.

As we have seen, the north-west of England was settled by Vikings of Norwegian origin whose immediate provenance was probably in most cases Ireland. In and around Cumbria are numerous Scandinavian names of towns, villages, streams, mountains and other natural features. Typical examples are *Bir(k) beck* < *birki* + *bekkr* 'birch-brook', *Caldbeck* 'coldbrook', *Gaisgill* < *gás* + *gil* 'goose-valley', *Reagill* < *refr* + *gil* 'fox valley', *Rossgill* < *hross* + *gil* 'horse-valley', *Scaleby* < *skáli* + *býr* 'hut town', *Gatesgill* < *geit* + *skáli* 'goat-shelter', *Sosgill* < *saurr* + *skáli* 'hut at a muddy place', *Witherslack* < *viðart* + *slakki* 'wooded hollow', *Brackenthwaite* < *brakni* + *veit* 'bracken clearing', *Satterthwaite* < *sætr* + *þveit* 'shieling clearing', *Threlkeld* < *þræll* + *kelda* 'spring of the thralls (serfs)', *Wasdale* < *vatns* + *dalr* 'water valley'.

The Isle of Man has its fair share of Scandinavian names, with *-ey* in *Ramsey*, *-by* in *Surby, Kirby, sker* and *staðr* in *Sherestal, vík* in *Dreswick*, and, of course, *Snaefell* 'snow mountain'.

Not concentrated but scattered round the coast of Wales are many more Scandinavian names (see Charles, 1934, 1938; Richards, 1962). Island names in *-ey* < *ey* and *-holm* < *holmr* abound: *Anglesey, Bardsey, Ramsey* (the first element in each case is a personal name), *Caldy* 'cold island', *Priestholm*

---

[3] For fuller information on individual place-names, see Kenneth Cameron, *The Place-Names of Derbyshire*, English Place-Name Society, Vols. 27–9, 1959, and J.E.B. Glover, Allen Mawer and F.M. Stenton, *The Place-Names of Nottinghamshire,* English Place-Name Society, Vol. 17, 1940.

< *prestr* 'priest' + *holmr, Grasshom* 'grass island', *Misland (Island)* < *meðal* 'mid' + *holmr, Skokholm* < *stokkr* 'stock, trunk' or *skokkr* 'trunk, chest' + *holmr, Flat Holm* and, across the Bristol Channel, *Lundy* (*lundi* 'puffin' + *ey*). Others on or near the Welsh coast are *Ormes (Head)* < *ormr* 'snake', *Fishguard* < *fisk* 'fish' + *garðr* 'enclosure', *Stackpole* < *stakkr* 'rock in the sea' + *pollr* 'pool, pond', *Milford* < *melr* 'sandbank' + *fjörðr* 'fiord'.

Old English and the contemporary Scandinavian dialects were closely related and it is a reasonable assumption that speakers of one would have no great difficulty, once they had become accustomed to it, in understanding much of what was said in the other. Otto Jespersen, for example, is of the view (1948:60) that 'an Englishman would have no great difficulty in understanding a viking, nay we have positive evidence that Norse people looked upon the English language as one with their own', and Barbara Strang considers (1970:255) that 'the languages were mutually comprehensible up to about the time of the Norman Conquest'. In these circumstances, it is not in the least surprising that a considerable number of Scandinavian words should have passed into English. What is perhaps surprising is how many common, everyday words are of Scandinavian origin, including the nouns *anger, bloom, dirt, egg, husband, knife, law, leg, neck, root, scrap, seat, skill, skin, sky, slaughter, snare, steak, window, wing,* the adjectives *flat, ill, loose, low, meek, odd, rotten, same, ugly, weak, wrong,* and the verbs *call, cast, die, gape, gasp, get, happen, hit, scare, take, think, thrust, trust,* and *want.* Even the pronouns *they* and *them* and the possessive *their* are of Scandinavian origin (the corresponding Old English forms were *hie, him, hiera,* the second of which remains in the familiar *'em* for *them*). Sometimes, both English and Scandinavian words remain as 'doublets', usually with a slight or occasionally considerable difference of meaning: e.g. English *ditch* ∽ Scandinavian *dike, leap* ∽ *lope, from* ∽ *fro, rear* ∽ *raise, shirt* ∽ *skirt, yard* ∽ *garth*.

So far, we have considered only literary English. There are many more Scandinavian elements in the dialects of northern England, where we find such words as *kyle* 'wedge', *lathe* 'barn', *lea* 'scythe', *lop* 'flea', *slem* 'mud', *stee* 'ladder', *glatten* 'slide', *slaip* 'slippery', while others that also occur in Scots include *bairn* 'child', *cleg* 'horse-fly', *grice* 'pig', *haver* 'oats', *neave* 'fist', *rowan* 'mountain ash', *steg* 'gander', *tyke* (< *tík* 'bitch'), *stour* 'large', *toom* 'empty', *hoast* 'to cough', *lait* 'to look for', *lake* 'to play'. Dialect forms from Scandinavian also provide doublets with more general forms that are of English origin, e.g. English *breeches* ∽ Scandinavian *breeks, shrill* ∽ *skirl, bridge* ∽ *brig, ridge* ∽ *rig*.

The Celtic languages of Britain, not being closely related to Scandinavian as English was, were much less profoundly affected by contact with the Vikings. Scandinavian influence on Welsh is negligible (though *iarll* 'earl' is certainly a borrowing from Scandinavian *jarl*), but somewhat more extensive in the case of the Gaelic languages, particularly Scots Gaelic which has far more Norse loanwords than Irish has. Some of these loanwords (see Henderson, 1910) are *coinne* 'woman, hussy' < *kona (kvenna), cròcan* 'crook' < *krókr, dail* 'dale' < *dalr, eilean* 'island' < *ey* + *land, fadhaill* 'ford' < *vaðill, gnìoba* 'peak' < *gnípa, òs* 'rivermouth' < *óss, rùta* 'ram' < *hrútr, sgeir* 'skerry, rock in the sea' < *sker, trosg* 'cod-fish' < *þorskr, ùig* 'cove' < *vík, uinneag* 'window' < *windauga* wind-eye, i.e. window'.

Some time before AD 200 or thereabouts the Scandinavians had acquired an alphabetic mode of writing in the form of the runes. This alphabet is sometimes known, from the first six letters, as the *futhark* (fig. 2). Although

f   u   th   a   r   k

Fig. 2   The first six characters of the runic alphabet or *futhark*.

the precise origins of the futhark are unknown, and have indeed been the subject of much debate, it is now fairly generally agreed that it is related to and probably derived from the Latin alphabet.

Most runic inscriptions in England are in Anglo-Saxon, many of them dating from the seventh and eighth centuries. There are about nine in specifically Scandinavian runes, but they are mainly of little interest for our purposes (see Page, 1973). A couple of them (one of them on a comb-case) were apparently worked in Scandinavia and brought to Britain, and the language of most others is either certainly English, or (as in the case of an inscription at Pennington Church in Lancashire) mixed Norse and English, or (in the case of some fragmentary ones) doubtful. The only one that is indisputably in Norse is scratched on one of the interior walls of Carlisle cathedral. Scotland however has over thirty Scandinavian runic inscriptions, a small number of them from Shetland, the Hebrides and the mainland, but the great majority of them from Orkney. A further twenty-nine are found in the Isle of Man. In general, these inscriptions are very brief, memorials to the dead, and so on, and have little linguistic and no literary significance. The Carlisle Cathedral inscription, for example, reads: *Tolfin urait þasi runr a þisi stain* ('Dolfin wrote these runes on this stone').

We now have to enquire how long the various Scandinavian languages continued to be spoken in these islands, and we must consider separately England and Scotland.

As far as the continuance of Danish in England is concerned, Ekwall (1930), while recognizing that there is no contemporary evidence for the survival of Scandinavian, considers that it could well have survived in some remote districts up to the eleventh or early twelfth century. More specifically, he argues that the evidence of place-names suggests that it survived in the Carlisle district about 1100, and that certain personal names in the East Riding of Yorkshire and Lincolnshire lead us to conclude that, there too, it was still in use in the mid-tenth century. All this however is very tentative, and R.I Page, in a scrutiny (1971) of the Norse inscriptions of the Danelaw, and English inscriptions showing Norse influence, is forced to the view that they 'tell us little of the continued use of the Norse tongue in the lands the Vikings settled'. He warns, on the other hand, that 'we cannot assume that because there are few Norse-influenced inscriptions there were few Norse speakers'.

In Scotland, not surprisingly, it remained a good deal longer. Einar Haugen (1976:332) dates the disappearance of Norse in the face of Scots or Gaelic to the fifteenth century in Caithness and to the sixteenth century in the Hebrides. There is firm evidence that in the Northern Isles it lingered appreciably longer even than that. The Norse (and originally Norwegian) dialects of Orkney and Shetland are commonly referred to as 'Norn', a term that derives from the Old Norse *norrœnt mál* 'northern speech'.

Although the medieval *Orkneyinga Saga* was almost certainly composed in Iceland, there is at least one literary text from Orkney in the poem *Jómsvíkinga drápa* by the twelfth-century bishop of Orkney, Bjarni Kolbeinsson. There are also four charters, the earliest dating from 1329 and the last from about 1426, described by H. Marwick (1929:xxxi) as 'the only records that can be regarded with certainty as examples of the Orkney Norn subsequent to the twelfth century'. The language of these texts is not however characterized by any features peculiar to Orkney.

Marwick considers that the influence of Lowland Scots in Orkney must have been slight before 1379 when the St Clairs succeeded to the earldom, and that, even thereafter, Scots would have been largely confined to the entourage of the Earl. There was a significant change after 1420, when Bishop Thomas Tulloch, a Scot, was entrusted with the administration of the earldom. It is significant, Marwick suggests (1929:xxii), that it is at that time that Norse gives way to Scots as the language of legal and official documents:

> A Scottish bishop would naturally employ notaries who used his own language, and even if the surviving Norn-speaking notaries continued for a time to practise, it would be essential that their documents should be duplicated in the language of their lord − be he earl or bishop.

It is worth recalling that, at this stage, the islands were still Danish territory (having passed into Danish possession in 1380 when the thrones of Norway and Denmark were united). In 1467, however, Orkney and Shetland came under Scottish control when Christian I of Denmark (who was unable to raise the full amount of the agreed dowry on the occasion of the marriage of his daughter to James III, King of Scots) pledged them as surety for the balance. Five years later, the islands were formally annexed by Scotland.

Thereafter, the fate of Norn was to be one of steady decline. Although George Buchanan could write in his (Latin) history of Scotland in 1582 that the islands still used 'the old Gothic tongue' (*vetus gothica lingua*),[4] by which he must surely have meant Norn, Dalrymple's translation of Leslye's *History* already records in 1596 that 'of the Iles of Orchnay, sum are Inglese, sum of the language of Norway', and as early as 1605 Sir Thomas Craig stated that in Orkney and Shetland, where in the previous century only Norse was spoken, English (i.e. Scots) was the language used in churches and was well enough understood. About 1670 Mathew Mackaill said of Orkney that the inhabitants spoke the Norn in 'only three or four parishes (especially upon the

---

[4] These and later quotations are taken from Marwick, 1929:224−7.

Mainland or Pomona) . . . and that chiefly when they are at their own houses, but all speak the Scots language'.

By the beginning of the eighteenth century, Norn was sufficiently uncommon for James Wallace, who reported in 1700 that 'all speak English, after the Scots way', to comment that 'some of the common People amongst themselves, speak a language they call Norns' and for the Revd John Brand the following year to report that 'there are . . . some who speak *Norse* especially in the *Mainland*, as in the parish of *Hara* there are a few yet living, who can speak no other thing, this Language not being quite extinct among them'.

Fifty years later, the end is nigh. Murdoch Mackenzie writes in 1750 of 'the Language, which they call *Noren*' that 'thirty or forty years ago this [*Noren*] was the vulgar Language of two parishes in *Pomona* Island: since which, by the Means of Charity-schools, it is so much wore out, as to be understood by none but old People; and in thirty Years more, it is probable, will not be understood there at all'. His comment on the influence of schools in hastening the extinction of Norn is echoed in the same year, 1750, by James Mackenzie who, apparently with reference to both Orkney and Shetland, refers to 'their language the Norse, or that dialect of the Gothic which is spoken in Norway, and disused only within this present age, by means of those English schools erected by the Society for Promoting Christian Knowledge. Nor to this very time is it quite disused, being still retained by old people, and in vulgar use amongst them at this day.'

Various witnesses testified at the Court of Session in 1757 that they remembered hearing Norse spoken in diverse localities when they were children, and one claimed 'that he knows some People, particularly three or four in the parishes of Harray and Firth, who speak that Language pretty fluently, as far as he can judge, at this day'. It is clear that we are now talking of the very last handful of speakers of the Orkney Norn, and only a very few years later, in 1773, the Revd George Low reported that though 'little more than half a century ago [Norn] was the prevailing tongue of two parishes in the Mainland [of Orkney]' it was, at the time he was writing, 'so much worn out, that I believe there is scarce a single man in the country who can express himself on the most ordinary occasion in the language,' and that 'even the Songs . . . are now (except a few of the most trifling) altogether lost'.

Not a single complete text, not even one sentence in the post-medieval Orkney Norn remains to us other than a partially garbled version of the Lord's Prayer taken down at the end of the seventeenth century by the Revd James Wallace and transcribed in his *Description of the Isles of Orkney* (1693):

> Favor i ir i chimeri. Helleur ir i nam thite, gilla cosdum thite cumma, veya thine mota vara gort o yurn sinna gort i chimeri, ga vus da on da dalight brow vora. Firgive vus sinna vora sin vee firgive sindara mutha vus, lyv vus ye i tumtation, min delivra vus fro olt ilt, Amen.

Norn has however left its mark on the present-day Scots dialect of the islands. Our principal source of information is Hugh Marwick's book, *The Orkney Norn* (1929), which lists some thousands of words of Norse origin, e.g. *andoo* 'to row a boat slowly' (cf. Old Norse *andœfa*, same meaning), *brisk* 'cartilage, gristle' (cf. Old Norse *brjósk*, same meaning), *brudge* 'to chop up' (cf. Old Norse *brytja*, same meaning), *forstaa* 'to understand' (cf. Old Norse *forstanda*, Norwegian *forstá*, same meaning), *gouster* 'a sharp breeze' (cf. Old Norse *gustr* 'gust'), *kreest* 'to squeeze' (cf. Old Norse *kreista*, same meaning), *mean*, 'ridge of a house (cf. Old Norse *mœnir*, same meaning), *owse* 'to bale out' (cf. Old Norse *ausa*, same meaning), *rivlin* 'kind of shoe' (cf. Old Norse *hriflingr*, same meaning).

In Shetland, the language lasted rather longer.[5] Jakob Jakobsen comments (1928–32:xvii) that as late as 1600 'the knowledge of English (Lowland Scottish) seems to have been very meagre in Shetland; for according to the "Fasti Ecclesiae Scotticanae", Magnus, surnamed "Norsk", minister of Unst (the most northerly of the Islands), made a voyage to Norway to learn the language spoken there, because his congregation did not understand any language other than "Norse" '. A century later, Brand's *Description of Orkney, Zetland, etc.* (1701) tells us that English (i.e. Scots) is 'the common language among the inhabitants of Shetland, yet many of the People speak Norse or corrupt Danish, especially such as live in the more Northern Isles, yea so ordinary is it in some places that it is the first Language their Children speak', and, on the basis of contemporary accounts of the continued use of Shetland dance-songs, Jakobsen concludes (*ibid.*) 'that the Shetland Norn was still a living language in the middle of the 18th century' and that 'even rather late in the 18th century, Norn songs and ballads survived in the mouths of the common people'. The last place where Norn was spoken was probably the westernmost and remotest Shetland island of Foula. In 1774 the Revd George Low discovered that 'the Norse Language is much worn out here, yet there are some who know a few words of it; it was the language of the last age, but will be entirely lost by the next'. Very few people, he says, could then speak the language: 'The best phrases are all gone, and nothing remains but a few names of things and two or three remnants of songs which one old man can repeat and that but indistinctly.'

The decline of Norn, in both Orkney and Shetland, was presumably hastened both by the advent of the Reformation (neither the Bible nor any other religious work was translated into Norn), and by the superior prestige enjoyed by Scots. In the words of Jakobsen (*ibid.*, xvi), 'bit by bit, the peasantry began to think it genteel to adopt Scottish words and modes of expression, and to feel ashamed of the old homely words, which they gradually came to look upon as lacking authority and justification. Moreover, once the development had taken this line, things went so far that in the eyes of many people the use of the pure old dialect was a mark of defective breeding.'

As for the last stages, a Shetland author, Arthur Edmonston wrote in 1809 in his book *A View of the Ancient and Present State of the Zetland Islands*: 'The old Norse has long been wearing out, and the change appears to have begun in the southern extremity and to have been gradually extended to the

---

[5] In what follows, our references to the situation of the Shetland Norn at various times are taken from pp. xvi–xviii of Jakobsen's *Etymological Dictionary of the Norn Language in Shetland*. 2 vols., London – Copenhagen, 1928–32. The dictionary was prepared in the late 1890s and was originally published in Danish in 1921.

northern parts of the country. The island of Unst was its last abode, and not more than thirty years ago several individuals there could speak it fluently.' Jakobsen himself comments (on the basis of his own experience when he first visited the islands in 1893) that, at that late date, 'there were people in Foula who could repeat sentences in Norn'. He further expresses the view that, apart from Foula, the language must have remained longest in the northernmost islands of Unst, Yell and Fetlar, where, when Jakobsen was there at the very end of the nineteenth century, the greatest number of Norn words remained and where the great majority of fragments of connected Norn were recorded. Again according to Jakobsen, the last man in Unst who was said to have been able to speak Norn, Walter Sutherland from Skaw, died about 1850, and in Foula, men who were living much later than that were said to have been able to speak it. Jakobsen acknowledges however that 'the Norn spoken towards the middle of the century and later can hardly have been of much account. The difference between it and the dialect of the oldest people of the present generation probably consisted in little more than the fact that the former contained a greater sprinkling of Norn words which the younger people did not understand' (*ibid.*, xix). His account (*ibid.*) of the probable manner in which Norn gave place to Scots − by gradual interpenetration of the two languages rather than by substitution of one language for the other − is worth quoting in full:

> The first portions of the old language to be affected, as one can easily imagine, and as appears from the fragments preserved, were the inflections, the grammatical endings, since assimilations became common, by degrees, as the forms were obliterated: next the minor words frequently recurring in speech, such as conjunctions, prepositions, pronouns, numerals, common adverbs; likewise adjectives and verbs in general use, as well as abstract nouns. As a rule the substantives, denoting visible things, inanimate objecs and living beings, have lasted longer.

Jakobsen had spent some two years in Shetland in 1893−95 and was also able to collect, in the islands of Foula, Unst and Yell, a few Norn sentences, riddles, proverbs and fragments of song, many of them however in such a corrupt form as to be barely intelligible. All these relics of Norn (poignantly referred to by one of Jackobsen's correspondents as 'the last lisp of a dying child') are gathered together in his dictionary.[6] Among the best preserved items are phrases such as *Kwarna fãrna*? 'Where have you been?' and *Farna sikən a droka* 'I have been to get something to drink', and a version of the Lord's Prayer, quoted in the form in which it was recorded by George Low in his *Tour through Orkney and Shetland* (1774):

> Fy vor or er i Chimeri. Halaght vara nam dit. La konungdum din cumma. La vill din vera guerde i vrildin sindaeri chimeri. Gav us dagh u dagloght brau. Forgive sindor wara sin vi forgiva gem ao sinda gainst wus. Lia wus ikè o vera tempa, but delivera was fro adlu idlu for do i ir konungdum, u puri, u glori, Amen.

[6] All the surviving fragments of Norn are set out in pages xci−cxvii.

Jakobsen also amassed over 10,000 Norn words remaining in the vocabulary of the Scots dialect of the different islands, though only half of them were by then in general use. They include, for example, *berk* 'skin on boiled milk' (cf. Icelandic and Faroese *börkur*, same meaning), *boltet* 'big, round, lumpy' (cf. Norwegian *bultutt* 'thick, clumsy'), *fann* 'heap of drifted snow' (cf. Old Norse *fönn* 'snow-drift'), *klud* 'neckerchief' (cf. Old Norse *klútr* 'rag'), *skorm* 'eggshell' (cf. Norwegian *skurm*, 'eggshell, nutshell'), *valin* 'benumbed with cold' (cf. Norwegian *valen*, same meaning).

There is some evidence to suggest that the last speakers of Norn, not differing in this respect from speakers of many other minority languages (and not only those that are in an advanced state of decline), themselves held their ancestral tongue in little esteem. Jakobsen had collected in both Unst and Foula versions of a Norn rhyme which (in the Foula version) runs, in translation: 'It was good when my son went south, for he learned to call *bugga* "bere" [i.e. "barley"] and *russa* "mare".' John Geipel is probably guilty of no exaggeration when he comments (1971:97):

> These lines reflect, pathetically, the fact that the autochthonous Scandinavian language was, by the eighteenth century, regarded by its speakers very much as an inferior tongue, and that the acquisition of the socially superior Scots was an accomplishment to be attained by all those who hoped to better themselves.

References

Cameron, Kenneth (1975). 'Scandinavian settlement in the territory of the Five Boroughs: the place-name evidence', in Kenneth Cameron (ed.), *Place-name Evidence for the Anglo-Saxon Invasion and Scandinavian Settlements*, Nottingham: English Place-Name Society, pp. 115–71.

Charles, B.G. (1934). *Old Norse Relations with Wales*. Cardiff: University of Wales Press.

—(1938). *Non-Celtic Place-names in Wales*. London: University College.

Ekwall, E. (1925). 'The Scandinavian element', in the English Place-Name Society, *Introduction to the Survey of English Place-Names* (= EPNS, Vol. 1), Part 1, Cambridge: Cambridge University Press, pp. 55–92.

—(1930). 'How long did the Scandinavian language survive in England?', in *A Grammatical Miscellany offered to Otto Jespersen*, Copenhagen: Levin & Munksgaard, London: Allen & Unwin; reprinted in E. Ekwall, *Selected Papers*, Lund: Gleerup, Copenhagen: Munksgaard (Lund Studies in English, 33), 1963, pp. 54–67.

Geipel, John (1971). *The Viking Legacy. The Scandinavian Influence on the English and Gaelic Languages*. Newton Abbot: David & Charles.

Gelling, Margaret (1978). *Signposts to the Past. Place-names and the History of England*. London: Dent.

Henderson, George (1910). *The Norse Influence on Celtic Scotland*. Glasgow: Maclehose.

Jackson, Kenneth (1962). 'The Celtic languages during the Viking period', in Ó Cuív (ed.), pp. 3–11.

Jakobsen, Jakob (1928–32). *An Etymological Dictionary of the Norn Language in Shetland*. 2 vols. London: Nutt; Copenhagen: Prior.

Jesperson, Otto (1948). *Growth and Structure of the English Language*. 9th ed. Oxford: Blackwell. (1st ed., Leipzig: 1909).

Loyn, H.R. (1977). *The Vikings in Britain*. London: Batsford.

Marwick, Hugh (1962). *The Orkney Norn*. London: Oxford University Press.

Ó Cuív, Brian (ed.) (1962). *Proceedings of the [Ninth] International Congress of Celtic Studies* [Dublin, July 1957]. Dublin: Dublin Institute for Advanced Studies.

Oftedal, Magne (1962). 'Norse place-names in Celtic Scotland', in Ó Cuív (ed.), pp. 43–50.

Page, R.I. (1971). 'How long did the Scandinavian language survive in England?', in P. Clemoes and Kathleen Hughes (eds.), *England before the Conquest*, London: Cambridge University Press, pp. 165–81.

—(1973). *An Introduction to English Runes*. London: Methuen. (See especially Chap. 12, 'Anglo-Saxon and Viking', pp. 190–9.)

Reaney, P.H. (1960). *The Origin of English Place Names*. London: Routledge & Kegan Paul. (See especially Chap. VII, 'The Scandinavian element', pp. 162–91.)

Strang, Barbara (1970). *A History of English*. London: Methuen.

Richards, Melville (1962). 'Norse place-names in Wales', in Ó Cuív (ed.), pp. 51–60.

16   French in the Channel Islands

The Channel Islands, known in French as 'les Îles Anglo-Normandes', lie off the west coast of the Cotentin peninsula in Normandy, and, in the Middle Ages, formed part of the duchy of Normandy (as in a sense they still do).[1] The duchy itself, as a distinct political entity, came into being in 911 when the French king, Charles the Simple, ceded an area around the lower reaches of the river Seine, including the town of Rouen, to Rollo, the leader of a Viking band that had settled there. In the course of the next quarter of a century, the 'Northmen' − whence the name 'Normans − had extended their duchy to take in first Bayeux and its hinterland, then the Cotentin peninsula, and finally the offshore islands of which Rollo's son, William Longsword, took possession in 933.

There can be no doubt that the original Normans, like those other Norwegians and Danes who settled in Britain and elsewhere, spoke Norse. There are indeed still a number of Norse elements, particularly seafaring terms, in the French dialect of Normandy, and some of them have become established in standard French (i.e. *crique* 'creek', *vague* 'wave', *marsouin* 'porpoise'). However, in the course of a very few generations the Normans abandoned their traditional Norse speech and when, only a century and a half after the foundation of the duchy, Duke William invaded England in 1066, the language he and his men took with them was Norman French. Its later fortunes in England are discussed in Chapter 17, 'Anglo-Norman'.

After the Conquest, William reigned in England as King and in Normandy as Duke, and at that period the Channel Islands remained as part of the Duchy of Normandy, not of the Kingdom of England. At the death of the Conqueror, his eldest son, Robert, became Duke of Normandy, and his second son, William Rufus, King of England. In 1100, Rufus was succeeded as King by his brother Henry who by 1106 also gained possession of Normandy. England and Normandy were once more separated during the reign of his successor, Stephen, but when he was succeeded in 1154 by Henry II, who was already Duke of Normandy, the two domains were united, in the person of the ruler if in no other sense.

The Channel Islands were finally severed administratively from mainland Normandy in 1204 when the French king, Philippe Auguste, conquered the rest of the duchy after King John had refused to do homage to him in respect of his lands in Normandy. John then established a jurisdiction of its own in

---

[1] The reigning King or Queen of England is still referred to in the islands as 'Duke of Normandy', although this is not in fact one of the officially recognized titles of the sovereign.

each island and so has a claim to be considered as the originator of the separate political identity of the islands and of the extensive degree of autonomy that they still enjoy. This separateness was duly recognized in 1360 when England formally ceded Normandy, with the specific exception of the Channel Islands, by treaty to France.

The term 'French' in relation to the Channel Islands refers to what are variously considered as two different languages or as two markedly different forms of the same language. On the one hand, there are the traditional spoken vernaculars of the Islands. These, as we shall see, are varieties of Norman French and the idea that they are a 'corruption' of standard French is devoid of all foundation. On the other hand, standard French, though it has never been an everyday spoken language in any of the islands, has served, and to some extent still serves, as an official language. For that reason, and although my concern in this book is primarily with spoken languages, I shall devote a few brief paragraphs at the end of this chapter to the role of French as an official language.

We know nothing of the linguistic history of the Channel Islands in the pre-French period, and there is indeed relatively little direct evidence even for the French-speaking period before the nineteenth century. It is however certain not only that Channel Islands French in the Middle Ages was basically Norman French, not Parisian French, but also that the modern dialects of the Islands are Norman dialects (see Collas, 1933–6, Spence, 1957, Brasseur, 1978). For example, a Latin *c*- became *ch*- (like English *ch*, but later simplified to English *sh*) before *a* in Parisian French, but remained (i.e. pronounced *k*) in the Norman dialect − so, for example, corresponding to standard French *chaleur* (from Latin *calorem*) 'heat', *champ* (from *campum*) 'field', *château* (from *castellum*) 'castle', we find in Jersey the forms *caleu, camp, câté*.[2] On the other hand, Latin *c*- before an *e* came to be pronounced *s* in Parisian French, but like English *ch* and later *sh* (or French *ch*) in Norman − so, corresponding to French *cent* 'a hundred' (from *centum*) and *cerveau* (from *cerebellum*), we have *chent, chèrvé*.

The four main islands are, in decreasing order of size, Jersey, Guernsey (in French, Guernesey), Alderney (Aurigny), and Sark (Sercq). Not only are there differences (sometimes major ones) between the dialects of the various islands, but it is also possible to distinguish local varieties within both Jèrriais[3] (in French, *jersiais*) or Jersey French (in particular, between eastern and western varieties) and Guernesiais or Guernsey French (in particular, between the speech of the Upper Parishes, i.e. the south of the island, and that of the Lower Parishes, i.e. the north of the island. The dialect of Sark is basically a dialect of Jersey French, as the island was colonized from Jersey in 1565.

One important Old French writer is known to have hailed from Jersey, namely Wace (*c.* 1100−75), the author of two lengthy historical poems, the

---

[2] The form *câté* now survives only in place-names (Le Maistre, 1966:89). English *castle* also derives from Old Norman French *castel* (corresponding to *chastel* in the Old French of the Parisian and other areas).

[3] Whereas standard French uses a lower case initial for names of languages and dialects (*le français, le jersiais*), it is customary in written Jèrriais and Guernesiais to use capitals.

Roman de Brut and the *Roman de Rou* (Rou being the Duke Rollo who gained possession of Normandy in 911). The following is an extract, in which he identifies himself, from the *Roman de Rou*:[4]

> Se l'on demande qui ço dist,
> Qui ceste estoire en romanz fist,
> Jo di e dirai que jo sui
> Wace de l'isle de Gersui,
> Qui est en mer vers occident,
> Al fieu de Normendie apent.

('If one asks who said this, who put this story into French ["Romance"], I say and will say that I am Wace of the Isle of Jersey, which is in the sea towards the west, and belongs to the fief of Normandy.')

Thereafter, there is nothing until the nineteenth century when a certain amount of verse was produced, in particular in Guernsey French which was used by such writers as Georges Métivier[5] (*Rimes guernesiaises*, 1831; *Fantaisies guernesiaises*, 1866; *Poësies guernesiaises et françaises*, 1883), Denys Corbet (*Les Feuilles de la forêt* [poems in Guernesiais, French and English], 1871; *Les Chants du draïn Rimeux* [Guernesiais and French], 1884), and Thomas Lenfestey (*Le Chant des fontaines*, 1875). Jersey French was mainly represented by A. Mourant's collection of *Rimes et poésies jersiaises* of 1865 and an anonymous and undated volume of *Rimes jersiaises*. More recently, Jean Du Nord has written Guernesiais plays for local drama contests and, in the 1960s, Marjorie Ozanne published tales in Guernesiais in the local press (see Tomlinson, 1981:354), while George F. Le Feuvre has produced the first ever volumes of prose to be published in Jèrriais, *Jèrri Jadis* (1973) and *Histouaithes et Gens d'Jèrri* (1976).

Métivier also translated the Gospel according to St Matthew into Guernesiais in 1863. The following is his version of Chapter 8, verses 1–4:

1 Quànd Jésus aeut d'vallaï avaû la montâigne, une grànd route de gens l'siévit:
2 Et en même temps ùn lépraeux vìnt à li et l'adorit, et lli dît: Signeur, s'ous voulaïz, vous pouvaïz m'guérìr.
3 Jésus étèndit sa maïn, l'touquit, et lli dît: Je l'veurs; séyiz guéri; et dans ùn môment sa lèpre fut guérie.
4 Et Jésus lli dît: Gardons bien d'pâlaïr d'chunchìn à persounne; mais allaïz vous mourtraïr au prêtre, et offraïz l'don ordounnaï par Moïse, à ceulle fìn qu' vlà qui leû serve de témouégnage.

As an example of Jersey French here is F. Le Maistre's rendering of the Gospel according to St Luke, Chapter 2, verses 8–10 (quoted after Don Balleine Trust, 1979, 5:2):

---

[4] Here quoted after the authoritative edition by A.J. Holden, Paris: Picard (Société des Anciens Textes Français), 3 vols, 1970–73. The *Roman de Brut* was edited in the same series by I. Arnold, 2 vols. 1938–40.
[5] On Métivier and other poets, see R.J. Lebarbenchon, *Des Filles, Une Sorcière, Dame Toumasse et quelques autres*, Azeville: Montebours, 1980.

Eh bien, i' y'avait dans la même contrée des bèrgers tchi couochaient
dans les clios, et y gardaient lus troupieaux en villiant d'ssus la niet.
Et tout à co un aunge du Seigneu sé préthentit à ieux, et la glouaithe du
Seigneu brilyit à l'entou d'ieux, et i' fûdrent saisis d'eune grant' peux.
Et l'ange lus dit: N'ayiz pon d'peux; car jé vouos annonce des
bounonnes nouvelles dé grand' jouaie tchi s'sont pouor tout l'monde.

The first lexicographical work on Channel Islands French was also due to
Georges Métivier, who in 1870 published a *Dictionnaire franco-normand ou
recueil des mots particuliers au dialecte de Guernesey* (London: Williams &
Norgate). As only Vol. I, the French–Guernesiais section of Sjögren's much
more scholarly dictionary (1964) has appeared, and as there is as yet no companion volume to the English–Guernesiais dictionary by Marie de Garis and
others (1967) (though one is forthcoming), Métivier's now aged work has not
been superseded. For Jersey French we have two glossaries, namely a
Glossaire du patois jersiais of 1924 and the much more recent one by Spence
(1960), and Le Maistre's monumental dictionary (1966).[6] There is virtually
nothing on pronunciation[7] and grammar other than Le Maistre's introduc-
tory sections on pronunciation and the morphology of verbs (1966:xxvii–
xxxiii), a brief but informative article by Spence (1965) on Jersey French, and
a few pages in the introduction to the most recent glossary of Guernsey
French (de Garis, 1967:xii–xviii).[8] Alderney and Sark figure, as do Guernsey
and Jersey, as points in the *Atlas linguistique de la France* (1903–10) by Jules
Gilliéron and Edmond Edmont, and Sark also figures, together with Guernsey and Jersey (but not Alderney, where the dialect is now extinct), in the new
linguistic atlas of Normandy that is in course of publication (Brasseur, 1980),
but otherwise there is nothing on the dialects of these smaller islands.

Societies have been formed in recent years in both Jersey and Guernsey for
the purpose of encouraging the use of the rapidly declining local speech. The
Assembliée d'Jèrriais (founded in 1951) and the *Assemblaïe d'Guernesiais*
(founded in 1956) each seems to have the support of a small but devoted band
of enthusiasts. The former published from 1952 to 1977 a quarterly bulletin
(*Bulletîn d'Quart d'An*, entirely in Jèrriais)[9] and the latter publishes an
annual bulletin. Neither society, however, has succeeded in touching the
mass of speakers, who tend to hold their traditional tongue in low esteem and
who (like many speakers of other minority languages under pressure from a
more prestigious language) are often indifferent as to its survival and sometimes overtly hostile. The Swedish scholar Albert Sjögren, for example

[6] Le Maistre's dictionary also contains a French – Jersiais vocabulary by Albert L. Carré who
has since published an *English–Jersey Language Vocabulary*, Jersey: Don Balleine Trust,
1972.

[7] Cassettes of a number of passages of Jèrriais are now available (see Don Balleine Trust, 1979).

[8] H. Tomlinson's doctoral thesis (1981) on the grammar and vocabulary of Guernesiais is not yet
published.

[9] This was the first regular periodical publication in Jèrriais. It was succeeded in 1979 by the half-
yearly *Chroniques du Don Balleine,* also entirely in Jèrriais, of which five issues had appeared
by the summer of 1982. There has never been anything resembling a newspaper or popular
magazine in Jèrriais, but the *Jersey Evening Post* has for many years given it house-room,
publishing at the moment a quarter-page contribution once a week in the language.

(1964:xiv–xviii), had the experience in 1926 of hearing local Guernsey children refer to the dialect as 'Guernsey gibberish', and a quarter of a century later Spence (1960:10) was to find in Jersey that 'although many dialect-speakers have shown an increased interest in and affection for "Jerriais" in recent years, there are many who are somewhat ashamed of it, considering it a corruption of "good French"'. Le Maistre too (1966:xviii) mentions the scorn in which it is held by the younger generation ('notre vieil idiome chancelant, méprisé par les jeunes').

It is impossible to estimate with any precision how many still speak the various dialects of Channel Islands French (the decennial census reports provide no information on the subject). It is clear however that it is everywhere in an advanced state of decline. Indeed, in Alderney, where some 30 people were still able to speak Auregnais in the 1930s (Le Maistre, 1947:3), it is already extinct.[10] The process of anglicization probably began in Alderney when large numbers of Irish and other English-speaking labourers were brought in for the construction between 1845 and 1864 of extensive naval and military installations, and was further encouraged by the permanent presence thereafter in the island of a large English-speaking garrison. The main factors in familiarizing the inhabitants of Sark (where, so a Methodist missionary reported to John Wesley in 1787, not a single family at that time understood English) with English were the importation of English-speaking miners from 1835 onwards, and then, during and after the 1850s, the growth of a flourishing tourist traffic (see Ewen and de Carteret, 1969:105–6). Although as recently as 1935 Le Maistre found the local Norman French 'excellent et bien vivant' (1949:211), there are now probably no more than a hundred in Sark who speak Sercquiais, and perhaps as few as sixty, out of a total population of some 600,[11] and no children who do so.

The anglicization of Guernsey began with the growth of tourism and trade in the nineteenth century, leading to a marked increase in the use of English in and around the capital, St Peter Port. However, in spite of the generalization of education through the medium of English towards the end of the century, Guernesiais remained the language of the home in most parts of the island (see Tomlinson, 1981:13). But when Sjögren investigated the situation of Guernesiais in 1926, he discovered that it was already seriously undermined by English, particularly in the north of the island (see Sjögren, 1964:xiv–xviii). In St Peter Port and the island's second town, St Sampson, English had already triumphed – those who spoke Guernesiais could be counted on one's fingers, and the number of those who understood it was not much greater. The local dialect was still spoken by some families in the rural parts of the parish of St Sampson, though not generally by the children. In the northernmost parish of the Vale, few of those under thirty spoke Guernesiais. In St Martin (adjoining St Peter Port to the south), the young people spoke almost exclusively English, and in the central parish of St Andrew only seven

---

[10] Although the last native speakers of Auregnais died some twenty-five years ago, Dr Frank Le Maistre, who, before the Second World War, knew well the island, its dialect and a number of the remaining speakers, has recently recorded a passage of some 400 words in Auregnais (Le Maistre, 1982).

[11] The population of the island at the 1971 census was 584. No census was taken on Sark in 1981.

of a class of forty ten-to-twelve-year-olds spoke Guernesiais at home (though some of the others used it with grandparents). Sjögren concluded however that the anglicization of St Andrew was a recent phenomenon, and in the northern rural parish of Câtel and in the south-western parishes of St Saviour, Forest, St Peter in the Wood, and Torteval, Guernesiais still flourished throughout the population and there even remained a very few elderly people who did not speak English. Furthermore, the pronunciation in the south was still authentic, whereas in the north it had been much influenced by English, as had the vocabulary and the syntax.

The linguistic situation in Guernsey was to deteriorate considerably in the half-century after Sjögren's visit.[12] As late as the beginning of the Second World War, there were some who could not express themselves in English, but the evacuation of the island's children to England in 1940 dealt the language a blow from which it has not recovered, for when they returned, the children were more at home in English than in Guernesiais. Consequently, when they were restored to their families, the language used tended to be English. For those of the succeeding generation, say those now aged under thirty, Guernesiais is unintelligible and looked down on. The influx in recent years of large numbers of outsiders, either as residents or as tourists, and the influence of radio and television have served to encourage the progressive anglicization of all parts of the island. Although there are some rural areas, particularly in the north and the south-west of the island, where Guernesiais is still the first language of a number of those aged over fifty, there is now no-one who does not understand English, and in and around St Peter Port Guernesiais has completely disappeared. Tomlinson's estimate – which in the circumstances cannot be more than a well-informed guess – is that there are now perhaps some 6000 speakers left (i.e. only about 11 per cent of the population, according to the 1981 census, of 53,268).

Things are no better in Jersey. Here, the beginnings of anglicization probably go back earlier than in Guernsey, and in particular to the early nineteenth century when, on the one hand, some 2000 workers were brought in from England and Ireland to work in the fisheries at Grouville Bay and, on the other hand, numerous veterans of the Napoleonic wars settled on the island. Increasing contacts with English throughout the century, with the development of steamer services and the beginnings of tourism, were to hasten the process, as was later the dominance of English in the fields of trade and education (see Hublart, 1978:26–30). As early as 1863, a French writer reported that, in Jersey, 'la langue anglaise est presque généralement employée dans les rapports de société et dans les relations de commerce' (Le Cerf, 1863:109).

Dr Frank Le Maistre, a life-long student of and enthusiast for Jèrriais, declared shortly after the Second World War (1947:3) that it was dying and that the disappearance of Norman French there, as also in Guernsey and in Sark, was only a matter of years. He estimated that, if a few elderly natives of the capital, St Helier, were still able to speak Jèrriais, no-one under fifty

---

[12] The following comments are based mainly on the introduction to Tomlinson's thesis (1981:11–18).

could do so. It was unlikely that there were any Jèrriais-speaking children left in the other southern parishes of St Brelade, St Saviour, St Clement and Grouville, and they were becoming fewer and fewer in the inland parishes of St Lawrence and St Peter, though there were more in the north-central parishes of St Mary and St John. The language was also declining rapidly in the north-eastern parishes of St Martin and Trinity. It was best preseved in St Ouen, in the north-west of the island, where it was still widely spoken, even by the children (though there were few who could not already speak English when they first attended school). It is there, says Le Maistre, that, at some future date, the funeral of 'la langue Jèrriaise' will take place. In 1982, he estimated that there were some 10,000 speakers of Jèrriais (out of a total population, according to the 1981 census, of some 76,000,[13] so about 13 per cent), many of whom rarely used the language, and that there was probably no-one under the age of twenty who could speak it and perhaps not more than three or four under the age of thirty who could so so.

Before we can consider the role of French (i.e. standard French, not the local Norman French dialects) as an official language, we must take a brief look at the constitutional position of the various islands. They comprise two Bailiwicks, namely Jersey and Guernsey. In each Bailiwick, the legislative assembly is known as the States. There is however a further complication in the case of the Bailiwick of Guernsey, which, in addition to the main island, includes the islands of Alderney and Sark, each of which is to some extent self-governing. In Alderney the legislative assembly (which sends two of its members to sit as deputies in the States of Guernsey) is also known as the States. That in Sark (which is not represented in the States of Guernsey) is known as the Chief Pleas. The highest judicial body in each Bailiwick is the Royal Court.

Technically, French is still an official language in both Bailiwicks. In practice, its role is almost entirely restricted to certain purely formal and ceremonial functions. The one exception, i.e. the one field in which it still serves in, so to speak, a productive role is that of property conveyancing in Jersey (where moves in 1982 to adopt English for the purpose were successfully resisted by the legal profession) and in Sark. English was adopted as the language of conveyancing in Alderney under the new Constitution that came into force in 1949, and in Guernsey in 1969.

It is only within living memory that English has replaced French as the language of legislation and debate in the legislative assemblies. The former Bailiff[14] of Jersey, Lord Countanche, commented in 1963 (1963:404) that, when he first entered the States as a Deputy some forty years earlier, 'French was the language largely in use in debate and almost exclusively for legislation'. In fact, a motion that members should have the right to address the States in English was adopted in 1900 by the States of Jersey, which seven years earlier had thrown out a similar proposal by a large majority. The first law in Jersey to be drafted in English ('because no-one could draft it in

---

[13] The official report (States of Jersey, *Report of the Census for 1981*, Jersey: States Greffe, 1982) records a population (excluding visitors) of 72,970 actually present on census night (5/6 April, 1981), but estimates the total resident population at 76,050.

[14] The Bailiff of each Bailiwick presides both over the States and over the Royal Court.

French', *ibid*.) was the Income Tax Law of 1928. Throughout the 1930s there was a gradual increase in legislation in English. Formal recognition of the *de facto* role of English was given when the States approved the view, almost unanimously expressed by those of its members who appeared before a Privy Council committee in 1946, that English should be the recognized language of the States, French being retained only for formal and official occasions (see Le Hérissier, n.d., p. 149). Nevertheless, it was not until States procedure was revised in 1966 that French, which had gradually been falling into disuse as the language in which the official record of States proceedings was kept, was finally supplanted here too by English (see Bois, 1976).

In Guernsey, the States resolved in 1898 that the use of English should be permitted in debate, and in 1926 that English should rank with French as an official language of the States for the purpose of written records. Legislation was rarely drafted in English before 1914, but since 1945 has invariably been drafted in English apart from amendments to existing laws the text of which is in French (and even here, where major amendments are involved, the practice is sometimes adopted of repealing the earlier legislation and re-enacting in English). States minutes, which for some years before 1946 had been kept partly in one language and partly in the other, since that date have been kept entirely in English.

In Alderney, the most thoroughly anglicized of the islands, bills were usually drafted in French (with an English translation) until the new Constitution came into force in January, 1949.

In the Royal Courts, too, the working language is now no longer French, as used to be the case, but English. In Jersey, where the language used in the Court at the beginning of the century was normally, though not invariably, French, it had become rare by the 1930s for a trial to be conducted in that language, though it was not until 1963 that this *fait accompli* was recognized when English was adopted as the language of record (Bois, 1976). However, the formal record of instruction by the Royal Court that Orders in Council and other texts be entered in the records of the Island ('enregistrés sur les records de l'Île') was still expressed in French up to June, 1972, since which date such formal notification has no longer been printed as a preamble to each such Order.[16] In Guernsey, a long-standing practice was formally recognized and regularized in 1946 when the States approved proposals made by the Royal Court that legal proceedings and documents should be either in English or in French at the option of the parties concerned. Since 1946, English has gradually come to replace French as the day-to-day language of record. The last entry in French in the Orders in Council dates from June, 1948.[17]

[15] I am much indebted to Her Majesty's Greffier for Guernsey, Mr K.H. Tough, for supplying me with the information on which my comments on the official position of French, including its role in the States and the Royal Court, are based.

[16] The title of the volume (published by the States Greffe of the States of Jersey) in which Orders in Council, etc., are collected was in French, viz. *Ile de Jersey, Ordres en Conseil, Lois, etc.*, up to and including the volume for 1963–65 (published 1966). Thereafter, i.e. from the volume for 1966–67 (published 1968), was it *Jersey, Orders in Council, Laws, etc.*

[17] The change in title from *Recueil d'Ordres en Conseil et d'autres matières d'un intérêt général enregistrés sur les records de l'Île de Guernsey, rédigé sous l'autorité de la Cour Royale* to

Although French no longer functions as a working language (apart from serving as the language of conveyancing in Jersey and Sark), it retains a residual role for certain purely formal and ceremonial purposes. It is still, for example, the language in which opening prayers are said at meetings of the States in Jersey, Guernsey and even Alderney, and of the Chief Pleas in Sark, and at sessions of the Royal Court in each Bailiwick. In the legislative assemblies (except the States of Alderney), when a vote by *appel nominal* is taken (i.e. when each member in turn gives his vote orally), members vote 'pour' or 'contre'. Also, in the States of Jersey and Guernsey, when the role is take at the beginning of each sitting, each member answers 'présent' or, if absent for good cause, is declared 'absent de l'île', 'malade' (Jersey) or 'indisposé' (Guernsey), or 'excusé' (Jersey), or, in Jersey, if absent without good cause is pronounced 'en défaut'. Among other formal or ceremonial uses of French, we may note the usher's call 'La Cour!', when bidding the public rise when the Bailiff or Deputy Bailiff and *jurats* enter the court-room for sittings of the Royal Court in either Bailiwick, and the use of occasional French phrases in the course of the proceedings, as when, in the Royal Court in Guernsey, an advocate making an *ex parte* application to the Court ends with the phrase 'J'en supplie' ('May the application be granted').[18] In Sark, public notices, signed by the Seigneur and the Seneschal, summoning meetings of Chief Pleas are still put up in French only.

In other public contexts, the use of French has to all practical intents and purposes ceased. Travelling around the islands, one occasionally sees the words 'École élémentaire' or 'Salle paroissiale' on the buildings in question, but what goes on inside is now in English. Le Maistre commented just after the Second World War (1947:9) that Wesleyan Methodism had 'contributed considerably to preserve the French language', but that, by then, very few services were in French. Now, apart from Roman Catholic masses held at one church in St Helier and one in St Peter Port (in the interests of French residents and visitors, not for the local population), there are now no regular services in French in the churches of any denomination. Nor is there any periodical press — the *Gazette de Guernesey* ceased publication in 1936 and the last remaining French-language newspaper, *Les Chroniques de Jersey*, at the end of 1959.

The prevailing pessimism one encounters everywhere in the islands among those who still maintain an interest in the maintenance there of French, whether it be the traditional native Norman French or standard French, seems all too well founded. It can only be a matter of a few decades at most before Jersey, Guernsey and Sark are as anglicized as Alderney already is.

Orders in Council and other matters of general interest registered on the records of the Isle of Guernsey, compiled under the authority of the Royal Court, was made even earlier, between Volumes IX (1931–34) and X (1935–36).

[18] It is worth noting that advocates wishing to practise in Guernsey (but not Jersey) are required to study law for one year at the University of Caen.

References

Bois, F. de L. (1976). 'The disappearance of official French.' *Jersey Evening Post,* 9 January 1976, p. 8.

Brasseur, Patrice (1978). 'Les principales caractéristiques phonétiques des parlers normands de Jersey, Sercq, Guernesey et Magneville (canton de Bricquebec, Manche).' *Annales de Normandie,* 28:49–64, 275–306.

—(1980). *Atlas linguistique et ethnographique normand,* Vol. 1, Paris: CNRS.

Collas, J.-P. (1933–36). 'Some aspects of the Norman dialect in the Channel Islands, with special reference to Guernsey.' *Transactions of La Société Guernesiaise,* 12:213–25.

de Garis, Marie *et al.* (1967). *Dictionnaire angllais–guernesiais.* Guernsey: La Société Guernesiaise (with a Supplement, 1973).

Don Balleine Trust (1979). *The Jersey Language.* Five cassettes and accompanying booklets. St Helier: Don Balleine Trust.

Coutanche, Lord (1963). 'A glance at the past ninety years.' Société Jersiaise, *Bulletin,* 18(1961–64):401–8.

Ewen, A.H. and Allan R. de Carteret (1969). *The Fief of Sark.* Guernsey: Guernsey Press Co. Ltd.

Hublart, Claude (1979). 'Le français de Jersey.' Unpublished dissertation, University of Mons.

Le Cert, Théodore (1863). *L'Archipel de Îles Normandes.* Paris: Plon.

Le Hérissier, R.G. (n.d.). *The Development of the Government of Jersey, 1771–1972.* Jersey: States of Jersey.

Le Maistre, Frank (1947). *The Jersey Language in its Present State. The Passing of a Norman Heritage.* London: The Jersey Society in London.

—(1949). 'Le normand dans les îles Anglo-Normandes.' *Le français moderne,* 17:211–18.

—(1966). *Dictionnaire jersiais–français.* Jersey: Don Balleine Trust.

—(1982). *The Language of Auregny: La Langue normande d'Auregny.* Jersey: Don Balleine Trust; Alderney: Alderney Society and Museum.

Lewis, Edwin Seelye (1895). *Guernsey: its People and Dialect.* Baltimore: Modern Language Association of America.

Sjögren, Albert (1964). *Les parlers bas-normands de l'île de Guernesey.* I, *Lexique français–guernesiais.* Paris: Klincksieck.

Spence, N.C.W. (1957). 'Jerriais and the dialects of the Norman mainland.' Société Jersiaise, *Bulletin,* 17:81–90.

—(1960). *A Glossary of Jersey French.* Oxford: Basil Blackwell, for The Philological Society.

—(1965). 'Jersey-French.' *The Linguist,* April (pp. 98–101), May (pp. 126–7), June (pp. 155–6).

Tomlinson, Harry (1981). 'Le Guernesiais – étude grammaticale et lexicale du parler normand de l'île de Guernesey.' Unpublished PhD dissertation, University of Edinburgh.

17 Anglo-Norman

The date 1066 is probably the best known in English history, and the linguistic effects of the Norman Conquest are still very much with us in the hundreds of words of French origin that are in daily use wherever English is spoken. (This is a topic we shall return to later.) Curiously, however, though we have a considerable number of literary, legal and other medieval texts written in England in French, great uncertainty remains as to the role of French as a spoken language in England.[1] Who spoke it? How well did they speak it? In what circumstances was it spoken? How long did it remain as a spoken language? To none of these quetions is there a sure answer. On the contrary, there is sharp disagreement and even controversy among scholars and, all too often, far-reaching conclusions have been based on slender or fragmentary evidence.

The origins of Anglo-Norman date from before 1066. Long before the arrival of the Conqueror, French influence was making itself felt at the court of the kings of England, in particular during the reign of Edward the Confessor, who was elected king after a period of 24 years of rule by Danish kings. Edward was then a man in his late thirties and had spent almost all his life in exile in Normandy. In order to have around him men whom he knew and trusted, he placed Normans in positions of power and influence in England (it was, for example, he who appointed the first Norman Archbishop of Canterbury, one Robert of Jumièges).

Nevertheless, during the reign of the Confessor, the effective control of England was in the hands of an English and English-speaking administration. After 1066, things were very different. The administration was now in the hands of the French-speaking Normans and the effects of this, and of the partial colonization of much of England and Wales that accompanied it, were early and widespread.

Anglo-Norman was extensively used in the official and public life of England until well into the fourteenth century. This was a consequence of the dominant role in society exercised for a time by the Norman invaders and their immediate descendants, and thereafter of the tradition of using French inherited from the period immediately following the Conquest. As the discrepancy between the official and public use of the two languages on the one hand and their role in everyday life on the other became more and more

---

[1] In referring to the French spoken and written in medieval England as 'Anglo-Norman', I follow a widespread practice. The terms 'Anglo-French' and 'Norman-French' are also sometimes used.

marked, so English began to retrieve its positions.

The events of 1204 were probably decisive. In that year, King John lost Normandy to the French king and, as a consequence, families that had lands on both sides of the Channel were in most cases obliged to give up either their English or their French estates. With the breaking of family ties with the Continent, 'we may be sure that after 1250 there was no reason for the nobility of England to consider itself anything but English. The most valid reason for its use of French was gone' (Baugh and Cable, 1978:129).[2]

So strongly was the French tide ebbing, that even a massive upsurge in the mid-thirteenth century was to have no long-term effects except, as we shall see, in terms of its influence on the vocabulary of English. The upsurge in question occurred during the reign of the intensely Francophile Henry III (1216–72), whose mother and wife were both Frenchwomen and exercised considerable influence over him. From 1233 onwards, some thousands of Frenchmen – ecclesiastics, noblemen, knights and others – mainly from Henry's lands in Poitou and the south of France, were encouraged to cross over to England and many of them were appointed to high and influential positions in Church and State. In the end, this provoked strong reaction and the accession of Edward I in 1272 inaugurated a period in which English was finally to triumph over French.

In the thirteenth and fourteenth centuries, regulations introduced at various newly founded colleges at Oxford and Cambridge requiring students to converse in French or (preferably) Latin, not English, and similar provisions in certain monasteries, seem to have been intended to prop up somewhat artificially the use of French. By the mid-fourteenth century it is clear that pressures in favour of the use of English at the highest levels of public life were virtually irresistible. In 1356 it was ordered that proceedings in the sheriff's courts of London and Middlesex were to be in English. In 1362, an act of parliament, the 'Statute of Pleading', attempted to substitute 'the language of the country', *la lange du paiis* (i.e. English), as the spoken language of the courts of law in place of 'the French language, which is too unknown', *la lange français, q'est trop desconue*. As it happens, this measure seems to have met with little success, but its evidential value as to the use made in reality of the two languages remains. What seems to have occurred is that French continued to be used as 'the language of "pleadings" properly so called, while English became the language of that "argument" which was slowly differentiated from out of the mixed process of arguing and pleading which is represented to us by the Year Books'[3] (Maitland, 1907:409).

In the field of education, French was still the normal medium of instruction in schools in the first half of the fourteenth century, but later, and particularly after the Black Death of 1349, the use of English became more widespread and, according John of Trevisa, was general by 1385.

---

[2] The following chapters of this standard history of the English language are of particular relevance to Anglo-Norman: Chap. 5, 'The Norman Conquest and the subjection of English, 1066–1200'; Chap. 6, 'The re-establishment of English, 1200–1500'.

[3] The 'Year Books' are a record in summary form of legal cases decided from the reign of Edward I to that of Henry VIII.

The earliest known post-Conquest will to be written in English dates from 1383, though few others are known before 1400, after which date English wills are commonly found. At this time, there is also an increasing use of English in local government. 'About 1430 a number of towns are seen translating their ordinances and their books of customs into English, and English becomes general in their transactions after 1450' (Baugh and Cable, 1970:153).

Although by the fifteenth century French had all but disappeared from most spheres of public as well as private life, in some fields it hung on tenaciously right through the century and even later. Parliamentary statutes were first written in English alongside of French in 1485, and after 1489 French is no longer found. 'Law French' survived very much longer, in an increasingly debased form. Important legal treatises were written in it for another two centuries, including the *Tenures* of Thomas Littleton (†1481), the *Perutilis tractatus sive explanatio quorundam capitulorum valde necessaria* by John Perkins or Parkins (⸢ 1544 or 1545), and *Les Plees del Coron divisees in plusors titles et common lieux* by William Stanford (†1558). In 1549, Archbishop Cranmer comments: 'I have heard suitors murmur at the bar because their attornies pleaded their causes in the French tongue which they understood not' (quoted after Maitland, 1907:409), and in the reign of Henry VIII, a suggested answer to the antagonism to 'thys barbarouse tong and Old French, whych now servyth to no purpose else' was, surprisingly, not that the use of French in the courts should be discontinued but that law students should be taught to plead in good French. In fact, 'law French' was still in use in the seventeenth century, by which time it had become 'increasingly mangled and reached a pitch of absurdity in Dyer's famous report of 1631 that a prisoner, venting his rage on the judge, "jecte un graund brickbat que narrowly mist"' (Baker, 1966:216). Maitland comments (1907:408):

> We know 'law French' in its last days, in the age that lies between the Restoration [1660] and the Revolution [1688], as a debased jargon. Lawyers still wrote it; lawyers still pronounced or pretended to pronounce it. Not only was it the language in which the moots were holden at the Inns of Court until those ancient exercises ceased, but it might sometimes be heard in the courts of law.

One final relic is still to be found in the formula expressing the royal assent to acts of parliament, viz. *La Reyne le veult.*

We now have to attempt some assessment of the extent to which French survived as a spoken language in England in the centuries following the Conquest. Given what we know about the role of, say, English or French on the one hand and indigenous languages on the other during the imperialist period in such countries as India, Kenya and Algeria, it is remarkable that serious scholars could have attempted to draw from the extent to which French was in public use in medieval England conclusions regarding its position as an everyday spoken language. But such is the case.

It can safely be assumed that, for many of those who came over with the Conqueror and stayed, French was their first and only language. Three hundred years later, in the second half of the fourteenth century, many and perhaps most of those who spoke it (after a fashion at least) were people who, whether they were of English, Norman or mixed descent, had English as their mother tongue. In so far as they had acquired French (as spoken in England), this was because it was fashionable to do so, or, if they were lawyers or clerics, because a knowledge of it was indispensable for professional purposes. But to determine the stages by which Anglo-Norman declined over a period of three centuries, even among the members of the aristocracy, is no easy task. It is even more difficult to come to any firm conclusions as to the extent to which the language was spoken or understood among other sections of society, among tradespeople and town dwellers in general, what one might now call the 'middle class', and among the peasants who made up the bulk of the population. As we shall see, French was used, well into the fourteenth century and in some cases later, for literary, legal and official purposes, but this fact is not in itself evidence of its widespread use as a spoken tongue. As Professor William Rothwell has said (1968b:185):

> Although there is a considerable amount of extant material in Anglo-Norman − literary, historical, legal, didactic and so on − extending into later periods in our history, this proves only that French retained its status as a literary and official language for some time, not that French was the normal tongue of English right up to the fifteenth century, as historians have claimed.

The root of the problem is that there are no reliable and unambiguous contemporary comments of a general nature about the extent to which English, French and Latin were used in different situations.[4] We depend entirely on anecdotes (of which there are not a few), passing references, and other scraps of evidence that are not always easy to interpret. For example, the historian Ordericus Vitalis, born in England in 1075 of a Norman father and (it is supposed) an English mother, was educated from the age of five at Shewsbury; at the age of ten he was sent to a monastery in Normandy where he came across a language he did not understand, which can only have been French. It has therefore been argued, not implausibly, that 'the ordinary speech of his father and mother must have been English, a fact which may be significant when we consider the intermarriage which must have taken place between Normans and Englishwomen in the years immediately following the Conquest' (Wilson, 1943:47). Much of this evidence was gathered together and shrewdly assessed in 1943 by R.M. Wilson, in the article from which the above quotation is taken. He concluded that, during the twelfth and thirteenth centuries, 'a knowledge of English amongst the clergy was desirable, and certainly far from unusual' (*ibid.*, 49) and that English also 'rapidly made its way into the higher classes of secular society' (*ibid.*, 54).

An important point at issue is the extent to which England was in fact colonized by the Normans. Vising, for example, had quoted (1923:9), apparently without demur, an earlier view that about a quarter of England's

---

[4] For a careful and well-documented study of the respective roles of English, French and Latin as written media in medieval England, see Clanchy (1979) and, in particular, Chapter 6, 'Languages of record' (pp. 151−74).

population of perhaps two million were killed or driven out during the reign of William I, and that, during that same period, about 200,000 Normans – not only noblemen and knights, but also clerics, teachers, merchants, townspeople, skilled workmen and others – settled in England, and had claimed that not only the ruling and cultivated classes but 'a great part of the working population' (*ibid.*, 12) were of French extraction. In an article published in the same year as Wilson's study, George E. Woodbine commented (1943:408) – and one cannot but agree with him – that estimates of the number of Norman immigrants are 'pure guesswork' and that 'some of the figures suggested make one wonder if any merchants or workmen were left in Normandy': 'it may be affirmed with assurance . . .', he continues, 'that the proposition that the Frenchifying of England and its language was inevitable because of the numerical weight of the early Normans, is one which the evidence most decidedly does not support.' Taking a similar stance, Wilson (1943:57) thinks it 'not improbable that the Conquest had a comparatively small effect on language. The conquerors were only a small minority, and by no means a linguistically homogeneous minority, since the army at Hastings contained adventurers from almost every part of France.'

As we have said, opinions are very much divided about the extent to which England became French-speaking. On the one hand, some very eminent scholars have held that Anglo-Norman came to occupy a dominant position in all sections of English society. Paul Studer for example contended (1911:9) that 'in the thirteenth and fourteenth centuries French had secured a firm footing in the towns of England, and was rapidly reaching the remotest country villages. It had become the fashionable language in all classes of society, and English was now little better than the despised speech of the ignorant Saxon peasant.' John Orr characterized the situation in the early thirteenth century as follows (1948:4–5):

> French is spoken practically everywhere, certainly everywhere that matters. It is the language of the court and society, it is the language of administration, of Parliament, and of the law-courts, it is the language of church and monastery, it is taught and spoken in the schools, where English is forbidden; it is a triumphant rival to English for literary purposes. It is the *sine qua non* for all social and administrative, legal, and ecclesiastical preferment . . . Although political events . . . prevented us from becoming an entirely French-speaking population, it must be obvious to any unbiased linguist that this state of almost complete bilingualism, to put it at its lowest, must have had an effect upon the then humbler medium of discourse much more far-reaching than a mere count of borrowed words, even running into thousands, as they do.

Professor Dominica Legge goes even further, referring (1950a:1) to 'the time when all England was bilingual, and much of it was trilingual [i.e. in English, French and Latin]' and suggesting that, as late as thirteenth century, 'French was very widely, almost universally, understood' (*ibid.*, 90). In a later book, she expresses the view (1963:4) that, by about 1170, 'most people, down to the very poorest, were bilingual'.

The most extreme view on the other side is that of an American scholar who once suggested that 'the only general definition of Anglo-Norman possible is that it is bad French as used in England' (Menger, 1904:4). More moderately, another American, George E. Woodbine, while recognizing that the upper strata of society must for a time have been generally bilingual, argued forcefully (1943:433) that 'there is no dependable evidence to show that French became either the language of law or the language of the English people generally, as a result of William I's invasion'. And in the same year, an English historian, acknowledging that the available evidence is fragmentary, anecdotal and difficult to evaluate, nevertheless considered it to be extensive and reliable enough to allow him to draw at least tentative general conclusions, which, it must be said, are characterized by a much greater measure of realism than the views of those who would have us believe that English was in danger of being superseded by French as the normal conversational idiom of the country. The evidence, he argues (Wilson, 1943:60), suggests that, up to 1300, the lower classes probably spoke English only, while many of the middle and upper classes and lower clergy spoke English and either French or Latin or, the case of the higher clergy, perhaps both:

> It seems fairly clear that the displacement of English, as a spoken language, by French is unsupported by any considerable body of evidence. After 1300 there can be no doubt that English is the language of the country, though French survives for some time in court circles as a literary language and, of course, in the law.

The pendulum now seems to be swinging decisively in the direction of the view that, though French was the first language of the original Norman invaders and probably of their immediate descendants, for two or three generations, it thereafter declined as a medium of everyday intercourse, even among the upper classes. Whitehead, for example, argued (1966–67:81) that late Anglo-Norman 'shows none of the characteristics of a living, freely evolving, spoken dialect of French'.

The most recent extensive survey is provided by Professor William Rothwell who seeks (1978) to answer the question, 'When did French cease to be spoken in England?' (see also Rothwell, 1976). He argues that those who think in terms of a far-reaching bilingualism are merely following Vising. Basing himself on the pieces of anecdotal and fragmentary evidence to which we have referred, Vising – who, be it said, seems to have lacked any imaginative appreciation of sociolinguistic realities and probabilities – had concluded as follows (1923:18):

> It cannot be denied that these statements furnish a very strong proof of the complete dominance of the Anglo-Norman language during the second half of the twelfth and most of the thirteenth century in nearly all conditions of life, and of its penetration even into the lower strata of society,[5]

---

[5] It is only fair, however, to add that Vising later expresses the view (1923:22) that 'it must, indeed, have been the fact that by about 1250 English was well on the way towards the recovery of its position as the common language of ordinary intercourse'.

−a conclusion which, as has recently been said (Short, 1979−80:467), 'offends common sense'. As Rothwell persuasively argues (1978:1081), the various comments from literary texts on which Vising relies prove no more than that French enjoyed great prestige as a cultural language in medieval England: 'Vising's fundamental mistake . . . is to confuse vernacular speech and cultural language.' Reassessing the evidence, and stressing the importance of French as a literary and cultural language, Rothwell comes to the eminently reasonable conclusion that there is nothing to justify the view that French remained a vernacular language in England for the great majority of the population until the middle of the thirteenth century or thereabouts. On the contrary, he is able to produce clear evidence from contemporary texts in favour of the view that 'French was a language needing to be learned by very many Englishmen, not a vernacular in almost universal use in England *at the opening of the thirteenth century* [my italics]' (Rothwell, 1976:452). Nevertheless, in the thirteenth century French was becoming, in England, a serious rival to Latin as a cultural language, including in fields such as law and theology. Furthermore, French was becoming an international cultural language understood and used over much of Europe, whereas English was not. It was important that the cultured sections of the community in England should have access to this language, and this, and this alone, is the reason why many manuals of French were composed in England in the thirteenth century.

Rothwell's assessment of the situation is supported by Professor Ian Short who draws attention (1979−80:478−9) to disparaging remarks about the French of England made by the twelfth-century writers and clerics Giraldus Cambrensis and Walter Map, remarks which invite the conclusion that, though Anglo-Norman probably still flourished as a language of everyday communication among the upper classes in the late twelfth century, for both Giraldus and Walter it seems to have been 'a coarse deformation of French'. Furthermore, there is a fair amount of evidence to suggest that, even if the aristocracy and higher clergy were largely bilingual, 'lower down the social scale, and at a point still far short of peasant status', the minor clergy were only English-speaking and that, 'to the vast bulk of the Anglo-Saxon population', Anglo-Norman French in the twelfth century was a completely alien tongue.

If one tries to envisage the situation with both realism and imagination, taking account not only of the known facts but also of what might reasonably be supposed to have occurred, one is almost inevitably led to accept that French and English were in a relationship of diglossia (on this, see above pp. 121, 126−7, 164) in which the standing of French as a prestige language did not reflect the extent to which it was used in the community in general. There can be little doubt that most people in most circumstances used English, but that, by an inherited convention, French retained many functions that it had acquired in such fields as administration, the law, the church, the schools and literature, at a time when it had been the natural medium of expression of the most influential section of the community. One must assume that the use of French became increasingly anachronistic and increasingly inappropriate, indeed inefficient, even for these purposes and that for this reason its functions were taken over, in one field after another, by English. It may well be imagined that French was seen to fall short in two respects. First, French, in spite of its great prestige, was no longer the usual language of any section of the community. Second, it is clear from the kind of French that was being written in England in the thirteenth and, even more so, in the fourteenth century that the writers had less than total command of the language. What generally passed for French in England lacked any real roots in contemporary society and was indeed a language in an advanced state of decline. Grammatically, it was often little more than 'bad French'. Perhaps even more serious is the fact that its vocabulary was being heavily infiltrated by anglicisms. It is undoubtedly true, as Rothwell has argued, that French had great prestige as a cultural and international language. But that was French French. Increasingly, Anglo-Norman, as we shall see, came to take on the appearance of a debased form of the language from which it had sprung. With hindsight, therefore, one should not be surprised that it eventually went out of use.

That Anglo-Norman should have come to diverge more and more from continental French as time went on is in itself not surprising. It is a normal phenomenon for a language to break up into different dialects and, often, different languages over a period of centuries, particularly when communication between different areas is restricted as a result of geographical features (forests, mountains, water) or social factors (such as political borders). Indeed, in the Old French period (corresponding roughly to the twelfth and thirteenth centuries) there were already marked differences between the French even of various regions with northern France itself (the Île-de-France, Normandy, Picardy, Champagne, Lorraine, and so on). However, late Anglo-Norman is characterized by so many and such marked deviations from any other kind of French of the time as to lead one to the view that what we have before us is not just another authentic variety of native-speaker French but incorrect French written by people for whom it was a foreign language and whose command of it was inadequate. This is particularly noticeable in respect of verbs, where we frequently find such forms as *vener* for *venir, entenda* for *entendit, appara* for *apparut, feserent* for *firent, baysir* for *baiser*. It is no exaggeration to say that 'in Later Anglo-Norman the growing confusion of [verb] endings and forms indicates the gradual disintegration of the whole system' (Pope, 1934:478). Nouns are given the wrong gender – in the first few pages of the fourteenth-century prose text *Fouke le Fitz Warin* (edited by E.J. Hathaway and others, Anglo-Norman Text Society, 1975), for example, we find the masculine nouns *pays* and *coup* treated as feminine (*de ceste pays, meynte dure coupe donnee*) and the feminine nouns *roche* and *tour* treated as masculines (*un grant roche, un tour* 'tower'). The same text has frequent examples of *a le, a les* and *de le* used instead of *al, as, del* (*dou*) (modern *au, aux, du*), e.g. *a le chastiel* (= *château*), *a les esposayles* (= *épousailles*), *de le prince, de le chyval* (= *cheval*). There are also various concealed anglicisms such as *donner sur* 'to give up' = 'to abandon' (e.g. *le counte ly dona sur Asshesdoune* 'the earl abandoned Ashdown to him'), *traviler* (= *travailler*) in the sense of 'to travel' rather than of 'to work' (e.g. *qe ele de yleqe ne poeit traviler* 'that she could not travel thence'), *mout le plus* 'all the more', and *la, les,* meaning 'to her, to them'

(e.g. *yl la dysent qe . . .* 'they told her that . . .', *la damoisele les promit qe
. . .*). Another text that survives only in a fourteenth-century manuscript, the
Pseudo-Turpin Chronicle of William de Briane, has, among many other
similar examples, *de les faus prestres* (= *des faux prêtres*), *soun propre
espeye* (= *sa propre épée*), *il le rendist la cité* (= *il lui rendit la cité*).

But, if Anglo-Norman finally died out leaving the English language
triumphant, it has not gone without trace. English − as it came to take over
from Anglo-Norman all those functions of a cultivated language that were
not reserved, wholly or in some measure, for Latin − drew extensively on the
lexical resources of its rival. Before turning our attention specifically to its
influence on the English language, however, we shall consider briefly another
major respect in which Anglo-Norman has left its mark in England, and that
is its literature.

Anglo-Norman had an important role as a literary medium, in a variety of
genres. Indeed, it has a unique place in the western European cultural tradition in that its literature can rightly be considered both as an important aspect
of medieval French literature and as part of the literary heritage of England.
No literature written in England in either French or English has come down to
us from the first thirty years or so after the Conquest. This does not
necessarily mean, of course, that none was composed − as Dominica Legge
comments (1963:7), 'from 1100 onwards Anglo-Norman writers were
amongst the pioneers of French literature, and it is difficult to believe that
these authors sprang from nothing'.

Curiously, whereas the authors of nearly all continental French texts from
the same period are unknown to us, we can put a name to the authors of many
of the earliest known Anglo-Norman texts, though it has to be recognized
that in many cases little is known about them apart from their names, not
even whether they were born in Normandy or in England of a family of
Norman origin. Two writers from the reign of Henry I (1100−35) are
Benedeit (probably a monk) and Philippe de Thaon. Benedeit's *Voyage of St
Brendan* is an adaptation (and by no means a mere translation) of a Latin
work, *Navigatio Sancti Brendani*, that recounts the semi-legendary travels of
an Irish monk and his companions who may indeed have sailed as far as the
coasts of North America. Philippe de Thaon − of whom Dominica Legge
comments (1963:19) that his 'literary qualities are . . . not of a high order' −
has left a work known as *Li Cumpoz*, a kind of ecclesiastical calendar in
verse, setting out with the accompaniment of a good deal of allegory the
principles for calculating the dates of Easter and other movable feasts and of
the seasons, and a Bestiary and a Lapidary in which beasts and precious
stones respectively provide the basis for further allegorical moralizing.

A little later, we have an account by one Gaimar of the story of the English
people, based partly (indeed, for the early period, entirely) on legend, partly,
as far as more recent events were concerned, on fact. As history, this *Estorie
des Englois* is more or less worthless, but as a linguistic and literary document
it is of considerable significance being the earliest known chronicle in French.
The earliest Anglo-Norman chronicle to merit attention as a source of
historical information is that of Jordan Fantosme, which deals with the
Anglo-Scottish wars of 1173−4 and was written within a very few years after

the events recorded. There are many later chronicles, some of them of minor importance in every respect, but including also, from the fourteenth century, Sir Thomas Gray of Heron's *Scalacronica* (based, like some earlier works of the kind, partly on legend, partly on recent events), Nicholas Trevet's prose history of the world from the Creation down to his own times, and, also in prose, a chronicle of the crusade and death of Richard I. Many of these texts, minor and major alike, are largely derivative but Legge refers to two of them in particular, namely an account (in verse − some 19,000 lines of it) of the life of William Marshall (†1219), and a late-fourteenth-century biography of the Black Prince, as 'primary sources for the history of the times'.

Dating probably from the second half of the twelfth century, perhaps from around 1165−70, is one of the two main versions in French of the Tristan story, by one Thomas, a text of outstanding importance in the field of medieval French literature and, in spite of the fact that only fragments of it remain, in the field of western Europe an medieval literature. The other main French 'Tristan', by Béroul, dating from about the same period, may or may not be Anglo-Norman. Other verse romances, written for the delectation of the nobility, were to follow before the end of the century, including two, *Ipomedon* and *Protheselaus*, by Hue of Rotelande (= Rhuddlan, in Clwyd), who probably lived near Hereford, a *Roman de toute chevalerie* by Thomas of Kent, and another, *Horn*, by a Thomas who was probably neither the author of the *Tristan* nor Thomas of Kent. Numerous other verse romances date from the thirteenth century, and one prose text, part romance, part chronicle, *Fouke le Fitz Warin*, in the defective French that was characteristic of the late period (see p. 224 above), from the fourteenth century.

An important area in which Anglo-Norman seems to have played a pioneering role, as compared with continental French, is that of biblical translations. From the first half of the twelfth century there is an as yet unprinted translation by Sanson de Nanteuil of the Proverbs of Solomon. The early thirteenth century (if not indeed the end of the twelfth) saw the production of an important translation of the Four Books of Kings and of two different versions of the Psalms (known respectively as the Oxford and the Cambridge psalters). And, though only parts of the Anglo-Norman Bible of the fourteenth century have come down to us, this may well have once comprised a complete version of both Testaments. But Anglo-Norman religious literature was by no means limited to translations of the Scriptures. Saints' lives figured largely, including in the twelfth century a life of St Edward the Confessor by an anonymous nun from Barking Abbey, three other lives of native English saints, namely St Osyth (an Anglo-Saxon princess), St Modwenna and St Audrey, and a thirteenth-century life of St John the Almsgiver. Unique in the whole field of medieval literature in French is a Passion of Judas.

The drama too had its origin in the church and one of the earliest medieval plays in any vernacular language is the highly important dramatization of the stories of Adam and Eve and Cain and Abel, now often called the *Mystère d'Adam*, that may well have been written in England about 1140.

Great impetus was given to the production of religious literature by the Fourth Lateran Council of 1215, the effect of which on Anglo-Norman literature was to give rise to 'a remarkable series of manuals, treatises and encyclopaedias of religious knowledge destined for the laity, or for the parish clergy who were to prepare them for confession' (Legge, 1963:312). Among the most significant figures in this field were Angier who wrote a life of Pope Gregory the Great and translated his *Dialogues*, Robert Grosseteste, Bishop of Lincoln, the author of various works in prose and verse, Peter of Peckham, whose *Lumere as Lais* (completed in 1267) was an attempt to interpret theology to the laity, and the Franciscan, Nicole Bozon, who, in the late thirteenth and early fourteenth centuries, produced a considerable amount of work in a variety of genres, including allegories, sermons and eleven saints' lives.

The late fourteenth century is marked by the literary output of the last major English writer in French, John Gower (*c.* 1330–1408), whose *balades* (over 50 of them) show 'what French poetry in England might have become if Chaucer had not flung his cap over the windmill and plunged into the English language' (Legge, 1963:357), and whose lengthy moralizing poem (some 30,000 lines), the *Mirour de l'omme* (probably written in the late 1370s), has been called 'the swan-song of Anglo-Norman literature' (*ibid.*, 220).

As we have already mentioned, the vocabulary of English was deeply marked by the influence of Anglo-Norman. One or two words (such as *proud* and *pride*) in fact entered English from French before the Conquest, and in the period up to 1250 some 900 words were borrowed, 'many of them [words] such as the lower classes would become familiar with through contact with a French-speaking nobility (*baron, noble, dame, servant, messenger, feast, minstrel, juggler, largess*)' (Baugh and Cable, 1978:168).[6] Words such as *story* and *rhyme* presumably came in via literary channels, and an important group of words was associated with the church. Paradoxically, however, it was after 1250, i.e. at a time when French as a widespread spoken language was on the decline in English, that its influence on English was at its height. The reason, Baugh suggests, was that 'those who had been accustomed to speak French were turning increasingly to the use of English' and, in so doing, either because the English language lacked the lexical resources they needed or because of their own inadequate command of the language, they 'carried over into English an astonishing number of common French words' (*ibid.*), However, as we have seen, formal links with Normandy were broken in 1204 when the duchy was lost to the French crown and later, in the reign of Henry III, and in particular from the 1230s onwards, large numbers of Frenchmen from other parts of France flocked to England. Furthermore, the growing prestige of Paris and Parisian French meant that, for literary purposes in particular, there was a tendency to borrow French words in their Parisian or 'Central French' form rather than their Anglo-Norman form. The difference between the two is particularly noticeable in respect of certain features of pronunciation. For example, a Latin initial *c-* when followed by *-a-* became *ch* (pronounced as in English) in Central French, but remained as *c-* (pronounced [k]) in northern dialects, including Norman and its derivative, Anglo-Norman. So, from Latin *capitalem* we have both *cattle* (of Anglo-Norman origin, and originally meaning 'property') and *chattel* (of Central

[6] In what follows, I draw heavily on this book. See also Pope, 1944.

French origin). The retention of initial *ca-* likewise indicates the Anglo-Norman origin of such words as English *caitiff, carry, case* ('box'), *castle, cauldron* (compare French *chétif, charrier, châsse, château* [Old French *chastel*], *chaudron*), whereas such words as *chain, chair, chamber, change, chapel, charge,* are of Central French origin. On the other hand, in words which in Latin began with *ce-* or *ci-*, northern dialects had *ch* (pronounced as in English) whereas Central French had *c-* (pronounced [ts] and later [s]), so we have, for example, English *chisel* and *cherry* (earlier *cherise*) but French *ciseau* and *cerise*. Similarly, an initial *w-* (mainly in words borrowed by French from the Germanic dialect of the Franks) remained as *w-* in the north, but developed an initial *g-* in Central French, giving a spelling *gu-* (pronounced [gw] and later [g]). Here again, English has 'doublets', one of each pair from Anglo-Norman and one from Central French, e.g. *wage* and *gage, ward* and *guard, warranty* and *guarantee, wile* and *guile*; contrast too English *warren, waste* and *wicket* with French *garenne, gâter* (Old French *guaster*) and *guichet*.

Baugh estimates that some ten thousand French words were borrowed by English in the Middle English period, i.e. between approximately 1150 and 1400, and that 75 per cent of them still remain in the language. To illustrate how deeply English has been influenced, we need only quote the following examples (from the much longer lists given by Baugh and Cable, 1978:168–72):

Governmental and administrative words:
government, crown, state, empire, reign, royal, sovereign, court, council, parliament, assembly, treaty, alliance, tax, subsidy, revenue, subject, traitor, public, liberty, office, minister, prince, duke, peasant, slave.

Ecclesiastical words:
sermon, prayer, lesson, clergy, dean, chaplain, parson, image, abbey, cloister, saviour, saint, miracle, mystery, faith, devotion, temptation, piety, mercy, pity, solemn, divine, preach, chant, repent, confess, convert, ordain.

Law:
justice, bar, assize, plea, judge, complaint, inquest, summons, jury, evidence, proof, verdict, sentence, decree, prison, gaol, accuse, blame, arrest, seize, condemn, convict, award, acquit, pardon, fraud, libel, slander, perjury, property, heir, innocent.

Military words:
army, navy, peace, enemy, arms, battle, combat, siege, defence, ambush, retreat, soldier, spy, captain, sergeant, lance, banner, archer, harness.

Fashion, meals and social life:
fashion, dress, garment, cloak, coat, collar, veil, button, garter, boot, satin, fur, jewel, ornament, brooch, ivory, ruby, pearl, diamond, dinner, supper, mackerel, sole, salmon, oyster, venison, beef, veal, mutton, pork, bacon, sausage, gravy, poultry, pigeon, biscuit, cream,

sugar, olive, salad, lettuce, fruit, date, grape, orange, lemon, peach, tart, jelly, spice, herb, mustard, vinegar, roast, boil, stew, fry, saucer, plate, curtain, chair, cushion, screen, lamp, blanket, towel, basin, wardrobe, leisure, dance, music, chess, rein, stable, terrier, partridge, pheasant, heron, squirrel, forest, park.

Art, Learning, Medicine:
art, music, colour, figure, image, tone, cathedral, palace, cellar, chimney, tower, column, pillar, poet, prose, romance, tragedy, title, paper, pen, study, grammar, noun, surgery, pain, leper, plague, remedy, ointment, poison.

General words:
nouns – age, air, bucket, city, coast, cost, country, coward, dozen, face, fame, flower, grain, grief, gum, hour, joy, labour, manner, mountain, noise, number, order, people, peril, person, piece, point, powder, power, rage, reason, river, season, sign, sound, spirit, square, sum, tailor, task, tavern, use, waste.
adjectives (nearly 1000 in Middle English) – able, actual, brief, calm, certain, clear, common, courteous, cruel, curious, eager, easy, faint, feeble, fierce, firm, foreign, frail, gentle, hasty, horrible, honest, innocent, jolly, large, mean, nice, plain, poor, probable, proper, pure, real, safe, savage, scarce, second, secret, simple, single, sober, solid, special, strange, sudden, sure, tender.
verbs – advance, advise, aim, allow, approach, arrive, betray, carry, change, chase, close, comfort, conceal, continue, cover, cry, deceive, defeat, defy, desire, destroy, embrace, enjoy, enter, flatter, flourish, form, join, marry, move, murmur, nourish, obey, pass, pay, pinch, please, praise, prefer, prove, push, receive, refuse, remember, reply, rob, satisfy, save, scald, serve, spoil, succeed, surprise, tempt, travel, trip, wait, waste.

Comparable in nature with the concealed anglicisms in *Fouke le Fitz Warin* that we referred to above, but vastly more significant in terms both of their number and of the depth to which they have penetrated the language, are the concealed gallicisms in English. John Orr claimed (1948:16), perhaps with some exaggeration but the claim has a good deal of substance, that 'infinitely numerous . . . are the English words which have taken up a special meaning or function possessed by their French equivalents', quoting among other examples *always* (*toutes voies*), *to bear illwill* (*porter male volonté*), *to lay a hand upon* (= 'to strike') (*metre la main sur*), *hot-foot* (*chaut pié*), *to make bold* (*se faire fier*), *to take heart* (*prendre cuer*), *to make way* (*faire voie*), *to wit* (*à savoir*).

There are also a few words in Welsh – though very few as compared with English – of undoubted French origin that came into the language in the medieval period, such as *tŵr* 'tower', *bwrdais* 'burgess', *cwarel* 'quarrel (cross-bow bolt)', and others that have since disappeared, such as *albras* 'cross-bow' (from *arbaleste*) and *orlaes* 'clock' (from *horloge*). However, there seem unfortunately to be no reliable criteria based on form or pronunciation on which we can decide with any certainty which such words were borrowed directly from French and which — as must have happened in many cases — came into Welsh via English. A book that Morgan Watkin once stated (1918–19:222) his intention of publishing, to be entitled *L'influence française sur la langue et la littérature galloises aux XIIe, XIIIe et XIVe siècles*, never appeared.[7] This is all the more regrettable in that Watkin was firmly of the view that there *was* considerable direct influence of French on Welsh, whereas others have tended to consider English as the prime source of French elements in Welsh. T.H. Parry-Williams, for example, in his book on English loanwords in Welsh recognizes (1923:49) that a problem exists, i.e. that there is no foolproof way of distinguishing between direct borrowings from French and those that passed through the channel of English, but nevertheless includes quantities of these doubtful items in his lists 'whenever it is *possible* [my italics] to derive these from forms found in English itself', on the ground that 'it is, perhaps, safer' to regard them as what he called 'Anglo-Romance' borrowings, i.e. borrowings via English. Whether or not one might in the end have been any more convinced by the case Morgan Watkin would have put than one is by Parry-Williams's assumptions, it would have been interesting to read his arguments. The problem of distinguishing between direct borrowings (if any) and borrowings via English, remains, then, to be solved. Meanwhile, it has at least been convincingly demonstrated that there are no *a priori* grounds for assuming that French words could *not* have entered Welsh directly. A number of possible channels have been suggested (see Surridge, 1966), among the more plausible being Norman settlements in the Welsh Marches and to some extent in Wales itself, mixed marriages both among the middle classes and between the families of Welsh lords and princes and the Anglo-Norman aristocracy, commercial links between Welsh traders and Normans in the towns founded by the Normans in Wales, and monastic (and in particular Cistercian) houses with their links with French parent houses.

References

Baker, Timothy (1966). *The Normans*. London: Cassell.
Baugh, Albert C. and Thomas Cable (1970). *A History of the English Language*. 3rd ed. London: Routledge & Kegan Paul.
Clanchy, M.T. (1979). *From Memory to Written Record. England 1066–1307.* London: Edward Arnold.
Legge, M. Dominica (1950a). *Anglo-Norman in the Cloisters*. Edinburgh: Edinburgh University Press.
—(1950b). 'The French language and the English cloister', in Veronica Ruffer and A.J. Taylor (eds), *Medieval Studies presented to Rose Graham,* Oxford: printed for the Subscribers at the University Press, pp. 146–62.
—(1963). *Anglo-Norman Literature and its Background*. Oxford: Clarendon Press.

---

[7] His article (1918–19) entitled 'The French linguistic influence in medieval Wales' deals only with French influence on Welsh orthography.

—(1979). 'Anglo-Norman as a spoken language', in R. Allen Brown (ed.), *Proceedings of the Battle Conference 1979*, Woodbridge: The Boydell Press, 1980, pp. 108–17.

Maitland, F.W. (1907). 'The Anglo-French law language', in *The Cambridge History of English Literature,* Cambridge: University Press, Vol. I, pp. 407–12.

Menger, L.E. (1904). *The Anglo-Norman Dialect.* New York: Columbia University.

Orr, John (1948). *The Impact of French upon English.* (The Taylorian Lecture, 1948.) Oxford: Clarendon Press.

Parry-Williams, T.H. (1923). *The English Element in Welsh.* London: Honourable Society of Cymmrodorion.

Pope, Mildred K. (1934). *From Latin to Modern French with Especial Consideration of Anglo-Norman.* Manchester: Manchester University Press. (2nd ed., 1952).

—(1944). *The Anglo-Norman Element in our Vocabulary: its Significance for our Civilization.* Manchester: Manchester University Press.

Rothwell, William (1968a). 'The teaching of French in medieval England.' *Modern Language Review*, 63:37–46.

—(1968b). 'Teaching French: old wine in new bottles.' *Bulletin of the John Rylands Library*, 51:184–99.

—(1976). 'The role of French in thirteenth-century England.' *Bulletin of the John Rylands University Library of Manchester*, 58:445–66.

—(1978). 'A quelle époque a-t-on cessé de parler français en Angleterre?', *in Mélanges de philologie romane offerts à Charles Camproux*, Montpellier: Centre d'études occitanes de l'Université Paul-Valéry, Vol. II, pp. 1075–89.

Short, Ian (1979–80). 'On bilingualism in Anglo-Norman England.' *Romance Philology*, 33:467–79.

Studer, Paul (ed.) (1911). *Supplement to the Oak Book of Southampton*. Southampton: Southampton Record Society.

Surridge, Marie (1966). 'Romance linguistic influence on Middle Welsh: a review of some problems.' *Studia Celtica*, 1:63–92.

Vising, Johan (1923). *Anglo-Norman Language and Literature.* London: Oxford University Press.

Watkin, Morgan (1918–19). 'The French linguistic influence in medieval Wales.' *Transactions of the Honourable Society of Cymmrodorion*, 1918–19: 146–222.

Whitehead, F. (1966–67). 'Norman French: the linguistic consequences of the Conquest.' *Memoirs and Proceedings of the Manchester Literary and Philosophical Society*, 109:78–83.

Wilson, R.M. (1943). 'English and French in England, 1100–1300.' *History,* 28:37–60.

Woodbine, George E. (1943). 'The language of English law.' *Speculum*, 1:395–436.

18   Romani

Romani – sometimes written 'Romany', and otherwise known as Romanés or Romanichel – is the language of the Gypsies. The name has nothing whatsoever to do with 'Rome' and 'Roman' but is derived from the Romani word *rom* 'husband'. Its origin, the stages by which it spread to many countries in various continents, and its present situation (in terms both of the extent to which it is spoken and the quality of spoken Romani) are all, as we shall see, to some extent obscure. One thing, however, is beyond dispute, namely that Romani originated in India and that it is a member of the Indo-European family of languages. This family also includes most of the languages of Europe (among them, the Germanic, Celtic, Romance and Slav languages and Greek, but not Basque, Finnish and Hungarian), Persian (but not, for example, Arabic, Hebrew or Turkish), and, as we shall see, Sanskrit and a number (though by no means all) of the present day languages of the Indian sub-continent often known collectively as the Indo-Aryan languages.

But if the Indian origin of Romani is certain, its precise relationship to the other Indo-Aryan languages is not. In many respects it seems closest to central Indo-Aryan languages (the best known of which is Hindi), but it also has some features in common with a north-western group (including Kashmiri, Punjabi and Sindhi). The most authoritative view is that of the eminent Sanskrit scholar, Sir Ralph Lilley Turner. In a monograph (Turner, 1927) devoted specifically to determining the position of Romani in the Indo-Aryan group of languages, he surveys the characteristic phonetic features (both conservative and innovatory) of Romani, and its lexicon, in the light of a comparison with Sanskrit and the modern Indo-Aryan languages. He concludes that the evidence indicates clearly that there was originally a connection with the Central group, which he defines (*ibid.*, 34) as a group which included the ancestors of Hindi and Rajasthani but excluded the ancestors of Sinhalese, Marathi, Sindhi, Landha, Punjabi, Dardic, and West Pahari, and probably Gujerati and Bengali. At some early stage, however, probably before 250 BC, the ancestors of the Gypsies migrated north-westwards and settled, probably in the Western Punjab or in the Peshawar district (see Turner, 1959:463), among speakers of north-western dialects. There they seem to have stayed for perhaps a thousand years or more, during which time their language came to be influenced, both phonetically and lexically, by those of the other Indo-Aryan tribes with whom they were now in contact. This, then, is the explanation for the north-western features still to be found in Romani.

At some indeterminate period, but certainly not later than the ninth century AD, the Romanis were on the move again. Migrating further and further westwards, they spread gradually over much of western Asia, throughout almost the whole of Europe and, eventually, to America. They were already in south-eastern Europe in the course of the fourteenth century (if not earlier), as there are references to their presence in Crete, Corfu and Serbia by the middle of the century and in Bulgaria and Romania towards its end (Vesey-Fitzgerald, 1944:6–7; Clébert, 1963:29–31; Kenrick and Puxon, 1972:14–15), and in the course of the fifteenth century they reached virtually every country in western Europe (see Bataillard, 1888–90; Fitzgerald, 1944, Chapter II, 'Recent history', pp. 12–42; Clébert, 1963:29–36).

It is not known precisely how or when the Gypsies (or 'Egyptians' as they were first known – 'Gypsies' is a deformation of the same word) first teached Britain, but there is every reason to suppose that they arrived here too in the course of the fifteenth century. It is more than likely that an Act of the Scottish Parliament of 1449, directed against unspecified 'sorners', 'vagabonds' and the like, was the first of many repressive measures passed by the Scottish, English and, later, British parliaments against the Gypsies. The first recorded mention of them by name (i.e. 'Egyptians') is also from Scotland, in the accounts of the Lord High Treasurer for Scotland of 22 April, 1505, and the earliest known reference to them (again as 'Egyptians') in England is in the *Dyalog of Syr Thomas More, Knyght*, of 1514. It is clear that they came across in substantial numbers, as there are estimated to have been 10,000 Gypsies in England in the reign of Elizabeth I.

In the course of the thousand years or so since they left India, the Gypsies have come into contact, perhaps sometimes close and prolonged contact, with many other peoples, whose languages have had far-reaching influence on Romani. The dispersion of the Romani community in so many different directions has of course meant that different groups have different patterns of borrowings, but the pattern in any given case is astonishingly varied. Turner estimated (1959:463) that the dialect of the Gypsies of Wales, for example, contains words from Persian, Armenian, Greek (the Greek element is particularly important), Romanian, Bulgarian, Serbian, Czech, German, French and English (and, one must add, Welsh).

The effects of geographical dispersion and contacts with other languages have not only affected the lexicon however. Grammar and pronunciation have evolved differently in different areas, and there are now many distinct dialects of Romani. That is not all. One can divide Gypsy communities, in terms of their use of Romani, into three broad, but not discrete, categories. There are those (as, for example, in parts of the Balkans) for whom Romani survives, with its own grammatical forms and structures, as a first language. Then there are those communities, perhaps consisting in some cases of no more than a single extended family, who speak 'jargons consisting of a framework of the local language, for example, English, in which a certain portion of the vocabulary is replaced by Gypsy words' (Turner, 1959:463). And finally, there are those who have lost the language almost entirely, and use for all purposes the language of their environment, incorporating in it an occasional word of Romani here and there. As we shall see, British Gypsies now fall mainly into the second category, though until recently some Welsh

Gypsies still knew and used enough of the grammatical forms of Romani to warrant inclusion on the fringes of the first category.

English Romani is first attested in 1547, when Andrew Borde included in his *Fyrst Boke of the Introduction of Knowledge* thirteen sentences, under the title 'A talk in Egyptian and English' (see Furnivall, 1870:318, and 1874), beginning:

Good morrow!	Lach ittur ydyues!
How farre is it to the next town?	Cater myla barforas?
You be welcome to the towne.	Maysta ves barforas.
Wyl you drynke some wine?	Mole pis lauena?

Thereafter, there is nothing more for well over two hundred years, until William Marsden (1784) included thirty-eight words of English Gypsy in an article in *Archaeologia* arguing (correctly) that Gypsy was connected with 'the Hindostanic languages' and, in the same volume, Jacob Bryant published a list of some 300 English Gypsy words.

In the course of the next hundred years there were a few, but only a few, minor items devoted to Romani (see Smart and Crofton, 1875:xii), but the seventies of the last century suddenly saw a heightening of serious interest in the Gypsies and their language, with the publication in successive years of three books devoted to it, namely Leland's *The English Gipsies and their Language* (1873), Borrow's *Romano Lavo-Lil* (sub-titled *Word-book of the Romany, or English Gypsy Language*) (1874), and, in particular, Smart and Crofton's *The Dialect of the English Gypsies* (1875), which contained a grammar, an extensive vocabulary, and a wide selection of miscellaneous texts.

By this time, the grammatical structure of the language of the English Gypsies was severely undermined. Leland comments (1873:ix) that 'the grammar has well nigh disappeared', though later (*ibid.*, xiii) he gives us to understand that this had happened only recently:

> Within the memory of man the popular Rommany of this country was really grammatical; that which is now spoken . . . is . . . almost entirely English as to its structure, although it still abounds in Hindu words to a far greater extent than has hitherto been supposed.

Borrow expresses a similar view: having estimated the 'scanty' vocabulary of English Gypsy speech at 'probably not more than fourteen hundred words' (1874:6), he goes on to say:

> With respect to Grammar, the English Gypsy is perhaps in a worse condition than with respect to words. Attention is seldom paid to gender . . . The proper Gypsy plural terminations are retained in nouns, but in declension prepositions are generally substituted for postpositions, and those prepositions English. The proper way of conjugating verbs is seldom or never observed, and the English method is followed (*ibid.*, 11).

Smart and Crofton (1875:xi) distinguish between 'the common widespread corrupt dialect . . . containing but few inflexions, and mixed to a greater or less extent with English, and conforming to the English method in the arrangement of the sentences. This is the vulgar tongue in every-day use by ordinary Gypsies' and 'the "Deep" or old dialect known only to a few aged Gypsies, which contains many inflexions and idioms; which has its own "ordo verborum"; which closely resembles the principal Continental Gypsy dialects, e.g., the German, Turkish, etc.; and which contains a minimum admixture of English words. This last, which will soon cease to exist, is *par excellence* the Gypsy language, of which the first is merely the corruption.'

Specific instances of the deterioration of the grammar are provided by Smart and Crofton when they discuss, for example, the definite article or the use of verb forms. Romani has a masculine article *o*, a feminine article *i*, but, they tell us (*ibid.*, 11), the English Gypsies 'now hardly employ any other than the English word *the*', except in a few set phrases like *le o gri* 'catch the horse', *paúdel i paáni* 'over the water'. With reference to 2nd person singular verb forms in *-ésa* (e.g. *dikésa* 'thou seest', *jinésa* 'thou knowest'), they comment (*ibid.*, 35) that 'a few of the old Gypsies still use this form'.

The following (from Leland, 1873:238) well illustrates that the kind of language that has been accurately described as 'really a register of English rather than a dialect of Romani', and which 'apart from the lexis . . . does not differ from the language spoken by Gajo (non-Gypsy) people of similar class and education' (Kenrick, 1979:111–12), was in use over a century ago:

> Mandy sūtto'd I was pirraben lang o' tute, an' I dicked mandy's pen odöi 'pre the choomber. Then I was pirryin' ajaw parl the puvius, an' I welled to the panni paul' the Beng's Choomber, an' adöi I dicked some rānis, saw nāngo barrin' a pauno plāchta 'pré lengis sherros, adree the panni pāsh their bukkos.

> ('I dreamed I was walking with you, and I saw my sister (a fortune-teller) there upon the hill. Then I (found myself) walking again over the field, and I came to the water near the Devil's Dyke, and there I saw some ladies, quite naked excepting a white cloth on their heads, in the water to the waists.')

This 'Anglo-Romani', as it is known, i.e. a speech form in which 'Romani words are fitted, inflected as English words, into sentences with English grammar and additional vocabulary' (Acton, 1974:56), seems to be still in widespread use among English Gypsies. Accounts of its use in different parts of England half a century ago are given, under the general title 'Anglo-Romani Gleanings', in the *Journal of the Gypsy Lore Society*, Third Series, Volumes 3 (1924):110–36 (on London Gypsies), 4 (1925):115–39 (Hampshire), 8 (1929):105–34 (East Anglia), and (by E.O. Winstedt) 27 (1948):83–110 and 28 (1949):50–61 (northern counties). In a foreword to the last of these, however, Archdeacon D.M.M. Bartlett comments (p. 83):

> It must be confessed that here in the North, just as he [i.e. Mr Winstedt] tells me it is happening in the South, the old *Romanes* . . . is now moribund, if not actually dead. Occasionally one comes across a Romani who can *roker* ['speak'] connectedly: but the 'younger end' . . . only know a few short everyday phrases, and have a smattering

of words which they try on the visitor, most of which are sadly distorted or used in a wrong sense.

On the other hand, Ian F. Hancock (1969) discovered that some Gypsies of the Lee family whom he met at Epsom Races in June 1968 had an extensive vocabulary. None of the Romani he then heard spoken was inflected but:

> it was still far from being English and I think it will be many more years before the language expires in Britain (Hancock, 1969:23).

But Donald Kenrick expresses a much more pessimistic view (1979:114):

> Nowadays, the everyday language in use among Gypsies in England is that of the surrounding urban or rural community in which they live and work: English. In addition, they possess a special lexis of between 100 and 1000 words which they can use to replace the English equivalents when they want or need to.

In fact, Anglo-Romani now seems not to be a language functioning as 'natural' languages do. This is indicated first by the fact that it is largely acquired not in early childhood but in adolescence:

> The average six-year-old hardly knows ten words of the lexis, and his knowledge does not exceed 50 before puberty. At this point the girls learn the language from the younger women and the boys from the younger men. During the long drives looking for work a boy can learn as many as thirty or forty words in a day, and as he learns them he gets into situations where he needs to use them and is allowed to do so (Kenrick, 1979:118–19),

and secondly by the fact that it is not used for normal everyday communicative and expressive purposes, but, primarily though not exclusively, for a restricted range of functions (see Kenrick, 1971:11, 1979:115–19). Among the more important are its use:

1 for identification purposes – a Gypsy may slip a word of Romani into a conversation to ascertain whether someone else present is also a Gypsy, or whether someone known to be a Gajo (non-Gypsy) is friendly or hostile; or the language may serve as a means of self-identification as a group member on the occasion of, say, family reunions;

2 as a source of specialized vocabulary in certain trades or professions, such as horse-dealing;

3 in songs and oaths;

4 above all, as a secret language that could be used by Gypsies to communicate with one another in the presence of strangers, a facility that is highly prized: 'The secretness of the language is such that young children are discouraged from giving words even to such friendly persons as volunteer teachers on the trailer sites' (Kenrick, 1979:117). Indeed, 'for many Gypsies it is important that even the *fact* that they have a secret language should be concealed' (*ibid*.), and 'the secretness of the language is one reason why it is not taught to young children. If they don't know it, then they can't reveal its secrets' (*ibid*., 118).

It has been estimated (Acton and Davies, 1979:100) that at least 50,000 people in England and Wales now speak Anglo-Romani, with up to 800 words being fairly commonly known, and a beginning has been made on teaching it in some of the Gypsy caravan schools that have recently come into existence. An elementary first reader, for example (Acton, 1977), has been issued, consisting of thirty-two pages of pictures with bilingual text, e.g.:

> p. 24: The rai-mush putches the chavvies to kek atch akai, or their dad will be lelled to stirapen/The gentleman asks the boys not to stop here, or their dad will be taken to prison.

It can be seen that the grammatical structure is English — English definite articles, plurals (*chavvies*), verb endings (*putches, lelled*), and prepositions.

It seems to have been widely assumed, on the basis of the work of people like Leland, Borrow, and Smart and Crofton, and the conclusions they had arrived at, that 'deep Romani', or inflected Romani, was virtually extinct not only in England but in Britain generally by the late nineteenth century. But then, to his astonishment, Dr John Sampson (later to become Librarian of the University of Liverpool), made a remarkable discovery:

> For several decades before the period when my own Gypsy studies began, Anglo-Romani, through the gradual loss of most of its inflections and a great part of its original vocabulary, had sunk to the level of a semi-jargon, while the so-called 'deep Gypsy' possessed by a few aged pundits of the tribe exhibited little more than the debris of a once stately and beautifully constructed language. It was therefore with sensations which will be readily understood by those who have indulged in dreams of treasure trove that in the summer of 1894, while on a caravan tour through North Wales, I chanced upon a Welsh Gypsy harper at Bala, and made the discovery that the ancient Romanī tongue, so long extinct in England and Scotland, had been miraculously preserved by the Gypsies of the Principality (Sampson, 1926:vii).

The harpist in question, Edward Wood, and his family proved to be 'the descendants of an eponymous ancestor Abram Wood, reputed King of the Gypsies, who was born before the close of the seventeenth century, and the dialect so religiously kept intact in the fastenesses of Cambria is thus a survival of the oldest and purest from of British Romanī' (*ibid.*). Furthermore, he was to discover that this Welsh Romani 'was still the mother-tongue of a large tribe, who spoke it habitually among themselves and only used Welsh or English when addressing strangers' (*ibid.*, viii).

Over a period of more than twenty years, Sampson came to know many of the Wood family in many localities in North Wales, and as far south as Newtown and Aberystwyth. Regarded by them as one of themselves from whom there was nothing to conceal, he enjoyed a unique opportunity of studying the people and their language:

> My note-books, over a hundred in number, have been filled while sitting beside the camp-fires of the Gypsies, or travelling in their company, on heaths, by the river-banks, at fairs, in village inns, or listening to their

stories in the barns, where by ancient use and wont they are allowed to lodge at night (Sampson, 1926:x).

Sampson's devoted and assiduous work on what he terms 'an Indian language spoken in the heart of Wales' (*ibid.*, vii) and 'perhaps the strangest of all the mother-tongues spoken in these islands' (*ibid.*, x) was to bear rich fruit. In 1907, he published in the *Journal of the Gipsy Lore Society* the first of forty-two folk-tales he had collected, the remainder of which were to appear over the next quarter of a century, the last of them posthumously in 1933 (Sampson having died in 1931) (see Sampson, 1907–33). The first of them, *I Kâli Râni* 'The Black Lady', collected from a member of the Wood family in Merioneth, begins:

Sas tārni čác wontsélas t'an te kel būtí. 'Yas t'an p'uri filišinátī. ('There was once a young girl who wanted a place to do work. She got a place at the old castle.')

(č = *ch*, š = *sh*, t' = *t + h* as in *ant-hill*, p' = *p + h* as in *uphill*, – indicates a long vowel, ′ indicates a stressed vowel; the word *wont(sélas)* is a borrowing from English *to want*.)

Of even greater importance than the folk-tales is Sampson's *magnum opus*, his volume entitled *The Dialect of the Gypsies of Wales, being the Older Form of British Romani preserved in the Speech of the Clan of Abram Wood* (1926). This monumental work of nearly seven hundred pages includes substantial sections on 'Phonology', 'Word-formation' and 'Inflection and syntax', and a vocabulary of over four hundred pages. The grammatical and lexical sections in particular are abundantly illustrated with examples, including thousands of complete sentences, the authenticity of which is vouched for by Sampson:

Every Romani sentence given in the Grammar or Vocabulary is the spontaneous utterance of some Welsh Gypsy, reflecting the life and lore, customs, beliefs, thought and feeling of the race (*ibid.*, x).

A very few examples must suffice = (ǰ = English *j* as in *judge*):

Kekār ātaváva tut me, 'I will nēver forgive you'; Nai 'doi kek t'an aré ī Walšī te na ǰuná kek, 'there is no place in Wales that I do not know'; Varesávī ǰuvel sas, na ǰuná lā mē kek, 'Whichever woman it was, I do not know her'.

Good evidence for the continued existence of 'deep Romani' among members of the Wood family on the eve of the Second World War is provided by sixteen letters dictated by the illiterate Harry Wood in 1935–39 to the postmaster at the village of Druid (near Corwen, Merioneth), Rowland Humphreys, and later published (Huth, 1940). The following extract, in Humphreys' orthography derived mainly from that of English, partly from that of Welsh (e.g. *w* = English *u*; *si* = English *sh*), shows how different this is from the 'Anglo-Romani' discussed above:

Kamlo Pal, Kam diom te shuna teeree chinimangeri ta shanes mishtol tai Rawni. Mwranes nashadoe siomes may pala twte. Fedader siom

Kanaw. ('Dear Brother, I liked to hear your letter, and that you were well, also the Lady. I was altogether lost without you. I am better now.')

There are no very clear indications as to how far Romani still remains at the level of richness and purity recorded by Sampson. In 1950, Dereck Tipler met a Gypsy family in Caernarfonshire and discovered that the older members spoke 'inflected Romani' (see Tipler, 1957). While some of the examples he quotes are uncorrupted (e.g. *Šomas uštilo 'dova bar* 'I was lifting that stone'; *Reperésa tū ō lav?* 'Do you remember the word?'), others show considerable influence of English or Welsh morphosyntax (e.g. latsiler'*d* 'kick*ed*', ǰiv*in*' 'liv*ing*', *wedi* parikedo 'thanked' = Welsh *wedi (diolch)* 'after (thanking)', ler les *evo* inka 'do it with ink' (Welsh *efo* 'with'). Furthermore, though 'the declensions of nouns and pronouns are in a good state of preservation, with the case-endings in the main as yet uncorrupted', mistakes in gender or false agreements in number and gender occurred, and the preterite tense was in 'the first stages of decay'. What is worse, 'the children, unfortunately, were no credit to their parents as regards the language, speaking a much more debased type of Romani'.

Recent statements to the effect that some, though not all, Welsh Gypsies 'can speak Romani inflected in such a way that English Gypsies cannot understand' (Acton, 1974:67), or that 'there is a small group of "North Welsh" Gypsies who speak an inflected dialect of Romanès, but their numbers are probably a few hundred at most' (Acton and Davies, 1979:106), or that 'the Romani language still survives in Wales' (Kenrick, 1979:114), must almost certainly be taken as referring to the kind of Romani recorded by Tipler in 1950. There seems no evidence that the relatively pure Romani discovered by Sampson at the turn of the century still survives. Indeed, the authors of the most recent book (in Welsh) on the Welsh gypsies are firmly of the view that it does not:

Welsh Romani in its pure state has now disappeared. Its lexicon and its morphology and syntax have been preserved in Sampson's dictionary and grammar. Sampson also described its sounds and transcribed them in a phonetic script. But it did not last long enough for researchers to have the opportunity of analysing its phonology using modern scientific methods (Jarman, 1979:147 – my translation from the original Welsh).

References

Acton, Thomas (1974). *Gypsy Politics and Social Change*. London: Routledge & Kegan Paul.
—(1977). *Mo Romano Lil*. Romanestan Publications: Gypsy Council School Book.
Acton, Thomas and Gerwyn Davies (1979). 'Educational policy and language use among English Romanies and Irish travellers (tinkers) in England and Wales.' *International Journal of the Sociology of Language*, No. 19 ('Romani Sociolinguistics'), 91–109.
Bataillard, Paul (1888–90). 'Immigration of the Gypsies into Western Europe in the

fifteenth century. First period, 1417–1438.' *Journal of the Gypsy Lore Society,* First Series, 1 (1888–89):185–212, 260–86, 324–45, 2(1890–91):27–53.

Borrow, George (1874). *Romano Lavo-Lil.* London: Murray.

Bryant, Jacob (1784). 'Collections on the Zingara, or Gypsey language.' *Archaeologia,* 7:388–94.

Clébert, Jean-Paul (1963). *The Gypsies.* New York: Dutton. (Originally published as *Les Tziganes,* Paris: Arthaud, 1961).

Furnivall, F.J. (ed.) (1870). Andrew Borde, *The Fyrst Boke of the Introduction of Knowledge.* London: Early English Texts Society (Extra Series, X).

Hancock, Ian F. (1969). 'Romanes numerals and innovations.' *Journal of the Gypsy Lore Society,* Third Series, 48:19–24.

Huth, F.G. (1940). 'Letters from a Welsh Gypsy to a Tarno Rai.' *Journal of the Gypsy Lore Society,* Third Series, 20:1–15, 150–62.

Jarman, Eldra and A.O.H. (1979). *Y Sipsiwn Cymreig* ('The Welsh Gypsies'.) Cardiff: University of Wales Press.

Kenrick, Donald (1979). 'Romani English,' *International Journal of the Sociology of Language,* No. 19 ('Romani Sociolinguistics'), 111–20.

—(1971). 'Anglo-Romani today', in T.A. Acton (ed.), *Current Changes among British Gypsies and their Place in International Patterns of Development* (Proceedings of the Research and Policy Conference of the National Gypsy Education Council, Oxford, 26–28 March, 1971), pp. 5–14.

Kenrick, Donald and Grattan Puxon (1972): *The Destiny of Europe's Gypsies.* London: Chatto, Heinemann, for Sussex University Press.

Leland, C.G. (1873). *The English Gypsies and their Language.* London: Trübner.

Marsden, William (1784). 'Observations on the language of the people commonly called Gypsies.' *Archaeologia,* 7:382–86.

Sampson, John (ed.) (1907–33). 'Welsh Gypsy folk-tales, Nos. 1–42.' *Journal of the Gypsy Lore Society,* Second Series, Vols. 1 (1907–08)–4 (1910–11), 8 (1914–15); Third Series, Vols 1 (1922) – 9 (1930), 12 (1933).

—(1926). *The Dialect of the Gypsies of Wales, being the older form of British Romani preserved in the speech of the clan of Abram Wood.* Oxford: Clarendon Press.

Smart, B. and S.T. Crofton (1875). *The Dialect of the English Gypsies.* 2nd ed. London: Asher.

Turner, Ralph L. (1927). *The Position of Romani in Indo-Aryan.* London. (Gypsy Lore Society, Monograph No. 4.)

—(1959). 'Romany Language'. *The Encyclopaedia Britannica,* Vol. 19, pp. 462–4.

Vesey-Fitzgerald, Brian (1944). *Gypsies of Britain. An Introduction to their History.* London: Chapman & Hall.

Conclusion

The linguistic pattern of these islands for the last two thousand years has been one of kaleidoscopic change. In late prehistoric times the Celts were everywhere, Q-Celts or P-Celts, sometimes and in some areas both. There were the enigmatic Picts. Then the Romans came, but Latin never took root here as it did in mainland provinces of the empire.

The Romans left and were succeeded by the English, whose speech spread, at times rapidly, at times more slowly, but constantly and relentlessly, submerging the languages of later arrivals, Norse (which however survived for nearly a thousand years in the Northern Isles) and Anglo-Norman (but not without being profoundly influenced by it in its vocabulary), displacing the traditional French of the Channel Islands, and steadily eroding the areas of Celtic speech.

Celtic in Britain was to crystallize in the course of time into five well-attested languages (and others of which we know little). Now there are two. Cornish expired two centuries ago and Manx has disappeared as a living language in the last few years, while Irish, though surviving somewhat precariously in western parts of the Republic, has virtually died out in Northern Ireland. Scottish Gaelic, ousted from all but two or three remote fragments of the mainland, maintains itself in some of the islands of the north-west, but not even there is it sheltered from the pervasiveness of English. Welsh has by no means succumbed as yet to powerful pressures and multifarious threats and even, in the opinion of some, shows signs of renewed vitality.

One can only speculate, but unprofitably, as to whether, a hundred years from now, the islands of Britain will, to their inestimable loss, have lapsed into (for 'achieved' is not the word) an unenviable linguistic uniformity that they have not known since their recorded history began.

Index